THE LOEB CLASSICAL LIBRARY

FOUNDED BY JAMES LOEB, LL.D.

EDITED BY

G. P. GOOLD, PH.D.

FORMER EDITORS

† T. E. PAGE, C.H., LITT.D.   † E. CAPPS, PH.D., LL.D.
† W. H. D. ROUSE, LITT.D.   † L. A. POST, L.H.D.
E. H. WARMINGTON, M.A., F.R.HIST.SOC.

THE APOSTOLIC FATHERS
I

THE APOSTOLIC FATHERS

WITH AN ENGLISH TRANSLATION BY
KIRSOPP LAKE

IN TWO VOLUMES

I

I CLEMENT   II CLEMENT   IGNATIUS
POLYCARP   DIDACHE
BARNABAS

CAMBRIDGE, MASSACHUSETTS
HARVARD UNIVERSITY PRESS

LONDON
WILLIAM HEINEMANN LTD
MCMLXXXV

American ISBN 0–674–99027–7
British ISBN 0 434 99024 8

First published September 1912
Reprinted July 1914 *and December* 1919
1925, 1930, 1946, 1949, 1952, 1959, 1965, 1970, 1975,
1977, 1985

Printed in Great Britain

CONTENTS

INTRODUCTION

THE name of "Apostolic Fathers" is so firmly established by usage that it will certainly never be abandoned; but it is not altogether a satisfactory title for the collection of writings to which it is given. It means that the writers in question may be supposed to have had personal knowledge of some of the Apostles, but not actually to have belonged to their number. Thus, for instance, Clement and Hermas are reckoned as disciples of St. Paul, and Polycarp as a disciple of St. John. It is not, however, always possible to maintain this view: Barnabas, to whom one of these writings is ascribed, was not merely a disciple of the Apostles, but belonged to their actual number, and the Didache claims in its title to belong to the circle of "the Twelve." It should also be noted that the title does not represent any ancient tradition: there are no traces of any early collection of "Apostolic Fathers," and each of them has a separate literary history.

There is very little important difference in the text of any of the more recent editions; but various discoveries of new MSS. and versions enable the text to be improved in detail from time to time. This is especially the case with I. Clement and Hermas.

For the purposes of the present publication the text has been revised, but it has not been possible to give critical notes unless the evidence was so balanced that more than one reading was capable of defence.

THE APOSTOLIC FATHERS

THE FIRST EPISTLE OF CLEMENT
TO THE CORINTHIANS

THE APOSTOLIC FATHERS

THE FIRST EPISTLE OF CLEMENT TO THE CORINTHIANS

THE writing which has always been known by this name is clearly, from internal evidence, a letter sent by the church of Rome to the church of Corinth in consequence of trouble in the latter community which had led to the deposition of certain Presbyters. The church of Rome writes protesting against this deposition, and the partizanship which has caused it.

The actual name of the writer is not mentioned in the letter itself: indeed, it clearly claims to be not the letter of a single person but of a church. Tradition, however, has always ascribed it to Clement, who was, according to the early episcopal lists,[1] the third or fourth bishop of Rome during the last decades of the first century. There is no reason for rejecting this tradition, for though it is not supported by any corroborative evidence in its favour there is nothing whatever against it.

Nothing certain is known of Clement; but from the amount of pseudepigraphic literature attributed to him it is probable that he was a famous man in his own time. Tradition has naturally identified him with the Clement who is mentioned in Philippians iv. 3.

---

[1] See Harnack, *Chronologie*, i. pp. 70-230.

A Clement is also mentioned in the Shepherd of Hermas, Vis. ii. 4, 3, in which it is stated that it was his duty to write to other churches. This certainly points to a Clement in Rome exercising the same functions as the writer of I. Clement; but Hermas is probably somewhat later than I. Clement, and the reference may be merely a literary device based on knowledge of the earlier book.

More complicated and more interesting are suggestions that Clement may be identified or at least connected with Titus Flavius Clemens, a distinguished Roman of the imperial Flavian family. This Titus Flavius Clemens was in 95 A.D. accused of treason or impiety (ἀθεότης) by Domitian, his cousin, owing, according to Dio Cassius, to his Jewish proclivities. He was put to death and his wife, Domitilla, was banished. There is no proof that he was really a Christian, but one of the oldest catacombs in Rome is supposed to have belonged to Domitilla, and certainly was connected with this family. It is not probable that T. Flavius Clemens was the writer of I. Clement, but it is an attractive and not improbable hypothesis that a slave or freedman of the Flavian family had the name of Clemens, and held a high position in the Christian community at Rome.

The date of I. Clement is fixed by the following considerations. It appears from chapter 5 to be later than the persecution in the time of Nero, and from chapters 42–44 it is clear that the age of the apostles is regarded as past. It can therefore scarcely be older than 75–80 A.D. On the other hand chapter 44 speaks of presbyters who were appointed by the apostles and were still alive, and there is no trace of any of the controversies or persecutions of the second century. It is therefore probably not much later than 100 A.D. If it be assumed that chapter 1, which speaks of trouble and perhaps of persecution, refers to the time of Domitian, it can probably be dated as c. 96 A.D.; but we know very little about the alleged persecution in the time of Domitian, and it would not be prudent to decide that the epistle cannot be another ten or fifteen years later. It is safest to say that it must be dated between 75 and 110 A.D.; but within these limits there is a general agreement among critics to regard as most probable the last decade of the first century.

The evidence for the text of the epistle is as follows:—

The *Codex Alexandrinus,* a Greek uncial of the fifth century in the British Museum, contains the whole text with the exception of one page. It can be consulted in the photographic edition of the whole codex published by the Trustees of the British Museum.

The *Codex Constantinopolitanus,* a Greek minuscule written by Leo the Notary in 1056 A.D. and discovered by Bryennius in Constantinople in 1875; it also contains the second epistle of Clement, the epistle of Barnabas, the Didache, and the interpolated text (see pp. 167 ff.) of the epistles of Ignatius. A photographic edition of the text is given in Lightfoot's edition of Clement.

The Syriac version, extant in only one MS. written in 1169 A.D. and now in the Library of Cambridge University (MS. add. 1700); the date of this version is unknown, but it is probably not early, and may perhaps best be placed in the eighth century. A collation is given in Lightfoot's edition, and the text has been published in full by R. H. Kennett (who took up the material of the late Prof. Bensley) in *The Epistles of St. Clement to the Corinthians in Syriac*, London, 1899.

The Latin version, also extant in only one MS which formerly belonged to the Monastery of Florennes, and is now in the Seminary at Namur. The MS. was probably written in the eleventh century, but the version which it represents is extremely ancient. It seems to have been used by Lactantius, and may perhaps be best regarded as a translation of the late second or early third century made in Rome. The text was published in 1894 by Dom Morin in *Anecdota Maredsolana* vol. 2 as *S. Clementis Romani ad Corinthios versio latina antiquissima.*

The Coptic version is extant in two MSS., neither complete, in the Akhmimic dialect. The older and better preserved is MS. orient, fol. 3065 in the Königliche Bibliothek in Berlin. This is a beautiful Papyrus of the fourth century from the famous 'White monastery' of Shenute. It was published in 1908 by C. Schmidt in *Texte und Untersuchungen*, xxxii. 1 as *Der erste Clemensbrief in altkoptischer Übersetzung.* The later and more fragmentary MS. is in Strassburg and was published in 1910 by F. Rösch as *Bruchstücke des I. Clemensbriefes* ; it probably was written in the seventh century.

Besides these MSS. and Versions exceptionally valuable evidence is given by numerous quotations in the Stromateis of Clement of Alexandria (flor. c. 200 A.D.). It is noteworthy that I. Clement appears to be treated by Clement of Alexandria as Scripture, and this, especially in connection with its position in the codex Alexandrinus and in the Strassburg

I. CLEMENT

Coptic MS., where it is directly joined on to the canonical books, suggests that at an early period in Alexandria and Egypt I. Clement was regarded as part of the New Testament.

The relations subsisting between these authorities for the text have not been finally established, but it appears clear that none of them can be regarded as undoubtedly superior to the others, so that any critical text is necessarily eclectic. At the same time there is very little range of variation, and the readings which are in serious doubt are few, and, as a rule, unimportant.

The symbols employed in quoting the textual evidence are as follows :—

A = Codex Alexandrinus.
C = Codex Constantinopolitanus.
L = Latin Version.
S = Syriac Version.
K = Coptic · Version (Kb = the Berlin MS., Ks = the Strassburg MS.).
Clem = Clement of Alexandria.

ΚΛΗΜΕΝΤΟΣ
ΠΡΟΣ ΚΟΡΙΝΘΙΟΥΣ Ᾱ

Ἡ ἐκκλησία τοῦ θεοῦ ἡ παροικοῦσα Ῥώμην τῇ ἐκκλησίᾳ τοῦ θεοῦ τῇ παροικούσῃ Κόρινθον, κλητοῖς ἡγιασμένοις ἐν θελήματι θεοῦ διὰ τοῦ κυρίου ἡμῶν Ἰησοῦ Χριστοῦ. χάρις ὑμῖν καὶ εἰρήνη ἀπὸ παντοκράτορος θεοῦ διὰ Ἰησοῦ Χριστοῦ πληθυνθείη.

Ι

1. Διὰ τὰς αἰφνιδίους καὶ ἐπαλλήλους γενομένας ἡμῖν συμφορὰς καὶ περιπτώσεις,[1] βράδιον νομίζομεν ἐπιστροφὴν πεποιῆσθαι περὶ τῶν ἐπιζητουμένων παρ᾽ ὑμῖν πραγμάτων, ἀγαπητοί, τῆς τε ἀλλοτρίας καὶ ξένης τοῖς ἐκλεκτοῖς τοῦ θεοῦ, μιαρᾶς καὶ ἀνοσίου στάσεως ἣν ὀλίγα πρόσωπα προπετῆ καὶ αὐθάδη ὑπάρχοντα εἰς τοσοῦτον ἀπονοίας ἐξέκαυσαν, ὥστε τὸ σεμνὸν καὶ περιβόητον καὶ πᾶσιν ἀνθρώποις ἀξιαγάπητον ὄνομα ὑμῶν μεγάλως βλασφημηθῆναι. 2. τίς γὰρ παρεπιδημήσας πρὸς ὑμᾶς τὴν πανάρετον καὶ βεβαίαν ὑμῶν πίστιν οὐκ ἐδοκίμασεν; τήν τε σώφρονα καὶ ἐπιεικῆ ἐν Χριστῷ εὐσέβειαν οὐκ ἐθαύμασεν; καὶ τὸ μεγαλοπρεπὲς τῆς φιλοξενίας ὑμῶν ἦθος οὐκ ἐκήρυξεν; καὶ τὴν τελείαν καὶ ἀσφαλῆ γνῶσιν

---

[1] C reads περιστάσεις which L perhaps represents by *impedimenta*, and Knopf accepts this.

THE FIRST EPISTLE OF CLEMENT
TO THE CORINTHIANS

THE Church of God which sojourns in Rome to the Salutation. Church of God which sojourns in Corinth, to those who are called and sanctified by the will of God through our Lord Jesus Christ. Grace and peace from God Almighty be multiplied to you through Jesus Christ.

I

1. OWING to the sudden and repeated mis- Reason for delay in writing fortunes and calamities[1] which have befallen us, we consider that our attention has been somewhat delayed in turning to the questions disputed among you, beloved, and especially the abominable and unholy sedition, alien and foreign to the elect of God, which a few rash and self-willed persons have made blaze up to such a frenzy that your name, venerable and famous, and worthy as it is of all men's love, has been much slandered. 2. For who has stayed with you without making The ancient fame of Corinth proof of the virtue and stedfastness of your faith? Who has not admired the sobriety and Christian gentleness of your piety? Who has not reported your character so magnificent in its hospitality? And who has not blessed your perfect and secure

[1] Or, with Knopf's text "critical circumstances."

οὐκ ἐμακάρισεν ; 3. ἀπροσωπολήμπτως γὰρ
πάντα ἐποιεῖτε καὶ ἐν τοῖς νομίμοις τοῦ θεοῦ ἐπο-
ρεύεσθε, ὑποτασσόμενοι τοῖς ἡγουμένοις ὑμῶν, καὶ
τιμὴν τὴν καθήκουσαν ἀπονέμοντες τοῖς παρ' ὑμῖν
πρεσβυτέροις· νέοις τε μέτρια καὶ σεμνὰ νοεῖν
ἐπετρέπετε· γυναιξίν τε ἐν ἀμώμῳ καὶ σεμνῇ καὶ
ἁγνῇ συνειδήσει πάντα ἐπιτελεῖν παρηγγέλλετε,
στεργούσας καθηκόντως τοὺς ἄνδρας ἑαυτῶν· ἔν τε
τῷ κανόνι τῆς ὑποταγῆς ὑπαρχούσας τὰ κατὰ τὸν
οἶκον σεμνῶς οἰκουργεῖν ἐδιδάσκετε, πάνυ σωφρονούσας.

II.

1. Πάντες τε ἐταπεινοφρονεῖτε μηδὲν ἀλαζο-
νευόμενοι, ὑποτασσόμενοι μᾶλλον ἢ ὑποτάσσοντες,
ἥδιον διδόντες ἢ λαμβάνοντες. τοῖς ἐφοδίοις τοῦ
Χριστοῦ[1] ἀρκούμενοι, καὶ προσέχοντες τοὺς λόγους
αὐτοῦ ἐπιμελῶς ἐνεστερνισμένοι ἦτε τοῖς σπλάγ-
χνοις, καὶ τὰ παθήματα αὐτοῦ ἦν πρὸ ὀφθαλμῶν
ὑμῶν. 2. οὕτως εἰρήνη βαθεῖα καὶ λιπαρὰ
ἐδέδοτο πᾶσιν καὶ ἀκόρεστος πόθος εἰς ἀγα-
θοποιΐαν, καὶ πλήρης πνεύματος ἁγίου ἔκχυσις
ἐπὶ πάντας ἐγίνετο· 3. μεστοί τε ὁσίας βουλῆς,
ἐν ἀγαθῇ προθυμίᾳ μετ' εὐσεβοῦς πεποιθήσεως
ἐξετείνετε τὰς χεῖρας ὑμῶν πρὸς τὸν παντοκράτορα
θεόν, ἱκετεύοντες αὐτὸν ἱλέως[2] γενέσθαι, εἴ τι ἄκοντες
ἡμάρτετε. 4. ἀγὼν ἦν ὑμῖν ἡμέρας τε καὶ νυκτὸς
ὑπὲρ πάσης τῆς ἀδελφότητος, εἰς τὸ σώζεσθαι μετ'

Acts 20, 35

---

[1] Θεοῦ " of God " is read by A.
[2] ἵλεων C.

knowledge ? **3.** For you did all things without respect of persons, and walked in the laws of God, obedient to your rulers, and paying all fitting honour to the older among you. On the young, too, you enjoined temperate and seemly thoughts, and to the women you gave instruction that they should do all things with a blameless and seemly and pure conscience, yielding a dutiful affection to their husbands. And you taught them to remain in the rule of obedience and to manage their households with seemliness, in all circumspection.

II

1. AND you were all humble-minded and in no wise arrogant, yielding subjection rather than demanding it, " giving more gladly than receiving," satisfied with the provision of Christ, and paying attention to his words you stored them up carefully in your hearts, and kept his sufferings before your eyes. **2.** Thus a profound and rich peace was given to all, you had an insatiable desire to do good, and the Holy Spirit was poured out in abundance on you all. **3.** You were full of holy plans, and with pious confidence you stretched out your hands to Almighty God in a passion of goodness, beseeching him to be merciful towards any unwilling sin. **4.** Day and night you strove on behalf of the whole brotherhood

ἐλέους[1] καὶ συνειδήσεως[2] τὸν ἀριθμὸν τῶν ἐκλεκτῶν
αὐτοῦ. 5. εἰλικρινεῖς καὶ ἀκέραιοι ἦτε καὶ ἀμνησί-
κακοι εἰς ἀλλήλους. 6. πᾶσα στάσις καὶ πᾶν σχίσμα βδελυκτὸν ἦν ὑμῖν. ἐπὶ τοῖς παραπτώμασιν τῶν
πλησίον ἐπενθεῖτε· τὰ ὑστερήματα αὐτῶν ἴδια
ἐκρίνετε. 7. ἀμεταμέλητοι ἦτε ἐπὶ πάσῃ ἀγαθο-

Tit. 3, 1 ποιΐᾳ, ἕτοιμοι εἰς πᾶν ἔργον ἀγαθόν. 8. τῇ
παναρέτῳ καὶ σεβασμίῳ πολιτείᾳ κεκοσμημένοι
πάντα ἐν τῷ φόβῳ αὐτοῦ ἐπετελεῖτε· τὰ προστάγματα καὶ τὰ δικαιώματα τοῦ κυρίου ἐπὶ τὰ

Prov. 7, 8 πλάτη τῆς καρδίας ὑμῶν ἐγέγραπτο.

III

Deut. 32, 15 1. Πᾶσα δόξα καὶ πλατυσμὸς ἐδόθη ὑμῖν, καὶ
ἐπετελέσθη τὸ γεγραμμένον· Ἔφαγεν καὶ ἔπιεν,
καὶ ἐπλατύνθη, καὶ ἐπαχύνθη, καὶ ἀπελάκτισεν
ὁ ἠγαπημένος. 2. ἐκ τούτου ζῆλος καὶ φθόνος,
καὶ ἔρις, καὶ στάσις, διωγμὸς καὶ ἀκαταστασία,
πόλεμος καὶ αἰχμαλωσία. 3. οὕτως ἐπηγέρθησαν

Is. 3, 5 οἱ ἄτιμοι ἐπὶ τοὺς ἐντίμους, οἱ ἄδοξοι ἐπὶ τοὺς
ἐνδόξους, οἱ ἄφρονες ἐπὶ τοὺς φρονίμους, οἱ νέοι

Is. 59, 14 ἐπὶ τοὺς πρεσβυτέρους. 4. διὰ τοῦτο πόρρω
ἄπεστιν ἡ δικαιοσύνη καὶ εἰρήνη, ἐν τῷ ἀπολιπεῖν
ἕκαστον τὸν φόβον τοῦ θεοῦ καὶ ἐν τῇ πίστει
αὐτοῦ ἀμβλυωπῆσαι, μηδὲ ἐν τοῖς νομίμοις τῶν

---

[1] δέους C.
[2] This must be corrupt: συναισθήσεως is perhaps the best
emendation.

that the number of his elect should be saved
with mercy and compassion.[1] 5. You were sincere
and innocent, and bore no malice to one another.
6. All sedition and all schism was abominable to you.
You mourned over the transgressions of your neighbours ; you judged their shortcomings as your own.
7. You were without regret in every act of kindness, "ready unto every good work." 8. You were
adorned by your virtuous and honourable citizenship
and did all things in the fear of God.[2] The
commandments and ordinances of the Lord were
"written on the tables of your heart."

III

1. ALL glory and enlargement was given to you, The
and that which was written was fulfilled, "My troubles
Beloved ate and drank, and he was enlarged and waxed at Corinth
fat and kicked." 2. From this arose jealousy and
envy, strife and sedition, persecution and disorder,
war and captivity. 3. Thus "the worthless" rose
up "against those who were in honour," those of
no reputation against the renowned, the foolish
against the prudent, the "young against the old."
4. For this cause righteousness and peace are far
removed, while each deserts the fear of God and the
eye of faith in him has grown dim, and men walk
neither in the ordinances of his commandments nor

[1] The MS. reading means "conscience," which gives no
sense. There is also a variant in the previous word ; the
inferior MS. (C) reads "fear" instead of "mercy."
[2] "God" is found only in L ; the other authorities have
"his fear," but the meaning is plain.

προσταγμάτων αὐτοῦ πορεύεσθαι, μηδὲ πολιτεύε-
σθαι κατὰ τὸ καθῆκον τῷ Χριστῷ, ἀλλὰ ἕκαστον
βαδίζειν κατὰ τὰς ἐπιθυμίας τῆς καρδίας αὐτοῦ
τῆς πονηρᾶς, ζῆλον ἄδικον καὶ ἀσεβῆ ἀνειληφότας,
Wisd. 2, 24   δι' οὗ καὶ θάνατος εἰσῆλθεν εἰς τὸν κόσμον.

IV

Gen. 4, 3-8   1. Γέγραπται γὰρ οὕτως· Καὶ ἐγένετο μεθ'
ἡμέρας, ἤνεγκεν Κάϊν ἀπὸ τῶν καρπῶν τῆς γῆς
θυσίαν τῷ θεῷ, καὶ Ἄβελ ἤνεγκεν καὶ αὐτὸς ἀπὸ
τῶν πρωτοτόκων τῶν προβάτων καὶ ἀπὸ τῶν
στεάτων αὐτῶν.   2. καὶ ἐπεῖδεν ὁ θεὸς ἐπὶ Ἄβελ
καὶ ἐπὶ τοῖς δώροις αὐτοῦ, ἐπὶ δὲ Κάϊν καὶ ἐπὶ
ταῖς θυσίαις αὐτοῦ οὐ προσέσχεν.   3. καὶ ἐλυ-
πήθη Κάϊν λίαν καὶ συνέπεσεν τῷ προσώπῳ
αὐτοῦ.   4. καὶ εἶπεν ὁ θεὸς πρὸς Κάϊν· Ἱνατί
περίλυπος ἐγένου, καὶ ἱνατί συνέπεσεν τὸ πρόσωπόν σου; οὐκ ἐὰν ὀρθῶς προσενέγκῃς, ὀρθῶς δὲ
μὴ διέλῃς, ἥμαρτες;   5. ἡσύχασον· πρὸς σὲ ἡ
ἀποστροφὴ αὐτοῦ, καὶ σὺ ἄρξεις αὐτοῦ.   6. καὶ
εἶπεν Κάϊν πρὸς Ἄβελ τὸν ἀδελφὸν αὐτοῦ· Διέλθωμεν εἰς τὸ πεδίον. καὶ ἐγένετο ἐν τῷ εἶναι αὐτοὺς
ἐν τῷ πεδίῳ, ἀνέστη Κάϊν ἐπὶ Ἄβελ τὸν ἀδελφὸν
αὐτοῦ καὶ ἀπέκτεινεν αὐτόν.   7. ὁρᾶτε, ἀδελφοί,
ζῆλος καὶ φθόνος ἀδελφοκτονίαν κατειργάσατο.
Gen. 27,41 ff.   8. διὰ ζῆλος ὁ πατὴρ ἡμῶν Ἰακὼβ ἀπέδρα ἀπὸ
Gen. 37   προσώπου Ἡσαῦ τοῦ ἀδελφοῦ αὐτοῦ.   9. ζῆλος
ἐποίησεν Ἰωσὴφ μέχρι θανάτου διωχθῆναι καὶ
μέχρι δουλείας εἰσελθεῖν.   10. ζῆλος φυγεῖν ἠνάγ-
κασεν Μωϋσῆν ἀπὸ προσώπου Φαραὼ βασιλέως
Αἰγύπτου ἐν τῷ ἀκοῦσαι αὐτὸν ἀπὸ τοῦ ὁμοφύλου·

use their citizenship worthily of Christ, but each goes according to the lusts of his wicked heart, and has revived the unrighteousness and impious envy, by which also "death came into the world."

IV

1. For it is written thus:—"And it came to pass after certain days that Cain offered to God a sacrifice of the fruits of the earth, and Abel himself also offered of the first-born of the sheep and of their fat. 2. And God looked on Abel and his gifts, but he had no respect to Cain and his sacrifices. 3. And Cain was greatly grieved and his countenance fell. 4. And God said to Cain, Why art thou grieved, and why is thy countenance fallen? If thou offeredst rightly, but didst not divide rightly, didst thou not sin?[1] 5. Be still: he shall turn to thee, and thou shalt rule over him. 6. And Cain said to Abel his brother, Let us go unto the plain. And it came to pass that, while they were in the plain, Cain rose up against Abel his brother and slew him." 7. You see, brethren,—jealousy and envy wrought fratricide. 8. Through jealousy our father Jacob ran from the face of Esau his brother. 9. Jealousy made Joseph to be persecuted to the death, and come into slavery. 10. Jealousy forced Moses to fly from the face of Pharaoh, King of Egypt, when his fellow countryman

Examples of jealousy.

Cain and Abel

Jacob and Esau

Joseph

Moses

---

[1] This is unintelligible, and does not agree with the Hebrew, which is also unintelligible. It is dealt with at length in all commentaries on Genesis.

Exod. 2, 14   Τίς σε κατέστησεν κριτὴν ἢ δικαστὴν ἐφ' ἡμῶν;
μὴ ἀνελεῖν με σὺ θέλεις, ὃν τρόπον ἀνεῖλες ἐχθὲς
Num. 12   τὸν Αἰγύπτιον;   11. διὰ ζῆλος Ἀαρὼν καὶ
Μαριὰμ ἔξω τῆς παρεμβολῆς ηὐλίσθησαν. 12.
Num. 16   ζῆλος Δαθὰν καὶ Ἀβειρὼν ζῶντας κατήγαγεν εἰς
ᾅδου διὰ τὸ στασιάσαι αὐτοὺς πρὸς τὸν θεράποντα
I Sam. 18 ff.   τοῦ θεοῦ Μωϋσῆν. 13. διὰ ζῆλος Δαυεὶδ φθόνον
ἔσχεν οὐ μόνον ὑπὸ τῶν ἀλλοφύλων, ἀλλὰ καὶ ὑπὸ
Σαοὺλ βασιλέως Ἰσραὴλ ἐδιώχθη.

V

1. Ἀλλ' ἵνα τῶν ἀρχαίων ὑποδειγμάτων παυ-
σώμεθα, ἔλθωμεν ἐπὶ τοὺς ἔγγιστα γενομένους
ἀθλητάς· λάβωμεν τῆς γενεᾶς ἡμῶν τὰ γενναῖα
ὑποδείγματα. 2. διὰ ζῆλον καὶ φθόνον οἱ μέγι-
στοι καὶ δικαιότατοι στῦλοι ἐδιώχθησαν καὶ ἕως
θανάτου ἤθλησαν. 3. λάβωμεν πρὸ ὀφθαλμῶν
ἡμῶν τοὺς ἀγαθοὺς ἀποστόλους· 4. Πέτρον, ὃς
διὰ ζῆλον ἄδικον οὐχ ἕνα οὐδὲ δύο, ἀλλὰ πλείονας
ὑπήνεγκεν πόνους καὶ οὕτω μαρτυρήσας ἐπορεύθη
εἰς τὸν ὀφειλόμενον τόπον τῆς δόξης. 5. διὰ ζῆλον
καὶ ἔριν Παῦλος ὑπομονῆς βραβεῖον ὑπέδειξεν,
6. ἑπτάκις δεσμὰ φορέσας, φυγαδευθείς, λιθα-
σθείς, κῆρυξ γενόμενος ἔν τε τῇ ἀνατολῇ καὶ ἐν τῇ
δύσει, τὸ γενναῖον τῆς πίστεως αὐτοῦ κλέος ἔλαβεν, 7. δικαιοσύνην διδάξας ὅλον τὸν κόσμον, καὶ
ἐπὶ τὸ τέρμα τῆς δύσεως ἐλθὼν καὶ μαρτυρήσας ἐπὶ
τῶν ἡγουμένων, οὕτως ἀπηλλάγη τοῦ κόσμου καὶ
εἰς τὸν ἅγιον τόπον ἀνελήμφθη,[1] ὑπομονῆς γενόμενος μέγιστος ὑπογραμμός.

---

[1] So SLK, ἐπορεύθη AC probably from v. 4.

said to him, "Who made thee a judge or a ruler
over us? Wouldest thou slay me as thou didst
slay the Egyptian yesterday?" 11. Through *Aaron and*
jealousy Aaron and Miriam were lodged outside the *Miriam*
camp. 12. Jealousy brought down Dathan and *Dathan and*
Abiram alive into Hades, because they rebelled *Abiram*
against Moses the servant of God. 13. Through
jealousy David incurred envy not only from *David*
strangers, but suffered persecution even from Saul,
King of Israel.

V

1. But, to cease from the examples of old time, let *Peter and*
us come to those who contended in the days nearest to *Paul*
us; let us take the noble examples of our own generation. 2. Through jealousy and envy the greatest and
most righteous pillars of the Church were persecuted
and contended unto death. 3. Let us set before our
eyes the good apostles: 4. Peter, who because of
unrighteous jealousy suffered not one or two but
many trials, and having thus given his testimony
went to the glorious place which was his due.
5. Through jealousy and strife Paul showed the way
to the prize of endurance; 6. seven times he was
in bonds, he was exiled, he was stoned, he was a
herald both in the East and in the West, he gained
the noble fame of his faith, 7. he taught righteousness to all the world, and when he had reached the
limits of the West he gave his testimony before the
rulers, and thus passed from the world and was
taken up into the Holy Place,—the greatest example
of endurance.

VI

1. Τούτοις τοῖς ἀνδράσιν ὁσίως πολιτευσαμένοις συνηθροίσθη πολὺ πλῆθος ἐκλεκτῶν, οἵτινες πολλαῖς αἰκίαις καὶ βασάνοις[1] διὰ ζῆλος παθόντες ὑπόδειγμα κάλλιστον ἐγένοντο ἐν ἡμῖν. 2. διὰ ζῆλος διωχθεῖσαι γυναῖκες Δαναΐδες καὶ Δίρκαι,[2] αἰκίσματα δεινὰ καὶ ἀνόσια παθοῦσαι, ἐπὶ τὸν τῆς πίστεως βέβαιον δρόμον κατήντησαν καὶ ἔλαβον γέρας γενναῖον αἱ ἀσθενεῖς τῷ σώματι. 3. ζῆλος ἀπηλλοτρίωσεν γαμετὰς ἀνδρῶν καὶ ἠλλοίωσεν τὸ ῥηθὲν ὑπὸ τοῦ πατρὸς ἡμῶν Ἀδάμ· Τοῦτο νῦν ὀστοῦν ἐκ τῶν ὀστέων μου καὶ σὰρξ ἐκ τῆς σαρκός μου. 4. ζῆλος καὶ ἔρις πόλεις μεγάλας κατέστρεψεν καὶ ἔθνη μεγάλα ἐξερίζωσεν.

Gen. 2, 23

VII

1. Ταῦτα, ἀγαπητοί, οὐ μόνον ὑμᾶς νουθετοῦντες ἐπιστέλλομεν, ἀλλὰ καὶ ἑαυτοὺς ὑπομιμνήσκοντες· ἐν γὰρ τῷ αὐτῷ ἐσμὲν σκάμματι, καὶ ὁ αὐτὸς ἡμῖν ἀγὼν ἐπίκειται. 2. διὸ ἀπολίπωμεν τὰς κενὰς καὶ ματαίας φροντίδας, καὶ ἔλθωμεν ἐπὶ τὸν εὐκλεῆ καὶ σεμνὸν τῆς παραδόσεως ἡμῶν κανόνα, 3. καὶ ἴδωμεν, τί καλὸν καὶ τί τερπνὸν καὶ τί προσδεκτὸν ἐνώπιον τοῦ ποιήσαντος ἡμᾶς. 4. ἀτενίσωμεν εἰς τὸ αἷμα τοῦ Χριστοῦ καὶ γνῶμεν, ὡς ἔστιν

---

[1] LK perhaps imply πολλὰς αἰκίας καὶ βασάνους.
[2] This is perhaps corrupt : but no satisfactory emendation is known.

VI

1. To these men with their holy lives was gathered The Christian martyrs a great multitude of the chosen, who were the victims of jealousy and offered among us the fairest example in their endurance under many indignities and tortures. 2. Through jealousy women were persecuted as Danaids and Dircae,[1] suffering terrible and unholy indignities; they stedfastly finished the course of faith, and received a noble reward, weak in the body though they were. 3. Jealousy has estranged wives from husbands, and made of no effect the saying of our father Adam, "This is now bone of my bone and flesh of my flesh." 4. Jealousy and strife have overthrown great cities, and rooted up mighty nations.

VII

1. WE are not only writing these things to you, Instances of repentance beloved, for your admonition, but also to remind ourselves; for we are in the same arena, and the same struggle is before us. 2. Wherefore let us put aside empty and vain cares, and let us come to the glorious and venerable rule of our tradition, 3. and let us see what is good and pleasing and acceptable in the sight of our Maker. 4. Let us fix our gaze on the Blood of Christ, and let us

[1] No satisfactory interpretation has ever been given of this phrase : either it refers to theatrical representations by condemned Christians, or the text is hopelessly corrupt.

THE APOSTOLIC FATHERS

τίμιον τῷ πατρὶ αὐτοῦ,[1] ὅτι διὰ τὴν ἡμετέραν
σωτηρίαν ἐκχυθὲν παντὶ τῷ κόσμῳ μετανοίας
χάριν ὑπήνεγκεν. 5. διέλθωμεν εἰς τὰς γενεὰς
πάσας, καὶ καταμάθωμεν ὅτι ἐν γενεᾷ καὶ γενεᾷ

Wisd. 12, 10 μετανοίας τόπον ἔδωκεν ὁ δεσπότης τοῖς βουλο-
Gen. 7 μένοις ἐπιστραφῆναι ἐπ' αὐτόν. 6. Νῶε ἐκήρυξεν
Jon. 3; μετάνοιαν, καὶ οἱ ὑπακούσαντες ἐσώθησαν. 7. Ἰω-
Mt. 12, 41 νᾶς Νινευΐταις καταστροφὴν ἐκήρυξεν· οἱ δὲ μετανοήσαντες ἐπὶ τοῖς ἁμαρτήμασιν αὐτῶν ἐξιλάσαντο
τὸν θεὸν ἱκετεύσαντες καὶ ἔλαβον σωτηρίαν, καίπερ ἀλλότριοι τοῦ θεοῦ ὄντες.

VIII

1. Οἱ λειτουργοὶ τῆς χάριτος τοῦ θεοῦ διὰ πνεύματος ἁγίου περὶ μετανοίας ἐλάλησαν, 2. καὶ
αὐτὸς δὲ ὁ δεσπότης τῶν ἁπάντων περὶ μετανοίας

Ezek. 38. ἐλάλησεν μετὰ ὅρκου· Ζῶ γὰρ ἐγώ, λέγει κύριος,
11-27 οὐ βούλομαι τὸν θάνατον τοῦ ἁμαρτωλοῦ ὡς
τὴν μετάνοιαν, προστιθεὶς καὶ γνώμην ἀγαθήν·
3. Μετανοήσατε, οἶκος Ἰσραήλ, ἀπὸ τῆς ἀνομίας
ὑμῶν· εἶπον τοῖς υἱοῖς τοῦ λαοῦ μου. Ἐὰν ὦσιν αἱ
ἁμαρτίαι ὑμῶν ἀπὸ τῆς γῆς ἕως τοῦ οὐρανοῦ καὶ
ἐὰν ὦσιν πυρρότεραι κόκκου καὶ μελανώτεραι σάκκου, καὶ ἐπιστραφῆτε πρός με ἐξ ὅλης τῆς καρδίας
καὶ εἴπητε· Πάτερ· ἐπακούσομαι ὑμῶν ὡς λαοῦ
ἁγίου. 4. καὶ ἐν ἑτέρῳ τόπῳ λέγει οὕτως·

[1] τῷ θεῷ καὶ πατρὶ αὐτοῦ A, τῷ πατρὶ αὐτοῦ τῷ θεῷ C. The
text is found in SLK.

know that it is precious to his Father,[1] because
it was poured out for our salvation, and brought the
grace of repentance to all the world.   5. Let us
review all the generations, and let us learn that in
generation after generation the Master has given a
place of repentance to those who will turn to him.
6. Noah preached repentance and those who obeyed   Noah
were saved.   7. Jonah foretold destruction to the Jonah and
men of Nineveh, but when they repented they   the
received forgiveness of their sins from God in answer   Ninevites
to their prayer, and gained salvation, though they
were aliens to God.

VIII

1. THE ministers of the grace of God spoke   Repentance
through the Holy Spirit concerning repentance, 2.   in the
and even the Master of the universe himself spoke   Prophets
with an oath concerning repentance ; " For as I live,
said the Lord, I do not desire the death of the
sinner so much as his repentance," and he added a
gracious declaration, 3. " Repent, O house of Israel,
from your iniquity.   Say to the sons of my people,
If your sins reach from the earth to Heaven, and if
they be redder than scarlet, and blacker than sackcloth, and ye turn to me with all your hearts and
say ' Father,' I will listen to you as a holy people."[2]
4. And in another place he speaks thus, " Wash

---

[1] The Greek MSS. insert " his God," but in different places,
and the evidence of the versions confirms Lightfoot's view
that the words are interpolated.

[2] The origin of this quotation is obscure : possibly
Clement's text of Ezekiel was different from ours and really
contained it.

Is. 1, 16-20 Λούσασθε καὶ καθαροὶ γένεσθε, ἀφέλεσθε τὰς πονηρίας ἀπὸ τῶν ψυχῶν ὑμῶν ἀπέναντι τῶν ὀφθαλμῶν μου· παύσασθε ἀπὸ τῶν πονηριῶν ὑμῶν, μάθετε καλὸν ποιεῖν, ἐκζητήσατε κρίσιν, ῥύσασθε ἀδικούμενον, κρίνατε ὀρφανῷ καὶ δικαιώσατε χήρᾳ· καὶ δεῦτε καὶ διελεγχθῶμεν, λέγει κύριος· καὶ ἐὰν ὦσιν αἱ ἁμαρτίαι ὑμῶν ὡς φοινικοῦν, ὡς χιόνα λευκανῶ· ἐὰν δὲ ὦσιν ὡς κόκκινον, ὡς ἔριον λευκανῶ· καὶ ἐὰν θέλητε καὶ εἰσακούσητέ μου, τὰ ἀγαθὰ τῆς γῆς φάγεσθε· ἐὰν δὲ μὴ θέλητε μηδὲ εἰσακούσητέ μου, μάχαιρα ὑμᾶς κατέδεται· τὸ γὰρ στόμα κυρίου ἐλάλησεν ταῦτα. 5. πάντας οὖν τοὺς ἀγαπητοὺς αὐτοῦ βουλόμενος μετανοίας μετασχεῖν ἐστήριξεν τῷ παντοκρατορικῷ βουλήματι αὐτοῦ.

IX

1. Διὸ ὑπακούσωμεν τῇ μεγαλοπρεπεῖ καὶ ἐνδόξῳ βουλήσει αὐτοῦ, καὶ ἱκέται γενόμενοι τοῦ ἐλέους καὶ τῆς χρηστότητος αὐτοῦ προσπέσωμεν καὶ ἐπιστρέψωμεν ἐπὶ τοὺς οἰκτιρμοὺς αὐτοῦ, ἀπολιπόντες τὴν ματαιοπονίαν τήν τε ἔριν καὶ τὸ εἰς θάνατον ἄγον ζῆλος. 2. ἀτενίσωμεν εἰς τοὺς τελείως λειτουργήσαντας τῇ μεγαλοπρεπεῖ δόξῃ αὐτοῦ.

Gen. 5, 24 ; Heb. 11, 5 3. λάβωμεν Ἐνώχ, ὃς ἐν ὑπακοῇ δίκαιος εὑρεθεὶς μετετέθη, καὶ οὐχ εὑρέθη αὐτοῦ θάνατος.

Gen. 6,8; 1,7; Heb. 11, 7; II Pet. 2, 5 4. Νῶε πιστὸς εὑρεθεὶς διὰ τῆς λειτουργίας αὐτοῦ παλιγγενεσίαν κόσμῳ ἐκήρυξεν, καὶ διέσωσεν δι' αὐτοῦ ὁ δεσπότης τὰ εἰσελθόντα ἐν ὁμονοίᾳ ζῷα εἰς τὴν κιβωτόν.

you, and make you clean, put away your wickedness from your souls before my eyes, cease from your wickedness, learn to do good, seek out judgment, rescue the wronged, give judgment for the orphan, do justice to the widow, and come and let us reason together, saith the Lord; and if your sins be as crimson, I will make them white as snow, and if they be as scarlet, I will make them white as wool, and if ye be willing and hearken to me, ye shall eat the good things of the land, but if ye be not willing, and hearken not to me, a sword shall devour you, for the mouth of the Lord has spoken these things." 5. Thus desiring to give to all his beloved a share in repentance, he established it by his Almighty will.

IX

1. WHEREFORE let us obey his excellent and glorious will; let us fall before him as suppliants of his mercy and goodness; let us turn to his pity, and abandon the vain toil and strife and jealousy which leads to death. 2. Let us fix our gaze on those who have rendered perfect service to his excellent glory. 3. Let us take Enoch, who was found righteous in obedience, and was translated, and death did not befall him. 4. Noah was found faithful in his service, in foretelling a new beginning to the world, and through him the Master saved the living creatures which entered in concord into the Ark.

Examples of obedience

Enoch

Noah

X

Is. 41, 8;
II Chron.
20, 7 ;
James 2, 28
1. Ἀβραάμ, ὁ φίλος προσαγορευθείς, πιστὸς εὑρέθη ἐν τῷ αὐτὸν ὑπήκοον γενέσθαι τοῖς ῥήμασιν τοῦ θεοῦ. 2. οὗτος δι᾿ ὑπακοῆς ἐξῆλθεν ἐκ τῆς γῆς αὐτοῦ καὶ ἐκ τῆς συγγενείας αὐτοῦ καὶ ἐκ τοῦ οἴκου τοῦ πατρὸς αὐτοῦ, ὅπως γῆν ὀλίγην καὶ συγγένειαν ἀσθενῆ καὶ οἶκον μικρὸν καταλιπὼν κληρονομήσῃ τὰς ἐπαγγελίας τοῦ θεοῦ. λέγει γὰρ αὐτῷ·

Gen. 12, 1-3
3. Ἄπελθε ἐκ τῆς γῆς σου καὶ ἐκ τῆς συγγενείας σου καὶ ἐκ τοῦ οἴκου τοῦ πατρός σου εἰς τὴν γῆν ἣν ἄν σοι δείξω· καὶ ποιήσω σε εἰς ἔθνος μέγα καὶ εὐλογήσω σε καὶ μεγαλυνῶ τὸ ὄνομά σου, καὶ ἔσῃ εὐλογημένος· καὶ εὐλογήσω τοὺς εὐλογοῦντάς σε καὶ καταράσομαι τοὺς καταρωμένους σε, καὶ εὐλογηθήσονται ἐν σοὶ πᾶσαι αἱ φυλαὶ τῆς γῆς. 4. καὶ πάλιν ἐν τῷ διαχωρισθῆναι

Gen. 13,
14-16
αὐτὸν ἀπὸ Λὼτ εἶπεν αὐτῷ ὁ θεός. Ἀναβλέψας τοῖς ὀφθαλμοῖς σου ἴδε ἀπὸ τοῦ τόπου, οὗ νῦν σὺ εἶ, πρὸς βορρᾶν καὶ λίβα καὶ ἀνατολὰς καὶ θάλασσαν, ὅτι πᾶσαν τὴν γῆν, ἣν σὺ ὁρᾷς, σοὶ δώσω αὐτὴν καὶ τῷ σπέρματί σου ἕως αἰῶνος. 5. καὶ ποιήσω τὸ σπέρμα σου ὡς τὴν ἄμμον τῆς γῆς· εἰ δύναταί τις ἐξαριθμῆσαι τὴν ἄμμον τῆς γῆς, καὶ τὸ σπέρμα σου ἐξαριθμηθήσεται. 6. καὶ

Gen. 15, 5. 6;
Rom. 4, 3
πάλιν λέγει· Ἐξήγαγεν ὁ θεὸς τὸν Ἀβραὰμ καὶ εἶπεν αὐτῷ· Ἀνάβλεψον εἰς τὸν οὐρανὸν καὶ ἀρίθμησον τοὺς ἀστέρας, εἰ δυνήσῃ ἐξαριθμῆσαι αὐτούς· οὕτως ἔσται τὸ σπέρμα σου. ἐπίστευσεν δὲ Ἀβραὰμ τῷ θεῷ, καὶ ἐλογίσθη αὐτῷ εἰς δικαιο-

Gen. 18, 21
σύνην. 7. διὰ πίστιν καὶ φιλοξενίαν ἐδόθη

X

1. ABRAHAM, who was called "the Friend", was Abraham found faithful in his obedience to the words of God. 2. He in obedience went forth from his country and from his kindred and from his father's house, that by leaving behind a little country and a feeble kindred and a small house he might inherit the promises of God. For God says to him, 3. "Depart from thy land and from thy kindred and from thy father's house to the land which I shall show thee, and I will make thee a great nation, and I will bless thee, and I will magnify thy name, and thou shalt be blessed ; and I will bless those that bless thee, and I will curse those that curse thee, and all the tribes of the earth shall be blessed in thee." 4. And again, when he was separated from Lot, God said to him, "Lift up thine eyes and look from the place where thou art now, to the North and to the South and to the East and to the West ; for all the land which thou seest, to thee will I give it and to thy seed for ever. 5. And I will make thy seed as the dust of the earth. If a man can number the dust of the earth thy seed shall also be numbered." 6. And again he says, "God led forth Abraham, and said to him, ' Look up to the Heaven and number the stars, if thou canst number them ; so shall thy seed be.' And Abraham believed God, and it was counted unto him for righteousness." 7. Because of his faith and hospitality a son was given him in

25

Gen. 22;
Heb. 11, 17

αὐτῷ υἱὸς ἐν γήρᾳ, καὶ δι' ὑπακοῆς προσήνεγκεν αὐτὸν θυσίαν τῷ θεῷ πρὸς τὸ ὄρος ὃ[1] ἔδειξεν αὐτῷ.

XI

Gen. 19;
II Pet. 2, 6. 7

1. Διὰ φιλοξενίαν καὶ εὐσέβειαν Λὼτ ἐσώθη ἐκ Σοδόμων, τῆς περιχώρου πάσης κριθείσης διὰ πυρὸς καὶ θείου, πρόδηλον ποιήσας ὁ δεσπότης, ὅτι τοὺς ἐλπίζοντας ἐπ' αὐτὸν οὐκ ἐγκαταλείπει, τοὺς δὲ ἑτεροκλινεῖς ὑπάρχοντας εἰς κόλασιν καὶ αἰκισμὸν τίθησιν. 2. συνεξελθούσης γὰρ αὐτῷ τῆς γυναικὸς ἑτερογνώμονος ὑπαρχούσης καὶ οὐκ ἐν ὁμονοίᾳ, εἰς τοῦτο σημεῖον ἐτέθη, ὥστε γενέσθαι αὐτὴν στήλην ἁλὸς ἕως τῆς ἡμέρας ταύτης, εἰς τὸ γνωστὸν εἶναι πᾶσιν, ὅτι οἱ δίψυχοι καὶ οἱ διστάζοντες περὶ τῆς τοῦ θεοῦ δυνάμεως εἰς κρίμα καὶ εἰς σημείωσιν πάσαις ταῖς γενεαῖς γίνονται.

XII

Josh. 2;
James 2, 25;
Heb. 11, 31
Josh. 2, 1-3

Josh. 2, 6

1. Διὰ πίστιν καὶ φιλοξενίαν ἐσώθη Ῥαὰβ ἡ πόρνη.[2] 2. ἐκπεμφθέντων γὰρ ὑπὸ Ἰησοῦ τοῦ τοῦ Ναυὴ κατασκόπων εἰς τὴν Ἱεριχώ, ἔγνω ὁ βασιλεὺς τῆς γῆς, ὅτι ἥκασιν κατασκοπεῦσαι τὴν χώραν αὐτῶν, καὶ ἐξέπεμψεν ἄνδρας τοὺς συλλημψομένους αὐτούς, ὅπως συλλημφθέντες θανατωθῶσιν. 3. ἡ οὖν φιλόξενος Ῥαὰβ εἰσδεξαμένη αὐτοὺς ἔκρυψεν εἰς τὸ ὑπερῷον ὑπὸ τὴν

---

[1] So L; ACSK conform to the LXX and read ἐν τῶν ὀρέων.
[2] ἡ ἐπιλεγομένη πόρνη CLSK perhaps from Hebr. 11, 31,
The text is found in A Clement.

his old age, and in his obedience he offered him as a
sacrifice to God on the mountain [1] which he showed
him.

XI

1. For his hospitality and piety Lot was saved out Lot
of Sodom when the whole countryside was judged
by fire and brimstone, and the Master made clear
that he does not forsake those who hope in him,
but delivers to punishment and torture those who
turn aside to others. 2. For of this a sign was given Lot's wife
when his wife went with him, but changed her mind
and did not remain in agreement with him, so that
she became a pillar of salt unto this day, to make
known to all, that those who are double-minded,
and have doubts concerning the power of God,
incur judgment and become a warning to all
generations.

XII

1. For her faith and hospitality Rahab the harlot [2] Rahab
was saved. 2. For when the spies were sent to
Jericho by Joshua the son of Nun, the King of
the land knew that they had come to spy out his
country, and sent men to take them, that they
might be captured and put to death. 3. So the
hospitable Rahab took them in, and hid them in the
upper room under the stalks of flax. 4. And when the

[1] Or possibly, with the other reading, "on one of the
mountains."
[2] Or possibly "who was called a harlot."

Josh. 2, 3 λινοκαλάμην. 4. ἐπισταθέντων δὲ τῶν παρὰ τοῦ βασιλέως καὶ λεγόντων· Πρὸς σὲ εἰσῆλθον οἱ κατάσκοποι τῆς γῆς ἡμῶν· ἐξάγαγε αὐτούς, ὁ γὰρ

Josh. 2, 4. 5 βασιλεὺς οὕτως κελεύει, ἥδε ἀπεκρίθη· Εἰσῆλθον μὲν οἱ ἄνδρες, οὓς ζητεῖτε, πρός με, ἀλλ᾽ εὐθέως ἀπῆλθον καὶ πορεύονται τῇ ὁδῷ· ὑποδεικνύουσα αὐτοῖς ἐναλλάξ. 5. καὶ εἶπεν πρὸς τοὺς ἄνδρας·

Josh. 2, 9–13 Γινώσκουσα γινώσκω ἐγώ, ὅτι κύριος ὁ θεὸς παραδίδωσιν ὑμῖν τὴν γῆν ταύτην· ὁ γὰρ φόβος καὶ ὁ τρόμος ὑμῶν ἐπέπεσεν τοῖς κατοικοῦσιν αὐτήν. ὡς ἐὰν οὖν γένηται λαβεῖν αὐτὴν ὑμᾶς, διασώσατέ με καὶ τὸν οἶκον τοῦ πατρός μου. 6. καὶ

Josh. 2, 14 εἶπαν αὐτῇ· Ἔσται οὕτως, ὡς ἐλάλησας ἡμῖν. ὡς ἐὰν οὖν γνῷς παραγινομένους ἡμᾶς, συνάξεις πάντας τοὺς σοὺς ὑπὸ τὸ στέγος σου, καὶ διασωθήσονται· ὅσοι γὰρ ἐὰν εὑρεθῶσιν ἔξω τῆς

Josh. 2, 18 οἰκίας, ἀπολοῦνται. 7. καὶ προσέθεντο αὐτῇ δοῦναι σημεῖον, ὅπως ἐκκρεμάσῃ ἐκ τοῦ οἴκου αὐτῆς κόκκινον, πρόδηλον ποιοῦντες, ὅτι διὰ τοῦ αἵματος τοῦ κυρίου λύτρωσις ἔσται πᾶσιν τοῖς πιστεύουσιν καὶ ἐλπίζουσιν ἐπὶ τὸν θεόν. 8. ὁρᾶτε, ἀγαπητοί, ὅτι οὐ μόνον πίστις, ἀλλὰ καὶ προφητεία ἐν τῇ γυναικὶ γέγονεν.

XIII

1. Ταπεινοφρονήσωμεν οὖν, ἀδελφοί, ἀποθέμενοι πᾶσαν ἀλαζονείαν καὶ τῦφος καὶ ἀφροσύνην καὶ ὀργάς, καὶ ποιήσωμεν τὸ γεγραμμένον, λέγει γὰρ

Jer. 9, 23–24; τὸ πνεῦμα τὸ ἅγιον· Μὴ καυχάσθω ὁ σοφὸς ἐν τῇ
I Sam. 2, 10; σοφίᾳ αὐτοῦ μηδὲ ὁ ἰσχυρὸς ἐν τῇ ἰσχύι αὐτοῦ
I Cor. 1, 31;
II Cor. 10, 17 μηδὲ ὁ πλούσιος ἐν τῷ πλούτῳ αὐτοῦ, ἀλλ᾽ ἢ ὁ

king's men came and said, "The spies of our land came in to thee, bring them out, for the king orders thus," she answered "The men whom ye seek did indeed come to me, but they went away forthwith, and are proceeding on their journey," and pointed in the wrong direction.   5. And she said to the men, "I know assuredly that the Lord God is delivering to you this land ; for the fear and dread of you has fallen on those who dwell in it.   When therefore it shall come to pass, that ye take it, save me and my father's house."   6. And they said to her, "It shall be as thou hast spoken to us ; when therefore thou knowest that we are at hand, thou shalt gather all thy folk under thy roof, and they shall be safe ; for as many as shall be found outside the house shall perish."   7. And they proceeded to give her a sign, that she should hang out a scarlet thread from her house, foreshowing that all who believe and · hope on God shall have redemption through the blood of the Lord.   8. You see, beloved, that the woman is an instance not only of faith but also of prophecy.

XIII

1. LET us, therefore, be humble-minded, brethren, putting aside all arrogance and conceit and foolishness and wrath, and let us do that which is written (for the Holy Spirit says, "Let not the wise man boast himself in his wisdom, nor the strong man in his strength, nor the rich man in his riches, but he

The need of humble-mindedness

καυχώμενος ἐν κυρίῳ καυχάσθω, τοῦ ἐκζητεῖν
αὐτὸν καὶ ποιεῖν κρίμα καὶ δικαιοσύνην· μάλιστα
μεμνημένοι τῶν λόγων τοῦ κυρίου Ἰησοῦ, οὓς
ἐλάλησεν διδάσκων ἐπιείκειαν καὶ μακροθυμίαν.
2. οὕτως γὰρ εἶπεν· Ἐλεᾶτε, ἵνα ἐλεηθῆτε·
ἀφίετε, ἵνα ἀφεθῇ ὑμῖν· ὡς ποιεῖτε, οὕτω ποιηθή-
σεται ὑμῖν· ὡς δίδοτε, οὕτως δοθήσεται ὑμῖν· ὡς
κρίνετε, οὕτως κριθήσεσθε· ὡς χρηστεύεσθε, οὕτως
χρηστευθήσεται ὑμῖν· ᾧ μέτρῳ μετρεῖτε, ἐν αὐτῷ
μετρηθήσεται ὑμῖν. 3. ταύτῃ τῇ ἐντολῇ καὶ τοῖς
παραγγέλμασιν τούτοις στηρίξωμεν ἑαυτοὺς εἰς
τὸ πορεύεσθαι ὑπηκόους ὄντας τοῖς ἁγιοπρεπέσι
λόγοις αὐτοῦ, ταπεινοφρονοῦντες· φησὶν γὰρ ὁ
ἅγιος λόγος· 4. Ἐπὶ τίνα ἐπιβλέψω, ἀλλ᾿ ἢ
ἐπὶ τὸν πραὺν καὶ ἡσύχιον καὶ τρέμοντά μου τὰ
λόγια.

Matt. 5, 7; 6,
14. 15 ; 7, 1.
2. 12 ;
Luke 6, 31.
36–38

Is. 66, 2

XIV

1. Δίκαιον οὖν καὶ ὅσιον, ἄνδρες ἀδελφοί,
ὑπηκόους ἡμᾶς μᾶλλον γενέσθαι τῷ θεῷ ἢ τοῖς ἐν
ἀλαζονείᾳ καὶ ἀκαταστασίᾳ μυσεροῦ ζήλους
ἀρχηγοῖς ἐξακολουθεῖν. 2. βλάβην γὰρ οὐ τὴν
τυχοῦσαν, μᾶλλον δὲ κίνδυνον ὑποίσομεν μέγαν,
ἐὰν ῥιψοκινδύνως ἐπιδῶμεν ἑαυτοὺς τοῖς θελήμασιν
τῶν ἀνθρώπων, οἵτινες ἐξακοντίζουσιν εἰς ἔριν καὶ
στάσεις, εἰς τὸ ἀπαλλοτριῶσαι ἡμᾶς τοῦ καλῶς
ἔχοντος. 3. χρηστευσώμεθα ἑαυτοῖς κατὰ τὴν
εὐσπλαγχνίαν καὶ γλυκύτητα τοῦ ποιήσαντος
ἡμᾶς. 4. γέγραπται γάρ· Χρηστοὶ ἔσονται οἰκή-
τορες γῆς, ἄκακοι δὲ ὑπολειφθήσονται ἐπ᾿ αὐτῆς·
οἱ δὲ παρανομοῦντες ἐξολεθρευθήσονται ἀπ᾿ αὐτῆς.

Prov. 2, 21.
22 ;
Ps. 37, 9. 38

that boasteth let him boast in the Lord, to seek him
out and to do judgment and righteousness"),
especially remembering the words of the Lord Jesus
which he spoke when he was teaching gentleness
and longsuffering. 2. For he spoke thus: "Be
merciful, that ye may obtain mercy. Forgive, that
ye may be forgiven. As ye do, so shall it be done
unto you. As ye give, so shall it be given unto you.
As ye judge, so shall ye be judged. As ye are kind,
so shall kindness be shewn you. With what measure
ye mete, it shall be measured to you." 3. With this
commandment and with these injunctions let us
strengthen ourselves to walk in obedience to his
hallowed words and let us be humble-minded, for the
holy word says, 4. "On whom shall I look, but on
the meek and gentle and him who trembles at my
oracles."

XIV

1. THEREFORE it is right and holy, my brethren,
for us to obey God rather than to follow those who
in pride and unruliness are the instigators of an
abominable jealousy. 2. For we shall incur no
common harm, but great danger, if we rashly yield
ourselves to the purposes of men who rush into
strife and sedition, to estrange us from what is right.
3. Let us be kind to one another, according to the
compassion and sweetness of our Maker. 4. For
it is written, "The kind shall inhabit the land,
and the guiltless shall be left on it, but they
who transgress shall be destroyed from off it."

Obedience to God, and abstinence from sedition.

THE APOSTOLIC FATHERS

Ps. 37, 35-37 5. καὶ πάλιν λέγει· Εἶδον ἀσεβῆ ὑπερυψούμενον καὶ ἐπαιρόμενον ὡς τὰς κέδρους τοῦ Λιβάνου· καὶ παρῆλθον, καὶ ἰδοὺ οὐκ ἦν, καὶ ἐξεζήτησα τὸν τόπον αὐτοῦ, καὶ οὐχ εὗρον. φύλασσε ἀκακίαν καὶ ἴδε εὐθύτητα, ὅτι ἐστὶν ἐγκατάλειμμα ἀνθρώπῳ εἰρηνικῷ.

XV

1. Τοίνυν κολληθῶμεν τοῖς μετ᾽ εὐσεβείας εἰρηνεύουσιν, καὶ μὴ τοῖς μεθ᾽ ὑποκρίσεως βουλομένοις
Is. 29, 13;
Mk. 7, 6 εἰρήνην. 2. λέγει γάρ που· Οὗτος ὁ λαὸς τοῖς
χείλεσίν με τιμᾷ, ἡ δὲ καρδία αὐτῶν πόρρω ἄπεστιν
Ps. 61, 5 ἀπ᾽ ἐμοῦ. 3. καὶ πάλιν· Τῷ στόματι αὐτῶν
εὐλογοῦσιν, τῇ δὲ καρδίᾳ αὐτῶν κατηρῶντο·
Ps. 77, 36. 37 4. καὶ πάλιν λέγει· Ἠγάπησαν αὐτὸν τῷ στόματι αὐτῶν καὶ τῇ γλώσσῃ αὐτῶν ἐψεύσαντο
αὐτόν, ἡ δὲ καρδία αὐτῶν οὐκ εὐθεῖα μετ᾽ αὐτοῦ,
Ps. 30, 19 οὐδὲ ἐπιστώθησαν ἐν τῇ διαθήκῃ αὐτοῦ. 5. διὰ
τοῦτο ἄλαλα γενηθήτω τὰ χείλη τὰ δόλια τὰ
λαλοῦντα κατὰ τοῦ δικαίου ἀνομίαν. καὶ πάλιν·
Ps. 12, 3-5 Ἐξολεθρεύσαι κύριος πάντα τὰ χείλη τὰ δόλια,[1]
γλῶσσαν μεγαλορήμονα, τοὺς εἰπόντας· Τὴν
γλῶσσαν ἡμῶν μεγαλυνοῦμεν, τὰ χείλη ἡμῶν
παρ᾽ ἡμῖν ἐστιν· τίς ἡμῶν κύριός ἐστιν; 6. ἀπὸ
τῆς ταλαιπωρίας τῶν πτωχῶν καὶ τοῦ στεν-
αγμοῦ τῶν πενήτων νῦν ἀναστήσομαι, λέγει κύριος·
θήσομαι ἐν σωτηρίῳ, 7. παρρησιάσομαι ἐν αὐτῷ.

---

[1] δόλια . . . δόλια are omitted by all the textual authorities
(including Clem.) except S. It is probable that this is a
primitive corruption in the text, and that the reading of
S is a correct emendation, which, it may be observed, was
independently made by Lightfoot before the discovery of S.

5. And again he says: "I saw the ungodly lifted high, and exalted as the cedars of Lebanon. And I went by, and behold he was not; and I sought his place, and I found it not. Keep innocence, and look on uprightness; for there is a remnant for a peaceable man."

XV

1. MOREOVER let us cleave to those whose Cleaving peacefulness is based on piety and not to those to the whose wish for peace is hypocrisy. 2. For it peaceable says in one place: "This people honoureth me with their lips, but their heart is far from me." 3. And again, "They blessed with their mouth, but cursed in their hearts." 4. And again it says "they loved him with their mouth, and they lied unto him with their tongue, and their heart was not right with him, nor were they faithful in his covenant." 5. Therefore "let the deceitful lips be dumb which speak iniquity against the righteous." And again, "May the Lord destroy all the deceitful lips, a tongue that speaketh great things, those who say, Let us magnify our tongue, our lips are our own, who is lord over us? 6. For the misery of the poor and groaning of the needy, now will I arise, saith the Lord, I will place him in safety, 7. I will deal boldly with him."

XVI

1. Ταπεινοφρονούντων γάρ ἐστιν ὁ Χριστός,
οὐκ ἐπαιρομένων ἐπὶ τὸ ποίμνιον αὐτοῦ. 2. τὸ
σκῆπτρον τῆς μεγαλωσύνης τοῦ θεοῦ, ὁ κύριος
Ἰησοῦς Χριστός, οὐκ ἦλθεν ἐν κόμπῳ ἀλαζονείας
οὐδὲ ὑπερηφανίας, καίπερ δυνάμενος, ἀλλὰ
ταπεινοφρονῶν, καθὼς τὸ πνεῦμα τὸ ἅγιον περὶ
Is. 53, 1-12 αὐτοῦ ἐλάλησεν· φησὶν γάρ· 3. Κύριε, τίς ἐπίστευσεν τῇ ἀκοῇ ἡμῶν ; καὶ ὁ βραχίων κυρίου
τίνι ἀπεκαλύφθη ; ἀνηγγείλαμεν ἐναντίον αὐτοῦ,
ὡς παιδίον, ὡς ῥίζα ἐν γῇ διψώσῃ· οὐκ ἔστιν
αὐτῷ εἶδος οὐδὲ δόξα, καὶ εἴδομεν αὐτόν, καὶ
οὐκ εἶχεν εἶδος οὐδὲ κάλλος, ἀλλὰ τὸ εἶδος αὐτοῦ
ἄτιμον, ἐκλεῖπον παρὰ τὸ εἶδος τῶν ἀνθρώπων·
ἄνθρωπος ἐν πληγῇ ὢν καὶ πόνῳ καὶ εἰδὼς φέρειν
μαλακίαν, ὅτι ἀπέστραπται τὸ πρόσωπον αὐτοῦ,
ἠτιμάσθη καὶ οὐκ ἐλογίσθη· 4. οὗτος τὰς
ἁμαρτίας ἡμῶν φέρει καὶ περὶ ἡμῶν ὀδυνᾶται, καὶ
ἡμεῖς ἐλογισάμεθα αὐτὸν εἶναι ἐν πόνῳ καὶ ἐν
πληγῇ καὶ ἐν κακώσει· 5. αὐτὸς δὲ ἐτραυματίσθη
διὰ τὰς ἁμαρτίας ἡμῶν καὶ μεμαλάκισται διὰ τὰς
ἀνομίας ἡμῶν. παιδεία εἰρήνης ἡμῶν ἐπ᾽ αὐτόν· τῷ
μώλωπι αὐτοῦ ἡμεῖς ἰάθημεν. 6. πάντες ὡς
πρόβατα ἐπλανήθημεν, ἄνθρωπος τῇ ὁδῷ αὐτοῦ
ἐπλανήθη· 7. καὶ κύριος παρέδωκεν αὐτὸν ὑπὲρ
τῶν ἁμαρτιῶν ἡμῶν, καὶ αὐτὸς διὰ τὸ κεκακῶσθαι
οὐκ ἀνοίγει τὸ στόμα. ὡς πρόβατον ἐπὶ σφαγὴν
ἤχθη, καὶ ὡς ἀμνὸς ἐναντίον τοῦ κείραντος ἄφωνος,
οὕτως οὐκ ἀνοίγει τὸ στόμα αὐτοῦ. ἐν τῇ ταπεινώσει ἡ κρίσις αὐτοῦ ἤρθη. 8. τὴν γενεὰν αὐτοῦ

XVI

1. For Christ is of those who are humble-minded, The
not of those who exalt themselves over His flock. humility
2. The sceptre of the greatness of God, the Lord of Christ
Jesus Christ, came not with the pomp of pride or of
arrogance, for all his power, but was humble-minded,
as the Holy Spirit spake concerning him. For it
says, 3. "Lord, who has believed our report, and to
whom was the arm of the Lord revealed? We
declared him before the Lord as a child, as a
root in thirsty ground; there is no form in him, nor
glory, and we saw him, and he had neither form nor
beauty, but his form was without honour, less than
the form of man, a man living among stripes and
toil, and acquainted with the endurance of weakness;
for his face was turned away, he was dishonoured,
and not esteemed. 4. He it is who beareth our sins,
and is pained for us, and we regarded him as subject
to pain, and stripes and affliction, 5. but he was
wounded for our sins and he has suffered for our
iniquities. The chastisement of our peace was upon
him; with his bruises were we healed. 6. All we
like sheep went astray, each man went astray in his
path; 7. and the Lord delivered him up for our sins,
and he openeth not his mouth because of his
affliction. As a sheep he was brought to the
slaughter, and as a lamb dumb before its shearer, so
he openeth not his mouth. In humiliation his
judgment was taken away. 8. Who shall declare

35

τίς διηγήσεται; ὅτι αἴρεται ἀπὸ τῆς γῆς ἡ ζωὴ
αὐτοῦ. 9. ἀπὸ τῶν ἀνομιῶν τοῦ λαοῦ μου ἥκει
εἰς θάνατον. 10. καὶ δώσω τοὺς πονηροὺς ἀντὶ
τῆς ταφῆς αὐτοῦ καὶ τοὺς πλουσίους ἀντὶ τοῦ
θανάτου αὐτοῦ· ὅτι ἀνομίαν οὐκ ἐποίησεν, οὐδὲ
εὑρέθη δόλος ἐν τῷ στόματι αὐτοῦ. καὶ κύριος
βούλεται καθαρίσαι αὐτὸν τῆς πληγῆς. 11. ἐὰν
δῶτε περὶ ἁμαρτίας, ἡ ψυχὴ ὑμῶν ὄψεται σπέρμα
μακρόβιον. 12. καὶ κύριος βούλεται ἀφελεῖν ἀπὸ
τοῦ πόνου τῆς ψυχῆς αὐτοῦ, δεῖξαι αὐτῷ φῶς καὶ
πλάσαι τῇ συνέσει, δικαιῶσαι δίκαιον εὖ δουλεύ-
οντα πολλοῖς. καὶ τὰς ἁμαρτίας αὐτῶν αὐτὸς
ἀνοίσει. 13. διὰ τοῦτο αὐτὸς κληρονομήσει
πολλοὺς καὶ τῶν ἰσχυρῶν μεριεῖ σκῦλα· ἀνθ᾽ ὧν
παρεδόθη εἰς θάνατον ἡ ψυχὴ αὐτοῦ, καὶ ἐν τοῖς
ἀνόμοις ἐλογίσθη. 14. καὶ αὐτὸς ἁμαρτίας πολλῶν
ἀνήνεγκεν καὶ διὰ τὰς ἁμαρτίας αὐτῶν παρεδόθη.
Ps. 22, 6-8 15. καὶ πάλιν αὐτός φησιν· Ἐγὼ δέ εἰμι σκώληξ
καὶ οὐκ ἄνθρωπος, ὄνειδος ἀνθρώπων καὶ ἐξουθέ-
νημα λαοῦ. 16. πάντες οἱ θεωροῦντές με ἐξεμυκ-
τήρισάν με, ἐλάλησαν ἐν χείλεσιν, ἐκίνησαν
κεφαλήν· Ἤλπισεν ἐπὶ κύριον, ῥυσάσθω αὐτόν,
σωσάτω αὐτόν, ὅτι θέλει αὐτόν. 17. ὁρᾶτε,
ἄνδρες ἀγαπητοί, τίς ὁ ὑπογραμμὸς ὁ δεδομένος
ἡμῖν· εἰ γὰρ ὁ κύριος οὕτως ἐταπεινοφρόνησεν, τί
ποιήσωμεν ἡμεῖς οἱ ὑπὸ τὸν ζυγὸν τῆς χάριτος
αὐτοῦ δι᾽ αὐτοῦ ἐλθόντες;

his generation? For his life is taken away from the earth. 9. For the iniquities of my people is he come to death. 10. And I will give the wicked for his burial, and the rich for his death; for he wrought no iniquity, nor was guile found in his mouth. And the Lord's will is to purify him from stripes. 11. If ye make an offering for sin, your soul shall see a long-lived seed. 12. And the Lord's will is to take of the toil of his soul, to show him light and to form him with understanding, to justify a righteous man who serveth many well. And he himself shall bear their sins. 13. For this reason shall he inherit many, and he shall share the spoils of the strong; because his soul was delivered to death, and he was reckoned among the transgressors. 14. And he bore the sins of many, and for their sins was he delivered up." 15. And again he says himself, " But I am a worm and no man, a reproach of men, and despised of the people. 16. All they who saw me mocked me, they spoke with their lips, they shook their heads; He hoped on the Lord, let him deliver him, let him save him, for he hath pleasure in him." 17. You see, Beloved, what is the example which is given to us; for if the Lord was thus humble-minded, what shall we do, who through him have come under the yoke of his grace?

XVII

Heb. 11, 37   1. Μιμηταὶ γενώμεθα κἀκείνων, οἵτινες ἐν δέρ-
μασιν αἰγείοις καὶ μηλωταῖς περιεπάτησαν
κηρύσσοντες τὴν ἔλευσιν τοῦ Χριστοῦ· λέγομεν
δὲ Ἠλίαν καὶ Ἐλισαιέ, ἔτι δὲ καὶ Ἰεζεκιήλ, τοὺς
προφήτας· πρὸς τούτοις καὶ τοὺς μεμαρτυρημένους.
2. ἐμαρτυρήθη μεγάλως Ἀβραὰμ καὶ φίλος προσ-
ηγορεύθη τοῦ θεοῦ, καὶ λέγει ἀτενίζων εἰς τὴν
Gen. 18, 27   δόξαν τοῦ θεοῦ ταπεινοφρονῶν· Ἐγὼ δέ εἰμι γῆ
καὶ σποδός. 3. ἔτι δὲ καὶ περὶ Ἰὼβ οὕτως
Job 1, 1   γέγραπται· Ἰὼβ δὲ ἦν δίκαιος καὶ ἄμεμπτος,
ἀληθινός, θεοσεβής, ἀπεχόμενος ἀπὸ παντὸς
κακοῦ. 4. ἀλλ᾽ αὐτὸς ἑαυτοῦ κατηγορεῖ λέγων·
Job 14, 4, 5   Οὐδεὶς καθαρὸς ἀπὸ ῥύπου, οὐδ᾽ ἂν μιᾶς ἡμέρας ἡ
Num. 12, 7   ζωὴ αὐτοῦ. 5. Μωϋσῆς πιστὸς ἐν ὅλῳ τῷ οἴκῳ αὐτοῦ
Heb 3, 2   ἐκλήθη, καὶ διὰ τῆς ὑπηρεσίας αὐτοῦ ἔκρινεν ὁ
θεὸς Αἴγυπτον διὰ τῶν μαστίγων καὶ τῶν αἰκισ-
μάτων αὐτῶν· ἀλλὰ κἀκεῖνος δοξασθεὶς μεγάλως
οὐκ ἐμεγαλορημόνησεν, ἀλλ᾽ εἶπεν ἐκ τῆς βάτου
Exod. 3, 11;   χρηματισμοῦ αὐτῷ διδομένου· Τίς εἰμι ἐγώ, ὅτι
4, 10   με πέμπεις; Ἐγὼ δέ εἰμι ἰσχνόφωνος καὶ βραδύ-
γλωσσος. 6. καὶ πάλιν λέγει· Ἐγὼ δέ εἰμι
ἀτμὶς ἀπὸ κύθρας.

XVIII

1. Τί δὲ εἴπωμεν ἐπὶ τῷ μεμαρτυρημένῳ Δαυείδ;
Ps. 89, 20;   ἐφ᾽ οὗ [1] εἶπεν ὁ θεός· Εὗρον ἄνδρα κατὰ τὴν
Acts 13, 22   καρδίαν μου, Δαυεὶδ τὸν τοῦ Ἰεσσαί, ἐν ἐλέει
αἰωνίῳ ἔχρισα αὐτόν. 2. ἀλλὰ καὶ αὐτὸς λέγει
Ps. 51, 1-17   πρὸς τὸν θεόν· Ἐλέησόν με, ὁ θεός, κατὰ τὸ μέγα

[1] So L Clem. πρὸς ὃν ACS.

38

XVII

1. LET us also be imitators of those who went about "in the skins of goats and sheep," heralding the coming of Christ; we mean Elijah and Elisha, and moreover Ezekiel, the prophets, and in addition to them the famous men of old. 2. Great fame was given to Abraham, and he was called 'the Friend of God, and he, fixing his gaze in' humility on the Glory of God, says "But I am dust and ashes." 3. Moreover it is also written thus concerning Job :—" Now Job was righteous and blameless, true, a worshipper of God, and kept himself from all evil." 4. But he accuses himself, saying, " No man is clean from defilement, not even if his life be but for a single day." 5. Moses was called " Faithful with all his house," and through his ministry God judged Egypt with their scourges and torments; but he, though he was given great glory, did not use great words, but, when an oracle was given to him from the bush, said :—" Who am I that thou sendest me ? Nay, I am a man of feeble speech, and a slow tongue." 6. And again he says, " But I am as smoke from a pot."

[margin: Humility in the Old Testament]

[margin: Abraham]

[margin: Job]

[margin: Moses]

XVIII

1. BUT what shall we say of the famous David ? Of him said God, " I have found a man after my own heart, David the son of Jesse, I have anointed him with eternal mercy;" 2. but he too says to God " Have mercy upon me, O God, according to thy

[margin: The humility of David]

THE APOSTOLIC FATHERS

ἔλεός σου, καὶ κατὰ τὸ πλῆθος τῶν οἰκτιρμῶν σου
ἐξάλειψον τὸ ἀνόμημά μου. 3. ἐπὶ πλεῖον πλῦνόν
με ἀπὸ τῆς ἀνομίας μου, καὶ ἀπὸ τῆς ἁμαρτίας μου
καθάρισόν με· ὅτι τὴν ἀνομίαν μου ἐγὼ γινώσκω,
καὶ ἡ ἁμαρτία μου ἐνώπιόν μου ἐστὶν διαπαντός.
4. σοὶ μόνῳ ἥμαρτον, καὶ τὸ πονηρὸν ἐνώπιόν σου
ἐποίησα, ὅπως ἂν δικαιωθῇς ἐν τοῖς λόγοις σου,
καὶ νικήσῃς ἐν τῷ κρίνεσθαί σε. 5. ἰδοὺ γὰρ ἐν
ἀνομίαις συνελήμφθην, καὶ ἐν ἁμαρτίαις ἐκίσσησέν
με ἡ μήτηρ μου. 6. ἰδοὺ γὰρ ἀλήθειαν ἠγάπησας·
τὰ ἄδηλα καὶ τὰ κρύφια τῆς σοφίας σου ἐδήλωσάς
μοι. 7. ῥαντιεῖς με ὑσσώπῳ, καὶ καθαρισθή-
σομαι· πλυνεῖς με, καὶ ὑπὲρ χιόνα λευκανθήσομαι.
8. ἀκουτιεῖς με ἀγαλλίασιν καὶ εὐφροσύνην.
ἀγαλλιάσονται ὀστᾶ τεταπεινωμένα. 9. ἀπό-
στρεψον τὸ πρόσωπόν σου ἀπὸ τῶν ἁμαρτιῶν μου,
καὶ πάσας τὰς ἀνομίας μου ἐξάλειψον. 10. καρδίαν καθαρὰν κτίσον ἐν ἐμοί, ὁ θεός, καὶ πνεῦμα
εὐθὲς ἐγκαίνισον ἐν τοῖς ἐγκάτοις μου. 11. μὴ
ἀπορίψῃς με ἀπὸ τοῦ προσώπου σου, καὶ τὸ
πνεῦμα τὸ ἅγιόν σου μὴ ἀντανέλῃς ἀπ' ἐμοῦ.
12. ἀπόδος μοι τὴν ἀγαλλίασιν τοῦ σωτηρίου σου,
καὶ πνεύματι ἡγεμονικῷ στήρισόν με. 13. διδάξω
ἀνόμους τὰς ὁδούς σου, καὶ ἀσεβεῖς ἐπιστρέψουσιν
ἐπὶ σέ. 14. ῥῦσαί με ἐξ αἱμάτων, ὁ θεός, ὁ θεὸς
τῆς σωτηρίας μου. 15. ἀγαλλιάσεται ἡ γλῶσσά
μου τὴν δικαιοσύνην σου. κύριε, τὸ στόμα μου
ἀνοίξεις, καὶ τὰ χείλη μου ἀναγγελεῖ τὴν αἴνεσίν
σου. 16. ὅτι εἰ ἠθέλησας θυσίαν, ἔδωκα ἄν·
ὁλοκαυτώματα οὐκ εὐδοκήσεις. 17. θυσία τῷ θεῷ
πνεῦμα συντετριμμένον· καρδίαν συντετριμμένην
καὶ τεταπεινωμένην ὁ θεὸς οὐκ ἐξουθενώσει.

great mercy, and according to the multitude of thy compassions, blot out my transgression. 3. Wash me yet more from mine iniquity, and cleanse me from my sin ; for I know my iniquity, and my sin is ever before me. 4. Against thee only did I sin, and did evil before thee, that thou mightest be justified in thy words, and mightest overcome when thou art judged. 5. For, lo, I was conceived in iniquity, and in sin did my mother bear me. 6. For, behold, thou hast loved truth, thou didst make plain to me the secret and hidden things of thy wisdom. 7. Thou shalt sprinkle me with hyssop, and I shall be cleansed ; thou shalt wash me, and I shall be whiter than snow. 8. Thou shalt make me hear joy and gladness ; the bones which have been humbled shall rejoice. 9. Turn thy face from my sins, and blot out all mine iniquities. 10. Create a clean heart in me, O God, and renew a right spirit in my inmost parts. 11. Cast me not away from thy presence, and take not thy Holy Spirit from me. 12. Give me back the gladness of thy salvation, strengthen me with thy governing spirit. 13. I will teach the wicked thy ways, and the ungodly shall be converted unto thee. 14. Deliver me from blood-guiltiness, O God, the God of my salvation. 15. My tongue shall rejoice in thy righteousness. O Lord, thou shalt open my mouth, and my lips shall tell of thy praise. 16. For if thou hadst desired sacrifice, I would have given it ; in whole burnt offerings thou wilt not delight. 17. The sacrifice unto God is a broken spirit, a broken and a humbled heart God shall not despise."

THE APOSTOLIC FATHERS

XIX

1. Τῶν τοσούτων οὖν καὶ τοιούτων οὕτως μεμαρτυρημένων τὸ ταπεινόφρον καὶ τὸ ὑποδεὲς διὰ τῆς ὑπακοῆς οὐ μόνον ἡμᾶς, ἀλλὰ καὶ τὰς πρὸ ἡμῶν γενεὰς βελτίους ἐποίησεν, τούς τε καταδεξαμένους τὰ λόγια αὐτοῦ ἐν φόβῳ καὶ ἀληθείᾳ.

Heb. 12, 1

2. πολλῶν οὖν καὶ μεγάλων καὶ ἐνδόξων μετειληφότες πράξεων ἐπαναδράμωμεν ἐπὶ τὸν ἐξ ἀρχῆς παραδεδομένον ἡμῖν τῆς εἰρήνης σκοπόν, καὶ ἀτενίσωμεν εἰς τὸν πατέρα καὶ κτίστην τοῦ σύμπαντος κόσμου καὶ ταῖς μεγαλοπρεπέσι καὶ ὑπερβαλλούσαις αὐτοῦ δωρεαῖς τῆς εἰρήνης εὐεργεσίαις τε κολληθῶμεν. 3. ἴδωμεν αὐτὸν κατὰ διάνοιαν καὶ ἐμβλέψωμεν τοῖς ὄμμασιν τῆς ψυχῆς εἰς τὸ μακρόθυμον αὐτοῦ βούλημα· νοήσωμεν, πῶς ἀόργητος ὑπάρχει πρὸς πᾶσαν τὴν κτίσιν αὐτοῦ.

XX

1. Οἱ οὐρανοὶ τῇ διοικήσει αὐτοῦ σαλευόμενοι ἐν εἰρήνῃ ὑποτάσσονται αὐτῷ. 2. ἡμέρα τε καὶ νὺξ τὸν τεταγμένον ὑπ’ αὐτοῦ δρόμον διανύουσιν, μηδὲν ἀλλήλοις ἐμποδίζοντα. 3. ἥλιός τε καὶ σελήνη, ἀστέρων τε χοροὶ κατὰ τὴν διαταγὴν αὐτοῦ ἐν ὁμονοίᾳ δίχα πάσης παρεκβάσεως ἐξελίσσουσιν τοὺς ἐπιτεταγμένους αὐτοῖς ὁρισμούς. 4. γῆ κυοφοροῦσα κατὰ τὸ θέλημα αὐτοῦ τοῖς ἰδίοις καιροῖς τὴν πανπληθῆ ἀνθρώποις τε καὶ θηρσὶν καὶ πᾶσιν τοῖς οὖσιν ἐπ’ αὐτῆς ζῴοις ἀνατέλλει τροφήν, μὴ διχοστατοῦσα μηδὲ ἀλλοιοῦσά

XIX

1. THE humility and obedient submission of so Exhortation to peace
many men of such great fame, have rendered better
not only us, but also the generations before us, who
received his oracles in fear and truth. 2. Seeing
then that we have received a share in many great
and glorious deeds, let us hasten on to the goal of
peace, which was given us from the beginning,
and let us fix our gaze on the Father and Creator of
the whole world and cleave to his splendid and
excellent gifts of peace, and to his good deeds to us.
3. Let us contemplate him with our mind, let us
gaze with the eyes of our soul on his long-suffering
purpose, let us consider how free from wrath he is
towards all his creatures.

XX

1. THE heavens moving at his appointment are The peace and harmony of the Universe
subject to him in peace ; 2. day and night follow
the course allotted by him without hindering each
other. 3. Sun and moon and the companies of
the stars roll on, according to his direction, in
harmony, in their appointed courses, and swerve
not from them at all. 4. The earth teems according
to his will at its proper seasons, and puts forth food in
full abundance for men and beasts and all the living
things that are on it, with no dissension, and changing

43

τι τῶν δεδογματισμένων ὑπ' αὐτοῦ. 5. ἀβύσσων τε ἀνεξιχνίαστα καὶ νερτέρων ἀνεκδιήγητα κλίματα [1] τοῖς αὐτοῖς συνέχεται προστάγμασιν. 6. τὸ κύτος τῆς ἀπείρου θαλάσσης κατὰ τὴν δημιουργίαν αὐτοῦ συσταθὲν εἰς τὰς συναγωγὰς οὐ παρεκβαίνει τὰ περιτεθειμένα αὐτῇ κλεῖθρα, ἀλλὰ καθὼς

Job 38, 11 διέταξεν αὐτῇ, οὕτως ποιεῖ. 7. εἶπεν γάρ· Ἕως ὧδε ἥξεις, καὶ τὰ κύματά σου ἐν σοὶ συντριβή- σεται. 8. ὠκεανὸς ἀπέραντος ἀνθρώποις καὶ οἱ μετ' αὐτὸν κόσμοι ταῖς αὐταῖς ταγαῖς τοῦ δεσπότου διευθύνονται. 9. καιροὶ ἐαρινοὶ καὶ θερινοὶ καὶ μετοπωρινοὶ καὶ χειμερινοὶ ἐν εἰρήνῃ μεταπαρα- διδόασιν ἀλλήλοις. 10. ἀνέμων σταθμοὶ κατὰ τὸν ἴδιον καιρὸν τὴν λειτουργίαν αὐτῶν ἀπρο- σκόπως ἐπιτελοῦσιν· ἀέναοί τε πηγαί, πρὸς ἀπόλαυσιν καὶ ὑγείαν δημιουργηθεῖσαι, δίχα ἐλλείψεως παρέχονται τοὺς πρὸς ζωῆς ἀνθρώ- ποις μαζούς· τά τε ἐλάχιστα τῶν ζώων τὰς συνελεύσεις αὐτῶν ἐν ὁμονοίᾳ καὶ εἰρήνῃ ποιοῦνται. 11. ταῦτα πάντα ὁ μέγας δημιουργὸς καὶ δεσπότης τῶν ἁπάντων ἐν εἰρήνῃ καὶ ὁμονοίᾳ προσέταξεν εἶναι, εὐεργετῶν τὰ πάντα, ὑπερεκπερισσῶς δὲ ἡμᾶς τοὺς προσπεφευγότας τοῖς οἰκτιρμοῖς αὐτοῦ διὰ τοῦ κυρίου ἡμῶν Ἰησοῦ Χριστοῦ, 12. ᾧ ἡ δόξα καὶ ἡ μεγαλωσύνη εἰς τοὺς αἰῶνας τῶν αἰώνων. ἀμήν.

---

[1] κρίματα AC, qui situ (sic) L, "boundaries" K. The emendation given in the text seems the most probable treat- ment of the difficulty.

none of his decrees. 5. The unsearchable places of the abysses and the unfathomable realms of the lower world are controlled by the same ordinances. 6. The hollow of the boundless sea is gathered by his working into its allotted places, and does not pass the barriers placed around it, but does even as he enjoined on it; 7. for he said "Thus far shalt thou come, and thy waves shall be broken within thee." 8. The ocean, which men cannot pass, and the worlds beyond it, are ruled by the same injunctions of the Master. 9. The seasons of spring, summer, autumn, and winter give place to one another in peace. 10. The stations of the winds fulfil their service without hindrance at the proper time. The everlasting springs, created for enjoyment and health, supply sustenance for the life of man without fail ; and the smallest of animals meet together in concord and peace. 11. All these things did the great Creator and Master of the universe ordain to be in peace and concord, and to all things does he do good, and more especially to us who have fled for refuge to his mercies through our Lord Jesus Christ, 12. to whom[1] be the glory and the majesty for ever and ever, Amen.

---

[1] The Latin has *per quem deo et patri,* "through whom to God and the Father."

XXI

1. Ὁρᾶτε, ἀγαπητοί, μὴ αἱ εὐεργεσίαι αὐτοῦ αἱ πολλαὶ γένωνται εἰς κρίμα¹ ἡμῖν, ἐὰν μὴ ἀξίως αὐτοῦ πολιτευόμενοι τὰ καλὰ καὶ εὐάρεστα ἐνώπιον αὐτοῦ ποιῶμεν μεθ' ὁμονοίας. 2. λέγει

Prov. 20, 27 γάρ που· Πνεῦμα κυρίου λύχνος ἐρευνῶν τὰ ταμιεῖα τῆς γαστρός· 3. ἴδωμεν,² πῶς ἐγγύς ἐστιν, καὶ ὅτι οὐδὲν λέληθεν αὐτὸν τῶν ἐννοιῶν ἡμῶν οὐδὲ τῶν διαλογισμῶν ὧν ποιούμεθα· 4. δίκαιον οὖν ἐστὶν μὴ λειποτακτεῖν ἡμᾶς ἀπὸ τοῦ θελήματος αὐτοῦ. 5. μᾶλλον ἀνθρώποις ἄφροσι καὶ ἀνοήτοις καὶ ἐπαιρομένοις καὶ ἐγκαυχωμένοις ἐν ἀλαζονείᾳ τοῦ λόγου αὐτῶν προσκόψωμεν ἢ τῷ θεῷ. 6. τὸν κύριον Ἰησοῦν Χριστόν, οὗ τὸ αἷμα ὑπὲρ ἡμῶν ἐδόθη, ἐντραπῶμεν, τοὺς προηγουμένους ἡμῶν αἰδεσθῶμεν, τοὺς πρεσβυτέρους τιμήσωμεν, τοὺς νέους παιδεύσωμεν τὴν παιδείαν τοῦ φόβου τοῦ θεοῦ, τὰς γυναῖκας ἡμῶν ἐπὶ τὸ ἀγαθὸν διορθωσώμεθα. 7. τὸ ἀξιαγάπητον τῆς ἁγνείας ἦθος ἐνδειξάσθωσαν, τὸ ἀκέραιον τῆς πραΰτητος αὐτῶν βούλημα ἀποδειξάτωσαν, τὸ ἐπιεικὲς τῆς γλώσσης αὐτῶν διὰ τῆς σιγῆς φανερὸν ποιησάτωσαν, τὴν ἀγάπην αὐτῶν μὴ κατὰ προσκλίσεις, ἀλλὰ πᾶσιν τοῖς φοβουμένοις τὸν θεὸν ὁσίως ἴσην παρεχέτωσαν. 8. τὰ τέκνα ἡμῶν τῆς ἐν Χριστῷ παιδείας μεταλαμβανέτωσαν· μαθέτωσαν, τί ταπεινοφροσύνη παρὰ θεῷ ἰσχύει, τί ἀγάπη ἁγνὴ παρὰ θεῷ δύναται, πῶς ὁ φόβος αὐτοῦ καλὸς καὶ μέγας καὶ

---

¹ A(C) read κρίμα πᾶσιν ἡμῖν.
² L implies εἴδωμεν (sciamus), "let us know."

XXI

1. TAKE heed, beloved, lest his many good works Christian towards us become a judgment on us, if we do virtues not good and virtuous deeds before him in concord, and be citizens worthy of him. 2. For he says in one place:—"The Spirit of the Lord is a lamp searching the inward parts." 3. Let us observe how near he is, and that nothing escapes him of our thoughts or of the devices which we make. 4. It is right, therefore, that we should not be deserters from his will. 5. Let us offend foolish and thoughtless men, who are exalted and boast in the pride of their words, rather than God. 6. Let us reverence the Lord Jesus Christ, whose blood was given for us, let us respect those who rule us, let us honour the aged,[1] let us instruct the young in the fear of God, let us lead our wives to that which is good. 7. Let them exhibit the lovely habit of purity, let them show forth the innocent will of meekness, let them make the gentleness of their tongue manifest by their silence, let them not give their affection by factious preference, but in holiness to all equally who fear God. 8. Let our children share in the instruction which is in Christ, let them learn the strength of humility before God, the power of pure love before God, how beautiful and great is his fear and how it

[1] Or possibly "the Presbyters," but the context makes this improbable.

σώζων πάντας τοὺς ἐν αὐτῷ ὁσίως ἀναστρεφο-
μένους ἐν καθαρᾷ διανοίᾳ. 9. ἐρευνητὴς γάρ ἐστιν
ἐννοιῶν ‘καὶ ἐνθυμήσεων· οὗ ἡ πνοὴ αὐτοῦ ἐν ἡμῖν
ἐστίν, καὶ ὅταν θέλῃ, ἀνελεῖ αὐτήν.

XXII

1. Ταῦτα δὲ πάντα βεβαιοῖ ἡ ἐν Χριστῷ πίστις·
καὶ γὰρ αὐτὸς διὰ τοῦ πνεύματος τοῦ ἁγίου οὕτως
Ps.34,11-17 προσκαλεῖται ἡμᾶς· Δεῦτε, τέκνα, ἀκούσατέ μου,
φόβον κυρίου διδάξω ὑμᾶς. 2. τίς ἐστιν ἄνθρωπος ὁ θέλων ζωήν, ἀγαπῶν ἡμέρας ἰδεῖν ἀγαθάς ;
3. παῦσον τὴν γλῶσσάν σου ἀπὸ κακοῦ, καὶ χείλη
σου τοῦ μὴ λαλῆσαι δόλον. 4. ἔκκλινον ἀπὸ
κακοῦ, καὶ ποίησον ἀγαθόν. 5. ζήτησον εἰρήνην,
καὶ δίωξον αὐτήν· 6. ὀφθαλμοὶ κυρίου ἐπὶ δικαίους, καὶ ὦτα αὐτοῦ πρὸς δέησιν αὐτῶν· πρόσωπον
δὲ κυρίου ἐπὶ ποιοῦντας κακά, τοῦ ἐξολεθρεῦσαι
ἐκ γῆς τὸ μνημόσυνον αὐτῶν. 7. ἐκέκραξεν ὁ
δίκαιος, καὶ ὁ κύριος εἰσήκουσεν αὐτοῦ, καὶ ἐκ
πασῶν τῶν θλίψεων αὐτοῦ ἐρύσατο αὐτόν.[1]
Ps. 32, 10 8. Πολλαὶ αἱ μάστιγες τοῦ ἁμαρτωλοῦ, τοὺς δὲ
ἐλπίζοντας ἐπὶ κύριον ἔλεος κυκλώσει.

XXIII

1. Ὁ οἰκτίρμων κατὰ πάντα καὶ εὐεργετικὸς
πατὴρ ἔχει σπλάγχνα ἐπὶ τοὺς φοβουμένους
αὐτόν, ἠπίως τε καὶ προσηνῶς τὰς χάριτας αὐτοῦ

Ps. 34, 19 [1] S adds πολλαὶ αἱ θλίψεις τοῦ δικαίου, καὶ ἐκ πασῶν αὐτῶν
ῥύσεται αὐτὸν ὁ κύριος, but the evidence of ACLK suggests that
it is an insertion from the text of LXX ; cf. I. Clem. XV. 5,
and the note on the text.

gives salvation to all who live holily in it with a pure mind. 9. For he is a searcher of thoughts and desires; his breath is in us, and when he will he shall take it away.

XXII

1. Now the faith which is in Christ confirms all these things, for he himself through his Holy Spirit calls us thus :—"Come, Children, hearken to me, I will teach you the fear of the Lord. 2. Who is the man that desireth life, that loveth to see good days? 3. Make thy tongue cease from evil, and thy lips that they speak no guile. 4. Depart from evil, and do good. 5. Seek peace, and pursue it. 6. The eyes of the Lord are upon the righteous, and his ears are open to their petition ; but the face of the Lord is against those that do evil, to destroy the memory of them from off the earth. 7. The righteous cried, and the Lord heard him, and delivered him out of all his afflictions.[1] 8. Many are the scourges of the sinner, but mercy shall encompass those that hope on the Lord."

The confirmation of this teaching in the Scriptures

XXIII

1. The all-merciful and beneficent Father has compassion on those that fear him, and kindly and lovingly bestows his favours on those that draw near

Humility and sincerity

---

[1] The Editors (except Knopf) add as v. 8, " Many are the afflictions of the righteous and out of them all will the Lord deliver him."

ἀποδιδοῖ τοῖς προσερχομένοις αὐτῷ ἁπλῇ διανοίᾳ.
2. διὸ μὴ διψυχῶμεν, μηδὲ ἰνδαλλέσθω ἡ ψυχὴ
ἡμῶν ἐπὶ ταῖς ὑπερβαλλούσαις καὶ ἐνδόξοις
δωρεαῖς αὐτοῦ. 3. πόρρω γενέσθω ἀφ' ἡμῶν ἡ
γραφὴ αὕτη, ὅπου λέγει· Ταλαίπωροί εἰσιν οἱ
δίψυχοι, οἱ διστάζοντες τῇ ψυχῇ, οἱ λέγοντες·
Ταῦτα ἠκούσαμεν καὶ ἐπὶ τῶν πατέρων ἡμῶν, καὶ
ἰδού, γεγηράκαμεν, καὶ οὐδὲν ἡμῖν τούτων συνβέ-
βηκεν. 4. ὦ ἀνόητοι, συμβάλετε ἑαυτοὺς ξύλῳ·
λάβετε ἄμπελον· πρῶτον μὲν φυλλοροεῖ, εἶτα
βλαστὸς γίνεται, εἶτα φύλλον, εἶτα ἄνθος, καὶ
μετὰ ταῦτα ὄμφαξ, εἶτα σταφυλὴ παρεστηκυῖα.
ὁρᾶτε, ὅτι ἐν καιρῷ ὀλίγῳ εἰς πέπειρον καταντᾷ ὁ
καρπὸς τοῦ ξύλου. 5. ἐπ' ἀληθείας ταχὺ καὶ
ἐξαίφνης τελειωθήσεται τὸ βούλημα αὐτοῦ, συν-
επιμαρτυρούσης καὶ τῆς γραφῆς, ὅτι ταχὺ ἥξει
καὶ οὐ χρονιεῖ, καὶ ἐξαίφνης ἥξει ὁ κύριος εἰς τὸν
ναὸν αὐτοῦ, καὶ ὁ ἅγιος, ὃν ὑμεῖς προσδοκᾶτε.

Isaiah
13, 22 (LXX)
Malach. 3, 1

XXIV

1. Κατανοήσωμεν, ἀγαπητοί, πῶς ὁ δεσπότης
ἐπιδείκνυται διηνεκῶς ἡμῖν τὴν μέλλουσαν ἀνάστασιν ἔσεσθαι, ἧς τὴν ἀπαρχὴν ἐποιήσατο τὸν
κύριον Ἰησοῦν Χριστὸν ἐκ νεκρῶν ἀναστήσας.
2. ἴδωμεν, ἀγαπητοί, τὴν κατὰ καιρὸν γινομένην
ἀνάστασιν. 3. ἡμέρα καὶ νὺξ ἀνάστασιν ἡμῖν δη-
λοῦσιν· κοιμᾶται ἡ νύξ, ἀνίσταται ἡ ἡμέρα· ἡ ἡμέρα
ἄπεισιν, νὺξ ἐπέρχεται. 4. λάβωμεν τοὺς καρπούς·

I Cor. 15, 20

to him with a simple mind. 2. Wherefore let us not be double-minded, nor let our soul be fanciful concerning his excellent and glorious gifts. 3. Let this Scripture be far from us in which he says " Wretched are the double-minded, who doubt in their soul and say ' We have heard these things even in the days of our fathers, and behold we have grown old, and none of these things has happened to us.' 4. Oh, foolish men, compare yourself to a tree : take a vine, first it sheds its leaves, then there comes a bud, then a leaf, then a flower, and after this the unripe grape, then the full bunch."[1] See how in a little time the fruit of the tree comes to ripeness. 5. Truly his will shall be quickly and suddenly accomplished, as the Scripture also bears witness that " he shall come quickly and shall not tarry ; and the Lord shall suddenly come to his temple, and the Holy One for whom ye look."

XXIV

1. Let us consider, beloved, how the Master continually proves to us that there will be a future resurrection, of which he has made the first-fruits, by raising the Lord Jesus Christ from the dead. 2. Let us look, beloved, at the resurrection which is taking place at its proper season. 3. Day and night show us a resurrection. The night sleeps, the day arises : the day departs, night comes on. 4. Let us take the crops : how and in what way does the

The resurrection foreshadowed in Nature

---

[1] This quotation which is also found in II. Clem. 11, 2, cannot be identified. Some think it is from the lost apocalypse of Eldad and Modad. Cf. Hermas, *Vis.* 2, 3.

Mk. 4, 3 and
cf. I Cor. 15,
36 ff. ὁ σπόρος πῶς καὶ τίνα τρόπον γίνεται; 5. ἐξῆλθεν
ὁ σπείρων καὶ ἔβαλεν εἰς τὴν γῆν ἕκαστον τῶν
σπερμάτων, ἅτινα πεσόντα εἰς τὴν γῆν ξηρὰ καὶ
γυμνὰ διαλύεται· εἶτ' ἐκ τῆς διαλύσεως ἡ μεγα-
λειότης τῆς προνοίας τοῦ δεσπότου ἀνίστησιν αὐτά,
καὶ ἐκ τοῦ ἑνὸς πλείονα αὔξει καὶ ἐκφέρει καρπόν.

XXV

1. Ἴδωμεν τὸ παράδοξον σημεῖον τὸ γινόμενον
ἐν τοῖς ἀνατολικοῖς τόποις, τουτέστιν τοῖς περὶ
τὴν Ἀραβίαν. 2. ὄρνεον γάρ ἐστιν, ὃ προσονο-
μάζεται φοῖνιξ· τοῦτο μονογενὲς ὑπάρχον ζῇ ἔτη
πεντακόσια, γενόμενόν τε ἤδη πρὸς ἀπόλυσιν τοῦ
ἀποθανεῖν αὐτό, σηκὸν ἑαυτῷ ποιεῖ ἐκ λιβάνου καὶ
σμύρνης καὶ τῶν λοιπῶν ἀρωμάτων, εἰς ὃν πληρω-
θέντος τοῦ χρόνου εἰσέρχεται καὶ τελευτᾷ. 3.
σηπομένης δὲ τῆς σαρκὸς σκώληξ τις γεννᾶται, ὃς
ἐκ τῆς ἰκμάδος τοῦ τετελευτηκότος ζῴου ἀνατρε-
φόμενος πτεροφυεῖ· εἶτα γενναῖος γενόμενος αἴρει
τὸν σηκὸν ἐκεῖνον, ὅπου τὰ ὀστᾶ τοῦ προγεγονότος
ἐστίν, καὶ ταῦτα βαστάζων διανύει ἀπὸ τῆς Ἀρα-
βικῆς χώρας ἕως τῆς Αἰγύπτου εἰς τὴν λεγομένην
Ἡλιούπολιν, 4. καὶ ἡμέρας, βλεπόντων πάντων,
ἐπιπτὰς ἐπὶ τὸν τοῦ ἡλίου βωμὸν τίθησιν αὐτὰ
καὶ οὕτως εἰς τοὐπίσω ἀφορμᾷ. 5. οἱ οὖν ἱερεῖς
ἐπισκέπτονται τὰς ἀναγραφὰς τῶν χρόνων καὶ
εὑρίσκουσιν αὐτὸν πεντακοσιοστοῦ ἔτους πεπλη-
ρωμένου ἐληλυθέναι.

sowing take place? 5. "The sower went forth" and cast each of the seeds into the ground, and they fall on to the ground, parched and bare, and suffer decay; then from their decay the greatness of the providence of the Master raises them up, and from one grain more grow and bring forth fruit.

XXV

1. LET us consider the strange sign which takes place in the East, that is in the districts near Arabia. 2. There is a bird which is called the Phoenix. This is the only one of its kind, and lives 500 years; and when the time of its dissolution in death is at hand, it makes itself a sepulchre of frankincense and myrrh and other spices, and when the time is fulfilled it enters into it and dies. 3. Now, from the corruption of its flesh there springs a worm, which is nourished by the juices of the dead bird, and puts forth wings. Then, when it has become strong, it takes up that sepulchre, in which are the bones of its predecessor, and carries them from the country of Arabia as far as Egypt until it reaches the city called Heliopolis, 4. and in the daylight in the sight of all it flies to the altar of the Sun, places them there, and then starts back to its former home. 5. Then the priests inspect the registers of dates, and they find that it has come at the fulfilment of the 500th year.[1]

The Phoenix as a sign of the resurrection

---

[1] The same story, with variations, is found in Herodotus (ii. 73), Pliny (*Nat. Hist.* x. 2), etc. It was supposed by Christians to be sanctioned by the LXX version of Ps. xcii. 12, where there is a confusion between φοῖνιξ = phoenix, and φοῖνιξ = palm tree.

XXVI

1. Μέγα καὶ θαυμαστὸν οὖν νομίζομεν εἶναι, εἰ ὁ δημιουργὸς τῶν ἁπάντων ἀνάστασιν ποιήσεται τῶν ὁσίως αὐτῷ δουλευσάντων ἐν πεποιθήσει πίστεως ἀγαθῆς, ὅπου καὶ δι' ὀρνέου δείκνυσιν ἡμῖν τὸ μεγαλεῖον τῆς ἐπαγγελίας αὐτοῦ; 2. λέγει γάρ που· Καὶ ἐξαναστήσεις με, καὶ ἐξομολογήσομαί σοι, καί· Ἐκοιμήθην καὶ ὕπνωσα, ἐξηγέρθην, ὅτι σὺ μετ' ἐμοῦ εἶ. 3. καὶ πάλιν Ἰὼβ λέγει· Καὶ ἀναστήσεις τὴν σάρκα μου ταύτην τὴν ἀναντλήσασαν ταῦτα πάντα.

Ps. 28, 7?
Ps. 3, 5
Job 19, 26

XXVII

1. Ταύτῃ οὖν τῇ ἐλπίδι προσδεδέσθωσαν αἱ ψυχαὶ ἡμῶν τῷ πιστῷ ἐν ταῖς ἐπαγγελίαις καὶ τῷ δικαίῳ ἐν τοῖς κρίμασιν. 2. ὁ παραγγείλας μὴ ψεύδεσθαι, πολλῷ μᾶλλον αὐτὸς οὐ ψεύσεται· οὐδὲν γὰρ ἀδύνατον παρὰ τῷ θεῷ εἰ μὴ τὸ ψεύσασθαι. 3. ἀναζωπυρησάτω οὖν ἡ πίστις αὐτοῦ ἐν ἡμῖν, καὶ νοήσωμεν ὅτι πάντα ἐγγὺς αὐτῷ ἐστιν. 4. ἐν λόγῳ τῆς μεγαλωσύνης αὐτοῦ συνεστήσατο τὰ πάντα, καὶ ἐν λόγῳ δύναται αὐτὰ καταστρέψαι. 5. Τίς ἐρεῖ αὐτῷ· Τί ἐποίησας; ἢ τίς ἀντιστήσεται τῷ κράτει τῆς ἰσχύος αὐτοῦ; ὅτε θέλει καὶ ὡς θέλει ποιήσει πάντα, καὶ οὐδὲν μὴ παρέλθῃ τῶν δεδογματισμένων ὑπ' αὐτοῦ. 6. πάντα ἐνώπιον αὐτοῦ εἰσίν, καὶ οὐδὲν λέληθεν τὴν βουλὴν αὐτοῦ, 7. εἰ οἱ οὐρανοὶ διηγοῦνται δόξαν θεοῦ,

Heb. 6, 18
Wisd. 12, 12
Ps. 19, 1-3

54

XXVI

1. Do we then consider it a great and wonderful thing that the creator of the universe will bring about the resurrection of those who served him in holiness, in the confidence of a good faith, when he shows us the greatness of his promise even through a bird ? 2. For he says in one place " And thou shalt raise me up, and I will praise thee," and " I laid me down and slept, I rose up, for thou art with me." 3. And again Job says " And thou shalt raise up this my flesh which has endured all these things." *The resurrection promised in the Scriptures*

XXVII

1. IN this hope then let our souls be bound to him who is faithful in his promises and righteous in his judgments. 2. He who has commanded not to lie shall much more not be a liar himself; for nothing is impossible with God save to lie. 3. Let therefore faith in him be kindled again in us, and let us consider that all things are near him. 4. By the word of his majesty did he establish all things, and by his word can he destroy them. 5. " Who shall say to him what hast thou done, or who shall resist the might of his strength ? " When he will, and as he will, he will do all things, and none of his decrees shall pass away. 6. All is in his sight and nothing has escaped from his counsel, 7. since " The heavens declare the glory of God and the firmament *The necessity of cleaving to God*

ποίησιν δὲ χειρῶν αὐτοῦ ἀναγγέλλει τὸ στερέωμα·
ἡ ἡμέρα τῇ ἡμέρᾳ ἐρεύγεται ῥῆμα, καὶ νὺξ νυκτὶ
ἀναγγέλλει γνῶσιν· καὶ οὐκ εἰσὶν λόγοι οὐδὲ
λαλιαί, ὧν οὐχὶ ἀκούονται αἱ φωναὶ αὐτῶν.

XXVIII

1. Πάντων οὖν βλεπομένων καὶ ἀκουομένων, φοβηθῶμεν αὐτόν, καὶ ἀπολίπωμεν φαύλων ἔργων μια-
ρὰς ἐπιθυμίας, ἵνα τῷ ἐλέει αὐτοῦ σκεπασθῶμεν ἀπὸ
τῶν μελλόντων κριμάτων· 2. ποῦ γάρ τις ἡμῶν
δύναται φυγεῖν ἀπὸ τῆς κραταιᾶς χειρὸς αὐτοῦ;
ποῖος δὲ κόσμος δέξεταί τινα τῶν αὐτομολούντων
Ps. 139, 7-8 ἀπ' αὐτοῦ; 3. λέγει γάρ που τὸ γραφεῖον· Ποῦ
ἀφήξω καὶ ποῦ κρυβήσομαι ἀπὸ τοῦ προσώπου
σου; ἐὰν ἀναβῶ εἰς τὸν οὐρανόν, σὺ ἐκεῖ εἶ· ἐὰν
ἀπέλθω εἰς τὰ ἔσχατα τῆς γῆς, ἐκεῖ ἡ δεξιά σου·
ἐὰν καταστρώσω εἰς τὰς ἀβύσσους, ἐκεῖ τὸ πνεῦμά
σου. 4. ποῖ οὖν τις ἀπέλθῃ ἢ ποῦ ἀποδράσῃ ἀπὸ
τοῦ τὰ πάντα ἐμπεριέχοντος;

XXIX

1. Προσέλθωμεν οὖν αὐτῷ ἐν ὁσιότητι ψυχῆς,
ἁγνὰς καὶ ἀμιάντους χεῖρας αἴροντες πρὸς αὐτόν,
ἀγαπῶντες τὸν ἐπιεικῆ καὶ εὔσπλαγχνον πατέρα
ἡμῶν, ὃς ἐκλογῆς μέρος ἡμᾶς ἐποίησεν ἑαυτῷ.
Deut. 32 8. 9 2. οὕτω γὰρ γέγραπται· Ὅτε διεμέριζεν ὁ ὕψιστος

telleth his handiwork, day uttereth speech unto day,
and night telleth knowledge to night. And there
are neither words nor speeches, and their voices are
not heard."

XXVIII

1. Since then all things are seen and heard by
him, let us fear him, and leave off from foul desires
of evil deeds, that we may be sheltered by his mercy
from the judgments to come. 2. For whither can
any of us fly from his mighty hand? And what
world shall receive those who seek to desert from
him? 3. For the Writing [1] says in one place:
" Where shall I go and where shall I hide from thy
presence? If I ascend into heaven thou art there,
if I depart to the ends of the earth there is thy
right hand; If I make my bed in the abyss there
is thy spirit." 4. Whither then shall a man depart
or where shall he escape from him who embraces all
things?

The omniscience of God

XXIX

1. Let us then approach him in holiness of soul,
raising pure and undefiled hands to him, loving our
gracious and merciful Father, who has made us the
portion of his choice for himself. 2. For thus it is
written : " When the most high divided the nations,

The privileges of Christians

---

[1] An accurate quotation of an unintelligible sentence. τὸ
γραφεῖον means the third division of the Jewish bible, sometimes called the "Hagiographa"; it was in a sense "Scripture" but not considered as important as the "Law" and
the "Prophets."

ἔθνη, ὡς διέσπειρεν υἱοὺς Ἀδάμ, ἔστησεν ὅρια ἐθνῶν κατὰ ἀριθμὸν ἀγγέλων θεοῦ. ἐγενήθη μερὶς κυρίου λαὸς αὐτοῦ Ἰακώβ, σχοίνισμα κληρονομίας αὐτοῦ Ἰσραήλ. 3. καὶ ἐν ἑτέρῳ τόπῳ λέγει· Ἰδού, κύριος λαμβάνει ἑαυτῷ ἔθνος ἐκ μέσου ἐθνῶν, ὥσπερ λαμβάνει ἄνθρωπος τὴν ἀπαρχὴν αὐτοῦ τῆς ἅλω· καὶ ἐξελεύσεται ἐκ τοῦ ἔθνους ἐκείνου ἅγια ἁγίων.

Deut. 4, 34;
Deut. 14, 2
Num. 18, 27;
II Chron.
31, 14;
Ezek. 48,
12;

XXX

1. Ἁγίου[1] οὖν μερὶς ὑπάρχοντες ποιήσωμεν τὰ τοῦ ἁγιασμοῦ πάντα, φεύγοντες καταλαλιάς, μιαράς τε καὶ ἀνάγνους συμπλοκάς, μέθας τε καὶ νεωτερισμοὺς καὶ βδελυκτὰς ἐπιθυμίας, μυσερὰν μοιχείαν, βδελυκτὴν ὑπερηφανίαν. 2. Θεὸς γάρ, φησίν, ὑπερηφάνοις ἀντιτάσσεται, ταπεινοῖς δὲ δίδωσιν χάριν. 3. κολληθῶμεν οὖν ἐκείνοις, οἷς ἡ χάρις ἀπὸ τοῦ θεοῦ δέδοται· ἐνδυσώμεθα τὴν ὁμόνοιαν ταπεινοφρονοῦντες, ἐγκρατευόμενοι, ἀπὸ παντὸς ψιθυρισμοῦ καὶ καταλαλιᾶς πόρρω ἑαυτοὺς ποιοῦντες, ἔργοις δικαιούμενοι, μὴ[2] λόγοις. 4. λέγει γάρ· Ὁ τὰ πολλὰ λέγων καὶ ἀντακούσεται· ἢ ὁ εὔλαλος οἴεται εἶναι δίκαιος; 5. εὐλογημένος γεννητὸς γυναικὸς ὀλιγόβιος. μὴ πολὺς ἐν ῥήμασιν γίνου. 6. ὁ ἔπαινος ἡμῶν ἔστω ἐν θεῷ καὶ μὴ ἐξ αὐτῶν· αὐτεπαινέτους γὰρ μισεῖ ὁ

Prov. 3, 34;
James 4, 6;
I Pet. 5, 5

Job 11, 2. 3

---

[1] A has ἁγίου οὖν μερίς : C has ἅγια οὖν μέρη : LS imply ἁγία οὖν μερίς "a holy portion" : K represents ἁγίων οὖν μέρις "portion of saints."
[2] μή CLK, καὶ μή AS.

when he scattered the sons of Adam, he established the bounds of the nations according to the number of the angels of God. His people Jacob became the portion of the Lord, Israel was the lot of his inheritance." 3. And in another place he says " Behold the Lord taketh to himself a nation from the midst of nations, as a man taketh the first-fruit of his threshing-floor, and the Holy of Holies shall come forth from that nation."[1]

XXX

1. SEEING then that we are the portion of one who is holy, let us do all the deeds of sanctification, fleeing from evil speaking, and abominable and impure embraces, drunkenness and youthful lusts, and abominable passion, detestable adultery, and abominable pride. 2. " For God," he says, " resisteth the proud but giveth grace to the humble." 3. Let us then join ourselves to those to whom is given grace from God ; let us put on concord in meekness of spirit and continence, keeping ourselves far from all gossip and evil speaking, and be justified by deeds, not by words. 4. For he says " He that speaketh much shall also hear much ; or doth he that is a good speaker think that he is righteous ? 5. Blessed is he that is born of woman and hath a short life. Be not profuse in speech." [2] 6. Let our praise be with God, and not from ourselves, for God hates

The duties of their privileges

[1] The passages quoted in the margin are those which most nearly resemble this quotation, but the difference is considerable, and Clement may be referring to some lost source.

[2] The text is here obviously corrupt ; but the corruption is in the LXX, not in Clement.

THE APOSTOLIC FATHERS

θεός. 7. ἡ μαρτυρία τῆς ἀγαθῆς πράξεως ἡμῶν
διδόσθω ὑπ᾿ ἄλλων, καθὼς ἐδόθη τοῖς πατράσιν
ἡμῶν τοῖς δικαίοις. 8. θράσος καὶ αὐθάδεια καὶ
τόλμα τοῖς κατηραμένοις ὑπὸ τοῦ θεοῦ· ἐπιείκεια
καὶ ταπεινοφροσύνη καὶ πραΰτης παρὰ τοῖς
ηὐλογημένοις ὑπὸ τοῦ θεοῦ.

XXXI

1. Κολληθῶμεν οὖν τῇ εὐλογίᾳ αὐτοῦ καὶ
ἴδωμεν, τίνες αἱ ὁδοὶ τῆς εὐλογίας. ἀνατυλίξωμεν
Gen. 21, 17 τὰ ἀπ᾿ ἀρχῆς γενόμενα. 2. τίνος χάριν ηὐλογήθη
ὁ πατὴρ ἡμῶν ᾿Αβραάμ, οὐχὶ δικαιοσύνην καὶ
Gen. 22 ἀλήθειαν διὰ πίστεως ποιήσας; 3. ᾿Ισαὰκ μετὰ
πεποιθήσεως γινώσκων τὸ μέλλον ἡδέως προσήγετο
Gen. 28 f. ·θυσία. 4. ᾿Ιακὼβ μετὰ ταπεινοφροσύνης ἐξε-
χώρησεν τῆς γῆς αὐτοῦ δι᾿ ἀδελφὸν καὶ ἐπορεύθη
πρὸς Λαβὰν καὶ ἐδούλευσεν, καὶ ἐδόθη αὐτῷ τὸ
δωδεκάσκηπτρον τοῦ ᾿Ισραήλ. ·

XXXII

1. ῝Ο ἐάν τις καθ᾿ ἓν ἕκαστον εἰλικρινῶς κατα-
νοήσῃ, ἐπιγνώσεται μεγαλεῖα τῶν ὑπ᾿ αὐτοῦ
δεδομένων δωρεῶν. 2. ἐξ αὐτοῦ γὰρ ἱερεῖς καὶ
Λευῖται πάντες οἱ λειτουργοῦντες τῷ θυσιαστηρίῳ

those who praise themselves. 7. Let testimony to our good deeds be given by others, as it was given to our fathers, the righteous. 8. Frowardness and arrogance and boldness belong to those that are accursed by God, gentleness and humility and meekness are with those who are blessed by God.

XXXI

1. LET us cleave, then, to his blessing and let us consider what are the paths of blessing. Let us unfold the deeds of old. 2. Why was our father Abraham blessed? Was it not because he wrought righteousness and truth through faith? 3. Isaac in confident knowledge of the future was gladly led as a sacrifice. 4. Jacob departed from his country in meekness because of his brother, and went to Laban and served him, and to him was given the sceptre of the twelve tribes of Israel.

The faith of the Patriarchs

XXXII

1. AND if anyone will candidly consider this in detail, he will recognize the greatness of the gifts given by him. 2. For from him [1] come the priests and all the Levites, who serve the altar

The greatness of Jacob's blessing

---

[1] The obscurity of this passage is partly due to an ambiguity in the Greek, partly to the faultiness of the chapter-divisions. The first verse of this chapter ought really to be closely connected with the last verse of Chapter XXXI; the "by him" in XXXII, 1 means "by God," and the "from him" in XXXII, 2 means from Jacob.

Rom. 9, 3   τοῦ θεοῦ· ἐξ αὐτοῦ ὁ κύριος Ἰησοῦς τὸ κατὰ σάρκα.
ἐξ αὐτοῦ βασιλεῖς καὶ ἄρχοντες καὶ ἡγούμενοι
κατὰ τὸν Ἰούδαν· τὰ δὲ λοιπὰ σκῆπτρα αὐτοῦ
οὐκ ἐν μικρᾷ δόξῃ ὑπάρχουσιν, ὡς ἐπαγγειλαμένου

Gen. 15, 5 ; τοῦ θεοῦ, ὅτι ἔσται τὸ σπέρμα σου ·ὡς οἱ ἀστέρες
22, 17 ; 26, 4 τοῦ οὐρανοῦ.   3. πάντες οὖν ἐδοξάσθησαν καὶ
ἐμεγαλύνθησαν οὐ δι᾽ αὐτῶν ἢ τῶν ἔργων αὐτῶν
ἢ τῆς δικαιοπραγίας ἧς κατειργάσαντο, ἀλλὰ διὰ
τοῦ θελήματος αὐτοῦ.   4. καὶ ἡμεῖς οὖν, διὰ
θελήματος αὐτοῦ ἐν Χριστῷ Ἰησοῦ κληθέντες, οὐ
δι᾽ ἑαυτῶν δικαιούμεθα, οὐδὲ διὰ τῆς ἡμετέρας
σοφίας ἢ συνέσεως ἢ εὐσεβείας ἢ ἔργων ὧν
κατειργασάμεθα ἐν ὁσιότητι καρδίας, ἀλλὰ διὰ
τῆς πίστεως, δι᾽ ἧς πάντας τοὺς ἀπ᾽ αἰῶνος ὁ
παντοκράτωρ θεὸς ἐδικαίωσεν· ᾧ ἔστω ἡ δόξα εἰς
τοὺς αἰῶνας τῶν αἰώνων.   ἀμήν.

XXXIII

Rom. 6, 1   1. Τί οὖν ποιήσωμεν, ἀδελφοί ; ἀργήσωμεν ἀπὸ
τῆς ἀγαθοποιΐας καὶ ἐγκαταλίπωμεν τὴν ἀγάπην ;
μηθαμῶς τοῦτο ἐάσαι ὁ δεσπότης ἐφ᾽ ἡμῖν γε
γενηθῆναι, ἀλλὰ σπεύσωμεν μετὰ ἐκτενείας καὶ
Tit. 3, 1 προθυμίας πᾶν ἔργον ἀγαθὸν ἐπιτελεῖν.   2. αὐτὸς
γὰρ ὁ δημιουργὸς καὶ δεσπότης τῶν ἁπάντων
ἐπὶ τοῖς ἔργοις αὐτοῦ ἀγαλλιᾶται.   3. τῷ γὰρ
παμμεγεθεστάτῳ αὐτοῦ κράτει οὐρανοὺς ἐστήρισεν
καὶ τῇ ἀκαταλήπτῳ αὐτοῦ συνέσει διεκόσμησεν
αὐτούς· γῆν τε διεχώρισεν ἀπὸ τοῦ περιέχοντος
αὐτὴν ὕδατος καὶ ἥδρασεν ἐπὶ τὸν ἀσφαλῆ τοῦ
ἰδίου βουλήματος θεμέλιον· τά τε ἐν αὐτῇ ζῷα

of God, from him comes the Lord Jesus according to the flesh, from him come the kings and rulers and governors in the succession of Judah, and the other sceptres of his tribes are in no small renown seeing that God promised that "thy seed shall be as the stars of heaven." 3. All of them therefore were all renowned and magnified, not through themselves or their own works or the righteous actions which they had wrought, but through his will; 4. and therefore we who by his will have been called in Christ Jesus, are not made righteous by ourselves, or by our wisdom or understanding or piety or the deeds which we have wrought in holiness of heart, but through faith, by which Almighty God has justified all men from the beginning of the world; to him be glory for ever and ever. Amen.

XXXIII

1. WHAT shall we do, then, brethren? Shall we be slothful in well-doing and cease from love? May the Master forbid that this should happen, at least to us, but let us be zealous to accomplish every good deed with energy and readiness. 2. For the Creator and Master of the universe himself rejoices in his works. 3. For by his infinitely great might did he establish the heavens, and by his incomprehensible understanding did he order them; and he separated the earth from the water that surrounds it, and fixed it upon the secure foundation of his own will; and the animals

Continuance in good works

φοιτῶντα τῇ ἑαυτοῦ διατάξει ἐκέλευσεν εἶναι·
θάλασσαν καὶ τὰ ἐν αὐτῇ ζῷα προετοιμάσας
ἐνέκλεισεν τῇ ἑαυτοῦ δυνάμει. 4. ἐπὶ πᾶσι τὸ
ἐξοχώτατον καὶ παμμέγεθες κατὰ διάνοιαν, ἄνθρωπον, ταῖς ἱεραῖς καὶ ἀμώμοις χερσὶν ἔπλασεν
τῆς ἑαυτοῦ εἰκόνος χαρακτῆρα. 5. οὕτως γὰρ
Gen.1, 26. 27 φησιν ὁ θεός· Ποιήσωμεν ἄνθρωπον κατ᾿ εἰκόνα
καὶ καθ᾿ ὁμοίωσιν ἡμετέραν· καὶ ἐποίησεν ὁ θεὸς
τὸν ἄνθρωπον, ἄρσεν καὶ θῆλυ ἐποίησεν αὐτούς.
6. ταῦτα οὖν πάντα τελειώσας ἐπήνεσεν αὐτὰ
Gen. 1, 28 καὶ ηὐλόγησεν καὶ εἶπεν· Αὐξάνεσθε καὶ πληθύνεσθε. 7. ἴδωμεν, ὅτι ἐν ἔργοις ἀγαθοῖς πάντες
ἐκοσμήθησαν οἱ δίκαιοι, καὶ αὐτὸς δὲ ὁ κύριος
ἔργοις ἀγαθοῖς ἑαυτὸν κοσμήσας ἐχάρη. 8. ἔχοντες
οὖν τοῦτον τὸν ὑπογραμμὸν ἀόκνως προσέλθωμεν
τῷ θελήματι αὐτοῦ· ἐξ ὅλης τῆς ἰσχύος ἡμῶν
ἐργασώμεθα ἔργον δικαιοσύνης.

XXXIV

1. Ὁ ἀγαθὸς ἐργάτης μετὰ παρρησίας λαμβάνει
τὸν ἄρτον τοῦ ἔργου αὐτοῦ, ὁ νωθρὸς καὶ παρειμένος
οὐκ ἀντοφθαλμεῖ τῷ ἐργοπαρέκτῃ αὐτοῦ. 2. δέον
οὖν ἐστιν προθύμους ἡμᾶς εἶναι εἰς ἀγαθοποιΐαν·
ἐξ αὐτοῦ γάρ ἐστιν τὰ πάντα. 3. προλέγει γὰρ
Is. 40, 10; ἡμῖν· Ἰδοὺ ὁ κύριος, καὶ ὁ μισθὸς αὐτοῦ πρὸ προσ-
62, 11 ;
Prov. 24, 12 ώπου αὐτοῦ, ἀποδοῦναι ἑκάστῳ κατὰ τὸ ἔργον
Rev. 22, 12 αὐτοῦ. 4. προτρέπεται οὖν ἡμᾶς πιστεύοντας ἐξ
ὅλης τῆς καρδίας ἐπ᾿ αὐτῷ, μὴ ἀργοὺς μηδὲ
Tit. 3, 1 παρειμένους εἶναι ἐπὶ πᾶν ἔργον ἀγαθόν. 5. τὸ

that move in it did he command to exist by his own decree; the sea and the living things in it did he make ready, and enclosed by his own power. 4. Above all, man, the most excellent and from his intellect the greatest of his creatures, did he form in the likeness of his own image by his sacred and faultless hands.[1] 5. For God spake thus: "Let us make man according to our image and likeness; and God made man, male and female made he them." 6. So when he had finished all these things he praised them and blessed them and said, "Increase and multiply." 7. Let us observe that all the righteous have been adorned with good works; and the Lord himself adorned himself with good works and rejoiced. 8. Having therefore this pattern let us follow his will without delay, let us work the work of righteousness with all our strength.

XXXIV

1. THE good workman receives the bread of his labour with boldness; the lazy and careless cannot look his employer in the face. 2. Therefore we must be prompt in well-doing: for all things are from him. 3. For he warns us: "Behold the Lord cometh, and his reward is before his face, to pay to each according to his work." 4. He exhorts us therefore if we believe on him with our whole heart not to be lazy or careless "in every good work." The reward of good works

[1] Or perhaps "did he form in accordance with his intellect."

65

καύχημα ἡμῶν καὶ ἡ παρρησία ἔστω ἐν αὐτῷ· ὑπο-
τασσώμεθα τῷ θελήματι αὐτοῦ· κατανοήσωμεν τὸ
πᾶν πλῆθος τῶν ἀγγέλων αὐτοῦ, πῶς τῷ θελήματι
αὐτοῦ λειτουργοῦσιν παρεστῶτες. 6. λέγει γὰρ
ἡ γραφή· Μύριαι μυριάδες παρειστήκεισαν αὐτῷ,
καὶ χίλιαι χιλιάδες ἐλειτούργουν αὐτῷ, καὶ
ἐκέκραγον, Ἅγιος, ἅγιος, ἅγιος κύριος σαβαώθ,
πλήρης πᾶσα ἡ κτίσις τῆς δόξης αὐτοῦ. 7. καὶ
ἡμεῖς, οὖν, ἐν ὁμονοίᾳ ἐπὶ τὸ αὐτὸ συναχθέντες τῇ
συνειδήσει, ὡς ἐξ ἑνὸς στόματος βοήσωμεν πρὸς
αὐτὸν ἐκτενῶς εἰς τὸ μετόχους ἡμᾶς γενέσθαι τῶν
μεγάλων καὶ ἐνδόξων ἐπαγγελιῶν αὐτοῦ. 8. λέγει γάρ· Ὀφθαλμὸς οὐκ εἶδεν, καὶ οὓς οὐκ ἤκουσεν,
καὶ ἐπὶ καρδίαν ἀνθρώπου οὐκ ἀνέβη, ὅσα
ἡτοίμασεν κύριος[1] τοῖς ὑπομένουσιν αὐτόν.

XXXV

1. Ὡς μακάρια καὶ θαυμαστὰ τὰ δῶρα τοῦ
θεοῦ, ἀγαπητοί. 2. ζωὴ ἐν ἀθανασίᾳ, λαμπρότης
ἐν δικαιοσύνῃ, ἀλήθεια ἐν παρρησίᾳ, πίστις ἐν
πεποιθήσει, ἐγκράτεια ἐν ἁγιασμῷ· καὶ ταῦτα
ὑπέπιπτεν πάντα ὑπὸ τὴν διάνοιαν ἡμῶν. 3. τίνα
οὖν ἄρα ἐστὶν τὰ ἑτοιμαζόμενα τοῖς ὑπομένουσιν ;
ὁ δημιουργὸς καὶ πατὴρ τῶν αἰώνων ὁ πανάγιος
αὐτὸς γινώσκει τὴν ποσότητα καὶ τὴν καλλονὴν
αὐτῶν. 4. ἡμεῖς οὖν ἀγωνισώμεθα εὑρεθῆναι ἐν
τῷ ἀριθμῷ τῶν ὑπομενόντων, ὅπως μεταλά-
βωμεν τῶν ἐπηγγελμένων δωρεῶν. 5. πῶς δὲ

---

[1] Κύριος CLS, ὁ θεός Clem. (so 1 Cor. 2, 9), A omits.

5. Let our glorying and confidence be in him; let us be subject to his will; let us consider the whole multitude of his angels, how they stand ready and minister to his will. 6. For the Scripture says " Ten thousand times ten thousand stood by him, and thousand thousands ministered to him, and they cried Holy, Holy, Holy is the Lord of Sabaoth, the whole creation is full of his glory." 7. Therefore, we too must gather together with concord in our conscience[1] and cry earnestly to him, as it were with one mouth, that we may share in his great and glorious promises, 8. for he says: " Eye hath not seen, and ear hath not heard, and it hath not entered into the heart of man, what things the Lord hath prepared for them that wait for him."

XXXV

1. How blessed and wonderful, beloved, are the gifts of God! 2. Life in immortality, splendour in righteousness, truth in boldness, faith in confidence, continence in holiness: and all these things are submitted to our understanding. 3. What, then, are the things which are being prepared for those who wait for him? The Creator and Father of the ages, the All-holy one, himself knows their greatness and beauty. 4. Let us then strive to be found among the number of those that wait, that we may receive a share of the promised gifts. 5. But how

The reward of good works, and how it may be gained

[1] Others translate "in concord and a good conscience": but it is not certain that συνείδησις can be the synonym of ἀγαθὴ συνείδησις.

ἔσται τοῦτο, ἀγαπητοί; ἐὰν ἐστηριγμένη ᾖ ἡ
διάνοια ἡμῶν πιστῶς πρὸς τὸν θεόν, ἐὰν ἐκζητῶμεν
τὰ εὐάρεστα καὶ εὐπρόσδεκτα αὐτῷ, ἐὰν ἐπιτελέ-
σωμεν τὰ ἀνήκοντα τῇ ἀμώμῳ βουλήσει αὐτοῦ,

Cf. Rom. 1, 29-32

καὶ ἀκολουθήσωμεν τῇ ὁδῷ τῆς ἀληθείας, ἀπορρί-
ψαντες ἀφ' ἑαυτῶν πᾶσαν ἀδικίαν καὶ πονηρίαν,
πλεονεξίαν, ἔρεις, κακοηθείας τε καὶ δόλους,
ψιθυρισμούς τε καὶ καταλαλιάς, θεοστυγίαν,
ὑπερηφανίαν τε καὶ ἀλαζονείαν, κενοδοξίαν τε καὶ
ἀφιλοξενίαν.[1] 6. ταῦτα γὰρ οἱ πράσσοντες στυγητοὶ
τῷ θεῷ ὑπάρχουσιν· οὐ μόνον δὲ οἱ πράσσοντες

Rom. 1, 32
Ps.50, 16-23

αὐτά, ἀλλὰ καὶ οἱ συνευδοκοῦντες αὐτοῖς. 7. λέγει
γὰρ ἡ γραφή· Τῷ δὲ ἁμαρτωλῷ εἶπεν ὁ θεός·
Ἱνατί σὺ διηγῇ τὰ δικαιώματά μου, καὶ ἀνα-
λαμβάνεις τὴν διαθήκην μου ἐπὶ στόματός σου;
8. σὺ δὲ ἐμίσησας παιδείαν καὶ ἐξέβαλες τοὺς
λόγους μου εἰς τὰ ὀπίσω. εἰ ἐθεώρεις κλέπτην,
συνέτρεχες αὐτῷ, καὶ μετὰ μοιχῶν τὴν μερίδα σου
ἐτίθεις. τὸ στόμα σου ἐπλεόνασεν κακίαν, καὶ ἡ
γλῶσσά σου περιέπλεκεν δολιότητα. καθήμενος
κατὰ τοῦ ἀδελφοῦ σου κατελάλεις, καὶ κατὰ τοῦ
υἱοῦ τῆς μητρός σου ἐτίθεις σκάνδαλον. 9. ταῦτα
ἐποίησας, καὶ ἐσίγησα· ὑπέλαβες, ἄνομε, ὅτι
ἔσομαί σοι ὅμοιος. 10. ἐλέγξω σε καὶ παρα-
στήσω σε κατὰ πρόσωπόν σου. 11. σύνετε δὴ
ταῦτα, οἱ ἐπιλανθανόμενοι τοῦ θεοῦ, μήποτε
ἁρπάσῃ ὡς λέων, καὶ μὴ ᾖ ὁ ῥυόμενος. 12. θυσία
αἰνέσεως δοξάσει με, καὶ ἐκεῖ ὁδός, ᾗ[2] δείξω αὐτῷ
τὸ σωτήριον τοῦ θεοῦ.

---

[1] The text is doubtful: A reads φιλοξενίαν, which is impossible, CS read ἀφιλοξενίαν, but L has *inhumilitatem*, which
Knopf believes to represent an original φιλοδοξίαν.
[2] ᾗ L (*in qua*) ἣν ACS with later LXX MSS.

shall this be, beloved? If our understanding be
fixed faithfully on God; if we seek the things which
are well-pleasing and acceptable to him; if we fulfil
the things which are in harmony with his faultless
will, and follow the way of truth, casting away from
ourselves all iniquity and wickedness, covetousness,
strife, malice and fraud, gossiping and evil speaking,
hatred of God, pride and arrogance, vain-glory and
inhospitality. 6. For those who do these things are
hateful to God, and "not only those who do them,
but also those who take pleasure in them." 7. For
the Scripture says: "But to the sinner said God:
Wherefore dost thou declare my ordinances, and
takest my covenant in thy mouth? 8. Thou hast
hated instruction, and cast my words behind thee.
If thou sawest a thief thou didst run with him, and
thou didst make thy portion with the adulterers.
Thy mouth hath multiplied iniquity, and thy tongue
did weave deceit. Thou didst sit to speak evil
against thy brother, and thou didst lay a stumbling-
block in the way of thy mother's son. 9. Thou
hast done these things and I kept silent; thou didst
suppose, O wicked one, that I shall be like unto thee.
10. I will reprove thee and set thyself before thy
face.[1] 11. Understand then these things, ye who
forget God, lest he seize you as doth a lion, and
there be none to deliver. 12. The sacrifice of
praise shall glorify me, and therein is a way in which
I will show to him the salvation of God."

[1] The Syriac reads "Set thy sins before thy face." This
is no doubt a guess, but it gives the meaning.

THE APOSTOLIC FATHERS

XXXVI

1. Αὕτη ἡ ὁδός, ἀγαπητοί, ἐν ᾗ εὕρομεν τὸ
σωτήριον ἡμῶν, Ἰησοῦν Χριστόν, τὸν ἀρχιερέα
τῶν προσφορῶν ἡμῶν, τὸν προστάτην καὶ βοηθὸν
τῆς ἀσθενείας ἡμῶν. 2. διὰ τούτου ἀτενίζομεν[1]
εἰς τὰ ὕψη τῶν οὐρανῶν, διὰ τούτου ἐνοπτριζόμεθα
τὴν ἄμωμον καὶ ὑπερτάτην ὄψιν αὐτοῦ, διὰ τούτου
ἠνεώχθησαν ἡμῶν οἱ ὀφθαλμοὶ τῆς καρδίας, διὰ
τούτου ἡ ἀσύνετος καὶ ἐσκοτωμένη διάνοια ἡμῶν
ἀναθάλλει εἰς τὸ φῶς, διὰ τούτου ἠθέλησεν ὁ δεσπότης τῆς ἀθανάτου γνώσεως ἡμᾶς γεύσασθαι, ὃς
ὢν ἀπαύγασμα τῆς μεγαλωσύνης αὐτοῦ, τοσούτῳ
μείζων ἐστὶν ἀγγέλων, ὅσῳ διαφορώτερον ὄνομα
κεκληρονόμηκεν. 3. γέγραπται γὰρ οὕτως· Ὁ
ποιῶν τοὺς ἀγγέλους αὐτοῦ πνεύματα καὶ τοὺς
λειτουργοὺς αὐτοῦ πυρὸς φλόγα. 4. ἐπὶ δὲ τῷ
υἱῷ αὐτοῦ οὕτως εἶπεν ὁ δεσπότης. Υἱός μου εἶ
σύ, ἐγὼ σήμερον γεγέννηκά σε· αἴτησαι παρ᾽ ἐμοῦ,
καὶ δώσω σοι ἔθνη τὴν κληρονομίαν σου καὶ τὴν
κατάσχεσίν σου τὰ πέρατα τῆς γῆς. 5. καὶ πάλιν
λέγει πρὸς αὐτόν· Κάθου ἐκ δεξιῶν μου, ἕως ἂν
θῶ τοὺς ἐχθρούς σου ὑποπόδιον τῶν ποδῶν σου.
6. τίνες οὖν οἱ ἐχθροί; οἱ φαῦλοι καὶ ἀντιτασσό-
μενοι τῷ θελήματι αὐτοῦ.

XXXVII

1. Στρατευσώμεθα οὖν, ἄνδρες ἀδελφοί, μετὰ
πάσης ἐκτενείας ἐν τοῖς ἀμώμοις προστάγμασιν
αὐτοῦ. 2. κατανοήσωμεν τοὺς στρατευομένους

----

[1] ἀτενίτωμεν A " let us fix our gaze."

Heb. 2, 18;
3, 1

Heb. 1, 3, 4

Heb. 1, 7;
Ps. 104, 4

Heb. 1, 5
Ps. 2, 7. 8

Heb. 1, 13;
Ps. 110, 1

XXXVI

1. This is the way, beloved, in which we found our salvation, Jesus Christ, the high priest of our offerings, the defender and helper of our weakness. 2. Through him we fix our gaze on the heights of heaven, through him we see the reflection of his faultless and lofty countenance, through him the eyes of our hearts were opened, through him our foolish and darkened understanding blossoms towards the light, through him the Master willed that we should taste the immortal knowledge ; "who, being the brightness of his majesty is by so much greater than angels as he hath inherited a more excellent name." 3. For it is written thus "Who maketh his angels spirits, and his ministers a flame of fire." 4. But of his son the Master said thus "Thou art my son : to-day have I begotten thee. Ask of me, and I will give thee the heathen for thine inheritance, and the ends of the earth for thy possession." 5. And again he says to him "Sit thou on my right hand until I make thine enemies a footstool of thy feet." 6. Who then are the enemies? Those who are wicked and oppose his will.

The reward is given through Christ

XXXVII

1. Let us then serve in our army, brethren, with all earnestness, following his faultless commands. 2. Let us consider those who serve our generals, with

The necessity for sub ordination

τοῖς ἡγουμένοις ἡμῶν, πῶς εὐτάκτως, πῶς ἐκτικῶς,[1] πῶς ὑποτεταγμένως ἐπιτελοῦσιν τὰ διατασσόμενα. 3. οὐ πάντες εἰσὶν ἔπαρχοι οὐδὲ χιλίαρχοι οὐδὲ ἑκα-

I Cor. 15, 23 τόνταρχαι οὐδὲ πεντηκόνταρχοι οὐδὲ τὸ καθεξῆς, ἀλλ᾿ ἕκαστος ἐν τῷ ἰδίῳ τάγματι τὰ ἐπιτασσόμενα ὑπὸ τοῦ βασιλέως καὶ τῶν ἡγουμένων ἐπιτελεῖ. 4. οἱ μεγάλοι δίχα τῶν μικρῶν οὐ δύνανται εἶναι, οὔτε οἱ μικροὶ δίχα τῶν μεγάλων· σύγκρασίς τίς ἐστιν ἐν πᾶσιν, καὶ ἐν τούτοις[2] χρῆσις. 5. λάβωμεν τὸ σῶμα ἡμῶν· ἡ κεφαλὴ δίχα τῶν ποδῶν οὐδέν

I Cor. 12, 21 ἐστιν, οὕτως οὐδὲ οἱ πόδες δίχα τῆς κεφαλῆς· τὰ δὲ ἐλάχιστα μέλη τοῦ σώματος ἡμῶν ἀναγκαῖα καὶ εὔχρηστά εἰσιν ὅλῳ τῷ σώματι· ἀλλὰ πάντα συνπνεῖ καὶ ὑποταγῇ μιᾷ χρῆται εἰς τὸ σώζεσθαι ὅλον τὸ σῶμα.

XXXVIII

1. Σωζέσθω οὖν ἡμῶν ὅλον τὸ σῶμα ἐν Χριστῷ Ἰησοῦ, καὶ ὑποτασσέσθω ἕκαστος τῷ πλησίον αὐτοῦ, καθὼς ἐτέθη ἐν τῷ χαρίσματι αὐτοῦ. 2. ὁ ἰσχυρὸς τημελείτω[3] τὸν ἀσθενῆ, ὁ δὲ ἀσθενὴς ἐντρεπέσθω τὸν ἰσχυρόν· ὁ πλούσιος ἐπιχορηγείτω τῷ πτωχῷ, ὁ δὲ πτωχὸς εὐχαριστείτω τῷ θεῷ, ὅτι ἔδωκεν αὐτῷ, δι᾿ οὗ ἀναπληρωθῇ αὐτοῦ τὸ ὑστέρημα· ὁ σοφὸς ἐνδεικνύσθω τὴν σοφίαν αὐτοῦ μὴ ἐν

---

[1] A reads ειεκτι... (the rest of the word has disappeared, though there is a trace either of ω. . or of ικ. .) A[1] has εὐεκτ. . .

[2] L seems to imply ἀλλήλοις "and one makes use of the other," which may be the original text.

[3] A has μη τητμμελειτω. This is perhaps a corruption of μὴ ἀτημελείτω "not neglect," which may be the true reading.

what good order, habitual readiness, and submissiveness they perform their commands. 3. Not all are prefects, nor tribunes, nor centurions, nor in charge of fifty men, or the like, but each carries out in his own rank the commands of the emperor and of the generals. 4. The great cannot exist without the small, nor the small without the great; there is a certain mixture among all, and herein lies the advantage. 5. Let us take our body; the head is nothing without the feet, likewise the feet are nothing without the head; the smallest members of our body are necessary and valuable to the whole body, but all work together and are united in a common subjection to preserve the whole body.

XXXVIII

1. Let, therefore, our whole body be preserved in Christ Jesus, and let each be subject to his neighbour, according to the position granted to him. 2. Let the strong care for the weak and let the weak reverence the strong. Let the rich man bestow help on the poor and let the poor give thanks to God, that he gave him one to supply his needs; let the wise manifest his wisdom not in words but in good deeds;

The duties of mutual help

λόγοις, ἀλλ' ἐν ἔργοις ἀγαθοῖς· ὁ ταπεινοφρονῶν
μὴ ἑαυτῷ μαρτυρείτω, ἀλλ' ἐάτω ὑφ' ἑτέρου
ἑαυτὸν μαρτυρεῖσθαι· ὁ ἁγνὸς ἐν τῇ σαρκὶ[1] μὴ
ἀλαζονευέσθω, γινώσκων ὅτι ἕτερός ἐστιν ὁ
ἐπιχορηγῶν αὐτῷ τὴν ἐγκράτειαν. 3. ἀναλογισώ-
μεθα οὖν, ἀδελφοί, ἐκ ποίας ὕλης ἐγενήθημεν, ποῖοι
καὶ τίνες εἰσήλθαμεν εἰς τὸν κόσμον, ἐκ ποίου
τάφου καὶ σκότους ὁ πλάσας ἡμᾶς καὶ δημιουρ-
γήσας εἰσήγαγεν εἰς τὸν κόσμον αὐτοῦ, προετοιμάσας τὰς εὐεργεσίας αὐτοῦ, πρὶν ἡμᾶς γεννηθῆναι.
4. ταῦτα οὖν πάντα ἐξ αὐτοῦ ἔχοντες ὀφείλομεν
κατὰ πάντα εὐχαριστεῖν αὐτῷ· ᾧ ἡ δόξα εἰς τοὺς
αἰῶνας τῶν αἰώνων. ἀμήν.

XXXIX

1. Ἄφρονες καὶ ἀσύνετοι καὶ μωροὶ καὶ ἀπαί-
δευτοι χλευάζουσιν ἡμᾶς καὶ μυκτηρίζουσιν,
ἑαυτοὺς βουλόμενοι ἐπαίρεσθαι ταῖς διανοίαις
αὐτῶν. 2. τί γὰρ δύναται θνητός ; ἢ τίς ἰσχὺς
γηγενοῦς ; 3. γέγραπται γάρ· Οὐκ ἦν μορφὴ πρὸ
ὀφθαλμῶν μου, ἀλλ' ἢ αὔραν καὶ φωνὴν ἤκουον·
4. Τί γάρ ; μὴ καθαρὸς ἔσται βροτὸς ἔναντι
κυρίου ; ἢ ἀπὸ τῶν ἔργων αὐτοῦ ἄμεμπτος ἀνήρ,
εἰ κατὰ παίδων αὐτοῦ οὐ πιστεύει, κατὰ δὲ
ἀγγέλων αὐτοῦ σκολιόν τι ἐπενόησεν ; 5. οὐρανὸς
δὲ οὐ καθαρὸς ἐνώπιον αὐτοῦ· ἔα δέ, οἱ κατοι-
κοῦντες οἰκίας πηλίνας, ἐξ ὧν καὶ αὐτοὶ ἐκ τοῦ

Job 4, 16–18;
15, 15 ; 4,
19–5, 5

[1] A reads καὶ μή preceded by a lacuna (the vellum has
been cut away). It is suggested that ἤτω should be supplied,
giving the meaning " Let him who is pure in the flesh, be so,
and not," etc.

let him who is humble-minded not testify to his own
humility, but let him leave it to others to bear him
witness ; let not him who is pure in the flesh be
boastful, knowing that it is another who bestows on
him his continence. 3. Let us consider, then,
brethren, of what matter we were formed, who we
are, and with what nature we came into the world,
and how he who formed and created us brought us
into his world from the darkness of a grave, and
prepared his benefits for us before we were born.
4. Since, therefore, we have everything from him we
ought in everything to give him thanks, to whom be
glory for ever and ever. Amen.

XXXIX

1. Foolish, imprudent, silly, and uninstructed men
mock and deride us, wishing to exalt themselves in
their own conceits. 2. For what can mortal man
do, or what is the strength of him who is a child of
earth ? 3. For it is written " There was no shape
before mine eyes, but I heard a sound and a voice.
4. What then ? Shall a mortal be pure before the
Lord ? Or shall a man be blameless in his deeds,
seeing that he believeth not in his servants, and hath
noted perversity in his angels ? 5. Yea, the heaven
is not pure before him. Away then, ye who inhabit
houses of clay, of which, even of the same clay,
we ourselves were made. He smote them as a

Exhortation against those who act otherwise

αὐτοῦ πηλοῦ ἐσμέν· ἔπαισεν αὐτοὺς σητὸς
τρόπον, καὶ ἀπὸ πρωΐθεν ἕως ἐσπέρας οὐκ ἔτι εἰσίν·
παρὰ τὸ μὴ δύνασθαι αὐτοὺς ἑαυτοῖς βοηθῆσαι
ἀπώλοντο. 6. ἐνεφύσησεν αὐτοῖς, καὶ ἐτελεύτη-
σαν παρὰ τὸ μὴ ἔχειν αὐτοὺς σοφίαν. 7. ἐπι-
κάλεσαι δέ, εἴ τίς σοι ὑπακούσεται, ἢ εἴ τινα ἁγίων
ἀγγέλων ὄψῃ· καὶ γὰρ ἄφρονα ἀναιρεῖ ὀργή,
πεπλανημένον δὲ θανατοῖ ζῆλος. 8. ἐγὼ δὲ
ἑώρακα ἄφρονας ῥίζας βάλλοντας,[1] ἀλλ᾽ εὐθέως
ἐβρώθη αὐτῶν ἡ δίαιτα. 9. πόρρω γένοιντο οἱ
υἱοὶ αὐτῶν ἀπὸ σωτηρίας· κολαβρισθείησαν ἐπὶ
θύραις ἡσσόνων, καὶ οὐκ ἔσται ὁ ἐξαιρούμενος· ἃ
γὰρ ἐκείνοις ἡτοίμασται, δίκαιοι ἔδονται, αὐτοὶ δὲ
ἐκ κακῶν οὐκ ἐξαίρετοι ἔσονται.

XL

1. Προδήλων οὖν ἡμῖν ὄντων τούτων, καὶ
ἐγκεκυφότες εἰς τὰ βάθη τῆς θείας γνώσεως,
πάντα τάξει ποιεῖν ὀφείλομεν, ὅσα ὁ δεσπότης
ἐπιτελεῖν ἐκέλευσεν κατὰ καιροὺς τεταγμένους.
2. τάς τε προσφορὰς καὶ λειτουργίας ἐπιτελεῖσθαι,
καὶ[2] οὐκ εἰκῆ ἢ ἀτάκτως ἐκέλευσεν γίνεσθαι, ἀλλ᾽
ὡρισμένοις καιροῖς καὶ ὥραις. · 3. ποῦ τε καὶ διὰ
τίνων ἐπιτελεῖσθαι θέλει, αὐτὸς ὥρισεν τῇ ὑπερ-
τάτῳ αὐτοῦ βουλήσει, ἵν᾽ ὁσίως πάντα γινόμενα
ἐν εὐδοκήσει εὐπρόσδεκτα εἴη τῷ θελήματι αὐτοῦ.
4. οἱ οὖν τοῖς προστεταγμένοις καιροῖς ποιοῦντες
τὰς προσφορὰς αὐτῶν εὐπρόσδεκτοί τε καὶ

---

[1] βαλόντας A, βάλλοντας CLS (LXX).
[2] ἐπιτελεῖσθαι καί AC, om. LS.

moth, and from morning until evening they do not
endure; they perished, without being able to help
themselves. 6. He breathed on them and they
died because they had no wisdom. 7. But call
now, if any shall answer thee, or if thou shalt see
any of the holy angels; for wrath destroyeth the
foolish, and envy putteth to death him that is in error.
8. I have seen the foolish taking root, but their
habitation was presently consumed. 9. Let their
sons be far from safety; let them be mocked in the
gates of those less than they, with none to deliver;
for what was prepared for them the righteous shall
eat, and they themselves shall not be delivered from
evil."

XL

1. Since then these things are manifest to us, The duty of
and we have looked into the depths of the divine observing
knowledge, we ought to do in order all things which religious
the Master commanded us to perform at appointed services
times. 2. He commanded us to celebrate sacrifices
and services, and that it should not be thoughtlessly
or disorderly, but at fixed times and hours. 3. He
has himself fixed by his supreme will the places and
persons whom he desires for these celebrations, in
order that all things may be done piously according
to his good pleasure, and be acceptable to his will.
4. So then those who offer their oblations at the
appointed seasons are acceptable and blessed, for

μακάριοι· τοῖς γὰρ νομίμοις τοῦ δεσπότου ἀκολου-
θοῦντες οὐ διαμαρτάνουσιν. 5. τῷ γὰρ ἀρχιερεῖ
ἴδιαι λειτουργίαι δεδομέναι εἰσίν, καὶ τοῖς ἱερεῦσιν
ἴδιος ὁ τόπος προστέτακται, καὶ Λευΐταις ἴδιαι
διακονίαι ἐπίκεινται· ὁ λαϊκὸς ἄνθρωπος τοῖς
λαϊκοῖς προστάγμασιν δέδεται.[1]

XLI

I Cor. 15, 23 1. Ἕκαστος ἡμῶν, ἀδελφοί, ἐν τῷ ἰδίῳ τάγματι
εὐαριστείτω[2] τῷ θεῷ ἐν ἀγαθῇ συνειδήσει
ὑπάρχων, μὴ παρεκβαίνων τὸν ὡρισμένον τῆς
λειτουργίας αὐτοῦ κανόνα, ἐν σεμνότητι. 2. οὐ
πανταχοῦ, ἀδελφοί, προσφέρονται θυσίαι ἐνδελε-
χισμοῦ ἢ εὐχῶν[3] ἢ περὶ ἁμαρτίας καὶ πλημμελείας,
ἀλλ᾽ ἢ ἐν Ἰερουσαλὴμ μόνῃ· κἀκεῖ δὲ οὐκ ἐν παντὶ
τόπῳ προσφέρεται, ἀλλ᾽ ἔμπροσθεν τοῦ ναοῦ πρὸς
τὸ θυσιαστήριον, μωμοσκοπηθὲν τὸ προσφερόμενον
διὰ τοῦ ἀρχιερέως καὶ τῶν προειρημένων λει-
τουργῶν. 3. οἱ οὖν παρὰ τὸ καθῆκον τῆς βουλή-
σεως αὐτοῦ ποιοῦντές τι θάνατον τὸ πρόστιμον
ἔχουσιν. 4. ὁρᾶτε, ἀδελφοί· ὅσῳ πλείονος κατη-
ξιώθημεν γνώσεως, τοσούτῳ μᾶλλον ὑποκείμεθα
κινδύνῳ.

XLII

1. Οἱ ἀπόστολοι ἡμῖν εὐηγγελίσθησαν ἀπὸ τοῦ
κυρίου Ἰησοῦ Χριστοῦ, Ἰησοῦς ὁ Χριστὸς ἀπὸ

---

[1] δέδεται A, δέδοται CLS.
[2] A reads εὐχαριστείτω, "join in the Eucharist," or less
probably, "give thanks."
[3] C reads προσευχῶν.

they follow the laws of the Master and do no sin.
5. For to the High Priest his proper ministrations
are allotted, and to the priests the proper place
has been appointed, and on Levites their proper
services have been imposed. The layman is bound
by the ordinances for the laity.

XLI

1. Let each one of us, brethren, be well The neces-
pleasing to God in his own rank, and have a good sity for a
conscience, not transgressing the appointed rules of functions in
his ministration, with all reverence. 2. Not in the church
every place, my brethren, are the daily sacrifices
offered or the free-will offerings,[1] or the sin-offerings
and trespass-offerings, but only in Jerusalem ; and
there also the offering is not made in every place,
but before the shrine, at the altar, and the offering
is first inspected by the High Priest and the ministers
already mentioned. 3. Those therefore who do anything contrary to that which is agreeable to his will
suffer the penalty of death. 4. You see, brethren,
that the more knowledge we have been entrusted
with, the greater risk do we incur.

XLII

1. The Apostles received the Gospel for us from The
the Lord Jesus Christ, Jesus the Christ was sent from Apostolic
foundation
of church
organisation

---

[1] If the reading of C be adopted, " Sacrifices of prayers."

τοῦ θεοῦ ἐξεπέμφθη. 2. ὁ Χριστὸς οὖν ἀπὸ τοῦ
θεοῦ καὶ οἱ ἀπόστολοι ἀπὸ τοῦ Χριστοῦ· ἐγένοντο
οὖν ἀμφότερα εὐτάκτως ἐκ θελήματος θεοῦ.
3. παραγγελίας οὖν λαβόντες καὶ πληροφορηθέντες
διὰ τῆς ἀναστάσεως τοῦ κυρίου ἡμῶν Ἰησοῦ
Χριστοῦ καὶ πιστωθέντες ἐν τῷ λόγῳ τοῦ θεοῦ,
μετὰ πληροφορίας πνεύματος ἁγίου ἐξῆλθον
εὐαγγελιζόμενοι, τὴν βασιλείαν τοῦ θεοῦ μέλλειν
ἔρχεσθαι. 4. κατὰ χώρας οὖν καὶ πόλεις κηρύσσοντες[1] καθίστανον τὰς ἀπαρχὰς αὐτῶν, δοκιμάσαντες τῷ πνεύματι, εἰς ἐπισκόπους καὶ διακόνους
τῶν μελλόντων πιστεύειν. 5. καὶ τοῦτο οὐ
καινῶς· ἐκ γὰρ δὴ πολλῶν χρόνων ἐγέγραπτο
Is. 60, 17 περὶ ἐπισκόπων καὶ διακόνων. οὕτως γάρ που
λέγει ἡ γραφή· Καταστήσω τοὺς ἐπισκόπους
αὐτῶν ἐν δικαιοσύνῃ καὶ τοὺς διακόνους αὐτῶν
ἐν πίστει.

XLIII

Num. 12, 7;
Heb. 3, 5 1. Καὶ τί θαυμαστόν, εἰ οἱ ἐν Χριστῷ πιστευ-
θέντες παρὰ θεοῦ ἔργον τοιοῦτο κατέστησαν τοὺς
προειρημένους; ὅπου καὶ ὁ μακάριος πιστὸς
θεράπων ἐν ὅλῳ τῷ οἴκῳ Μωϋσῆς τὰ διατεταγμένα
αὐτῷ πάντα ἐσημειώσατο ἐν ταῖς ἱεραῖς βίβλοις,
ᾧ καὶ ἐπηκολούθησαν οἱ λοιποὶ προφῆται, συνεπι-
μαρτυροῦντες τοῖς ὑπ' αὐτοῦ νενομοθετημένοις.
Num. 17 2. ἐκεῖνος γάρ, ζήλου ἐμπεσόντος περὶ τῆς ἱερω-
σύνης καὶ στασιαζουσῶν τῶν φυλῶν, ὁποία αὐτῶν
εἴη τῷ ἐνδόξῳ ὀνόματι κεκοσμημένη, ἐκέλευσεν

---

[1] L adds *eos qui obaudiebant voluntati Dei baptizantes.*
"baptising those who were obedient to the will of God."

God. 2. The Christ therefore is from God and the Apostles from the Christ. In both ways,[1] then, they were in accordance with the appointed order of God's will. 3. Having therefore received their commands, and being fully assured by the resurrection of our Lord Jesus Christ, and with faith confirmed by the word of God, they went forth in the assurance of the Holy Spirit preaching the good news that the Kingdom of God is coming. 4. They preached from district to district, and from city to city, and they appointed their first converts, testing them by the Spirit, to be bishops and deacons of the future believers. 5. And this was no new method, for many years before had bishops and deacons been written of; for the scripture says thus in one place " I will establish their bishops in righteousness, and their deacons in faith."

XLIII

1. And what wonder is it if those who were in Christ, and were entrusted by God with such a duty, established those who have been mentioned? Since the blessed Moses also " A faithful servant in all his house" noted down in the sacred books all the injunctions which were given him; and the other prophets followed him, bearing witness with him to the laws which he had given. 2. For when jealousy arose concerning the priesthood, and the tribes were quarrelling as to which of them was adorned with that glorious title, Moses himself commanded the

The action of Moses as a type of church organisation

---

[1] ἀμφότερα "both" is probably adverbial rather than the subject of ἐγένοντο.

τοὺς δώδεκα φυλάρχους προσενεγκεῖν αὐτῷ ῥάβδους
ἐπιγεγραμμένας ἑκάστης φυλῆς κατ᾽ ὄνομα· καὶ
λαβὼν αὐτὰς ἔδησεν καὶ ἐσφράγισεν τοῖς δακτυ-
λίοις τῶν φυλάρχων, καὶ ἀπέθετο αὐτὰς εἰς τὴν
σκηνὴν τοῦ μαρτυρίου ἐπὶ τὴν τράπεζαν τοῦ θεοῦ.
3. καὶ κλείσας τὴν σκηνὴν ἐσφράγισεν τὰς κλεῖδας
ὡσαύτως καὶ τὰς ῥάβδους, 4. καὶ εἶπεν αὐτοῖς·
Ἄνδρες ἀδελφοί, ἧς ἂν φυλῆς ἡ ῥάβδος βλαστήσῃ,
ταύτην ἐκλέλεκται ὁ θεὸς εἰς τὸ ἱερατεύειν καὶ
λειτουργεῖν αὐτῷ. 5. πρωΐας δὲ γενομένης συνε-
κάλεσεν πάντα τὸν Ἰσραήλ, τὰς ἑξακοσίας χιλι-
άδας τῶν ἀνδρῶν, καὶ ἐπεδείξατο τοῖς φυλάρχοις
τὰς σφραγῖδας, καὶ ἤνοιξεν τὴν σκηνὴν τοῦ μαρτυρίου καὶ προεῖλεν τὰς ῥάβδους· καὶ εὑρέθη ἡ
ῥάβδος Ἀαρὼν οὐ μόνον βεβλαστηκυῖα, ἀλλὰ καὶ
καρπὸν ἔχουσα. 6. τί δοκεῖτε, ἀγαπητοί; οὐ
προῄδει Μωϋσῆς τοῦτο μέλλειν ἔσεσθαι; μάλιστα
ᾔδει· ἀλλ᾽ ἵνα μὴ ἀκαταστασία γένηται ἐν τῷ
Ἰσραήλ, οὕτως ἐποίησεν, εἰς τὸ δοξασθῆναι τὸ
Cf. Joh. 17, 3 ὄνομα τοῦ ἀληθινοῦ καὶ μόνου θεοῦ.[1] ᾧ ἡ δόξα εἰς
τοὺς αἰῶνας τῶν αἰώνων. ἀμήν.

XLIV

1. Καὶ οἱ ἀπόστολοι ἡμῶν ἔγνωσαν διὰ τοῦ κυρίου
ἡμῶν Ἰησοῦ Χριστοῦ, ὅτι ἔρις ἔσται ἐπὶ τοῦ
ὀνόματος τῆς ἐπισκοπῆς. 2. διὰ ταύτην οὖν τὴν
αἰτίαν πρόγνωσιν εἰληφότες τελείαν κατέστησαν

---

[1] θεοῦ "God" KS, κυρίου "Lord" S, L omits and has
merely "the true and only one," A is missing.

rulers of the twelve tribes to bring him rods, with the name of a tribe written on each; and he took them, and bound them, and sealed them with the rings of the rulers of the tribes, and put them away in the Tabernacle of Testimony on the table of God. 3. And he shut the Tabernacle, and sealed the keys, as he had done with the rods, 4. and he said to them, "Brethren, of whichsoever tribe the rod shall bud, this has God chosen for his priesthood and ministry." 5. And when it was daylight he called together all Israel, six hundred thousand men, and showed the seals to the rulers of the tribes, and opened the Tabernacle of Testimony, and took forth the rods, and the rod of Aaron was found not only to have budded, but also to be bearing fruit. 6. What do you think, beloved? That Moses did not know beforehand that this was going to happen? Assuredly he knew, but he acted thus that there should be no disorder in Israel, to glorify the name of the true and only God, to whom be the glory for ever and ever. Amen.

XLIV

1. Our Apostles also knew through our Lord Jesus Christ that there would be strife for the title of bishop. 2. For this cause, therefore, since they had received perfect foreknowledge, they appointed

The application of these facts to the situation at Corinth

τοὺς προειρημένους, καὶ μιταξὺ ἐπινομὴν[1] δεδώ-
κασιν, ὅπως, ἐὰν κοιμηθῶσιν, διαδέξωνται ἕτεροι
δεδοκιμασμένοι ἄνδρες τὴν λειτουργίαν αὐτῶν.
3. τοὺς οὖν κατασταθέντας ὑπ' ἐκείνων ἢ μεταξὺ
ὑφ' ἑτέρων ἐλλογίμων ἀνδρῶν συνευδοκησάσης τῆς
ἐκκλησίας πάσης, καὶ λειτουργήσαντας ἀμέμπτως
τῷ ποιμνίῳ τοῦ Χριστοῦ μετὰ ταπεινοφροσύνης,
ἡσύχως καὶ ἀβαναύσως, μεμαρτυρημένους τε
πολλοῖς χρόνοις ὑπὸ πάντων, τούτους οὐ δικαίως
νομίζομεν ἀποβάλλεσθαι τῆς λειτουργίας. 4.
ἁμαρτία γὰρ οὐ μικρὰ ἡμῖν ἔσται, ἐὰν τοὺς
ἀμέμπτως καὶ ὁσίως προσενεγκόντας τὰ δῶρα
τῆς ἐπισκοπῆς ἀποβάλωμεν. 5. μακάριοι οἱ
προοδοιπορήσαντες πρεσβύτεροι, οἵτινες ἔγκαρπον
καὶ τελείαν ἔσχον τὴν ἀνάλυσιν· οὐ γὰρ εὐλα-
βοῦνται μή τις αὐτοὺς μεταστήσῃ ἀπὸ τοῦ
ἱδρυμένου αὐτοῖς τόπου. 6. ὁρῶμεν γάρ, ὅτι
ἐνίους ὑμεῖς μετηγάγετε καλῶς πολιτευομένους ἐκ
τῆς ἀμέμπτως αὐτοῖς τετιμημένης λειτουργίας.

XLV

1. Φιλόνεικοι ἔστε, ἀδελφοί, καὶ ζηλωταὶ περὶ
τῶν ἀνηκόντων εἰς σωτηρίαν. 2. ἐγκεκύφατε εἰς
τὰς ἱερὰς γραφάς, τὰς ἀληθεῖς, τὰς διὰ τοῦ

---

[1] ἐπινομὴν A, ἐπιδομήν C, legem L (= ἔτι νόμον?), the
equivalent of ἐπιδοκιμήν S, "And gave to those who were
after them" K.   ἐπινομήν seems to be the most probable
reading as L more or less supports the -νομήν and CS support
the ἐπι- ; but the translation is doubtful, as it is difficult to
obtain any sense unless it be supposed that ἐπινομήν has the
meaning "codicil" which usually belongs to the cognate word
ἐπινομίς.   Lightfoot emends to ἐπιμονήν, "permanence."

those who have been already mentioned, and afterwards added the codicil that if they should fall
asleep, other approved men should succeed to their
ministry. 3. We consider therefore that it is not
just to remove from their ministry those who were
appointed by them, or later on by other eminent
men, with the consent of the whole Church, and
have ministered to the flock of Christ without blame,
humbly, peaceably, and disinterestedly, and for
many years have received a universally favourable
testimony. 4. For our sin is not small, if we eject
from the episcopate those who have blamelessly and
holily offered its sacrifices. 5. Blessed are those
Presbyters who finished their course before now, and
have obtained a fruitful and perfect release in the
ripeness of completed work, for they have now
no fear that any shall move them from the place
appointed to them. 6. For we see that in spite
of their good service you have removed some from
the ministry which they fulfilled blamelessly.[1]

XLV

1. You are contentious,[2] brethren, and zealous for
the things which lead to salvation. 2. You have studied
the Holy Scriptures, which are true, and given by

The
persecution
of the just
in the Old
Testament

---

[1] It is doubtful if this translation is right, and the Greek
is perhaps corrupt. Lightfoot emends τετιμημένης to τετηρη-
μένης "which they preserved." The translation given is
supported by L *facto* (probably a corruption of *functo*).
[2] Or possibly, " Be contentious."

πνεύματος τοῦ ἁγίου. 3. ἐπίστασθε, ὅτι οὐδὲν
ἄδικον οὐδὲ παραπεποιημένον γέγραπται ἐν αὐταῖς.
οὐχ εὑρήσετε δικαίους ἀποβεβλημένους ἀπὸ ὁσίων
ἀνδρῶν. 4. ἐδιώχθησαν δίκαιοι, ἀλλ᾽ ὑπὸ ἀνόμων·
ἐφυλακίσθησαν, ἀλλ᾽ ὑπὸ ἀνοσίων· ἐλιθάσθησαν
ὑπὸ παρανόμων· ἀπεκτάνθησαν ὑπὸ τῶν μιαρὸν καὶ
ἄδικον ζῆλον ἀνειληφότων. 5. ταῦτα πάσχοντες
Dan. 6, 16   εὐκλεῶς ἤνεγκαν. 6. τί γὰρ εἴπωμεν, ἀδελφοί ;
Δανιὴλ ὑπὸ τῶν φοβουμένων τὸν θεὸν ἐβλήθη εἰς
Dan. 3, 19 ff.   λάκκον λεόντων ; 7. ἢ Ἀνανίας καὶ Ἀζαρίας καὶ
Μισαὴλ ὑπὸ τῶν θρησκευόντων τὴν μεγαλοπρεπῆ
καὶ ἔνδοξον θρησκείαν τοῦ ὑψίστου κατείρχθησαν
εἰς κάμινον πυρός ; μηθαμῶς τοῦτο γένοιτο. τίνες
οὖν οἱ ταῦτα δράσαντες ; οἱ στυγητοὶ καὶ πάσης
κακίας πλήρεις εἰς τοσοῦτο ἐξήρισαν θυμοῦ, ὥστε
τοὺς ἐν ὁσίᾳ καὶ ἀμώμῳ προθέσει δουλεύοντας τῷ
θεῷ εἰς αἰκίαν περιβαλεῖν, μὴ εἰδότες ὅτι ὁ
ὕψιστος ὑπέρμαχος καὶ ὑπερασπιστής ἐστιν τῶν
ἐν καθαρᾷ συνειδήσει λατρευόντων τῷ παναρέτῳ
ὀνόματι αὐτοῦ· ᾧ ἡ δόξα εἰς τοὺς αἰῶνας τῶν
αἰώνων. ἀμήν. 8. οἱ δὲ ὑπομένοντες ἐν πεποιθήσει
δόξαν καὶ τιμὴν ἐκληρονόμησαν, ἐπήρθησάν τε
καὶ ἔγγραφοι ἐγένοντο ἀπὸ τοῦ θεοῦ ἐν τῷ
μνημοσύνῳ αὐτοῦ[1] εἰς τοὺς αἰῶνας τῶν αἰώνων.
ἀμήν.

XLVI

1. Τοιούτοις οὖν ὑποδείγμασιν κολληθῆναι καὶ
ἡμᾶς δεῖ, ἀδελφοί. 2. γέγραπται γάρ· Κολλᾶσθε
τοῖς ἁγίοις, ὅτι οἱ κολλώμενοι αὐτοῖς ἁγιασθή-

---

[1] μνημοσύνῳ αὐτῶν A, "their memorial."

the Holy Spirit. 3. You know that nothing unjust or counterfeit is written in them. You will not find that the righteous have been cast out by holy men. 4. The righteous were persecuted; but it was by the wicked. They were put in prison; but it was by the unholy. They were stoned by law-breakers, they were killed by men who had conceived foul and unrighteous envy. 5. These things they suffered, and gained glory by their endurance. 6. For what shall we say, brethren? Was Daniel cast into the lions' den by those who feared God? 7. Or were Ananias, Azarias, and Misael shut up in the fiery furnace by those who ministered to the great and glorious worship of the Most High? God forbid that this be so. Who then were they who did these things? Hateful men, full of all iniquity, were roused to such a pitch of fury, that they inflicted torture on those who served God with a holy and faultless purpose, not knowing that the Most High is the defender and protector of those who serve his excellent name with a pure conscience, to whom be glory for ever and ever. Amen. But they who endured in confidence obtained the inheritance of glory and honour; they were exalted, and were enrolled by God in his memorial for ever and ever. Amen.

XLVI

1. WE also, brethren, must therefore cleave to such examples. 2. For it is written, " Cleave to the holy, for they who cleave to them shall be made holy."[1]

Exhortation against schism

---

[1] The source of this quotation is unknown.

THE APOSTOLIC FATHERS

σονται. 3. καὶ πάλιν ἐν ἑτέρῳ τόπῳ λέγει· Μετὰ

Ps. 17, 26 f. ἀνδρὸς ἀθῴου ἀθῷος ἔσῃ καὶ μετὰ ἐκλεκτοῦ
ἐκλεκτὸς ἔσῃ, καὶ μετὰ στρεβλοῦ διαστρέψεις.
4. κολληθῶμεν οὖν τοῖς ἀθῴοις καὶ δικαίοις· εἰσὶν
δὲ οὗτοι ἐκλεκτοὶ τοῦ θεοῦ. 5. ἱνατί ἔρεις καὶ
θυμοὶ καὶ διχοστασίαι καὶ σχίσματα πόλεμός τε
Eph. 4, 4-6 ἐν ὑμῖν; 6. ἢ οὐχὶ ἕνα θεὸν ἔχομεν καὶ ἕνα
Χριστὸν καὶ ἓν πνεῦμα τῆς χάριτος τὸ ἐκχυθὲν
ἐφ' ἡμᾶς; καὶ μία κλῆσις ἐν Χριστῷ; 7. ἱνατί
διέλκομεν καὶ διασπῶμεν τὰ μέλη τοῦ Χριστοῦ
καὶ στασιάζομεν πρὸς τὸ σῶμα τὸ ἴδιον, καὶ εἰς
τοσαύτην ἀπόνοιαν ἐρχόμεθα, ὥστε ἐπιλαθέσθαι
ἡμᾶς, ὅτι μέλη ἐσμὲν ἀλλήλων; μνήσθητε τῶν
λόγων τοῦ κυρίου Ἰησοῦ.[1] 8. εἶπεν γάρ· Οὐαὶ
Mt. 26. 24 τῷ ἀνθρώπῳ ἐκείνῳ· καλὸν ἦν αὐτῷ, εἰ οὐκ
(Mk. 14, 21 ;
Luke 22, 22); ἐγεννήθη, ἢ ἕνα τῶν ἐκλεκτῶν μου σκανδαλίσαι·
Luke 17, 2 κρεῖττον ἦν αὐτῷ περιτεθῆναι μύλον καὶ καταπον-
(Mt. 18, 6 ;
Mk. 9, 42) τισθῆναι εἰς τὴν θάλασσαν, ἢ ἕνα τῶν ἐκλεκτῶν
μου διαστρέψαι.[2] 9. τὸ σχίσμα ὑμῶν πολλοὺς
διέστρεψεν, πολλοὺς εἰς ἀθυμίαν ἔβαλεν, πολλοὺς
εἰς δισταγμόν, τοὺς πάντας ἡμᾶς εἰς λύπην· καὶ
ἐπίμονος ὑμῶν ἐστιν ἡ στάσις.

XLVII

I Cor.1, 10 ff. 1. Ἀναλάβετε τὴν ἐπιστολὴν τοῦ μακαρίου
Παύλου τοῦ ἀποστόλου. 2. τί πρῶτον ὑμῖν ἐν

---

[1] Ἰησοῦ τοῦ κυρίου ἡμῶν Α, τοῦ κυρίου ἡμῶν Ἰησοῦ Χριστοῦ
CSK, *domini Ihesu* (τοῦ κυρίου Ἰησοῦ) L. The other readings
appear to be semi-liturgical expansions of the simple form
found in L.

[2] τῶν ἐκλεκτῶν μου διαστρέψαι LSK Clem. τῶν μικρῶν μου
σκανδαλίσαι " offend one of my little ones " AC.

88

3. And again in another place it says, "With the innocent man thou shalt be innocent, and with the elect man thou shalt be elect, and with the perverse man thou shalt do perversely."[1] 4. Let us then cleave to the innocent and righteous, for these are God's elect. 5. Why are there strife and passion and divisions and schisms and war among you? 6. Or have we not one God, and one Christ, and one Spirit of grace poured out upon us? And is there not one calling in Christ? 7. Why do we divide and tear asunder the members of Christ, and raise up strife against our own body, and reach such a pitch of madness as to forget that we are members one of another? Remember the words of the Lord Jesus; 8. for he said, "Woe unto that man: it were good for him if he had not been born, than that he should offend one of my elect; it were better for him that a millstone be hung on him, and he be cast into the sea, than that he should turn aside one of my elect." 9. Your schism has turned aside many, has cast many into discouragement, many to doubt, all of us to grief; and your sedition continues

XLVII

1. TAKE up the epistle of the blessed Paul the Apostle. 2. What did he first write to you at the

The example and teaching of St. Paul, and the early parties at Corinth

[1] Clement takes the word for "with" ($\mu\epsilon\tau\acute{a}$) to mean "in the company of": in Ps. 17 (in Hebrew and English Ps. 18) it means "in the case of," and the subject of the verbs is God.

ἀρχῇ τοῦ εὐαγγελίου ἔγραψεν; 3. ἐπ' ἀληθείας
πνευματικῶς ἐπέστειλεν ὑμῖν περὶ ἑαυτοῦ τε καὶ
Κηφᾶ τε καὶ 'Απολλώ, διὰ τὸ καὶ τότε προσκλίσεις ὑμᾶς πεποιῆσθαι. 4. ἀλλ' ἡ πρόσκλισις
ἐκείνη ἥττονα ἁμαρτίαν ὑμῖν προσήνεγκεν· προσ-
εκλίθητε γὰρ ἀποστόλοις μεμαρτυρημένοις καὶ
ἀνδρὶ δεδοκιμασμένῳ παρ' αὐτοῖς. 5. νυνὶ δὲ
κατανοήσατε, τίνες ὑμᾶς διέστρεψαν καὶ τὸ σεμνὸν τῆς περιβοήτου φιλαδελφίας ὑμῶν ἐμείωσαν.
6. αἰσχρά, ἀγαπητοί, καὶ λίαν αἰσχρά, καὶ ἀνάξια
τῆς ἐν Χριστῷ ἀγωγῆς ἀκούεσθαι, τὴν βεβαιοτά-
την καὶ ἀρχαίαν Κορινθίων ἐκκλησίαν δι' ἓν ἢ
δύο πρόσωπα στασιάζειν πρὸς τοὺς πρεσβυτέρους·
7. καὶ αὕτη ἡ ἀκοὴ οὐ μόνον εἰς ἡμᾶς ἐχώρησεν,
ἀλλὰ καὶ εἰς τοὺς ἑτεροκλινεῖς ὑπάρχοντας ἀφ'
ἡμῶν, ὥστε καὶ βλασφημίας ἐπιφέρεσθαι τῷ
ὀνόματι κυρίου διὰ τὴν ὑμετέραν ἀφροσύνην,
ἑαυτοῖς δὲ κίνδυνον ἐπεξεργάζεσθαι.

XLVIII

1. 'Εξάρωμεν οὖν τοῦτο ἐν τάχει καὶ προσπέσωμεν τῷ δεσπότῃ καὶ κλαύσωμεν ἱκετεύοντες
αὐτόν, ὅπως ἵλεως γενόμενος ἐπικαταλλαγῇ ἡμῖν
καὶ ἐπὶ τὴν σεμνὴν τῆς φιλαδελφίας ἡμῶν ἁγνὴν
ἀγωγὴν ἀποκαταστήσῃ ἡμᾶς. 2. πύλη γὰρ δικαιοσύνης ἀνεῳγυῖα εἰς ζωὴν αὕτη, καθὼς γέγραπται·
Ps.118,19,20 'Ανοίξατέ μοι πύλας δικαιοσύνης, ἵνα εἰσελθὼν ἐν
αὐταῖς ἐξομολογήσωμαι[1] τῷ κυρίῳ. 3. αὕτη ἡ

[1] ἵνα εἰσελθών . . . ἐξομολογήσωμαι SK Clem., εἰσελθών . . . ,
ἐξομολογήσομαι (I will enter . . . and praise) ACL.

beginning of his preaching? 3. With true inspiration he charged you concerning himself and Cephas and Apollos, because even then you had made yourselves partisans. 4. But that partisanship entailed less guilt on you; for you were partisans of Apostles of high reputation, and of a man approved by them. 5. But now consider who they are who have perverted you, and have lessened the respect due to your famous love for the brethren. 6. It is a shameful report, beloved, extremely shameful, and unworthy of your training in Christ, that on account of one or two persons the stedfast and ancient church of the Corinthians is being disloyal to the presbyters. 7. And this report has not only reached us, but also those who dissent from us, so that you bring blasphemy on the name of the Lord through your folly, and are moreover creating danger for yourselves.

XLVIII

1. LET us then quickly put an end to this, and let us fall down before the Master, and beseech him with tears that he may have mercy upon us, and be reconciled to us, and restore us to our holy and seemly practice of love for the brethren. 2. For this is the gate of righteousness which opens on to life, as it is written "Open me the gates of righteousness, that I may enter into them and praise the Lord;

Exhortation to be reconciled

πύλη τοῦ κυρίου· δίκαιοι εἰσελεύσονται ἐν αὐτῇ. 4. πολλῶν οὖν πυλῶν ἀνεῳγυιῶν ἡ ἐν δικαιοσύνῃ αὕτη ἐστὶν ἡ ἐν Χριστῷ, ἐν ᾗ μακάριοι πάντες οἱ εἰσελθόντες καὶ κατευθύνοντες τὴν πορείαν αὐτῶν

Luke 1. 75 ἐν ὁσιότητι καὶ δικαιοσύνῃ, ἀταράχως πάντα
I Cor. 12, 8, 9 ἐπιτελοῦντες. 5. ἤτω τις πιστός, ἤτω δυνατὸς γνῶσιν ἐξειπεῖν, ἤτω σοφὸς ἐν διακρίσει λόγων, ἤτω ἁγνὸς[1] ἐν ἔργοις. 6. τοσούτῳ γὰρ μᾶλλον ταπεινοφρονεῖν ὀφείλει, ὅσῳ δοκεῖ μᾶλλον μείζων εἶναι, καὶ ζητεῖν τὸ κοινωφελὲς πᾶσιν, καὶ μὴ τὸ ἑαυτοῦ.

XLIX

1. Ὁ ἔχων ἀγάπην ἐν Χριστῷ ποιησάτω τὰ τοῦ Χριστοῦ παραγγέλματα. 2. τὸν δεσμὸν τῆς ἀγάπης τοῦ θεοῦ τίς δύναται ἐξηγήσασθαι; 3. τὸ μεγαλεῖον τῆς καλλονῆς αὐτοῦ τίς ἀρκετὸς ἐξειπεῖν; 4. τὸ ὕψος, εἰς ὃ ἀνάγει ἡ ἀγάπη, ἀνεκδι-

I Pet. 4, 8 ήγητόν ἐστιν. 5. ἀγάπη κολλᾷ ἡμᾶς τῷ θεῷ, ἀγάπη καλύπτει πλῆθος ἁμαρτιῶν, ἀγάπη πάντα

I Cor. 13, 4-7 ἀνέχεται, πάντα μακροθυμεῖ· οὐδὲν βάναυσον ἐν ἀγάπῃ, οὐδὲν ὑπερήφανον· ἀγάπη σχίσμα οὐκ ἔχει, ἀγάπη οὐ στασιάζει, ἀγάπη πάντα ποιεῖ ἐν ὁμονοίᾳ· ἐν τῇ ἀγάπῃ ἐτελειώθησαν πάντες οἱ ἐκλεκτοὶ τοῦ θεοῦ, δίχα ἀγάπης οὐδὲν εὐάρεστόν ἐστιν[2] τῷ θεῷ. 6. ἐν ἀγάπῃ προσελάβετο ἡμᾶς ὁ δεσπότης· διὰ τὴν ἀγάπην, ἣν ἔσχεν πρὸς ἡμᾶς,

---

[1] Clement twice quotes this passage with γοργός (energetic) instead of ἁγνός before ἐν ἔργοις, but the second time he adds ἤτω ἁγνός as well.

[2] ἐστίν om. L. Clem.

3. this is the gate of the Lord, the righteous shall enter in by it." 4. So then of the many gates which are opened, that which is in righteousness is the one in Christ, in which are blessed all who enter and make straight their way in holiness and righteousness, accomplishing all things without disorder. 5. Let a man be faithful, let him have power to utter "Knowledge,"[1] let him be wise in the discernment of arguments, let him be pure in his deeds; 6. for the more he seems to be great, the more ought he to be humble-minded, and to seek the common good of all and not his own benefit.

XLIX

1. Let him who has love in Christ perform the commandments of Christ. 2. Who is able to explain the bond of the love of God? 3. Who is sufficient to tell the greatness of its beauty? 4. The height to which love lifts us is not to be expressed. 5. Love unites us to God. "Love covereth a multitude of sins. Love beareth all things, is long-suffering in all things. There is nothing base, nothing haughty in love; love admits no schism, love makes no sedition, love does all things in concord. In love were all the elect of God made perfect. Without love is nothing well pleasing to God. 6. In love did the Master receive us; for the sake of the love which he

Panegyric on love

---

[1] "Knowledge" is here no doubt used in the almost technical sense of "secret knowledge, conveying power, and specially revealed," approaching closely to the meaning which it had in the various "Gnostic" systems and in the Mystery religions.

τὸ αἷμα αὐτοῦ ἔδωκεν ὑπὲρ ἡμῶν Ἰησοῦς Χριστὸς
ὁ κύριος ἡμῶν ἐν θελήματι θεοῦ, καὶ τὴν σάρκα
ὑπὲρ τῆς σαρκὸς ἡμῶν καὶ τὴν ψυχὴν ὑπὲρ τῶν
ψυχῶν ἡμῶν.

L

1. Ὁρᾶτε, ἀγαπητοί, πῶς μέγα καὶ θαυμαστόν
ἐστιν ἡ ἀγάπη, καὶ τῆς τελειότητος αὐτῆς οὐκ
ἔστιν ἐξήγησις. 2. τίς ἱκανὸς ἐν αὐτῇ εὑρεθῆναι,
εἰ μὴ οὓς ἂν καταξιώσῃ ὁ θεός; δεώμεθα οὖν καὶ
αἰτώμεθα ἀπὸ τοῦ ἐλέους αὐτοῦ, ἵνα ἐν ἀγάπῃ
εὑρεθῶμεν δίχα προσκλίσεως ἀνθρωπίνης, ἄμωμοι.
3. αἱ γενεαὶ πᾶσαι ἀπὸ Ἀδὰμ ἕως τῆσδε τῆς
ἡμέρας παρῆλθον, ἀλλ᾽ οἱ ἐν ἀγάπῃ τελειωθέντες
κατὰ τὴν τοῦ θεοῦ χάριν ἔχουσιν χῶρον εὐσεβῶν,
οἳ φανερωθήσονται ἐν τῇ ἐπισκοπῇ τῆς βασιλείας
τοῦ Χριστοῦ.[1] 4. γέγραπται γάρ· Εἰσέλθετε εἰς τὰ
ταμεῖα μικρὸν ὅσον ὅσον, ἕως οὗ παρέλθῃ ἡ ὀργὴ
καὶ ὁ θυμός μου, καὶ μνησθήσομαι ἡμέρας ἀγαθῆς,
καὶ ἀναστήσω ὑμᾶς ἐκ τῶν θηκῶν ὑμῶν. 5. μα-
κάριοί ἐσμεν, ἀγαπητοί, εἰ τὰ προστάγματα τοῦ
θεοῦ ἐποιοῦμεν[2] ἐν ὁμονοίᾳ ἀγάπης, εἰς τὸ ἀφεθῆναι ἡμῖν δι᾽ ἀγάπης τὰς ἁμαρτίας. 6. γέγραπται γάρ· Μακάριοι, ὧν ἀφέθησαν αἱ ἀνομίαι καὶ
ὧν ἐπεκαλύφθησαν αἱ ἁμαρτίαι· μακάριος ἀνήρ,
οὗ οὐ μὴ λογίσηται κύριος ἁμαρτίαν, οὐδέ ἐστιν
ἐν τῷ στόματι αὐτοῦ δόλος· 7. οὗτος ὁ μακαρι-

Is. 26, 20;
Ezek. 37, 12

Ps. 32, 1, 2;
Rom. 4, 7-9

---

[1] Χριστοῦ (A)LK Clem., θεοῦ CS.
[2] This seems corrupt : a present is required.

ħad towards us did Jesus Christ our Lord give his blood by the will of God for us, and his flesh for our flesh, and his soul[1] for our souls."

L

1. SEE, beloved, how great and wonderful is love, and that of its perfection there is no expression. 2. Who is able to be found in it save those to whom God grants it? Let us then beg and pray of his mercy that we may be found in love, without human partisanship, free from blame. 3. All the generations from Adam until this day have passed away; but those who were perfected in love by the grace of God have a place among the pious who shall be made manifest at the visitation of the Kingdom of Christ. 4. For it is written, "Enter into thy chambers for a very little while, until my wrath and fury pass away, and I will remember a good day, and will raise you up out of your graves." 5. Blessed are we, beloved, if we perform the commandments of God in the concord of love, that through love our sins may be forgiven. 6. For it is written "Blessed are they whose iniquities are forgiven, and whose sins are covered; blessed is the man whose sin the Lord will not reckon, and in whose mouth is no guile."

Exhortation to pray for love

---

[1] Or, perhaps "life for our lives"; but there seems to be an antithesis in the Greek between σάρξ, flesh, and ψυχή, soul.

σμὸς ἐγένετο ἐπὶ τοὺς ἐκλελεγμένους ὑπὸ τοῦ θεοῦ διὰ Ἰησοῦ Χριστοῦ τοῦ κυρίου ἡμῶν, ᾧ ἡ δόξα εἰς τοὺς αἰῶνας τῶν αἰώνων. ἀμήν.

LI

1. Ὅσα οὖν παρεπέσαμεν καὶ ἐποιήσαμεν διά τινας παρεμπτώσεις [1] τοῦ ἀντικειμένου, ἀξιώσωμεν ἀφεθῆναι ἡμῖν. καὶ ἐκεῖνοι δέ, οἵτινες ἀρχηγοὶ στάσεως καὶ διχοστασίας ἐγενήθησαν, ὀφείλουσιν τὸ κοινὸν τῆς ἐλπίδος σκοπεῖν. 2. οἱ γὰρ μετὰ φόβου καὶ ἀγάπης πολιτευόμενοι ἑαυτοὺς θέλουσιν μᾶλλον αἰκίαις περιπίπτειν ἢ τοὺς πλησίον· μᾶλλον δὲ ἑαυτῶν κατάγνωσιν φέρουσιν ἢ τῆς παραδεδομένης ἡμῖν καλῶς καὶ δικαίως ὁμοφωνίας, 3. καλὸν γὰρ ἀνθρώπῳ ἐξομολογεῖσθαι περὶ τῶν παραπτωμάτων ἢ σκληρῦναι τὴν καρδίαν αὐτοῦ,

Num. 16

καθὼς ἐσκληρύνθη ἡ καρδία τῶν στασιαζόντων πρὸς τὸν θεράποντα τοῦ θεοῦ Μωϋσῆν, ὧν τὸ κρίμα

Num. 16, 33
Ps. 49, 14

πρόδηλον ἐγενήθη, 4. κατέβησαν γὰρ εἰς ᾅδου ζῶντες, καὶ θάνατος ποιμανεῖ αὐτούς. 5. Φαραὼ καὶ ἡ στρατιὰ αὐτοῦ καὶ πάντες οἱ ἡγούμενοι

Exod. 14, 23

Αἰγύπτου, τά τε ἅρματα καὶ οἱ ἀναβάται αὐτῶν οὐ δι᾽ ἄλλην τινὰ αἰτίαν ἐβυθίσθησαν εἰς θάλασσαν ἐρυθρὰν καὶ ἀπώλοντο, ἀλλὰ διὰ τὸ σκληρυνθῆναι αὐτῶν τὰς ἀσυνέτους καρδίας μετὰ τὸ γενέσθαι τὰ σημεῖα καὶ τὰ τέρατα ἐν γῇ Αἰγύπτου διὰ τοῦ θεράποντος τοῦ θεοῦ Μωϋσέως.

---

[1] The text is doubtful : διὰ τὰς παρεμπτώσεις Clem., *propter quasdam incursiones* L, the equivalent of διὰ τὰς παρεμπτώσεις τινῶν (τὰς) K, διὰ τινὸς τῶν ACS.

7. This blessing was given to those who have been chosen by God through Jesus Christ our Lord, to whom be the glory for ever and ever. Amen.

LI

1. LET us then pray that for our transgressions, And for and for what we have done through any attacks of forgiveness the adversary, forgiveness may be granted to us. And those also who were the leaders of sedition and disagreement are bound to consider the common hope. 2. For those who live in fear and love are willing to suffer torture themselves rather than their neighbours, and they suffer the blame of themselves, rather than that of our tradition of noble and righteous harmony, 3. for it is better for man to confess his transgressions than to harden his heart, even as the heart of those was hardened who rebelled against God's servant Moses, and their condemnation was made manifest, 4. for "they went down into Hades alive" and "death shall be their shepherd." 5. Pharaoh and his army and all the rulers of Egypt, "the chariots and their riders," were sunk in the Red Sea, and perished for no other cause than that their foolish hearts were hardened, after that signs and wonders had been wrought in the land of Egypt by God's servant Moses.

LII

1. Ἀπροσδεής, ἀδελφοί, ὁ δεσπότης ὑπάρχει τῶν ἁπάντων· οὐδὲν οὐδενὸς χρήζει εἰ μὴ τὸ ἐξομολογεῖσθαι αὐτῷ. **2.** φησὶν γὰρ ὁ ἐκλεκτὸς Ps. 69, 30-32 Δαυείδ· Ἐξομολογήσομαι τῷ κυρίῳ, καὶ ἀρέσει αὐτῷ ὑπὲρ μόσχον νέον κέρατα ἐκφέροντα καὶ ὁπλάς· ἰδέτωσαν πτωχοὶ καὶ εὐφρανθήτωσαν. Ps. 50, 14. 15 **3.** καὶ πάλιν λέγει· Θῦσον τῷ θεῷ θυσίαν αἰνέσεως καὶ ἀπόδος τῷ ὑψίστῳ τὰς εὐχάς σου· καὶ ἐπικάλεσαί με ἐν ἡμέρᾳ θλίψεώς σου, καὶ Ps. 51, 17 ἐξελοῦμαί σε, καὶ δοξάσεις με. **4.** θυσία γὰρ τῷ θεῷ πνεῦμα συντετριμμένον.

LIII

1. Ἐπίστασθε γὰρ καὶ καλῶς ἐπίστασθε τὰς ἱερὰς γραφάς, ἀγαπητοί, καὶ ἐγκεκύφατε εἰς τὰ λόγια τοῦ θεοῦ. πρὸς ἀνάμνησιν οὖν ταῦτα γράφομεν. **2.** Μωϋσέως γὰρ ἀναβάντος εἰς τὸ ὄρος καὶ ποιήσαντος τεσσαράκοντα ἡμέρας καὶ τεσσαράκοντα νύκτας ἐν νηστείᾳ καὶ ταπεινώσει, εἶπεν Deut. 9, 12 πρὸς αὐτὸν ὁ θεός· Κατάβηθι[1] τὸ τάχος ἐντεῦθεν, (Exod. 32, 7-8) ὅτι ἠνόμησεν ὁ λαός σου, οὓς ἐξήγαγες ἐκ γῆς Αἰγύπτου· παρέβησαν ταχὺ ἐκ τῆς ὁδοῦ ἧς ἐνετείλω αὐτοῖς, ἐποίησαν ἑαυτοῖς χωνεύματα. **3.** καὶ εἶπεν κύριος πρὸς αὐτόν· Λελάληκα Deut. 9,13.14 πρός σε ἅπαξ καὶ δὶς λέγων· Ἑώρακα τὸν λαὸν (Exod. 32, 9-10) τοῦτον, καὶ ἰδού ἐστιν σκληροτράχηλος· ἔασόν

---

[1] Μωυσῆ, Μωυσῆ κατάβηθι Α(C) om. Μωυσῆ, Μωυσῆ LSK.

LII

1. THE Master, brethren, is in need of nothing: he asks nothing of anyone, save that confession be made to him. 2. For David the chosen says:—"I will confess to the Lord, and it shall please him more than a young calf that groweth horns and hoofs: let the poor see it and be glad." 3. And again he says "Sacrifice to God a sacrifice of praise, and pay to the Highest thy vows; and call upon me in the day of thy affliction, and I will deliver thee and thou shalt glorify me. 4. For the sacrifice of God is a broken spirit." *Let the wrongdoers confess their sins*

LIII

1. FOR you have understanding, you have a good understanding of the sacred Scriptures, beloved, and you have studied the oracles of God. Therefore we write these things to remind you. 2. For when Moses went up into the mountain, and passed forty days and forty nights in fasting and humiliation, God said to him:—"Go down hence quickly, for thy people, whom thou didst bring out of the land of Egypt, have committed iniquity; they have quickly gone aside out of the way which thou didst command them; they have made themselves molten images." 3. And the Lord said to him:—"I have spoken to thee once and twice, saying, I have seen this people, and behold it is stiffnecked; suffer *The example of Moses*

Exod. 32,
31. 32

με ἐξολεθρεῦσαι αὐτούς, καὶ ἐξαλείψω τὸ ὄνομα
αὐτῶν ὑποκάτωθεν τοῦ οὐρανοῦ, καὶ ποιήσω σε
εἰς ἔθνος μέγα καὶ θαυμαστὸν καὶ πολὺ μᾶλλον
ἢ τοῦτο.   4. καὶ εἶπεν Μωϋσῆς· Μηδαμῶς, κύριε·
ἄφες τὴν ἁμαρτίαν τῷ λαῷ τούτῳ, ἢ κἀμὲ ἐξάλειψον ἐκ βίβλου ζώντων. 5. ὦ μεγάλης ἀγάπης,
ὦ τελειότητος ἀνυπερβλήτου. παρρησιάζεται
θεράπων πρὸς κύριον, αἰτεῖται ἄφεσιν τῷ πλήθει,
ἢ καὶ ἑαυτὸν ἐξαλειφθῆναι μετ᾽ αὐτῶν ἀξιοῖ.

LIV

1. Τίς οὖν ἐν ὑμῖν γενναῖος, τίς εὔσπλαγχνος,
τίς πεπληροφορημένος ἀγάπης; 2. εἰπάτω· Εἰ
δι᾽ ἐμὲ στάσις καὶ ἔρις καὶ σχίσματα, ἐκχωρῶ,
ἄπειμι, οὗ ἐὰν βούλησθε, καὶ ποιῶ τὰ προστασσό-
μενα ὑπὸ τοῦ πλήθους· μόνον τὸ ποίμνιον τοῦ
Χριστοῦ εἰρηνευέτω μετὰ τῶν καθεσταμένων πρεσβυτέρων. 3. τοῦτο ὁ ποιήσας ἑαυτῷ μέγα κλέος
ἐν Χριστῷ περιποιήσεται, καὶ πᾶς τόπος δέξεται
αὐτόν, τοῦ γὰρ κυρίου ἡ γῆ καὶ τὸ πλήρωμα
αὐτῆς. 4. ταῦτα οἱ πολιτευόμενοι τὴν ἀμε-
ταμέλητον πολιτείαν τοῦ θεοῦ ἐποίησαν καὶ
ποιήσουσιν.

Ps. 24, 1

LV

1. Ἵνα δὲ καὶ ὑποδείγματα ἐθνῶν ἐνέγκωμεν.
πολλοὶ βασιλεῖς καὶ ἡγούμενοι, λοιμικοῦ τινος
ἐνστάντος καιροῦ, χρησμοδοτηθέντες παρέδωκαν
ἑαυτοὺς εἰς θάνατον, ἵνα ῥύσωνται διὰ τοῦ ἑαυτῶν
αἵματος τοὺς πολίτας· πολλοὶ ἐξεχώρησαν ἰδίων

me to destroy them, and I will wipe out their name from under heaven, and thee will I make into a nation great and wonderful and much more than this." 4. And Moses said, " Not so, Lord ; pardon the sin of this people, or blot me also out of the book of the living." 5. O great love ! O unsurpassable perfection ! The servant is bold with the Lord, he asks forgiveness for the people, or begs that he himself may be blotted out together with them.

LIV

1. Who then among you is noble, who is compassionate, who is filled with love ? 2. Let him cry :—" If sedition and strife and divisions have arisen on my account, I will depart, I will go away whithersoever you will, and I will obey the commands of the people ; only let the flock of Christ have peace with the presbyters set over it." 3. He who does this will win for himself great glory in Christ, and every place will receive him, for " the earth is the Lord's, and the fullness of it." 4. This has been in the past, and will be in the future, the conduct of those who live without regrets as citizens in the city of God.

Application to the Corinthians

LV

1. Let us also bring forward examples from the heathen. Many kings and rulers, when a time of pestilence has set in, have followed the counsel of oracles, and given themselves up to death, that they might rescue their subjects through their own blood.

Other examples of loving self-sacrifice

πόλεων, ἵνα μὴ στασιάζωσιν ἐπὶ πλεῖον. 2. ἐπι-
στάμεθα πολλοὺς ἐν ἡμῖν παραδεδωκότας ἑαυτοὺς
εἰς δεσμά, ὅπως ἑτέρους λυτρώσονται· πολλοὶ
ἑαυτοὺς παρέδωκαν εἰς δουλείαν, καὶ λαβόντες
τὰς τιμὰς αὐτῶν ἑτέρους ἐψώμισαν. 3. πολλαὶ
γυναῖκες ἐνδυναμωθεῖσαι διὰ τῆς χάριτος τοῦ
Judith 8 ff. θεοῦ ἐπετελέσαντο πολλὰ ἀνδρεῖα. 4. Ἰουδὶθ ἡ
μακαρία, ἐν συγκλεισμῷ οὔσης τῆς πόλεως,
ᾐτήσατο παρὰ τῶν πρεσβυτέρων ἐαθῆναι αὐτὴν
ἐξελθεῖν εἰς τὴν παρεμβολὴν τῶν ἀλλοφύλων.
5. παραδοῦσα οὖν ἑαυτὴν τῷ κινδύνῳ ἐξῆλθεν δι'
ἀγάπην τῆς πατρίδος καὶ τοῦ λαοῦ τοῦ ὄντος ἐν
συγκλεισμῷ, καὶ παρέδωκεν κύριος Ὀλοφέρνην ἐν
Esther 7, χειρὶ θηλείας. 6. οὐχ ἧττον[1] καὶ ἡ τελεία κατὰ
πίστιν Ἐσθὴρ κινδύνῳ ἑαυτὴν παρέβαλεν, ἵνα
τὸ ἔθνος[2] τοῦ Ἰσραὴλ μέλλον ἀπολέσθαι ῥύσηται·
Esther 4, 16 διὰ γὰρ τῆς νηστείας καὶ τῆς ταπεινώσεως αὐτῆς
ἠξίωσεν τὸν παντεπόπτην δεσπότην[3] τῶν αἰώνων·
ὃς ἰδὼν τὸ ταπεινὸν τῆς ψυχῆς αὐτῆς ἐρύσατο τὸν
λαόν, ὧν χάριν ἐκινδύνευσεν.

LVI

1. Καὶ ἡμεῖς οὖν ἐντύχωμεν περὶ τῶν ἔν τινι
παραπτώματι ὑπαρχόντων, ὅπως δοθῇ αὐτοῖς
ἐπιείκεια καὶ ταπεινοφροσύνη εἰς τὸ εἶξαι αὐτοὺς
μὴ ἡμῖν ἀλλὰ τῷ θελήματι τοῦ θεοῦ· οὕτως γὰρ
ἔσται αὐτοῖς ἔγκαρπος καὶ τελεία ἡ πρὸς τὸν θεὸν

---

[1] ἧττον CSK, ἧττονι A ("to no less danger").
[2] ἔθνος LSK, δωδεκάφυλον ("the twelve tribes") AC.
[3] δεσπότην LK, δεσπότην θεόν A, θεόν C (S also inserts θεόν
but after τῶν αἰώνων).

Many have gone away from their own cities, that sedition might have an end. 2. We know that many among ourselves have given themselves to bondage that they might ransom others. Many have delivered themselves to slavery, and provided food for others with the price they received for themselves. 3. Many women have received power through the grace of God and have performed many deeds of manly valour. 4. The blessed Judith, when her city was besieged, asked the elders to suffer her to go out into the camp of the strangers. 5. So she gave herself up to danger, and went forth for love of her country and her people in their siege, and the Lord delivered over Holofernes by the hand of a woman. 6. Not less did Esther also, who was perfect in faith, deliver herself to danger, that she might rescue the nation of Israel from the destruction that awaited it; for with fasting and humiliation she besought the all-seeing Master of the Ages, and he saw the meekness of her soul, and rescued the people for whose sake she had faced peril.

LVI

1. LET then us also intercede for those who have fallen into any transgression, that meekness and humility be given to them, that they may submit, not to us, but to the will of God; for so will they have fruitful and perfect remembrance before God

Exhortation to humility

καὶ τοὺς ἁγίους μετ᾽ οἰκτιρμῶν μνεία. 2. ἀναλά-
βωμεν παιδείαν, ἐφ᾽ ᾗ οὐδεὶς ὀφείλει ἀγανακτεῖν,
ἀγαπητοί. ἡ νουθέτησις, ἣν ποιούμεθα εἰς ἀλλήλους, καλή ἐστιν καὶ ὑπεράγαν ὠφέλιμος· κολλᾷ
γὰρ ἡμᾶς τῷ θελήματι τοῦ θεοῦ. 3. οὕτως γάρ

Ps. 118, 18   φησιν ὁ ἅγιος λόγος· Παιδεύων ἐπαίδευσέν με ὁ
Prov. 3, 12   κύριος, καὶ τῷ θανάτῳ οὐ παρέδωκέν με· 4. ὃν
(Heb. 12, 6)   γὰρ ἀγαπᾷ κύριος παιδεύει, μαστιγοῖ δὲ πάντα
Ps. 141, 5   υἱὸν ὃν παραδέχεται. 5. Παιδεύσει με γάρ,
               φησίν, δίκαιος ἐν ἐλέει καὶ ἐλέγξει με, ἔλαιον
               δὲ ἁμαρτωλῶν μὴ λιπανάτω τὴν κεφαλήν μου.
Job. 5, 17-26 6. καὶ πάλιν λέγει· Μακάριος ἄνθρωπος, ὃν
               ἤλεγξεν ὁ κύριος· νουθέτημα δὲ παντοκράτορος
               μὴ ἀπαναίνου· αὐτὸς γὰρ ἀλγεῖν ποιεῖ, καὶ πάλιν
               ἀποκαθίστησιν· 7. ἔπαισεν, καὶ αἱ χεῖρες αὐτοῦ
               ἰάσαντο. 8. ἑξάκις ἐξ ἀναγκῶν ἐξελεῖταί σε, ἐν
               δὲ τῷ ἑβδόμῳ οὐχ ἅψεταί σου κακόν. 9. ἐν λιμῷ
               ῥύσεταί σε ἐκ θανάτου, ἐν πολέμῳ δὲ ἐκ χειρὸς
               σιδήρου λύσει σε· 10. καὶ ἀπὸ μάστιγος γλώσσης
               σε κρύψει, καὶ οὐ μὴ φοβηθήσῃ κακῶν ἐπερχο-
               μένων. 11. ἀδίκων καὶ ἀνόμων καταγελάσῃ, ἀπὸ
               δὲ θηρίων ἀγρίων οὐ μὴ φοβηθῇς· 12. θῆρες γὰρ
               ἄγριοι εἰρηνεύσουσίν σοι. 13. εἶτα γνώσῃ, ὅτι
               εἰρηνεύσει σου ὁ οἶκος, ἡ δὲ δίαιτα τῆς σκηνῆς
               σου οὐ μὴ ἁμάρτῃ. 14. γνώσῃ δέ, ὅτι πολὺ τὸ
               σπέρμα σου, τὰ δὲ τέκνα σου ὥσπερ τὸ παμ-
               βότανον τοῦ ἀγροῦ. 15. ἐλεύσῃ δὲ ἐν τάφῳ
               ὥσπερ σῖτος ὥριμος κατὰ καιρὸν θεριζόμενος, ἢ

and the saints, and find compassion. 2. Let us receive correction, which none should take amiss, beloved. The admonition which we make one to another is good and beyond measure helpful, for it unites us to the will of God. 3. For the holy word The teach-says thus : " With chastisement did the Lord chastise ing of the Scriptures me, and he delivered me not over unto death ; 4. for whom the Lord loveth he chasteneth, and scourgeth every son whom he receiveth." 5 " For," he says, " the righteous shall chasten me with mercy, and reprove me, but let not the oil of sinners anoint my head." 6. And again he says " Blessed is the man whom the Lord did reprove ; and reject not thou the admonition of the Almighty, for he maketh to suffer pain and again he restoreth ; 7. he wounded, and his hands healed. 8. Six times shall he deliver thee from troubles, and the seventh time evil shall not touch thee. 9. In famine he shall rescue thee from death, and in war he shall free thee from the hand of the sword. 10. And he shall hide thee from the scourge of the tongue and thou shalt not fear when evils approach. 11. Thou shalt laugh at the unrighteous and wicked, and thou shalt not be afraid of wild beasts ; 12. for wild beasts shall be at peace with thee. 13. Then thou shalt know that thy house shall have peace, and the habitation of thy tabernacle shall not fail. 14. And thou shalt know that thy seed shall be many and thy children like the herb of the field. 15. And thou shalt come to the grave like ripened corn that is harvested in its due season, or like a heap on the threshing-floor

ὥσπερ θημωνιὰ ἅλωνος καθ᾽ ὥραν συγκομισθεῖσα.
16. βλέπετε, ἀγαπητοί, πόσος ὑπερασπισμός ἐστιν
τοῖς παιδευομένοις ὑπὸ τοῦ δεσπότου· πατὴρ γὰρ
ἀγαθὸς ὢν παιδεύει εἰς τὸ ἐλεηθῆναι ἡμᾶς διὰ τῆς
ὁσίας παιδείας αὐτοῦ.

LVII

1. Ὑμεῖς οὖν οἱ τὴν καταβολὴν τῆς στάσεως
ποιήσαντες ὑποτάγητε τοῖς πρεσβυτέροις καὶ
παιδεύθητε εἰς μετάνοιαν, κάμψαντες τὰ γόνατα
τῆς καρδίας ὑμῶν. 2. μάθετε ὑποτάσσεσθαι,
ἀποθέμενοι τὴν ἀλαζόνα καὶ ὑπερήφανον τῆς
γλώσσης ὑμῶν αὐθάδειαν· ἄμεινον γάρ ἐστιν
ὑμῖν, ἐν τῷ ποιμνίῳ τοῦ Χριστοῦ μικροὺς καὶ
ἐλλογίμους εὑρεθῆναι, ἢ καθ᾽ ὑπεροχὴν δοκοῦντας
ἐκριφθῆναι ἐκ τῆς ἐλπίδος αὐτοῦ. 3. οὕτως γὰρ
Prov.1,23-33 λέγει ἡ πανάρετος σοφία· Ἰδού, προήσομαι ὑμῖν
ἐμῆς πνοῆς ῥῆσιν, διδάξω δὲ ὑμᾶς τὸν ἐμὸν λόγον.
4. ἐπειδὴ ἐκάλουν καὶ οὐχ ὑπηκούσατε, καὶ
ἐξέτεινον λόγους καὶ οὐ προσείχετε, ἀλλὰ ἀκύρους
ἐποιεῖτε τὰς ἐμὰς βουλάς, τοῖς δὲ ἐμοῖς ἐλέγχοις
ἠπειθήσατε· τοιγαροῦν κἀγὼ τῇ ὑμετέρᾳ ἀπωλείᾳ
ἐπιγελάσομαι, καταχαροῦμαι δὲ ἡνίκα ἂν ἔρχηται
ὑμῖν ὄλεθρος καὶ ὡς ἂν ἀφίκηται ὑμῖν ἄφνω θόρυ-
βος, ἡ δὲ καταστροφὴ ὁμοία καταιγίδι παρῇ, ἢ ὅταν
ἔρχηται ὑμῖν θλῖψις καὶ πολιορκία. 5. ἔσται γὰρ
ὅταν ἐπικαλέσησθέ με, ἐγὼ δὲ οὐκ εἰσακούσομαι

which is gathered together at the appointed time."
16. You see, beloved, how great is the protection Application given to those that are chastened by the Master, for to the Corinthians he is a good father and chastens us that we may obtain mercy through his holy chastisement.

LVII

1. You therefore, who laid the foundation of the sedition, submit to the presbyters, and receive the correction of repentance, bending the knees of your hearts. 2. Learn to be submissive, putting aside the boastful and the haughty self-confidence of your tongue, for it is better for you to be found small but honourable in the flock of Christ, than to be pre-eminent in repute but to be cast out from his hope. 3. For "the excellent wisdom"[1] says thus :— Warning from Scripture "Behold I will bring forth to you the words of my spirit, 4. and I will teach you my speech, since I called and ye did not obey, and I put forth my words and ye did not attend, but made my counsels of no effect, and disobeyed my reproofs ; therefore will I also laugh at your ruin, and I will rejoice when destruction cometh upon you, and when sudden confusion overtaketh you and catastrophe cometh as a storm, or when persecution or siege cometh upon you. 5. For it shall come to pass when ye call upon me, I will not hear you. The evil shall seek me and they shall not find me. For they hated wisdom and they

---

[1] " The excellent wisdom " is a title used (a) of Proverbs, (b) of Proverbs, Ecclesiasticus, and Ecclesiastes, (c) of the third division of the O.T. (Hagiographa or " Writings ") as a whole. Cf. note on p. 57.

ὑμῶν· ζητήσουσίν με κακοί, καὶ οὐχ εὑρήσουσιν.
ἐμίσησαν γὰρ σοφίαν, τὸν δὲ φόβον τοῦ κυρίου
οὐ προείλαντο, οὐδὲ ἤθελον ἐμαῖς προσέχειν
βουλαῖς, ἐμυκτήριζον δὲ ἐμοὺς ἐλέγχους. 6. τοιγαροῦν ἔδονται τῆς ἑαυτῶν ὁδοῦ τοὺς καρπούς, καὶ
τῆς ἑαυτῶν ἀσεβείας πλησθήσονται·[1] 7. ἀνθ᾽ ὧν
γὰρ ἠδίκουν νηπίους φονευθήσονται, καὶ ἐξετασμὸς
ἀσεβεῖς ὀλεῖ· ὁ δὲ ἐμοῦ ἀκούων κατασκηνώσει ἐπ᾽
ἐλπίδι πεποιθὼς καὶ ἡσυχάσει ἀφόβως ἀπὸ παντὸς
κακοῦ.

LVIII

1. Ὑπακούσωμεν οὖν τῷ παναγίῳ καὶ ἐνδόξῳ
ὀνόματι αὐτοῦ φυγόντες τὰς προειρημένας διὰ τῆς
σοφίας τοῖς ἀπειθοῦσιν ἀπειλάς, ἵνα κατασκηνώσω-
μεν πεποιθότες ἐπὶ τὸ ὁσιώτατον τῆς μεγαλωσύνης
αὐτοῦ ὄνομα. 2. δέξασθε τὴν συμβουλὴν ἡμῶν,
καὶ ἔσται ἀμεταμέλητα ὑμῖν. ζῇ γὰρ ὁ θεὸς καὶ
ζῇ[2] ὁ κύριος Ἰησοῦς Χριστὸς καὶ τὸ πνεῦμα τὸ
ἅγιον, ἥ τε πίστις καὶ ἡ ἐλπὶς τῶν ἐκλεκτῶν, ὅτι
ὁ ποιήσας ἐν ταπεινοφροσύνῃ μετ᾽ ἐκτενοῦς ἐπιεικείας ἀμεταμελήτως τὰ ὑπὸ τοῦ θεοῦ δεδομένα
δικαιώματα καὶ προστάγματα, οὗτος ἐντεταγμένος
καὶ ἐλλόγιμος ἔσται εἰς τὸν ἀριθμὸν τῶν σωζομέ-
νων διὰ Ἰησοῦ Χριστοῦ, δι᾽ οὗ ἐστιν αὐτῷ ἡ δόξα
εἰς τοὺς αἰῶνας τῶν αἰώνων. ἀμήν.

---

[1] A is missing from here to the beginning of Chapter LXIV.
[2] ζῇ 2° CS, om. LK and quotation by Basil.

chose not the fear of the Lord, neither would they attend to my counsels but mocked my reproofs. 6. Therefore shall they eat the fruits of their own way, and shall be filled with their own wickedness; 7. for because they wronged the innocent they shall be put to death, and inquisition shall destroy the wicked. But he who heareth me shall tabernacle with confidence in his hope, and shall be in rest with no fear of any evil."

LVIII

1. LET us then be obedient to his most holy and glorious name, and escape the threats which have been spoken by wisdom aforetime to the disobedient, that we may tabernacle in confidence on the most sacred name of his majesty. 2. Receive our counsel, and there shall be nothing for you to regret, for as God lives and as the Lord Jesus Christ lives and the Holy Spirit, the faith and hope of the elect, he who with lowliness of mind and eager gentleness has without backsliding performed the decrees and commandments given by God shall be enrolled and chosen in the number of those who are saved through Jesus Christ, through whom is to him the glory for ever and ever. Amen.

Further application and exhortation to the Corinthian dissidents

LIX

1. Ἐὰν δέ τινες ἀπειθήσωσιν τοῖς ὑπ' αὐτοῦ δι' ἡμῶν εἰρημένοις, γινωσκέτωσαν ὅτι παραπτώσει καὶ κινδύνῳ οὐ μικρῷ ἑαυτοὺς ἐνδήσουσιν. 2. ἡμεῖς δὲ ἀθῷοι ἐσόμεθα ἀπὸ ταύτης τῆς ἁμαρτίας καὶ αἰτησόμεθα ἐκτενῆ τὴν δέησιν καὶ ἱκεσίαν ποιούμενοι, ὅπως τὸν ἀριθμὸν τὸν κατηριθμημένον τῶν ἐκλεκτῶν αὐτοῦ ἐν ὅλῳ τῷ κόσμῳ διαφυλάξῃ ἄθραυστον ὁ δημιουργὸς τῶν ἁπάντων διὰ τοῦ ἠγαπημένου παιδὸς αὐτοῦ Ἰησοῦ Χριστοῦ, δι' οὗ

Acts 26, 18 — ἐκάλεσεν ἡμᾶς ἀπὸ σκότους εἰς φῶς, ἀπὸ ἀγνωσίας εἰς ἐπίγνωσιν δόξης ὀνόματος αὐτοῦ, 3. . . . ἐλπί-ζειν[1] ἐπὶ τὸ ἀρχεγόνον πάσης κτίσεως ὄνομά σου,

Eph. 1, 18 — ἀνοίξας τοὺς ὀφθαλμοὺς τῆς καρδίας ἡμῶν εἰς τὸ
Is. 57, 15 — γινώσκειν σε τὸν μόνον ὕψιστον ἐν ὑψίστοις,
Is. 13, 11
Ps. 32, 10 — ἅγιον ἐν ἁγίοις ἀναπαυόμενον. τὸν ταπεινοῦντα ὕβριν ὑπερηφάνων, τὸν διαλύοντα λογισμοὺς
Job 5, 11 — ἐθνῶν, τὸν ποιοῦντα ταπεινοὺς εἰς ὕψος καὶ τοὺς
I Sam. 2, 7; — ὑψηλοὺς ταπεινοῦντα, τὸν πλουτίζοντα καὶ πτω-
cf. Luke 1, 53 — χίζοντα, τὸν ἀποκτείνοντα καὶ ζῆν ποιοῦντα,[2]
Deut. 32, 39; — μόνον εὑρέτην[3] πνευμάτων καὶ θεὸν πάσης σαρ-
cf. I Sam. 2, 6;
II Kings 5, 7 — κός· τὸν ἐπιβλέποντα ἐν τοῖς ἀβύσσοις, τὸν ἐπόπ-
Num. 16, 22; — την ἀνθρωπίνων ἔργων, τὸν τῶν κινδυνευόντων
27. 16

[1] There appears to be a lacuna in the Greek: Lightfoot supplies Δὸς ἡμῖν, κύριε.

[2] καὶ σώζοντα appears to be inserted before καὶ ζῆν by SL, but is omitted by CK.

[3] εὐεργέτην ("benefactor") C, "creator" K; the text is doubtful but εὑρέτην (LS) seems more likely to be implied by K than εὐεργέτην, and is therefore slightly more probable.

LIX

1. BUT if some be disobedient to the words which have been spoken by him through us, let them know that they will entangle themselves in transgression and no little danger ; 2. but we shall be innocent of this sin, and will pray with eager entreaty and supplication that the Creator of the Universe may guard unhurt the number of his elect that has been numbered in all the world through his beloved child Jesus Christ, through whom he called us from darkness to light, from ignorance to the full knowledge of the glory of his name. Warnings to the dissidents

3. Grant us[1] to hope on thy name, the source of all creation, open the eyes of our heart to know thee, that thou alone art the highest in the highest and remainest holy among the holy. Thou dost humble the pride of the haughty, thou dost destroy the imaginings of nations, thou dost raise up the humble and abase the lofty, thou makest rich and makest poor, thou dost slay and make alive, thou alone art the finder of spirits and art God of all flesh, thou dost look on the abysses, thou seest into the works of man, thou art the helper of those in danger, the saviour of those in despair, the Prayer to God

---

[1] Some such addition, though not in any authority for the text, appears to be necessary.

Dan. 3, 31
(Vulg. 3, 55);
cf. Sirach 16,
18. 19
Judith 9, 11
βοηθόν, τὸν τῶν ἀπηλπισμένων σωτῆρα, τὸν
παντὸς πνεύματος κτίστην καὶ ἐπίσκοπον· τὸν
πληθύνοντα ἔθνη ἐπὶ γῆς καὶ ἐκ πάντων ἐκλεξά-
μενον τοὺς ἀγαπῶντάς σε διὰ Ἰησοῦ Χριστοῦ τοῦ
ἠγαπημένου παιδός σου, δι' οὗ ἡμᾶς ἐπαίδευσας,
Ps. 118, 114;
cf. Judith 9,
11
ἡγίασας, ἐτίμησας· 4. ἀξιοῦμέν σε, δέσποτα,
βοηθὸν γενέσθαι καὶ ἀντιλήπτορα ἡμῶν. τοὺς ἐν
θλίψει ἡμῶν σῶσον, τοὺς ταπεινοὺς ἐλέησον, τοὺς
πεπτωκότας ἔγειρον, τοῖς δεομένοις ἐπιφάνηθι,
τοὺς ἀσθενεῖς ἴασαι, τοὺς πλανωμένους τοῦ λαοῦ
σου ἐπίστρεψον· χόρτασον τοὺς πεινῶντας, λύ-
τρωσαι τοὺς δεσμίους ἡμῶν, ἐξανάστησον τοὺς
ἀσθενοῦντας, παρακάλεσον τοὺς ὀλιγοψυχοῦντας·
I Kings 8, 60;
II Kings 19,
19;
Ezek. 36, 23
Ps. 78, 13;
94, 7; 99, 3
γνώτωσάν σε ἅπαντα τὰ ἔθνη, ὅτι σὺ εἶ ὁ θεὸς
μόνος καὶ Ἰησοῦς Χριστὸς ὁ παῖς σου καὶ ἡμεῖς
λαός σου καὶ πρόβατα τῆς νομῆς σου.

LX

1. Σὺ γὰρ τὴν ἀέναον τοῦ κόσμου σύστασιν διὰ
τῶν ἐνεργουμένων ἐφανεροποίησας· σύ, κύριε, τὴν
οἰκουμένην ἔκτισας, ὁ πιστὸς ἐν πάσαις ταῖς
γενεαῖς, δίκαιος ἐν τοῖς κρίμασιν, θαυμαστὸς ἐν
ἰσχύϊ καὶ μεγαλοπρεπείᾳ, ὁ σοφὸς ἐν τῷ κτίζειν
καὶ συνετὸς ἐν τῷ τὰ γενόμενα ἑδράσαι, ὁ ἀγαθὸς
ἐν τοῖς ὁρωμένοις καὶ χρηστὸς ἐν τοῖς πεποιθόσιν
Joel 2, 13;
Sirach 2, 11;
II Chron.
30, 9
ἐπὶ σέ, ἐλεῆμον καὶ οἰκτίρμον, ἄφες ἡμῖν τὰς
ἀνομίας ἡμῶν καὶ τὰς ἀδικίας καὶ τὰ παραπτώματα καὶ πλημμελείας. 2. μὴ λογίσῃ πᾶσαν
ἁμαρτίαν δούλων σου καὶ παιδισκῶν, ἀλλὰ καθά-
ρισον ἡμᾶς τὸν καθαρισμὸν τῆς σῆς ἀληθείας, καὶ

creator and watcher over every spirit; thou dost
multiply nations upon earth and hast chosen out
from them all those that love thee through Jesus
Christ thy beloved child, and through him hast thou
taught us, made us holy, and brought us to honour.

4. We beseech thee, Master, to be our " help and For help
succour." Save those of us who are in affliction,
have mercy on the lowly, raise the fallen, show
thyself to those in need, heal the sick, turn
again the wanderers of thy people, feed the hungry,
ransom our prisoners, raise up the weak, comfort the
faint-hearted ; let all " nations know thee, that thou
art God alone," and that Jesus Christ is thy child,
and that " we are thy people and the sheep of thy
pasture."

LX

1. For thou through thy operations didst make
manifest the eternal fabric of the world; thou,
Lord, didst create the earth.   Thou that art faithful
in all generations, righteous in judgment, wonderful in strength and majesty, wise in thy creation,
and prudent in establishing thy works, good in the
things which are seen, and gracious among those that
trust in thee, O "merciful and compassionate,"
forgive us our iniquities and unrighteousness, and
transgressions, and short-comings. 2. Reckon not For mercy
every sin of thy servants and handmaids, but

Pss. 40, 2;
119, 133
I Kings 9, 4
Deut. 12, 25,
28; 13, 18;
21, 9
Ps. 67, 1; 80,
3. 7. 19;
Num. 6, 25, 26
Gen. 50, 20;
Jer. 21, 10;
24, 6;
Am. 9, 4;
Deut. 30, 9
Exod. 6, 1;
Deut. 4, 34;
5, 15;
Jer. 32, 21;
Ezek. 20,
33. 34

κατεύθυνον τὰ διαβήματα ἡμῶν ἐν ὁσιότητι καρδίας πορεύεσθαι καὶ ποιεῖν τὰ καλὰ καὶ εὐάρεστα
ἐνώπιόν σου καὶ ἐνώπιον τῶν ἀρχόντων ἡμῶν.
3. ναί, δέσποτα, ἐπίφανον τὸ πρόσωπόν σου ἐφ᾿
ἡμᾶς εἰς ἀγαθὰ ἐν εἰρήνῃ, εἰς τὸ σκεπασθῆναι
ἡμᾶς τῇ χειρί σου τῇ κραταιᾷ καὶ ῥυσθῆναι ἀπὸ
πάσης ἁμαρτίας τῷ βραχίονί σου τῷ ὑψηλῷ, καὶ
ῥῦσαι ἡμᾶς ἀπὸ τῶν μισούντων ἡμᾶς ἀδίκως.
4. δὸς ὁμόνοιαν καὶ εἰρήνην ἡμῖν τε καὶ πᾶσιν
τοῖς κατοικοῦσιν τὴν γῆν, καθὼς ἔδωκας τοῖς
πατράσιν ἡμῶν, ἐπικαλουμένων σε αὐτῶν ὁσίως ἐν
πίστει καὶ ἀληθείᾳ, ὑπηκόους γινομένους τῷ
παντοκράτορι καὶ ἐνδόξῳ ὀνόματί σου, τοῖς τε
ἄρχουσιν καὶ ἡγουμένοις ἡμῶν ἐπὶ τῆς γῆς.

LXI

1. Σύ, δέσποτα, ἔδωκας τὴν ἐξουσίαν τῆς
βασιλείας αὐτοῖς διὰ τοῦ μεγαλοπρεποῦς καὶ
ἀνεκδιηγήτου κράτους σου, εἰς τὸ γινώσκοντας
ἡμᾶς τὴν ὑπὸ σοῦ αὐτοῖς δεδομένην δόξαν καὶ
τιμὴν ὑποτάσσεσθαι αὐτοῖς, μηδὲν ἐναντιουμένους
τῷ θελήματί σου· οἷς δός, κύριε, ὑγίειαν, εἰρήνην,
ὁμόνοιαν, εὐστάθειαν, εἰς τὸ διέπειν αὐτοὺς τὴν
ὑπὸ σοῦ δεδομένην αὐτοῖς ἡγεμονίαν ἀπροσκόπως.

I Tim. 5, 17;
Tob. 13, 6. 10

2. σὺ γάρ, δέσποτα ἐπουράνιε, βασιλεῦ τῶν
αἰώνων, δίδως τοῖς υἱοῖς τῶν ἀνθρώπων δόξαν καὶ
τιμὴν καὶ ἐξουσίαν τῶν ἐπὶ τῆς γῆς ὑπαρχόντων·
σύ, κύριε, διεύθυνον τὴν βουλὴν αὐτῶν κατὰ τὸ

Deut. 12, 25.
28; 13, 18

καλὸν καὶ εὐάρεστον ἐνώπιόν σου, ὅπως διέποντες
ἐν εἰρήνῃ καὶ πραΰτητι εὐσεβῶς τὴν ὑπὸ σοῦ

cleanse us with the cleansing of thy truth, and
" guide our steps to walk in holiness of heart,
to do the things which are good and pleasing before
thee " and before our rulers.   3. Yea, Lord, " make
thy face to shine upon us " in peace " for our good "
that we may be sheltered by thy mighty hand, and
delivered from all sin by " thy uplifted arm," and
deliver us from them that hate us wrongfully. 4. Give For peace
concord and peace to us and to all that dwell on the
earth, as thou didst give to our fathers who called on
thee in holiness with faith and truth, and grant that
we may be obedient to thy almighty and glorious
name, and to our rulers and governors upon the
earth.

LXI

1. Thou, Master, hast given the power of On behalf
sovereignty to them through thy excellent and of rulers
inexpressible might, that we may know the glory
and honour given to them by thee, and be subject to
them, in nothing resisting thy will.   And to them,
Lord, grant health, peace, concord, firmness that
they may administer the government which thou
hast given them without offence.   2. For thou,
heavenly Master, king of eternity, hast given to the
sons of men glory and honour and power over the
things which are on the earth ; do thou, O Lord,
direct their counsels according to that which is
" good and pleasing " before thee, that they may
administer with piety in peace and gentleness the
power given to them by thee, and may find mercy

αὐτοῖς δεδομένην ἐξουσίαν ἵλεώ σου τυγχάνωσιν. 3. ὁ μόνος δυνατὸς ποιῆσαι ταῦτα καὶ περισσότερα ἀγαθὰ μεθ᾿ ἡμῶν, σοὶ ἐξομολογούμεθα διὰ τοῦ ἀρχιερέως καὶ προστάτου τῶν ψυχῶν ἡμῶν Ἰησοῦ Χριστοῦ, δι᾿ οὗ σοι ἡ δόξα καὶ ἡ μεγαλωσύνη καὶ νῦν καὶ εἰς γενεὰν γενεῶν καὶ εἰς τοὺς αἰῶνας τῶν αἰώνων. ἀμήν.

LXII

1. Περὶ μὲν τῶν ἀνηκόντων τῇ θρησκείᾳ ἡμῶν καὶ τῶν ὠφελιμωτάτων εἰς ἐνάρετον βίον τοῖς θέλουσιν[1] εὐσεβῶς καὶ δικαίως διευθύνειν, ἱκανῶς ἐπεστείλαμεν ὑμῖν, ἄνδρες ἀδελφοί. 2. περὶ γὰρ πίστεως καὶ μετανοίας καὶ γνησίας ἀγάπης καὶ ἐγκρατείας καὶ σωφροσύνης καὶ ὑπομονῆς πάντα τόπον ἐψηλαφήσαμεν, ὑπομιμνήσκοντες δεῖν ὑμᾶς ἐν δικαιοσύνῃ καὶ ἀληθείᾳ καὶ μακροθυμίᾳ τῷ παντοκράτορι θεῷ ὁσίως εὐαρεστεῖν, ὁμονοοῦντας ἀμνησικάκως ἐν ἀγάπῃ καὶ εἰρήνῃ μετὰ ἐκτενοῦς ἐπιεικείας, καθὼς καὶ οἱ προδεδηλωμένοι πατέρες ἡμῶν εὐηρέστησαν ταπεινοφρονοῦντες τὰ πρὸς τὸν πατέρα καὶ κτίστην θεὸν[2] καὶ πάντας ἀνθρώπους. 3. καὶ ταῦτα τοσούτῳ ἥδιον ὑπεμνήσαμεν, ἐπειδὴ σαφῶς ἤδειμεν γράφειν ἡμᾶς ἀνδράσιν πιστοῖς καὶ ἐλλογιμωτάτοις καὶ ἐγκεκυφόσιν εἰς τὰ λόγια τῆς παιδείας τοῦ θεοῦ.

[1] τοῖς θέλουσιν ἐνάρετον βίον SL, εἰς ἐνάρετον βίον τοῖς θέλουσιν CK.
[2] κτίστην θεόν SL, θεὸν καὶ κτίστην C.

in thine eyes. 3. O thou who alone art able to do these things and far better things for us, we praise thee through Jesus Christ, the high priest and guardian of our souls, through whom be glory and majesty to thee, both now and for all generations and for ever and ever. Amen.

LXII

1. WE have now written to you, brethren, suf- Summary ficiently touching the things which befit our worship, of letter and are most helpful for a virtuous life to those who wish to guide their steps in piety and righteousness. 2. For we have touched on every aspect of faith and repentance and true love and self-control and sobriety and patience, and reminded you that you are bound to please almighty God with holiness in righteousness and truth and long-suffering, and to live in concord, bearing no malice, in love and peace with eager gentleness, even as our fathers, whose example we quoted, were well-pleasing in their humility towards God, the Father and Creator, and towards all men. 3. And we had the more pleasure in reminding you of this, because we knew quite well that we were writing to men who were faithful and distinguished and had studied the oracles of the teaching of God.

LXIII

1. Θεμιτὸν οὖν ἐστὶν τοῖς τοιούτοις καὶ τοσού-
τοις ὑποδείγμασιν προσελθόντας ὑποθεῖναι τὸν
τράχηλον καὶ τὸν τῆς ὑπακοῆς τόπον ἀναπληρῶ-
σαι, ὅπως ἡσυχάσαντες τῆς ματαίας στάσεως ἐπὶ
τὸν προκείμενον ἡμῖν ἐν ἀληθείᾳ σκοπὸν δίχα
παντὸς μώμου καταντήσωμεν. 2. χαρὰν γὰρ καὶ
ἀγαλλίασιν ἡμῖν παρέξετε, ἐὰν ὑπήκοοι γενόμενοι
τοῖς ὑφ᾽ ἡμῶν γεγραμμένοις διὰ τοῦ ἁγίου πνεύματος ἐκκόψητε τὴν ἀθέμιτον τοῦ ζήλους ὑμῶν
ὀργὴν κατὰ τὴν ἔντευξιν, ἣν ἐποιησάμεθα περὶ εἰρήνης καὶ ὁμονοίας ἐν τῇδε τῇ ἐπιστολῇ. 3. ἐπέμψαμεν δὲ ἄνδρας πιστοὺς καὶ σώφρονας ἀπὸ
νεότητος ἀναστραφέντας ἕως γήρους ἀμέμπτως ἐν
ἡμῖν, οἵτινες καὶ μάρτυρες ἔσονται μεταξὺ ὑμῶν
καὶ ἡμῶν. 4. τοῦτο δὲ ἐποιήσαμεν, ἵνα εἰδῆτε,
ὅτι πᾶσα ἡμῖν φροντὶς καὶ γέγονεν καὶ ἔστιν εἰς
τὸ ἐν τάχει ὑμᾶς εἰρηνεῦσαι.

LXIV

1. Λοιπὸν ὁ παντεπόπτης θεὸς καὶ δεσπότης
τῶν πνευμάτων καὶ κύριος πάσης σαρκός, ὁ
ἐκλεξάμενος τὸν κύριον Ἰησοῦν Χριστὸν καὶ ἡμᾶς
Num. 16, 22; δι᾽ αὐτοῦ εἰς λαὸν περιούσιον, δῴη πάσῃ ψυχῇ
27, 16 ;
fc. Heb. 12,9 ἐπικεκλημένῃ τὸ μεγαλοπρεπὲς καὶ ἅγιον ὄνομα
Deut. 14, 2 αὐτοῦ πίστιν, φόβον, εἰρήνην, ὑπομονὴν καὶ
μακροθυμίαν, ἐγκράτειαν, ἁγνείαν, σωφροσύνην,[1]

---

[1] σωφροσύνην CLK, καὶ σωφ. AS.

LXIII

1. It is therefore right that we should respect so many and so great examples, and bow the neck, and take up the position of obedience, so that ceasing from vain sedition we may gain without any fault the goal set before us in truth. 2. For you will give us joy and gladness, if you are obedient to the things which we have written through the Holy Spirit, and root out the wicked passion of your jealousy according to the entreaty for peace and concord which we have made in this letter. 3. And we have sent faithful and prudent men, who have lived among us without blame from youth to old age, and they shall be witnesses between you and us. 4. We have done this that you may know that our whole care has been and is directed to your speedy attainment of peace.

Introduction for representatives from Rome

LXIV

1. Now may God, the all-seeing, and the master of spirits, and the Lord of all flesh, who chose out the Lord Jesus Christ, and us through him for "a peculiar people," give unto every soul that is called after his glorious and holy name, faith, fear, peace, patience and long-suffering, self-control, purity, sobriety, that they may be well-pleasing to his

Blessing

119

εἰς εὐαρέστησιν τῷ ὀνόματι αὐτοῦ διὰ τοῦ ἀρχιερέως καὶ προστάτου ἡμῶν Ἰησοῦ Χριστοῦ, δι'
οὗ αὐτῷ δόξα καὶ μεγαλωσύνη, κράτος καὶ τιμή,
καὶ νῦν καὶ εἰς πάντας τοὺς αἰῶνας τῶν αἰώνων.
ἀμήν.

LXV

1. Τοὺς δὲ ἀπεσταλμένους ἀφ' ἡμῶν Κλαύδιον
Ἔφηβον καὶ Οὐαλέριον Βίτωνα σὺν καὶ Φορτου-
νάτῳ ἐν εἰρήνῃ μετὰ χαρᾶς ἐν τάχει ἀναπέμψατε
πρὸς ἡμᾶς, ὅπως θᾶττον τὴν εὐκταίαν καὶ ἐπιπο-
θήτην ἡμῖν εἰρήνην καὶ ὁμόνοιαν ἀπαγγέλλωσιν,
εἰς τὸ τάχιον καὶ ἡμᾶς χαρῆναι περὶ τῆς εὐστα-
θείας ὑμῶν.
2. Ἡ χάρις τοῦ κυρίου ἡμῶν Ἰησοῦ Χριστοῦ
μεθ' ὑμῶν καὶ μετὰ πάντων πανταχῆ τῶν κεκλη-
μένων ὑπὸ τοῦ θεοῦ δι' αὐτοῦ,[1] δι' οὗ αὐτῷ
δόξα, τιμή, κράτος καὶ μεγαλωσύνη, θρόνος
αἰώνιος, ἀπὸ τῶν αἰώνων εἰς τοὺς αἰῶνας τῶν
αἰώνων. ἀμήν.

Ἐπιστολὴ τῶν Ῥωμαίων πρὸς τοὺς Κορινθίους.

---

[1] δι' αὐτοῦ CL(K), καὶ δι' αὐτοῦ AS.

name through our high priest and guardian Jesus
Christ, through whom be to him glory and majesty,
might and honour, both now and to all eternity.
Amen.

LXV

1. SEND back quickly to us our messengers Claudius Message as
to Roman
Ephebus and Valerius Vito and Fortunatus, in peace representa-
with gladness, in order that they may report the tives
sooner the peace and concord which we pray for and
desire, that we also may the more speedily rejoice
in your good order.

2. The grace of our Lord Jesus Christ be with you Final blessing and
and with all, in every place, who have been called doxology
by God through him, through whom be to him
glory, honour, power and greatness and eternal
dominion, from eternity to eternity. Amen.

The Epistle of the Romans to the Corinthians.[1]

[1] This form of subscription is found only in the Coptic
version, though it was probably also known to Clement of
Alexandria, and is undoubtedly correct. The other MSS.
all attribute it directly to Clement.

THE
SECOND EPISTLE OF CLEMENT
TO THE CORINTHIANS

SECOND EPISTLE OF CLEMENT
TO THE CORINTHIANS

THE so-called second epistle of Clement is found
in the two Greek MSS. (AC) of I. Clement, and in
the Syriac version (S), but it is not in the Latin or
Coptic versions (LK), and it is never quoted by
Clement of Alexandria, though apparent reminis-
cences of its language have given rise to the view
that he was acquainted with it. It is clear from the
MS. tradition that at least as early as the fifth
century, and probably earlier, it was in some circles
closely associated with I. Clement, though this was
not the case in the Coptic church, which perhaps
represents early Alexandrian tradition, or in the
Latin Church. Western writers do, it is true, seem
to speak of a " second epistle " of Clement, but they
refer not to our II. Clement, but to the pseudepigraphic epistle of Clement to James.

II. Clement is a letter only in form, and scarcely in
that, for the writer distinctly states (cf. Cap. XIX) that
he is reading aloud, and implies that he is doing
so in a meeting for religious worship : it is thus
clear that it is really more a sermon than a letter.
The main object of the writer is to inculcate a

125

high Christology, a pure life, and a belief in the resurrection of the flesh. So much is generally agreed and it is, moreover, clear that it cannot have been written by the author of I. Clement; but there is no commonly accepted view as to the community to which it was sent. Three views may be mentioned.

1. Harnack thinks that it is the letter which Soter (bishop of Rome— c. 166–174) is related to have sent to Corinth (cf. Eus. *Hist. Eccl.* iv. 23. 11). He thinks that Soter probably used an old homily which seemed to him to be suitable. This letter was kept in the archives of the church at Corinth together with I Clement, which had also come from Rome; later on, when they were both copied, the real facts were forgotten and both were supposed to be letters of Clement (Harnack, *Chronologie* I, pp. 438 ff.).

2. Lightfoot is inclined to think that it was an ancient homily of some unknown person in the church at Corinth. He lays stress on the imagery from the games, and suggests that this was inspired by the Isthmian games. Like Harnack's this theory has the advantage of explaining why the document came to be connected with Clement,—it was found in the Corinthian archives together with I. Clement.

3. Other scholars, regarding the external evidence as practically valueless, have thought that II. Clement was originally an Alexandrian homily. Their reasons are the theological character of the book, and its possible use of the Gospel of the Egyptians. This theory explains the contents of the book more naturally than do the views of Harnack and Lightfoot, but fails to show why it was ever connected with I. Clement.

II. CLEMENT

Equally uncertain is the date of the book. In the absence of any direct references to contemporary events, it can only be dated by considering its place in the general development of Christian doctrine. This is a very insecure guide, but probably the half century between 120 and 170 A.D. is the period chosen by the general opinion of the best critics, and within these limits ± 150 A.D. is most usually accepted, except by those who agree with Harnack to identify II. Clement with the letter of Soter to the Corinthians.

ΚΛΗΜΕΝΤΟΣ

ΠΡΟΣ ΚΟΡΙΝΘΙΟΥΣ Β̄

I

1. Ἀδελφοί, οὕτως δεῖ ἡμᾶς φρονεῖν περὶ Ἰησοῦ Χριστοῦ, ὡς περὶ θεοῦ, ὡς περὶ κριτοῦ ζώντων καὶ νεκρῶν· καὶ οὐ δεῖ ἡμᾶς μικρὰ φρονεῖν περὶ τῆς σωτηρίας ἡμῶν. 2. ἐν τῷ γὰρ φρονεῖν ἡμᾶς μικρὰ περὶ αὐτοῦ, μικρὰ καὶ ἐλπίζομεν λαβεῖν· καὶ οἱ ἀκούοντες ὡς περὶ μικρῶν ἁμαρτάνουσιν, καὶ ἡμεῖς [1] ἁμαρτάνομεν οὐκ εἰδότες, πόθεν ἐκλήθημεν καὶ ὑπὸ τίνος καὶ εἰς ὃν τόπον, καὶ ὅσα ὑπέμεινεν Ἰησοῦς Χριστὸς παθεῖν ἕνεκα ἡμῶν. 3. τίνα οὖν ἡμεῖς αὐτῷ δώσομεν ἀντιμισθίαν, ἢ τίνα καρπὸν ἄξιον οὗ ἡμῖν αὐτὸς ἔδωκεν; πόσα δὲ αὐτῷ ὀφείλομεν ὅσια; 4. τὸ φῶς γὰρ ἡμῖν ἐχαρίσατο, ὡς πατὴρ υἱοὺς ἡμᾶς προσηγόρευσεν, ἀπολλυμένους ἡμᾶς ἔσωσεν. 5. ποῖον οὖν αἶνον αὐτῷ δώσομεν ἢ μισθὸν ἀντιμισθίας ὧν ἐλάβομεν; 6. πηροὶ ὄντες τῇ διανοίᾳ, προσκυνοῦντες λίθους καὶ ξύλα καὶ χρυσὸν καὶ ἄργυρον καὶ χαλκόν, ἔργα ἀνθρώπων· καὶ ὁ βίος ἡμῶν ὅλος ἄλλο οὐδὲν ἦν εἰ μὴ θάνατος. ἀμαύρωσιν οὖν περικείμενοι καὶ τοιαύτης ἀχλύος γέμοντες ἐν

---

[1] Om. ἁμαρτάνουσιν, καὶ ἡμεῖς AC.

Acts. 10, 42

THE

SECOND EPISTLE OF CLEMENT
TO THE CORINTHIANS

I

1. Brethren, we must think of Jesus Christ as of God, as of " the Judge of the living and the dead " and we must not think little of our salvation, 2. for if we think little of him we also hope to obtain but little. And those who listen as though it were a little matter are sinning, and we also are sinning, if we do not know whence and by whom, and to what place we were called, and how great sufferings Jesus Christ endured for our sake. 3. What return, then, shall we make to him, or what fruit shall we offer worthy of that which he has given us ? And how great a debt of holiness do we owe him ? 4. For he gave us the light, he called us " son," as a Father, he saved us when we were perishing. 5. What praise, then, or what reward shall we give him in return for what we received ? 6. We were maimed in our understanding, worshipping stone, and wood, and gold, and silver, and copper, the works of men, and our whole life was nothing else than death. We were covered with darkness, and our eyes were full of mist ; but we

The need for thinking highly of Christ, and prizing our salvation

The state of the unconverted

τῇ ὁράσει, ἀνεβλέψαμεν ἀποθέμενοι ἐκεῖνο ὃ περικείμεθα νέφος τῇ αὐτοῦ θελήσει. 7. ἠλέησεν γὰρ ἡμᾶς καὶ σπλαγχνισθεὶς ἔσωσεν, θεασάμενος ἐν ἡμῖν πολλὴν πλάνην καὶ ἀπώλειαν, καὶ μηδεμίαν ἐλπίδα ἔχοντας σωτηρίας, εἰ μὴ τὴν παρ᾽ αὐτοῦ. 8. ἐκάλεσεν γὰρ ἡμᾶς οὐκ ὄντας καὶ ἠθέλησεν ἐκ μὴ ὄντος εἶναι ἡμᾶς.

II

1. Εὐφράνθητι, στεῖρα ἡ οὐ τίκτουσα, ῥῆξον καὶ βόησον, ἡ οὐκ ὠδίνουσα, ὅτι πολλὰ τὰ τέκνα τῆς ἐρήμου μᾶλλον ἢ τῆς ἐχούσης τὸν ἄνδρα. ὃ εἶπεν· Εὐφράνθητι, στεῖρα ἡ οὐ τίκτουσα, ἡμᾶς εἶπεν· στεῖρα γὰρ ἦν ἡ ἐκκλησία ἡμῶν πρὸ τοῦ δοθῆναι αὐτῇ τέκνα. 2. ὃ δὲ εἶπεν· Βόησον, ἡ οὐκ ὠδίνουσα, τοῦτο λέγει· τὰς προσευχὰς ἡμῶν ἁπλῶς ἀναφέρειν πρὸς τὸν θεόν, μὴ ὡς αἱ ὠδίνουσαι ἐγκακῶμεν, 3. ὃ δὲ εἶπεν· Ὅτι πολλὰ τὰ τέκνα τῆς ἐρήμου μᾶλλον ἢ τῆς ἐχούσης τὸν ἄνδρα· ἐπεὶ ἔρημος ἐδόκει εἶναι ἀπὸ τοῦ θεοῦ ὁ λαὸς ἡμῶν, νυνὶ δὲ πιστεύσαντες πλείονες ἐγενόμεθα τῶν δοκούντων ἔχειν θεόν. 4. καὶ ἑτέρα δὲ γραφὴ λέγει, ὅτι οὐκ ἦλθον καλέσαι δικαίους, ἀλλὰ ἁμαρτωλούς· 5. τοῦτο λέγει, ὅτι δεῖ τοὺς ἀπολλυμένους σώζειν. 6. ἐκεῖνο γάρ ἐστιν μέγα καὶ θαυμαστὸν οὐ τὰ ἑστῶτα στηρίζειν, ἀλλὰ τὰ πίπτοντα. 7. οὕτως καὶ ὁ Χριστὸς ἠθέλησεν σῶσαι τὰ ἀπολλύμενα, καὶ ἔσωσεν πολλούς, ἐλθὼν καὶ καλέσας ἡμᾶς ἤδη ἀπολλυμένους.

Is. 54, 1;
Gal. 4, 27

Mt. 9, 13,
Mk. 2, 17;
Luke 5, 32

Luke 19, 10

have received our sight, and by his will we have cast off the cloud which covered us. 7. For he had pity on us, and saved us in his mercy, and regarded the great error and destruction which was in us, and our hopelessness of salvation save from him; 8. for he called us when we were not, and it was his will that out of nothing we should come to being.

II

1. "Rejoice thou barren that barest not; break Prophecies forth and cry thou that travailest not; for the of the church, and children of the deserted are many more than hers their inter- pretation that hath a husband." In saying, "Rejoice thou barren that barest not," he meant us, for our church was barren before children were given her. 2. And in saying, "Cry thou that travailest not," he means this,—that we should offer our prayers in sincerity to God, and not grow weary as women that give birth. 3. And in saying, "For the children of the deserted are many more than hers that hath a husband," he meant that our people seemed to be deserted by God, but that now we who have believed have become many more than those who have seemed to have God. 4. And another Scripture also says, "I came not to call righteous, but sinners"; 5. He means that those who are perishing must be saved, 6. for it is great and wonderful to give strength, not to the things which are standing, but to those which are falling. 7. So Christ also willed to save the perishing, and he saved many, coming and calling us who were already perishing.

III

1. Τοσοῦτον οὖν ἔλεος ποιήσαντος αὐτοῦ εἰς ἡμᾶς, πρῶτον μέν, ὅτι ἡμεῖς οἱ ζῶντες τοῖς νεκροῖς θεοῖς οὐ θύομεν καὶ οὐ προσκυνοῦμεν αὐτοῖς, ἀλλὰ ἔγνωμεν δι᾽ αὐτοῦ τὸν πατέρα τῆς ἀληθείας· τίς ἡ γνῶσις ἡ πρὸς αὐτόν, ἢ τὸ μὴ ἀρνεῖσθαι δι᾽

Mt. 10, 32; Luke 12, 8

οὗ ἔγνωμεν αὐτόν; 2. λέγει δὲ καὶ αὐτός· Τὸν ὁμολογήσαντά με ἐνώπιον τῶν ἀνθρώπων,[1] ὁμολογήσω αὐτὸν ἐνώπιον τοῦ πατρός μου. 3. οὗτος οὖν ἐστιν ὁ μισθὸς ἡμῶν, ἐὰν οὖν ὁμολογήσωμεν δι᾽ οὗ ἐσώθημεν. 4. ἐν τίνι δὲ αὐτὸν ὁμολογοῦμεν; ἐν τῷ ποιεῖν ἃ λέγει καὶ μὴ παρακούειν αὐτοῦ τῶν ἐντολῶν, καὶ μὴ μόνον χείλεσιν αὐτὸν τιμᾶν, ἀλλὰ ἐξ ὅλης καρδίας καὶ ἐξ ὅλης τῆς διανοίας. 5. λέγει

Is. 29, 13; Mt. 15, 8; Mk. 7, 6

δὲ καὶ ἐν τῷ Ἡσαΐα· Ὁ λαὸς οὗτος τοῖς χείλεσίν με τιμᾷ, ἡ δὲ καρδία αὐτῶν πόρρω ἄπεστιν ἀπ᾽ ἐμοῦ.

IV

Mt. 7, 21

1. Μὴ μόνον οὖν αὐτὸν καλῶμεν κύριον· οὐ γὰρ τοῦτο σώσει ἡμᾶς. 2. λέγει γάρ· Οὐ πᾶς ὁ λέγων μοι· Κύριε, κύριε, σωθήσεται, ἀλλ᾽ ὁ ποιῶν τὴν δικαιοσύνην. 3. ὥστε οὖν, ἀδελφοί, ἐν τοῖς ἔργοις αὐτὸν ὁμολογῶμεν, ἐν τῷ ἀγαπᾶν ἑαυτούς, ἐν τῷ μὴ μοιχᾶσθαι μηδὲ καταλαλεῖν ἀλλήλων μηδὲ ζηλοῦν, ἀλλ᾽ ἐγκρατεῖς εἶναι, ἐλεήμονας, ἀγαθούς· καὶ συμπάσχειν ἀλλήλοις ὀφείλομεν,

---

[1] ἐνώπιον τῶν ἀνθρώπων AC, om. S.

III

1. Seeing, then, that he has shewn such mercy towards us, first that we who are living do not sacrifice to the dead gods, and do not worship them, but through him know the father of truth, what is the true knowledge concerning him [1] except that we should not deny him through whom we knew him? 2. And he himself also says, " Whosoever confessed me before men, I will confess him before my Father " ; 3. this then is our reward, if we confess him through whom we were saved. 4. But how do we confess him? By doing what he says, and not disregarding his commandments, and honouring him not only with our lips, but " with all our heart and all our mind." 5. And he says also in Isaiah, " This people honoureth me with their lips, but their heart is far from me."

IV

1. Let us, then, not merely call him Lord, for this will not save us. 2. For he says, " Not everyone that saith to me Lord, Lord, shall be saved, but he that doeth righteousness." 3. So then, brethren, let us confess him in our deeds, by loving one another, by not committing adultery, nor speaking one against another, nor being jealous, but by being self-controlled, merciful, good; and we ought to

[1] The Greek is as ambiguous as the English, but this " him " no doubt refers to the " father of truth."

καὶ μὴ φιλαργυρεῖν. ἐν τούτοις τοῖς ἔργοις
ὁμολογῶμεν αὐτὸν καὶ μὴ ἐν τοῖς ἐναντίοις· 4.
καὶ οὐ δεῖ ἡμᾶς φοβεῖσθαι τοὺς ἀνθρώπους μᾶλλον,
ἀλλὰ τὸν θεόν. 5. διὰ τοῦτο, ταῦτα ὑμῶν
πρασσόντων, εἶπεν ὁ κύριος· Ἐὰν ἦτε μετ᾽ ἐμοῦ
συνηγμένοι ἐν τῷ κόλπῳ μου καὶ μὴ ποιῆτε τὰς
ἐντολάς μου, ἀποβαλῶ ὑμᾶς καὶ ἐρῶ ὑμῖν· Ὑπάγετε
ἀπ᾽ ἐμοῦ, οὐκ οἶδα ὑμᾶς, πόθεν ἐστέ, ἐργάται
ἀνομίας.

?Ev.
Aegypt.

V

1. Ὅθεν, ἀδελφοί, καταλείψαντες τὴν παροι-
κίαν τοῦ κόσμου τούτου ποιήσωμεν τὸ θέλημα τοῦ
καλέσαντος ἡμᾶς, καὶ μὴ φοβηθῶμεν ἐξελθεῖν ἐκ
τοῦ κόσμου τούτου. 2. λέγει γὰρ ὁ κύριος
Ἔσεσθε ὡς ἀρνία ἐν μέσῳ λύκων. 3. ἀποκριθεὶς
δὲ ὁ Πέτρος αὐτῷ λέγει· Ἐὰν οὖν διασπαράξωσιν
οἱ λύκοι τὰ ἀρνία ; 4. εἶπεν ὁ Ἰησοῦς τῷ Πέτρῳ·
Μὴ φοβείσθωσαν τὰ ἀρνία τοὺς λύκους μετὰ τὸ
ἀποθανεῖν αὐτά· καὶ ὑμεῖς μὴ φοβεῖσθε τοὺς
ἀποκτέννοντας ὑμᾶς καὶ μηδὲν ὑμῖν δυναμένους
ποιεῖν, ἀλλὰ φοβεῖσθε τὸν μετὰ τὸ ἀποθανεῖν
ὑμᾶς ἔχοντα ἐξουσίαν ψυχῆς καὶ σώματος τοῦ
βαλεῖν εἰς γέενναν πυρός. 5. καὶ γινώσκετε,
ἀδελφοί, ὅτι ἡ ἐπιδημία ἡ ἐν τῷ κόσμῳ τούτῳ τῆς
σαρκὸς ταύτης μικρά ἐστιν καὶ ὀλιγοχρόνιος, ἡ δὲ
ἐπαγγελία τοῦ Χριστοῦ μεγάλη καὶ θαυμαστή ἐστιν,
καὶ ἀνάπαυσις τῆς μελλούσης βασιλείας καὶ ζωῆς

Ev.
Aegypt.

sympathise with each other, and not to be lovers of money. By these deeds we confess him, and not by the opposite kind. 4. And we must not fear men rather than God. 5. For this reason, if you do these things, the Lord said, " If ye be gathered together with me in my bosom, and do not my commandments, I will cast you out, and will say to you, Depart from me, I know not whence ye are, ye workers of iniquity." [1]

V

1. WHEREFORE, brethren, let us forsake our sojourning in this world, and do the will of him who called us, and let us not fear to go forth from this world, 2. for the Lord said, " Ye shall be as lambs in the midst of wolves," 3. and Peter answered and said to him, " If then the wolves tear the lambs? " 4. Jesus said to Peter, " Let the lambs have no fear of the wolves after their death ; and do ye have no fear of those that slay you, and can do nothing more to you, but fear him who after your death hath power over body and soul, to cast them into the flames of hell." 5. And be well assured, brethren, that our sojourning in this world in the flesh is a little thing and lasts a short time, but the promise of Christ is great and wonderful, and brings us rest, in the kingdom which is to come and in everlasting life. 6. What then shall

Exhortation to abandon the world

---

[1] The source of this and the quotation in v. 2-4 is unknown : it is often supposed to have been the Gospel of the Egyptians, but there is no clear evidence of this.

αἰωνίου. 6. τί οὖν ἐστὶν ποιήσαντας ἐπιτυχεῖν αὐτῶν, εἰ μὴ τὸ ὁσίως καὶ δικαίως ἀναστρέφεσθαι καὶ τὰ κοσμικὰ ταῦτα ὡς ἀλλότρια ἡγεῖσθαι καὶ μὴ ἐπιθυμεῖν αὐτῶν; 7. ἐν γὰρ τῷ ἐπιθυμεῖν ἡμᾶς κτήσασθαι ταῦτα ἀποπίπτομεν τῆς ὁδοῦ τῆς δικαίας.

VI

Luke 16, 13 ;
Mt. 6, 24

Mt. 16, 26 ;
Mk. 8, 36 ;
Luke 9, 25

1. Λέγει δὲ ὁ κύριος· Οὐδεὶς οἰκέτης δύναται δυσὶ κυρίοις δουλεύειν. ἐὰν ἡμεῖς θέλωμεν καὶ θεῷ δουλεύειν καὶ μαμωνᾷ, ἀσύμφορον ἡμῖν ἐστίν. 2. τί γὰρ τὸ ὄφελος, ἐάν τις τὸν κόσμον ὅλον κερδήσῃ, τὴν δὲ ψυχὴν ζημιωθῇ; 3. ἔστιν δὲ οὗτος ὁ αἰὼν καὶ ὁ μέλλων δύο ἐχθροί. 4. οὗτος λέγει μοιχείαν καὶ φθορὰν καὶ φιλαργυρίαν καὶ ἀπάτην, ἐκεῖνος δὲ τούτοις ἀποτάσσεται. 5. οὐ δυνάμεθα οὖν τῶν δύο φίλοι εἶναι· δεῖ δὲ ἡμᾶς τούτῳ ἀποταξαμένους ἐκείνῳ χρᾶσθαι. 6. οἰόμεθα,[1] ὅτι βέλτιόν ἐστιν τὰ ἐνθάδε μισῆσαι, ὅτι μικρὰ καὶ ὀλιγοχρόνια καὶ φθαρτά, ἐκεῖνα δὲ ἀγαπῆσαι, τὰ ἀγαθὰ τὰ ἄφθαρτα. 7. ποιοῦντες γὰρ τὸ θέλημα τοῦ Χριστοῦ εὑρήσομεν ἀνάπαυσιν· εἰ δὲ μήγε, οὐδὲν ἡμᾶς ῥύσεται ἐκ τῆς αἰωνίου κολάσεως, ἐὰν παρακούσωμεν τῶν ἐντολῶν αὐτοῦ.

Ezek. 14,
14. 18, 20

8. λέγει δὲ καὶ ἡ γραφὴ ἐν τῷ Ἰεζεκιήλ, ὅτι ἐὰν ἀναστῇ Νῶε καὶ Ἰὼβ καὶ Δανιήλ, οὐ ῥύσονται τὰ τέκνα αὐτῶν ἐν τῇ αἰχμαλωσίᾳ. 9. εἰ δὲ καὶ οἱ τοιοῦτοι δίκαιοι οὐ δύνανται ταῖς ἑαυτῶν δικαιοσύναις ῥύσασθαι τὰ τέκνα αὐτῶν, ἡμεῖς, ἐὰν μὴ

---

[1] οἰόμεθα ACS, but Lightfoot emends to οἰώμεθα " Let us etc."

we do to attain these things save lead a holy and righteous life, and regard the things of this world as not our own, and not desire them? 7. For by desiring to obtain these things we fall from the way of righteousness.

VI

1. AND the Lord says:—"No servant can serve two masters." If we desire to serve both God and Mammon it is unprofitable to us, 2. "For what is the advantage if a man gain the whole world but lose his soul?" 3. Now the world that is, and the world to come are two enemies. 4. This world speaks of adultery, and corruption, and love of money, and deceit, but that world bids these things farewell. 5. We cannot then be the friends of both; but we must bid farewell to this world, to consort with that which is to come. 6. We reckon that it is better to hate the things which are here, for they are little, and short-lived, and corruptible, but to love the things which are there, the good things which are incorruptible. 7. For if we do the will of Christ we shall gain rest; but if not, nothing shall rescue us from eternal punishment, if we neglect his commandments. 8. And the Scripture also says in Ezekiel that, "if Noah and Job and Daniel arise, they shall not rescue their children in the captivity." 9. But if even such righteous men as these cannot save their children by their own righteousness, with

The opposition between this world and the world to come

Cf. Mt. 22.
11 ff.

τηρήσωμεν τὸ βάπτισμα ἁγνὸν καὶ ἀμίαντον,
ποίᾳ πεποιθήσει εἰσελευσόμεθα εἰς τὸ βασίλειον
τοῦ θεοῦ; ἢ τίς ἡμῶν παράκλητος ἔσται, ἐὰν μὴ
εὑρεθῶμεν ἔργα ἔχοντες ὅσια καὶ δίκαια;

VII

1. Ὥστε οὖν, ἀδελφοί μου, ἀγωνισώμεθα εἰδότες, ὅτι ἐν χερσὶν ὁ ἀγὼν καὶ ὅτι εἰς τοὺς φθαρτοὺς
ἀγῶνας καταπλέουσιν πολλοί, ἀλλ' οὐ πάντες
στεφανοῦνται, εἰ μὴ οἱ πολλὰ κοπιάσαντες καὶ
καλῶς ἀγωνισάμενοι. 2. ἡμεῖς οὖν ἀγωνισώμεθα,
ἵνα πάντες στεφανωθῶμεν. 3. ὥστε θέωμεν[1] τὴν
ὁδὸν τὴν εὐθεῖαν, ἀγῶνα τὸν ἄφθαρτον, καὶ
πολλοὶ εἰς αὐτὸν καταπλεύσωμεν καὶ ἀγωνισώμεθα, ἵνα καὶ στεφανωθῶμεν· καὶ εἰ μὴ δυνάμεθα
πάντες στεφανωθῆναι, κἂν ἐγγὺς τοῦ στεφάνου
γενώμεθα. 4. εἰδέναι ἡμᾶς δεῖ, ὅτι ὁ τὸν φθαρτὸν
ἀγῶνα ἀγωνιζόμενος, ἐὰν εὑρεθῇ φθείρων, μαστι-
γωθεὶς αἴρεται καὶ ἔξω βάλλεται τοῦ σταδίου.
5. τί δοκεῖτε; ὁ τὸν τῆς ἀφθαρσίας ἀγῶνα φθείρας τί παθεῖται; 6. τῶν γὰρ μὴ τηρησάντων,
φησίν, τὴν σφραγῖδα ὁ σκώληξ αὐτῶν οὐ τελευτήσει καὶ τὸ πῦρ αὐτῶν οὐ σβεσθήσεται, καὶ
ἔσονται εἰς ὅρασιν πάσῃ σαρκί.

Is. 66, 24;
cf. Mk. 9, 44.
46. 48

---

[1] AC read θῶμεν, but the Syriac implies θέωμεν and is
probably right.

what confidence shall we enter into the palace of God, if we keep not our baptism pure and undefiled? Or who shall be our advocate if we be not found to have pious and righteous works?

VII

1. So then, my brethren, let us contend, knowing that the contest is close at hand, and that many make voyages for corruptible prizes, but not all are crowned, save those who have toiled much, and contended well. 2. Let us then contend that we may all be crowned. 3. Let us run the straight course, the immortal contest, and let many of us sail to it, and contend, that we may also receive the crown, and if we cannot all receive the crown, let us at least come near to it. 4. We must remember that if he who takes part in the contest for a corruptible prize be detected in unfairness, he is flogged, taken up, and thrown off the course. 5. What do you think? What shall he suffer who cheats in the contest for that which is incorruptible? 6. For of those who have not kept the seal of baptism he says:—"Their worm shall not die, and their fire shall not be quenched, and they shall be a spectacle for all flesh."

Exhortation to strive well in the contest of life

VIII

1. Ὡς οὖν ἐσμὲν ἐπὶ γῆς, μετανοήσωμεν. 2. πηλὸς γάρ ἐσμεν εἰς τὴν χεῖρα τοῦ τεχνίτου· ὃν τρόπον γὰρ ὁ κεραμεύς, ἐὰν ποιῇ σκεῦος καὶ ἐν ταῖς χερσὶν αὐτοῦ διαστραφῇ ἢ συντριβῇ, πάλιν αὐτὸ ἀναπλάσσει, ἐὰν δὲ προφθάσῃ εἰς τὴν κάμινον τοῦ πυρὸς αὐτὸ βαλεῖν, οὐκέτι βοηθήσει αὐτῷ· οὕτως καὶ ἡμεῖς, ἕως ἐσμὲν ἐν τούτῳ τῷ κόσμῳ, ἐν τῇ σαρκὶ ἃ ἐπράξαμεν πονηρὰ μετανοήσωμεν ἐξ ὅλης τῆς καρδίας, ἵνα σωθῶμεν ὑπὸ τοῦ κυρίου, ἕως ἔχομεν καιρὸν μετανοίας. 3. μετὰ γὰρ τὸ ἐξελθεῖν ἡμᾶς ἐκ τοῦ κόσμου οὐκέτι δυνάμεθα ἐκεῖ ἐξομολογήσασθαι ἢ μετανοεῖν ἔτι. 4. ὥστε, ἀδελφοί, ποιήσαντες τὸ θέλημα τοῦ πατρὸς καὶ τὴν σάρκα ἁγνὴν τηρήσαντες καὶ τὰς ἐντολὰς τοῦ κυρίου φυλάξαντες ληψόμεθα ζωὴν αἰώνιον. 5. λέγει γὰρ ὁ κύριος ἐν τῷ εὐαγγελίῳ·

Luke 16, 10–12

Εἰ τὸ μικρὸν οὐκ ἐτηρήσατε, τὸ μέγα τίς ὑμῖν δώσει; λέγω γὰρ ὑμῖν, ὅτι ὁ πιστὸς ἐν ἐλαχίστῳ καὶ ἐν πολλῷ πιστός ἐστιν. 6. ἆρα οὖν τοῦτο λέγει· τηρήσατε τὴν σάρκα ἁγνὴν καὶ τὴν σφραγῖδα ἄσπιλον, ἵνα τὴν αἰώνιον ζωὴν ἀπολάβωμεν.

IX

1. Καὶ μὴ λεγέτω τις ὑμῶν, ὅτι αὕτη ἡ σὰρξ οὐ κρίνεται οὐδὲ ἀνίσταται. 2. γνῶτε· ἐν τίνι ἐσώθητε, ἐν τίνι ἀνεβλέψατε, εἰ μὴ ἐν τῇ σαρκὶ ταύτῃ ὄντες; 3. δεῖ οὖν ἡμᾶς ὡς ναὸν θεοῦ φυλάσσειν τὴν

140

VIII

1. LET us repent then while we are on the earth. Call to repentance and purity
2. For we are clay in the hand of the workman;
for just as the potter, if he make a vessel, and it be
bent or broken in his hand, models it afresh, but if
he has come so far as to put it into the fiery oven, he
can do nothing to mend it any more ; so also let us,
so long as we are in this world, repent with all our
heart of the wicked deeds which we have done in
the flesh, that we may be saved by the Lord, while
we have a time for repentance. 3. For after we
have departed from this world, we can no longer
make confession, or repent any more in that place.
4. So then, brethren, if we do the will of the Father,
if we keep the flesh pure, and if we observe the commandments of the Lord, we shall obtain eternal
life. 5. For the Lord says in the Gospel, "If ye
did not guard that which is small, who shall give
you that which is great? For I tell you that he
who is faithful in that which is least, is faithful also
in that which is much." 6. He means, then, this :—
Keep the flesh pure, and the seal of baptism undefiled,
that we may obtain eternal life.

IX

1. AND let none of you say that this flesh is not The resurrection of the flesh
judged and does not rise again. 2. Understand : in
what state did you receive salvation, in what state did
you receive your sight, except in this flesh ? 3. We

σάρκα· 4. ὃν τρόπον γὰρ ἐν τῇ σαρκὶ ἐκλήθητε,
καὶ ἐν τῇ σαρκὶ ἐλεύσεσθε. 5. εἰ Χριστός, ὁ
κύριος ὁ σώσας ἡμᾶς, ὢν μὲν τὸ πρῶτον πνεῦμα,
ἐγένετο σὰρξ καὶ οὕτως ἡμᾶς ἐκάλεσεν· οὕτως καὶ
ἡμεῖς ἐν ταύτῃ τῇ σαρκὶ ἀποληψόμεθα τὸν μισθόν.
6. ἀγαπῶμεν οὖν ἀλλήλους, ὅπως ἔλθωμεν πάντες
εἰς τὴν βασιλείαν τοῦ θεοῦ. 7. ὡς ἔχομεν καιρὸν
τοῦ ἰαθῆναι, ἐπιδῶμεν ἑαυτοὺς τῷ θεραπεύοντι
θεῷ, ἀντιμισθίαν αὐτῷ διδόντες. 8. ποίαν ; τὸ
μετανοῆσαι ἐξ εἰλικρινοῦς καρδίας. 9. προγνώστης
γάρ ἐστιν τῶν πάντων καὶ εἰδὼς ἡμῶν τὰ ἐν
καρδίᾳ. 10. δῶμεν οὖν αὐτῷ αἶνον,[1] μὴ ἀπὸ
στόματος μόνον, ἀλλὰ καὶ ἀπὸ καρδίας, ἵνα ἡμᾶς
προσδέξηται ὡς υἱούς. 11. καὶ γὰρ εἶπεν ὁ
κύριος· Ἀδελφοί μου οὗτοί εἰσιν οἱ ποιοῦντες τὸ
θέλημα τοῦ πατρός μου.

Mt. 12, 50 ;
Mk. 3, 35 ;
Luke 8, 21

X

1. Ὥστε, ἀδελφοί μου, ποιήσωμεν τὸ θέλημα
τοῦ πατρὸς τοῦ καλέσαντος ἡμᾶς, ἵνα ζήσωμεν,
καὶ διώξωμεν μᾶλλον τὴν ἀρετήν, τὴν δὲ κακίαν
καταλείψωμεν ὡς προοδοιπόρον τῶν ἁμαρτιῶν
ἡμῶν, καὶ φύγωμεν τὴν ἀσέβειαν, μὴ ἡμᾶς καταλάβῃ κακά. 2. ἐὰν γὰρ σπουδάσωμεν ἀγαθοποιεῖν,
διώξεται ἡμᾶς εἰρήνη. 3. διὰ ταύτην γὰρ τὴν
αἰτίαν οὐκ ἔστιν εὑρεῖν[2] ἄνθρωπον, οἵτινες

---

[1] αἶνον CS, αἰώνιον A ; Lightfoot thinks that the original
text was αἶνον αἰώνιον (everlasting praise).

[2] Lightfoot emends εὑρεῖν to εὐημερεῖν (to prosper), but even
so the Greek is very obscure and probably there is a primitive
corruption, perhaps the omission of a whole line.

must therefore guard the flesh as a temple of God, 4. for as you were called in the flesh, you shall also come in the flesh. 5. If Christ, the Lord who saved us, though he was originally spirit, became flesh and so called us, so also we shall receive our reward in this flesh. 6. Let us then love one another, that we may all attain to the kingdom of God.

7. While we have opportunity to be healed let us give ourselves to God, who heals us, giving him his recompense. 8. What recompense? Repentance from a sincere heart. 9. For he has knowledge of all things beforehand, and knows the things in our hearts. 10. Let us then give him praise, not only with our mouth, but also from our heart, that he may receive us as sons. 11. For the Lord said " My brethren are these who do the will of my Father." *Call to repentance*

X

1. WHEREFORE, my brethren, let us do the will of the father who called us, that we may live, and let us rather follow after virtue, but give up vice as the forerunner of our sins, and let us flee from ungodliness lest evil overtake us. 2. For, if we are zealous to do good, peace will follow after us. 3. For this cause it is not possible for a man to find it,[1] when they bring in human fears, and prefer the pleasures *Exhortation to godliness and warning against vice*

---

[1] *i.e.* peace.

παράγουσι φόβους ἀνθρωπίνους, προῃρημένοι
μᾶλλον τὴν ἐνθάδε ἀπόλαυσιν ἢ τὴν μέλλουσαν
ἐπαγγελίαν. 4. ἀγνοοῦσιν γὰρ ἡλίκην ἔχει
βάσανον ἡ ἐνθάδε ἀπόλαυσις, καὶ οἵαν τρυφὴν
ἔχει ἡ μέλλουσα ἐπαγγελία. 5. καὶ εἰ μὲν αὐτοὶ
μόνοι ταῦτα ἔπρασσον, ἀνεκτὸν ἦν· νῦν δὲ ἐπι-
μένουσιν κακοδιδασκαλοῦντες τὰς ἀναιτίους ψυχάς,
οὐκ εἰδότες, ὅτι δισσὴν ἕξουσιν τὴν **κρίσιν, αὐτοί**
τε καὶ οἱ ἀκούοντες αὐτῶν.

XI

1. Ἡμεῖς οὖν ἐν καθαρᾷ καρδίᾳ δουλεύσωμεν
τῷ θεῷ, καὶ ἐσόμεθα δίκαιοι· ἐὰν δὲ μὴ δουλεύσωμεν διὰ τὸ μὴ πιστεύειν ἡμᾶς τῇ ἐπαγγελίᾳ
τοῦ θεοῦ, ταλαίπωροι ἐσόμεθα. 2. λέγει γὰρ
καὶ ὁ προφητικὸς λόγος· Ταλαίπωροί εἰσιν οἱ
δίψυχοι, οἱ διστάζοντες τῇ καρδίᾳ, οἱ λέγοντες·
Ταῦτα πάλαι[1] ἠκούσαμεν καὶ ἐπὶ τῶν πατέρων
ἡμῶν, ἡμεῖς δὲ ἡμέραν ἐξ ἡμέρας προσδεχόμενοι
οὐδὲν τούτων ἑωράκαμεν. 3. ἀνόητοι, συμβάλετε
ἑαυτοὺς ξύλῳ· λάβετε ἄμπελον· πρῶτον μὲν
φυλλοροεῖ, εἶτα βλαστὸς γίνεται, μετὰ ταῦτα
ὄμφαξ, εἶτα σταφυλὴ παρεστηκυῖα. 4. οὕτως
καὶ ὁ λαός μου ἀκαταστασίας καὶ θλίψεις ἔσχεν·
ἔπειτα ἀπολήψεται τὰ ἀγαθά. 5. ὥστε, ἀδελφοί
μου, μὴ διψυχῶμεν, ἀλλὰ ἐλπίσαντες ὑπομείνω-
μεν, ἵνα καὶ τὸν μισθὸν κομισώμεθα. 6. πιστὸς
γάρ ἐστιν ὁ ἐπαγγειλάμενος τὰς ἀντιμισθίας
ἀποδιδόναι ἑκάστῳ τῶν ἔργων αὐτοῦ. 7. ἐὰν οὖν

cf. 1 Clement
23, 3. 4

Heb. 10, 23

---

[1] πάλαι CS, πάντα A.

of the present to the promises of the future. 4. For they do not know how great torment the pleasures of the present entail, and what is the joy of the promised future. 5. And if they did these things by themselves it could be endured, but, as it is, they are continuing in teaching evil to innocent souls, and do not know that they will incur a double judgment, both themselves and their hearers.

XI

1. LET us then serve God with a pure heart, and we shall be righteous, but if we do not serve him, because we do not believe the promise of God, we shall be miserable. 2. For the prophetic word also says :—" Miserable are the double-minded that doubt in their heart, who say, These things we heard long ago and in the time of our fathers, but we have waited from day to day, and have seen none of them. 3. O foolish men! compare yourselves to a tree ; take a vine ; first it sheds its leaves, then there comes a bud, after this the unripe grape, then the full bunch. 4. So also my people has had tumults and afflictions ; afterwards it shall receive the good things." [1] 5. Therefore, my brethren, let us not be double-minded, but let us be patient in hope, that we may also receive the reward. 6. " For he is faithful who promised" to pay to each man the recompense of his deeds. 7. If then we do righteousness before

Warning against doubt

---

[1] The additional clause at the end of this quotation seems to show that it is not derived from I. Clement, but directly from the "prophetic word," cf. note on p. 51.

THE APOSTOLIC FATHERS

1 Cor. 2, 9 ποιήσωμεν τὴν δικαιοσύνην ἐναντίον τοῦ θεοῦ, εἰσήξομεν εἰς τὴν βασιλείαν αὐτοῦ καὶ ληψόμεθα τὰς ἐπαγγελίας, ἃς οὓς οὐκ ἤκουσεν οὐδὲ ὀφθαλμὸς εἶδεν, οὐδὲ ἐπὶ καρδίαν ἀνθρώπου ἀνέβη.

XII

1. Ἐκδεχώμεθα οὖν καθ' ὥραν τὴν βασιλείαν τοῦ θεοῦ ἐν ἀγάπῃ καὶ δικαιοσύνῃ, ἐπειδὴ οὐκ οἴδαμεν τὴν ἡμέραν τῆς ἐπιφανείας τοῦ θεοῦ. 2. ἐπερωτηθεὶς γὰρ αὐτὸς ὁ κύριος ὑπό τινος,

Ev. Aegypt. (?) πότε ἥξει αὐτοῦ ἡ βασιλεία, εἶπεν· "Οταν ἔσται τὰ δύο ἕν, καὶ τὸ ἔξω ὡς τὸ ἔσω, καὶ τὸ ἄρσεν μετὰ τῆς θηλείας οὔτε ἄρσεν οὔτε θῆλυ. 3. τὰ δύο δὲ ἕν ἐστιν, ὅταν λαλῶμεν ἑαυτοῖς ἀλήθειαν καὶ ἐν δυσὶ σώμασιν ἀνυποκρίτως εἴη μία ψυχή. 4. καὶ τὸ ἔξω ὡς τὸ ἔσω, τοῦτο λέγει· τὴν ψυχὴν λέγει τὸ ἔσω, τὸ δὲ ἔξω τὸ σῶμα λέγει. ὃν τρόπον οὖν σου τὸ σῶμα φαίνεται, οὕτως καὶ ἡ ψυχή σου δῆλος ἔστω ἐν τοῖς καλοῖς ἔργοις. 5. καὶ τὸ ἄρσεν μετὰ τῆς θηλείας, οὔτε ἄρσεν οὔτε θῆλυ, τοῦτο[1] λέγει· ἵνα ἀδελφὸς ἰδὼν ἀδελφὴν οὐδὲν[2] φρονῇ περὶ

---

[1] From this point A is wanting.
[2] μηδέν seems required by the grammar of the sentence, but οὐδέν is probably a solecism of the writer rather than a corruption of the text.

146

God we shall enter into his kingdom, and shall receive the promises "which ear hath not heard, nor hath eye seen, neither hath it entered into the heart of man."

XII

1. LET us then wait for the kingdom of God, from hour to hour, in love and righteousness, seeing that we know not the day of the appearing of God. 2. For when the Lord himself was asked by someone when his kingdom would come, he said : " When the two shall be one, and the outside as the inside, and the male with the female neither male nor female." [1] 3. Now "the two are one" when we speak with one another in truth, and there is but one soul in two bodies without dissimulation. 4. And by "the outside as the inside" he means this, that the inside is the soul, and the outside is the body. Therefore, just as your body is visible, so let your soul be apparent in your good works. 5. And by "the male with the female neither male nor female" he means this, that when a brother sees a sister he should have no

Interpretation of a Saying of the Lord

[1] The same saying, or very nearly so, is quoted from Cassianus by Clement of Alexandria (*Strom.* iii. 13), and the latter states that it is from the Gospel of the Egyptians. But the whole question has been complicated by the discovery of Grenfell and Hunt's "Lost Gospel" (*Oxyrhynchus papyri*, vol. iv. pp. 22 ff.), which seems to refer to a similar saying, and the problem of the mutual relations between these documents is still unsolved.

αὐτῆς θηλυκόν, μηδὲ φρονῇ τι περὶ αὐτοῦ ἀρσε-
νικόν. 6. ταῦτα ὑμῶν ποιούντων, φησίν, ἐλεύσεται
ἡ βασιλεία τοῦ πατρός μου.

XIII

1. Ἀδελφοὶ οὖν, ἤδη ποτὲ μετανοήσωμεν, νήψω-
μεν ἐπὶ τὸ ἀγαθόν· μεστοὶ γάρ ἐσμεν πολλῆς
ἀνοίας καὶ πονηρίας. ἐξαλείψωμεν ἀφ᾽ ἡμῶν τὰ
πρότερα ἁμαρτήματα καὶ μετανοήσαντες ἐκ ψυχῆς
σωθῶμεν, καὶ μὴ γινώμεθα ἀνθρωπάρεσκοι μηδὲ
θέλωμεν μόνον ἑαυτοῖς ἀρέσκειν, ἀλλὰ καὶ τοῖς
ἔξω ἀνθρώποις ἐπὶ τῇ δικαιοσύνῃ, ἵνα τὸ ὄνομα δι᾽
ἡμᾶς μὴ βλασφημῆται. 2. λέγει γὰρ ὁ κύριος·
Is. 52, 5 Διὰ παντὸς τὸ ὄνομά μου βλασφημεῖται ἐν πᾶσιν
? τοῖς ἔθνεσιν, καὶ πάλιν· Οὐαὶ δι᾽ ὃν βλασφημεῖται τὸ ὄνομά μου. ἐν τίνι βλασφημεῖται; ἐν
τῷ μὴ ποιεῖν ὑμᾶς ἃ βούλομαι. 3. τὰ ἔθνη γὰρ
ἀκούοντα ἐκ τοῦ στόματος ἡμῶν τὰ λόγια τοῦ θεοῦ
ὡς καλὰ καὶ μεγάλα θαυμάζει· ἔπειτα καταμα-
θόντα τὰ ἔργα ἡμῶν ὅτι οὐκ ἔστιν ἄξια τῶν ῥημά-
των ὧν λέγομεν, ἔνθεν εἰς βλασφημίαν τρέπονται,
λέγοντες εἶναι μῦθόν τινα καὶ πλάνην. 4. ὅταν
Luke 6, 32. γὰρ ἀκούσωσιν παρ᾽ ἡμῶν, ὅτι λέγει ὁ θεός· Οὐ
35 χάρις ὑμῖν, εἰ ἀγαπᾶτε τοὺς ἀγαπῶντας ὑμᾶς,
ἀλλὰ χάρις ὑμῖν, εἰ ἀγαπᾶτε τοὺς ἐχθροὺς καὶ
τοὺς μισοῦντας ὑμᾶς· ταῦτα ὅταν ἀκούσωσιν, θαυ-

thought of her as female, nor she of him as male.[1]
6. When you do this, he says, the kingdom of my
Father will come.

XIII

1. THEREFORE, brethren, let us at last repent
forthwith, and be sober for our good, for we are full
of much folly and wickedness; let us wipe off from
ourselves our former sins, and let us gain salvation by
repenting with all our souls. Let us not be men-
pleasers, and let us wish to please by our righteousness not ourselves alone, but also those who are
without, that the name be not blasphemed on our
account. 2. For the Lord says, " Every way is my
name blasphemed among all the heathen," and again,
"Woe unto him on whose account my name is
blasphemed." [2] Wherein is it blasphemed? 3. In
that you do not do what I desire. For when the
heathen hear from our mouth the oracles of God,
they wonder at their beauty and greatness; afterwards, when they find out that our deeds are unworthy of the words which we speak, they turn from
their wonder to blasphemy, saying that it is a myth
and delusion. 4. For when they hear from us
that God says : "It is no credit to you, if ye love
them that love you, but it is a credit to you, if ye
love your enemies, and those that hate you";—
when they hear this they wonder at this extra-

The need for repentance

The impression made on "those without"

---

[1] Or, if αὑτοῦ be read instead of αὐτοῦ, "nor have any
thought of himself as male."
[2] The source of this quotation is unknown.

μάζουσιν τὴν ὑπερβολὴν τῆς ἀγαθότητος· ὅταν
δὲ ἴδωσιν, ὅτι οὐ μόνον τοὺς μισοῦντας οὐκ
ἀγαπῶμεν, ἀλλ᾽ ὅτι οὐδὲ τοὺς ἀγαπῶντας, κατα-
γελῶσιν ἡμῶν, καὶ βλασφημεῖται τὸ ὄνομα.

XIV

"Ωστε, ἀδελφοί, ποιοῦντες τὸ θέλημα τοῦ πατρὸς ἡμῶν θεοῦ ἐσόμεθα ἐκ τῆς ἐκκλησίας τῆς
πρώτης, τῆς πνευματικῆς, τῆς πρὸ ἡλίου καὶ
σελήνης ἐκτισμένης. ἐὰν δὲ μὴ ποιήσωμεν τὸ θέλημα κυρίου, ἐσόμεθα ἐκ τῆς γραφῆς τῆς λεγούσης·
'Εγενήθη ὁ οἶκός μου σπήλαιον λῃστῶν. ὥστε οὖν
αἱρετισώμεθα ἀπὸ τῆς ἐκκλησίας τῆς ζωῆς εἶναι,
ἵνα σωθῶμεν. 2. οὐκ οἴομαι δὲ ὑμᾶς ἀγνοεῖν, ὅτι
ἐκκλησία ζῶσα σῶμά ἐστιν Χριστοῦ· λέγει γὰρ ἡ
γραφή· 'Εποίησεν ὁ θεὸς τὸν ἄνθρωπον ἄρσεν καὶ
θῆλυ· τὸ ἄρσεν ἐστιν ὁ Χριστός, τὸ θῆλυ ἡ ἐκ-
κλησία· καὶ ἔτι[1] τὰ βιβλία καὶ οἱ ἀπόστολοι
τὴν ἐκκλησίαν οὐ νῦν εἶναι λέγουσιν[2] ἀλλὰ
ἄνωθεν. ἦν γὰρ πνευματική, ὡς καὶ ὁ 'Ιησοῦς
ἡμῶν, ἐφανερώθη δὲ ἐπ᾽ ἐσχάτων τῶν ἡμερῶν, ἵνα
ἡμᾶς σώσῃ. 3. ἡ ἐκκλησία δὲ πνευματικὴ οὖσα
ἐφανερώθη ἐν τῇ σαρκὶ Χριστοῦ, δηλοῦσα ἡμῖν,
ὅτι ἐάν τις ἡμῶν τηρήσῃ αὐτὴν ἐν τῇ σαρκὶ καὶ μὴ
φθείρῃ, ἀπολήψεται αὐτὴν ἐν τῷ πνεύματι τῷ

Jer. 7, 11 ;
Mt. 21, 13

Eph. 1, 22.

Gen. 1, 27

I Pet. 1, 20

---

[1] ὅτι C, "and moreover" (ἔτι) S.
[2] λέγουσι om. C. Some such word is necessary to the
grammar of the sentence, and is implied by S, but whether it
was λέγουσι or φασί, and its exact place in the sentence is of
course uncertain. S also adds "of the prophets" after "the
books."

ordinary goodness; but when they see that we not only do not love those that hate us, but not even those who love us, they laugh us to scorn, and the name is blasphemed.

XIV

1. Thus, brethren, if we do the will of our Father, God, we shall belong to the first Church, the spiritual one which was created before the sun and moon; but if we do not the will of the Lord, we shall fall under the scripture, which says, "My house became a den of brigands." Therefore let us choose to belong to the Church of life, that we may win salvation. 2. Now I imagine that you are not ignorant that the living "Church is the body of Christ." For the scripture says, "God made man male and female"; the male is Christ, the female is the Church. And moreover the books and the Apostles declare that the Church belongs not to the present, but has existed from the beginning; for she was spiritual, as was also our Jesus, but he was made manifest in the last days that he might save us;[1] 3. and the Church, which is spiritual, was made manifest in the flesh of Christ, showing us that if any of us guard her in the flesh without corruption, he shall receive her back again in the Holy Spirit.

The pre-existent Church

---

[1] The translation "she was made . . . that she might save us" is grammatically more probable, but seems to be excluded both by the context and by the history of doctrine.

ἁγίῳ· ἡ γὰρ σὰρξ αὕτη ἀντίτυπός ἐστιν τοῦ
πνεύματος· οὐδεὶς οὖν τὸ ἀντίτυπον φθείρας τὸ
αὐθεντικὸν μεταλήψεται. ἄρα οὖν τοῦτο λέγει,
ἀδελφοί· τηρήσατε τὴν σάρκα, ἵνα τοῦ πνεύματος
μεταλάβητε. 4. εἰ δὲ λέγομεν εἶναι τὴν σάρκα
τὴν ἐκκλησίαν καὶ τὸ πνεῦμα Χριστόν, ἄρα οὖν ὁ
ὑβρίσας τὴν σάρκα ὕβρισεν τὴν ἐκκλησίαν. ὁ
τοιοῦτος οὖν οὐ μεταλήψεται τοῦ πνεύματος, ὅ
ἐστιν ὁ Χριστός. 5. τοσαύτην δύναται ἡ σὰρξ
αὕτη μεταλαβεῖν ζωὴν καὶ ἀφθαρσίαν κολληθέντος
αὐτῇ τοῦ πνεύματος τοῦ ἁγίου, οὔτε ἐξειπεῖν τις
δύναται οὔτε λαλῆσαι ἃ ἡτοίμασεν ὁ κύριος τοῖς
ἐκλεκτοῖς αὐτοῦ.

I Cor. 2, 9

XV

1. Οὐκ οἴομαι δέ, ὅτι μικρὰν συμβουλίαν
ἐποιησάμην περὶ ἐγκρατείας, ἣν ποιήσας τις οὐ
μετανοήσει, ἀλλὰ καὶ ἑαυτὸν σώσει κἀμὲ τὸν
συμβουλεύσαντα. μισθὸς γὰρ οὔκ ἐστιν μικρὸς
πλανωμένην ψυχὴν καὶ ἀπολλυμένην ἀποστρέψαι
εἰς τὸ σωθῆναι. 2. ταύτην γὰρ ἔχομεν τὴν ἀντιμισθίαν ἀποδοῦναι τῷ θεῷ τῷ κτίσαντι ἡμᾶς, ἐὰν
ὁ λέγων καὶ ἀκούων μετὰ πίστεως καὶ ἀγάπης καὶ
λέγῃ καὶ ἀκούῃ. 3. ἐμμείνωμεν οὖν ἐφ᾿ οἷς
ἐπιστεύσαμεν δίκαιοι καὶ ὅσιοι, ἵνα μετὰ παρρησίας
αἰτῶμεν τὸν θεὸν τὸν λέγοντα· Ἔτι λαλοῦντός
σου ἐρῶ· ἰδοὺ πάρειμι. 4. τοῦτο γὰρ τὸ ῥῆμα
μεγάλης ἐστιν ἐπαγγελίας σημεῖον· ἑτοιμότερον
γὰρ ἑαυτὸν λέγει ὁ κύριος εἰς τὸ διδόναι τοῦ
αἰτοῦντος. 5. τοσαύτης οὖν χρηστότητος μετα-
λαμβάνοντες μὴ φθονήσωμεν ἑαυτοῖς τυχεῖν

For this flesh is an anti-type of the Spirit; no one therefore who has corrupted the anti-type shall receive the reality. So, then, he means this, brethren: Guard the flesh, that you may receive the Spirit. 4. Now if we say that the flesh is the Church, and the Spirit is Christ, of course he who has abused the flesh, has abused the Church. Such a one therefore will not receive the Spirit, which is Christ. 5. So great a gift of life and immortality has this flesh the power to receive, if the Holy Spirit be joined to it, nor can any man express or speak of the things "which the Lord hath prepared" for his elect.

The Flesh and the Spirit

XV

1. Now I think that I have given no mean advice concerning self-control, and if any man follow it, he shall have no regret, but shall save both himself and me his counsellor; for it is no small reward to turn to salvation a soul that is wandering and perishing. 2. For this is the recompense which we can pay to God, who created us, if he who speaks and hears both speak and hear with faith and love. 3. Let us then remain righteous and holy in our faith, that we may pray with confidence to God, who says, " While thou art speaking I will say, Behold here am I." 4. For this saying is the sign of a great promise; for the Lord says that he is more ready to give than we to ask. 5. Let us then accept such great goodness, and not grudge ourselves the gaining of such benefits,

Exhortation to holiness and prayer

τοσούτων ἀγαθῶν. ὅσην γὰρ ἡδονὴν ἔχει τὰ
ῥήματα ταῦτα τοῖς ποιήσασιν αὐτά, τοσαύτην
κατάκρισιν ἔχει τοῖς παρακούσασιν.

XVI

1. Ὥστε, ἀδελφοί, ἀφορμὴν λαβόντες οὐ μικρὰν
εἰς τὸ μετανοῆσαι, καιρὸν ἔχοντες ἐπιστρέψωμεν
ἐπὶ τὸν καλέσαντα ἡμᾶς θεόν, ἕως ἔτι ἔχομεν τὸν
παραδεχόμενον ἡμᾶς. 2. ἐὰν γὰρ ταῖς ἡδυπαθείαις
ταύταις ἀποταξώμεθα καὶ τὴν ψυχὴν ἡμῶν
νικήσωμεν ἐν τῷ μὴ ποιεῖν τὰς ἐπιθυμίας αὐτῆς
τὰς πονηράς, μεταληψόμεθα τοῦ ἐλέους Ἰησοῦ.

Malach. 4, 1 3. γινώσκετε δέ, ὅτι ἔρχεται ἤδη ἡ ἡμέρα τῆς
Is. 34, 4 κρίσεως ὡς κλίβανος καιόμενος, καὶ τακήσονταί
τινες¹ τῶν οὐρανῶν καὶ πᾶσα ἡ γῆ ὡς μόλιβος
ἐπὶ πυρὶ τηκόμενος· καὶ τότε φανήσεται τὰ κρύφια
καὶ φανερὰ ἔργα τῶν ἀνθρώπων. 4. καλὸν οὖν
ἐλεημοσύνη ὡς μετάνοια ἁμαρτίας· κρείσσων
νηστεία προσευχῆς, ἐλεημοσύνη δὲ ἀμφοτέρων·
I Pet. 4, 8 ἀγάπη δὲ καλύπτει πλῆθος ἁμαρτιῶν, προσευχὴ
δὲ ἐκ καλῆς συνειδήσεως ἐκ θανάτου ῥύεται.
μακάριος πᾶς ὁ εὑρεθεὶς ἐν τούτοις πλήρης·
ἐλεημοσύνη γὰρ κούφισμα ἁμαρτίας γίνεται.

¹ Lightfoot conjectures δυνάμεις, which is found in the LXX
text of Is. xxxiv. 4, to which the writer is alluding.

for as great joy as these words offer to those who do them so severe a condemnation do they threaten to the disobedient.

XVI

1. SEEING therefore, brethren, that we have received no small opportunity for repentance; let us, now that we have time, turn to the God who calls us, while we still have one who awaits us. 2. For if we bid farewell to these enjoyments, and conquer our soul, by giving up its wicked lusts, we shall share in the mercy of Jesus. 3. But you know that "the day" of judgment is already "approaching as a burning oven, and some [1] of the heavens shall melt," and the whole earth shall be as lead melting in the fire, and then shall be made manifest the secret and open deeds of men. 4. Almsgiving is therefore good even as penitence for sin; fasting is better than prayer, but the giving of alms is better than both; and love "covers a multitude of sins," but prayer from a good conscience rescues from death. Blessed is every man who is found full of these things; for almsgiving lightens sin.

The profit of repentance

The danger of the Judgment

Almsgiving

---

[1] Possibly the text is corrupt: Lightfoot's conjecture would be translated, "the powers of heaven," but the text may be defended as a reference to the early Christian belief in seven concentric heavens surrounding the Earth.

XVII

1. Μετανοήσωμεν οὖν ἐξ ὅλης καρδίας, ἵνα μή τις ἡμῶν παραπόληται. εἰ γὰρ ἐντολὰς ἔχομεν, ἵνα καὶ τοῦτο πράσσωμεν, ἀπὸ τῶν εἰδώλων ἀποσπᾶν καὶ κατηχεῖν, πόσῳ μᾶλλον ψυχὴν ἤδη γινώσκουσαν τὸν θεὸν οὐ δεῖ ἀπόλλυσθαι; 2. συλλάβωμεν οὖν ἑαυτοῖς καὶ τοὺς ἀσθενοῦντας ἀνάγειν περὶ[1] τὸ ἀγαθόν, ὅπως σωθῶμεν ἅπαντες καὶ ἐπιστρέψωμεν ἀλλήλους καὶ νουθετήσωμεν. 3. καὶ μὴ μόνον ἄρτι δοκῶμεν πιστεύειν καὶ προσέχειν ἐν τῷ νουθετεῖσθαι ἡμᾶς ὑπὸ τῶν πρεσβυτέρων, ἀλλὰ καὶ ὅταν εἰς οἶκον ἀπαλλαγῶμεν,[2] μνημονεύωμεν τῶν τοῦ κυρίου ἐνταλμάτων καὶ μὴ ἀντιπαρελκώμεθα ἀπὸ τῶν κοσμικῶν ἐπιθυμιῶν, ἀλλὰ πυκνότερον προσερχόμενοι πειρώμεθα προκόπτειν ἐν ταῖς ἐντολαῖς τοῦ κυρίου, ἵνα πάντες τὸ αὐτὸ φρονοῦντες συνηγμένοι ὦμεν ἐπὶ τὴν ζωήν· 4. εἶπεν γὰρ ὁ κύριος· Ἔρχομαι συναγαγεῖν πάντα τὰ ἔθνη, φυλὰς καὶ γλώσσας· τοῦτο δὲ λέγει τὴν ἡμέραν τῆς ἐπιφανείας αὐτοῦ, ὅτε ἐλθὼν λυτρώσεται ἡμᾶς, ἕκαστον κατὰ τὰ ἔργα αὐτοῦ. 5. καὶ ὄψονται τὴν δόξαν αὐτοῦ καὶ τὸ κράτος οἱ ἄπιστοι, καὶ ξενισθήσονται ἰδόντες τὸ βασίλειον τοῦ κόσμου ἐν τῷ Ἰησοῦ, λέγοντες· Οὐαὶ ἡμῖν, ὅτι σὺ ἦς, καὶ οὐκ ᾔδειμεν καὶ οὐκ ἐπιστεύομεν καὶ οὐκ ἐπειθόμεθα τοῖς πρεσβυτέροις τοῖς ἀναγγέλλουσιν ἡμῖν περὶ τῆς σωτηρίας ἡμῶν. καὶ ὁ σκώληξ αὐτῶν οὐ τελευτήσει καὶ τὸ πῦρ αὐτῶν οὐ σβεσθήσεται, καὶ ἔσονται εἰς ὅρασιν

Rom. 12, 16 ;
cf. Phil. 2, 2
Is. 66, 18

Is. 66, 24

Is. 66, 24

---

[1] S perhaps implies πρός "bring back to goodness."
[2] S adds "and have ceased from all."

XVII

1. LET us then repent with our whole heart, that none of us perish by the way. For if we have commandments to do this also, to tear men away from idols and to instruct them, how much more is it our duty to save from perishing a soul that already knows God? 2. Let us then help one another, and bring back those that are weak in goodness, that we may all be saved, and convert and exhort one another. 3. And let us not merely seem to believe and pay attention now, while we are being exhorted by the Elders, but also when we have gone home let us remember the commandments of the Lord, and let us not be dragged aside by worldly lusts, but let us try to come here more frequently, and to make progress in the commands of the Lord; that we may "all have the same mind" and be gathered together unto life. 4. For the Lord said: "I come to gather together all the nations, tribes, and languages." Now by this he means the day of his appearing, when he will come and ransom each of us according to his works. 5. And the unbelievers "shall see his glory" and might, and they shall be amazed when they see the sovereignty of the world given to Jesus and shall say: Woe unto us, that it was thou, and we knew it not, and did not believe, and were not obedient to the Elders, when they told us of our salvation. "And their worm shall not die and their fire shall not be quenched, and they shall be a

Exhortation to repentance

Not merely during the exhortation of the Elders

Warning of the Judgment

πάσῃ σαρκί. 6. τὴν ἡμέραν ἐκείνην λέγει τῆς κρί
σεως, ὅταν ὄψονται τοὺς ἐν ἡμῖν ἀσεβήσαντας καὶ
παραλογισαμένους τὰς ἐντολὰς Ἰησοῦ Χριστοῦ.
7. οἱ δὲ δίκαιοι εὐπραγήσαντες καὶ ὑπομείναντες τὰς
βασάνους καὶ μισήσαντες τὰς ἡδυπαθείας τῆς
ψυχῆς, ὅταν θεάσωνται τοὺς ἀστοχήσαντας καὶ
ἀρνησαμένους διὰ τῶν λόγων ἢ διὰ τῶν ἔργων τὸν
Ἰησοῦν, ὅπως κολάζονται δειναῖς βασάνοις πυρὶ
Apoc. 11, 13 ἀσβέστῳ, ἔσονται δόξαν διδόντες τῷ θεῷ αὐτῶν
λέγοντες, ὅτι ἔσται ἐλπὶς τῷ δεδουλευκότι θεῷ
ἐξ ὅλης καρδίας.

XVIII

1. Καὶ ἡμεῖς οὖν γενώμεθα ἐκ τῶν εὐχαρι
στούντων, δεδουλευκότων τῷ θεῷ, καὶ μὴ ἐκ τῶν
κρινομένων ἀσεβῶν. 2. καὶ γὰρ αὐτὸς πανθα
μαρτωλὸς ὢν καὶ μήπω φυγὼν τὸν πειρασμόν,
ἀλλ' ἔτι ὢν ἐν μέσοις τοῖς ὀργάνοις τοῦ διαβόλου
σπουδάζω τὴν δικαιοσύνην διώκειν, ὅπως ἰσχύσω
κἂν ἐγγὺς αὐτῆς γενέσθαι, φοβούμενος τὴν κρίσιν
τὴν μέλλουσαν.

XIX

1. Ὥστε, ἀδελφοὶ καὶ ἀδελφαί, μετὰ τὸν θεὸν
τῆς ἀληθείας ἀναγινώσκω ὑμῖν ἔντευξιν εἰς τὸ
προσέχειν τοῖς γεγραμμένοις, ἵνα καὶ ἑαυτοὺς
σώσητε καὶ τὸν ἀναγινώσκοντα ἐν ὑμῖν. μισθὸν
γὰρ αἰτῶ ὑμᾶς τὸ μετανοῆσαι ἐξ ὅλης καρδίας,
σωτηρίαν ἑαυτοῖς καὶ ζωὴν διδόντας. τοῦτο γὰρ
ποιήσαντες σκοπὸν πᾶσιν τοῖς νέοις θήσομεν, τοῖς

spectacle to all flesh." 6. He means that day of judgment, when they shall see those who were ungodly among us and perverted the commandments of Jesus Christ. 7. But the righteous who have done good, and have endured torture, and have hated the indulgences of the soul, when they see how those who have done amiss, and denied Jesus by word or deed, are punished with terrible torture in unquenchable fire, shall give " glory to their God," saying, There shall be hope for him who has served God with all his heart.

XVIII

1. Let us then also belong to them who give thanks, who have served God, and not to the ungodly who are judged. 2. For I myself too am altogether sinful, and I have not yet escaped temptation, but I am still in the midst of the devices of the devil, yet I am striving to follow after righteousness, that I may have the strength at least to draw near to it, in fear of the judgment to come. *The need of striving*

XIX

1. Therefore, brothers and sisters, following the God of truth, I am reading you an exhortation to pay attention to that which is written, that you may both save yourselves and him who is the reader[1] among you. For as a reward I beg of you that you repent with all your heart, and give to yourselves salvation and life. For if we do this we shall set a mark for all the *Attention to the Scriptures*

[1] It is probable though not quite certain that this refers to a definite order of "Readers" in the Church.

βουλομένοις περὶ τὴν εὐσέβειαν καὶ τὴν χρηστό-
τητα τοῦ θεοῦ φιλοπονεῖν. 2. καὶ μὴ ἀηδῶς ἔχωμεν
καὶ ἀγανακτῶμεν οἱ ἄσοφοι, ὅταν τις ἡμᾶς νουθετῇ
καὶ ἐπιστρέφῃ ἀπὸ τῆς ἀδικίας εἰς τὴν δικαιοσύνην.
ἐνίοτε γὰρ πονηρὰ πράσσοντες οὐ γινώσκομεν διὰ
τὴν διψυχίαν καὶ ἀπιστίαν τὴν ἐνοῦσαν ἐν τοῖς
Eph. 4, 18   στήθεσιν ἡμῶν, καὶ ἐσκοτίσμεθα τὴν διάνοιαν ὑπὸ
τῶν ἐπιθυμιῶν τῶν ματαίων. 3. πράξωμεν οὖν
τὴν δικαιοσύνην, ἵνα εἰς τέλος σωθῶμεν. μακάριοι
οἱ τούτοις ὑπακούοντες τοῖς προστάγμασιν· κἂν
ὀλίγον χρόνον κακοπαθήσωσιν ἐν τῷ κόσμῳ
τούτῳ,[1] τὸν ἀθάνατον τῆς ἀναστάσεως καρπὸν
τρυγήσουσιν. 4. μὴ οὖν λυπείσθω ὁ εὐσεβής,
ἐὰν ἐπὶ τοῖς νῦν χρόνοις ταλαιπωρῇ· μακάριος
αὐτὸν ἀναμένει χρόνος· ἐκεῖνος ἄνω μετὰ τῶν
πατέρων ἀναβιώσας εὐφρανθήσεται εἰς τὸν
ἀλύπητον αἰῶνα.

XX

1. Ἀλλὰ μηδὲ ἐκεῖνο τὴν διάνοιαν ὑμῶν ταρασ-
σέτω, ὅτι βλέπομεν τοὺς ἀδίκους πλουτοῦντας καὶ
στενοχωρουμένους τοὺς τοῦ θεοῦ δούλους. 2.
πιστεύωμεν οὖν, ἀδελφοὶ καὶ ἀδελφαί· θεοῦ ζῶντος
πεῖραν ἀθλοῦμεν καὶ γυμναζόμεθα τῷ νῦν βίῳ,
ἵνα τῷ μέλλοντι στεφανωθῶμεν. 3. οὐδεὶς τῶν
δικαίων ταχὺν καρπὸν ἔλαβεν, ἀλλ᾽ ἐκδέχεται
αὐτόν. 4. εἰ γὰρ τὸν μισθὸν τῶν δικαίων ὁ θεὸς
συντόμως ἀπεδίδου, εὐθέως ἐμπορίαν ἠσκοῦμεν
καὶ οὐ θεοσέβειαν· ἐδοκοῦμεν γὰρ εἶναι δίκαιοι, οὐ
τὸ εὐσεβές, ἀλλὰ τὸ κερδαλέον διώκοντες. καὶ

---

[1] τούτῳ om. S, in Lightfoot's opinion correctly.

younger, who wish to work in the cause of piety and the goodness of God. 2. And let us not be displeased or be vexed in our foolishness when any one admonishes us, and turns us from unrighteousness to righteousness. For sometimes when we do evil we do not know it because of the double-mindedness and unbelief which is in our breasts, and we are "darkened in our understanding" by vain desires. 3. Let us then do righteousness, that we may be saved at the end. Blessed are they who obey these instructions: though they suffer for a short time in this world, they shall gather the immortal fruit of the resurrection. 4. Let not, then, the pious grieve if he endure sorrow at this present time; a time of blessedness awaits him; he shall live again with the fathers above, and rejoice to an eternity wherein is no sorrow.

XX

1. But neither let it grieve your mind that we see the unrighteous enjoying wealth, and the servants of God oppressed. 2. Let us then have faith, brothers and sisters: we are contending in the contest of the living God, and we are being trained by the life which now is, that we may gain the crown in that which is to come. 3. None of the righteous has attained a reward quickly, but waits for it; 4. for if God should pay the recompense of the righteous speedily, we should immediately be training ourselves in commerce and not in godliness; for we should seem to be righteous when we were pursuing not

The prosperity of the righteous

διὰ τοῦτο θεία κρίσις ἔβλαψεν πνεῦμα μὴ ὂν δίκαιον, καὶ ἐβάρυνεν δεσμοῖς.

I Tim. 1, 17
5. Τῷ μόνῳ θεῷ ἀοράτῳ, πατρὶ τῆς ἀληθείας, τῷ ἐξαποστείλαντι ἡμῖν τὸν σωτῆρα καὶ ἀρχηγὸν τῆς ἀφθαρσίας, δι' οὗ καὶ ἐφανέρωσεν ἡμῖν τὴν ἀλήθειαν καὶ τὴν ἐπουράνιον ζωήν, αὐτῷ ἡ δόξα εἰς τοὺς αἰῶνας τῶν αἰώνων. ἀμήν.

Κλήμεντος πρὸς Κορινθίους ἐπιστολὴ β̄.

piety but gain. For this reason divine judgment punishes[1] a spirit which is not righteous and loads it with chains.

5. To the only invisible God, the father of truth, Doxology who sent forth to us the Saviour and prince of immortality, through whom he also made manifest to to us truth and the life of heaven, to him be the glory for ever and ever. Amen.

The Second Epistle of Clement to the Corinthians.

[1] This translation takes the aorist as gnomic, and regards "spirit" as meaning a human spirit. But Harnack prefers to take the aorist as historical and refers the passage to the fall of Satan.

THE EPISTLES OF IGNATIUS

THE EPISTLES OF IGNATIUS

THE epistles or letters of Ignatius are among the most famous documents of early Christianity, and have a curiously complicated literary history. Eusebius in *Historia Ecclesiastica* iii. 36 tells the story of Ignatius. He was the third bishop[1] of Antioch in Syria, and was condemned to be sent to Rome to be killed by the beasts in the amphitheatre. His journey took him through various churches in Asia Minor and while he was in Smyrna he wrote letters to Ephesus, Magnesia, Tralles, and Rome, and later on, when he reached Troas he wrote to the Philadelphians, Smyrnaeans, and Polycarp the bishop of Smyrna. In his *chronicon* Eusebius fixes the date of his martyrdom in Rome in the tenth year of Trajan, *i.e.* 108 A.D.

Modern critics are by no means unanimous as to the correctness of this date, but, though each has his own special preferences, there is a general tendency to think that Ignatius was really a martyr in Rome in the time of Trajan (98–117 A.D.)

The immediate purpose of each of the letters, except that to the Romans, is to thank the recipients for the kindness which they had shown to Ignatius. The "Romans" has the object of preventing the

---

[1] According to tradition Peter was the first and Euodius the second (Eus. *Hist. Eccl.* iii. 22).

Christians at Rome from making any efforts to save
Ignatius from the beasts in the arena, and so
robbing him of the crown of martyrdom. But
besides this immediate purpose the writer is
influenced by three other motives, all or some of
which can be traced in each letter.

(1) Ignatius is exceedingly anxious in each community to strengthen respect for the bishop and
presbyters. He ascribes the fullest kind of divine
authority to their organisation, and recognises as
valid no church, institution, or worship without their
sanction.

(2) He protests against the form of heresy called
docetism (δοκεῖν), which regarded the sufferings, and
in some cases the life, of Jesus as merely an
appearance. He also protests against any tendency
to Judaistic practices, but it is disputed whether he
means that this was an evil found in docetic circles,
or that it was a danger threatening the church from
other directions.

(3) He is also anxious to secure the future of his
own church in Antioch by persuading other com-
munities to send helpers.

Of the letters of Ignatius there are extant three
recensions.

1. *The long recension.*—The most widely found
contains not only the seven letters of which Eusebius
speaks, but also six others. In this collection the
chronological scheme (not however followed in the
MSS.) is :—

(1) *From Antioch.* A letter from a certain Mary
of Cassobola (a neighbouring town) to Ignatius, and
a letter from him in reply.

(2) *From Smyrna.* Letters to Ephesus, Magnesia, Tralles, and Rome.

(3) *From Troas.* Letters to Philadelphia, Smyrna, and Polycarp.

(4) *From Philippi.* Letters to Tarsus, Antioch, and Hero (the successor of Ignatius as bishop of Antioch).

(5) *From Italy.* Letter to Philippi.

There is also an appendix in the Latin version of Grosseteste containing letters from and to S. John and the Virgin Mary.

2. *The short recension.*—It was early seen that the long recension contained several letters which were clearly not genuine, and that those which had the most claim to acceptance, as having been mentioned by Eusebius, were greatly corrupted by obvious interpolations. Fortunately the remnants of an early collection have been found which originally contained only the seven Eusebian letters.

The text of this recension is nowhere extant in a pure form. All the known MSS. of Ignatius (with the possible exception of the Berlin papyrus) which contain the seven Eusebian letters belong in some degree to the " Long recension," but this degree fortunately varies. Two classes of MSS. must be distinguished. (1) MSS. containing the additional epistles of the " Long recension," but preserving the uninterpolated text of the seven Eusebian letters. (2) MSS. containing the additional epistles and the interpolated text of the Eusebian letters. It is obvious that the second class are genuine MSS. of the " Long recension," and that the former class are MSS. of the " Short recension," copied from originals containing only the Eusebian letters, to which the copyist has supplied the additional material of the "Long recension" from some other original, but luckily without correcting the text of the seven letters from this second source. Having, therefore, the information of Eusebius to define the extent of the original collection of letters we can use this class of MSS. to determine its text.

3. *The Syriac abridgment.*—In 1845 Dr. Cureton discovered a Syriac text of a collection of three epistles, Ephesians, Romans, and Polycarp, and there was for a time a tendency to think that this might be the original text. Lightfoot however and others showed it to be merely an abridgment from a Syriac text of the short recension. It has therefore more or less disappeared from the field of study except as evidence for the text of the short recension, in the same way as the 'long recension' is only valuable for the light which the interpolations throw on the doctrinal development of Christianity, and in a few places as a help to reconstructing the true text where the short recension has been corrupted.

The history of the discovery of the text of the short recension is worth mentioning, though it is here only possible to give it in outline. In the early middle ages the long recension was generally current, and in the west this included the correspondence between Ignatius and the Virgin Mary and St. John. This last addition was soon rejected as a forgery, but until the time of Archbishop Ussher only the long recension was known, though its genuineness was often doubted. In 1644 Ussher published an edition of Ignatius in which he restored the text of the short recension by the aid of a Latin version made in 1250 A.D. by Robert Grosseteste of Lincoln from a lost Greek original which belonged to the long recension but had the uninterpolated text of the Eusebian epistles. In 1646 Isaac Vossius published a Greek text of the same kind from *Cod. Medic. Laur.* lxii. 7 at Florence, which is however not complete, and omits the epistle to the Romans. This deficiency was supplied in 1689 by Ruinart in his *Acta Martyrum Sincera* from a Paris MS. (Paris Graec. 1451) of the 10th century.

In 1783 an Armenian version was published in Constantinople by Bishop Minas from five Armenian MSS., some of which are now extant, and this was reprinted and translated by Petermann in 1849. It is not a version made directly from the Greek, but from a lost Syriac version, of which however some fragments were published in 1849 in Cureton's *Corpus Ignatianum,* and some more by Lightfoot in his *Ignatius* (2nd edition) in 1889. In 1883 Ciasca, and in 1885 Lightfoot in his *Ignatius* (1st edition), published a Sahidic fragment containing part of the epistle to the Smyrnaeans, from MS. Borg. 248 in the Museo Nazionale at Naples. Finally, in 1910 a papyrus fragment of the 5th century (Berlin P. 10581) was published by C. Schmidt and W. Schubert in their *Altchristliche Texte (Berliner Klassikertexte, heft vi.)* ; this contains Smyrnaeans iii. 3–xii. 1. The text based on these sources may be regarded as fairly accurate, though it is probably by no means so good as that of I. Clement.

The symbols employed for referring to these MSS. and versions are as follows :—

IGNATIUS

G_1 = Codex Mediceus Laurentius lxii. 7 (the Vossian MS.).

g = the text of the interpolated epistles in the long recension.

L = the Latin version of Grosseteste. (L^c = codex Caiensis, L^m = codex Montacutianus, known only from the collation of Ussher.)

A = the Armenian version.

S = the Syriac version ($S_{1\,2\,3\,4}$ = the various fragments of the unabridged texts, Σ = Cureton's abridgment).

C = the Sahidic version.

B = the Berlin papyrus.

It is perhaps also desirable to note that Lightfoot and some other writers refer to the Syriac abridgment as the "short recension," and use the name of "middle recension" for the "short recension." The "Vossian epistles" is also a name sometimes used for the "short recension."

ΤΟΥ ΑΓΙΟΥ ΙΓΝΑΤΙΟΥ
ΕΠΙΣΤΟΛΑΙ

ΠΡΟΣ ΕΦΕΣΙΟΥΣ ΙΓΝΑΤΙΟΣ

Ἰγνάτιος, ὁ καὶ Θεοφόρος, τῇ εὐλογημένῃ ἐν
μεγέθει θεοῦ πατρὸς πληρώματι, τῇ προω-
ρισμένῃ πρὸ αἰώνων εἶναι διὰ παντὸς εἰς
δόξαν παράμονον ἄτρεπτον, ἡνωμένῃ καὶ
ἐκλελεγμένῃ ἐν πάθει ἀληθινῷ, ἐν θελήματι
τοῦ πατρὸς καὶ Ἰησοῦ Χριστοῦ τοῦ θεοῦ
ἡμῶν, τῇ ἐκκλησίᾳ τῇ ἀξιομακαρίστῳ, τῇ
οὔσῃ ἐν Ἐφέσῳ τῆς Ἀσίας, πλεῖστα ἐν
Ἰησοῦ Χριστῷ καὶ ἐν ἀμώμῳ χαρᾷ χαίρειν.

I

1. Ἀποδεξάμενος ἐν θεῷ τὸ πολυαγάπητόν σου
ὄνομα, ὃ κέκτησθε φύσει δικαίᾳ[1] κατὰ πίστιν καὶ
ἀγάπην ἐν Χριστῷ Ἰησοῦ, τῷ σωτῆρι ἡμῶν·
μιμηταὶ ὄντες θεοῦ, ἀναζωπυρήσαντες ἐν αἵματι
θεοῦ τὸ συγγενικὸν ἔργον τελείως ἀπηρτίσατε·
2. ἀκούσαντες γὰρ δεδεμένον ἀπὸ Συρίας ὑπὲρ

---

[1] "Truly immaculate will," A(S).

THE EPISTLES OF SAINT IGNATIUS

I.—IGNATIUS TO THE EPHESIANS

IGNATIUS, who is also called Theophorus,[1] to Greeting
the Church, worthy of all felicitation, which is
at Ephesus in Asia,—blessed with greatness
by the fulness of God the Father, predestined
from eternity for abiding and unchangeable
glory, united and chosen through true suffering
by the will of the Father and Jesus Christ our
God,—abundant greeting in Jesus Christ and in
blameless joy.

I

1. I BECAME acquainted through God with your The fame
much beloved name, which you have obtained by of the Ephesians
your righteous nature, according to faith and love in
Christ Jesus our Saviour. You are imitators of God,
and, having kindled your brotherly [2] task by the blood
of God, you completed it perfectly. 2. For when you

---

[1] *i.e.* "The God-bearer." In the 3rd century Acts of
Ignatius the Emperor asks "And who is Theophorus?" and
Ignatius replied "He who has Christ in his heart."
[2] Or "natural," "congenial," as Lightfoot suggests: the
translation given is that of Zahn.

τοῦ κοινοῦ ὀνόματος καὶ ἐλπίδος, ἐλπίζοντα τῇ
προσευχῇ ὑμῶν ἐπιτυχεῖν ἐν Ῥώμῃ θηριομαχῆσαι,
ἵνα διὰ τοῦ ἐπιτυχεῖν δυνηθῶ μαθητὴς εἶναι, ἰδεῖν
ἐσπουδάσατε· [1] 3. ἐπεὶ οὖν τὴν πολυπλήθειαν
ὑμῶν ἐν ὀνόματι θεοῦ ἀπείληφα ἐν Ὀνησίμῳ,
τῷ ἐν ἀγάπῃ ἀδιηγήτῳ, ὑμῶν δὲ ἐπισκόπῳ,[2]
ὃν εὔχομαι κατὰ Ἰησοῦν Χριστὸν ὑμᾶς ἀγαπᾶν
καὶ πάντας ὑμᾶς αὐτῷ ἐν ὁμοιότητι εἶναι.
εὐλογητὸς γὰρ ὁ χαρισάμενος ὑμῖν ἀξίοις οὖσι
τοιοῦτον ἐπίσκοπον κεκτῆσθαι.

II

1. Περὶ δὲ τοῦ συνδούλου μου Βούρρου, τοῦ
κατὰ θεὸν διακόνου ὑμῶν ἐν πᾶσιν εὐλογημένου,
εὔχομαι παραμεῖναι αὐτὸν εἰς τιμὴν ὑμῶν καὶ τοῦ
ἐπισκόπου· καὶ Κρόκος δέ, ὁ θεοῦ ἄξιος καὶ ὑμῶν,
ὃν ἐξεμπλάριον τῆς ἀφ᾽ ὑμῶν ἀγάπης ἀπέλαβον,
κατὰ πάντα με ἀνέπαυσεν, ὡς καὶ αὐτὸν ὁ πατὴρ
Ἰησοῦ Χριστοῦ ἀναψύξαι, ἅμα Ὀνησίμῳ καὶ
Βούρρῳ καὶ Εὔπλῳ καὶ Φρόντωνι, δι᾽ ὧν πάντας
ὑμᾶς κατὰ ἀγάπην εἶδον. 2. ὀναίμην ὑμῶν διὰ
παντός, ἐάνπερ ἄξιος ὦ. πρέπον οὖν ἐστὶν κατὰ
πάντα τρόπον δοξάζειν Ἰησοῦν Χριστὸν τὸν
δοξάσαντα ὑμᾶς, ἵνα ἐν μιᾷ ὑποταγῇ κατηρ-
τισμένοι, ὑποτασσόμενοι τῷ ἐπισκόπῳ καὶ τῷ
πρεσβυτερίῳ, κατὰ πάντα ἦτε ἡγιασμένοι.

---

[1] ἰδεῖν ἐσπουδάσατε om. Gg, the text is restored from ALS,
but Lightfoot prefers ἱστορῆσαι to ἰδεῖν.
[2] ἐν σαρκὶ ἐπισκ. GL, "your bishop in the flesh."

heard that I had been sent a prisoner from Syria for the sake of our common name and hope, in the hope of obtaining by your prayers the privilege of fighting with beasts at Rome, that by so doing I might be enabled to be a true disciple, you hastened to see me. 3. Seeing then that I received in the name of God your whole congregation in the person of Onesimus, a man of inexpressible love and your bishop, I beseech you by Jesus Christ to love him, and all to resemble him. For blessed is he who granted you to be worthy to obtain such a bishop.

The bishop, Onesimus

II

1. Now concerning my fellow servant, Burrhus, your deacon by the will of God, who is blessed in all things, I beg that he may stay longer, for your honour and for that of the bishop. And Crocus also, who is worthy of God and of you, whom I received as an example of your love, has relieved me in every way,—may the Father of Jesus Christ refresh him in like manner,—together with Onesimus and Burrhus and Euplus and Fronto, in whose persons I have seen you all in love. 2. May I ever have joy of you, if I be but worthy. It is, therefore, seemly in every way to glorify Jesus Christ, who has glorified you, that you may be joined together in one subjection, subject to the bishop and to the presbytery, and may in all things be sanctified.

Other members of the Ephesian church

III

1. Οὐ διατάσσομαι ὑμῖν ὡς ὤν τις. εἰ γὰρ καὶ δέδεμαι ἐν τῷ ὀνόματι, οὔπω ἀπήρτισμαι ἐν Ἰησοῦ Χριστῷ· νῦν γὰρ ἀρχὴν ἔχω τοῦ μαθητεύεσθαι, καὶ προσλαλῶ ὑμῖν ὡς συνδιδασκαλίταις μου. ἐμὲ γὰρ ἔδει ὑφ' ὑμῶν ὑπαλειφθῆναι πίστει, νουθεσίᾳ, ὑπομονῇ, μακροθυμίᾳ. 2. ἀλλ' ἐπεὶ ἡ ἀγάπη οὐκ ἐᾷ με σιωπᾶν περὶ ὑμῶν, διὰ τοῦτο προέλαβον παρακαλεῖν ὑμᾶς, ὅπως συντρέχητε τῇ γνώμῃ τοῦ θεοῦ. καὶ γὰρ Ἰησοῦς Χριστός, τὸ ἀδιάκριτον ἡμῶν ζῆν, τοῦ πατρὸς ἡ γνώμη, ὡς καὶ οἱ ἐπίσκοποι, οἱ κατὰ τὰ πέρατα ὁρισθέντες, ἐν Ἰησοῦ Χριστοῦ γνώμῃ εἰσίν.

IV

1. Ὅθεν πρέπει ὑμῖν συντρέχειν τῇ τοῦ ἐπισκόπου γνώμῃ, ὅπερ καὶ ποιεῖτε. τὸ γὰρ ἀξιονόμαστον ὑμῶν πρεσβυτέριον, τοῦ θεοῦ ἄξιον, οὕτως συνήρμοσται τῷ ἐπισκόπῳ, ὡς χορδαὶ κιθάρᾳ. διὰ τοῦτο ἐν τῇ ὁμονοίᾳ ὑμῶν καὶ συμφώνῳ ἀγάπῃ Ἰησοῦς Χριστὸς ᾄδεται. 2. καὶ οἱ κατ' ἄνδρα δὲ χορὸς γίνεσθε, ἵνα σύμφωνοι ὄντες ἐν ὁμονοίᾳ, χρῶμα θεοῦ λαβόντες ἐν ἑνότητι, ᾄδητε ἐν φωνῇ μιᾷ διὰ Ἰησοῦ Χριστοῦ τῷ πατρί, ἵνα ὑμῶν καὶ ἀκούσῃ καὶ ἐπιγινώσκῃ, δι' ὧν εὖ πράσσετε, μέλη

III

1. I DO not give you commands as if I were some one great, for though I am a prisoner for the Name, I am not yet perfect in Jesus Christ; for now I do but begin to be a disciple, and I speak to you as to my fellow learners. For I needed to be prepared[1] by you in faith, exhortation, endurance, long-suffering. 2. But since love does not suffer me to be silent concerning you, for this reason I have taken upon me to exhort you that you live[2] in harmony with the will of God. For Jesus Christ, our inseparable life, is the will of the Father, even as the bishops, who have been appointed throughout the world, are by the will of Jesus Christ.

Exhortation to Unity

IV

1. THEREFORE it is fitting that you should live in harmony with the will of the bishop, as indeed you do. For your justly famous presbytery, worthy of God, is attuned to the bishop as the strings to a harp. Therefore by your concord and harmonious love Jesus Christ is being sung. 2. Now do each of you join in this choir, that being harmoniously in concord you may receive the key[3] of God in unison, and sing with one voice through Jesus Christ to the Father, that he may both hear you and may recognise, through your good works, that you are

Obedience to the Bishop

---

[1] Literally "anointed." The allusion is to the preparation of a gymnast or gladiator.
[2] Literally "run."
[3] *i.e.* in the musical sense of the word.

ὄντας τοῦ υἱοῦ αὐτοῦ. χρήσιμον οὖν ἐστὶν ὑμᾶς ἐν ἀμώμῳ ἑνότητι εἶναι, ἵνα καὶ θεοῦ πάντοτε μετέχητε.

V

1. Εἰ γὰρ ἐγὼ ἐν μικρῷ χρόνῳ τοιαύτην συνήθειαν ἔσχον πρὸς τὸν ἐπίσκοπον ὑμῶν, οὐκ ἀνθρωπίνην οὖσαν, ἀλλὰ πνευματικήν, πόσῳ μᾶλλον ὑμᾶς μακαρίζω τοὺς ἐγκεκραμένους[1] οὕτως, ὡς ἡ ἐκκλησία Ἰησοῦ Χριστῷ, καὶ ὡς Ἰησοῦς Χριστὸς τῷ πατρί, ἵνα πάντα ἐν ἑνότητι σύμφωνα ᾖ; 2. μηδεὶς πλανάσθω· ἐὰν μή τις ᾖ ἐντὸς τοῦ θυσιαστηρίου, ὑστερεῖται τοῦ ἄρτου τοῦ θεοῦ. εἰ γὰρ ἑνὸς καὶ δευτέρου προσευχὴ τοσαύτην ἰσχὺν ἔχει, πόσῳ μᾶλλον ἥ τε τοῦ ἐπισκόπου καὶ πάσης τῆς ἐκκλησίας; 3. ὁ οὖν μὴ ἐρχόμενος ἐπὶ τὸ αὐτὸ οὗτος ἤδη ὑπερηφανεῖ καὶ ἑαυτὸν διέκρινεν. γέγραπται γάρ· Ὑπερηφάνοις ὁ θεὸς ἀντιτάσσεται, σπουδάσωμεν οὖν μὴ ἀντιτάσσεσθαι τῷ ἐπισκόπῳ, ἵνα ὦμεν θεῷ[2] ὑποτασσόμενοι.

Joh. 6, 33

Prov. 3, 34 ; James 4, 6 ; I Pet. 5, 5

VI

1. Καὶ ὅσον βλέπει τις σιγῶντα ἐπίσκοπον, πλειόνως αὐτὸν φοβείσθω· πάντα γάρ, ὃν πέμπει ὁ οἰκοδεσπότης εἰς ἰδίαν οἰκονομίαν, οὕτως δεῖ

---

[1] ἀνακεκραμένους g, which Lightfoot prefers.
[2] θεοῦ is found in G and Lightfoot prefers it for transcriptional probability, but θεῷ is supported by LS and some patristic quotations.

members of his Son. It is therefore profitable for you to be in blameless unity, in order that you may always commune with God.

V

1. For if I in a short time gained such fellowship with your bishop as was not human but spiritual, how much more do I count you blessed who are so united with him as the Church is with Jesus Christ, and as Jesus Christ is with the Father, that all things may sound together in unison! 2. Let no man be deceived: unless a man be within the sanctuary he lacks the bread of God, for if the prayer of one or two has such might, how much more has that of the bishop and of the whole Church? 3. So then he who does not join in the common assembly, is already haughty, and has separated himself.[1] For it is written " God resisteth the proud :" let us then be careful not to oppose the bishop, that we may be subject to God.[2]

The necessity of sub-ordination to the bishop

VI

1. And the more anyone sees that the bishop is silent, the more let him fear him. For every one whom the master of the house sends to do his

The silence of the bishop

---

[1] There is a curious mixture of tenses in the Greek: Lightfoot takes the final aorist as gnomic : but it is possible that Ignatius is, at least in part, referring to some special instance.

[2] Or, with the alternative reading, "by our submission we may belong to God."

ἡμᾶς αὐτὸν δέχεσθαι, ὡς αὐτὸν τὸν πέμψαντα. τὸν οὖν ἐπίσκοπον δῆλον ὅτι ὡς αὐτὸν κύριον δεῖ προσβλέπειν. 2. αὐτὸς μὲν οὖν Ὀνήσιμος ὑπερεπαινεῖ ὑμῶν τὴν ἐν θεῷ εὐταξίαν, ὅτι πάντες κατὰ ἀλήθειαν ζῆτε καὶ ὅτι ἐν ὑμῖν οὐδεμία αἵρεσις κατοικεῖ· ἀλλ᾽ οὐδὲ ἀκούετέ τινος πλέον, ἢ περὶ[1] Ἰησοῦ Χριστοῦ λαλοῦντος ἐν ἀληθείᾳ.

VII

1. Εἰώθασιν γάρ τινες δόλῳ πονηρῷ τὸ ὄνομα περιφέρειν, ἄλλα τινὰ πράσσοντες ἀνάξια θεοῦ· οὓς δεῖ ὑμᾶς ὡς θηρία ἐκκλίνειν· εἰσὶν γὰρ κύνες λυσσῶντες, λαθροδῆκται· οὓς δεῖ ὑμᾶς φυλάσσεσθαι ὄντας δυσθεραπεύτους. 2. εἷς ἰατρός ἐστιν, σαρκικός τε καὶ πνευματικός, γεννητὸς καὶ ἀγέννητος, ἐν ἀνθρώπῳ[2] θεός, ἐν θανάτῳ ζωὴ ἀληθινή, καὶ ἐκ Μαρίας καὶ ἐκ θεοῦ, πρῶτον παθητὸς καὶ τότε ἀπαθής, Ἰησοῦς Χριστὸς ὁ κύριος ἡμῶν.

VIII

1. Μὴ οὖν τις ὑμᾶς ἐξαπατάτω, ὥσπερ οὐδὲ ἐξαπατᾶσθε, ὅλοι ὄντες θεοῦ. ὅταν γὰρ μηδεμία ἔρις[3] ἐνήρεισται ἐν ὑμῖν ἡ δυναμένη ὑμᾶς βασανί-

---

[1] The reading of G is εἴπερ; the Latin is *aliquem amplius quam Iesum Christum loquentem*; the Armenian supports the text (ἢ περί) which is Lightfoot's emendation.

[2] This reading is justified by early patristic quotation, and (slightly corrupted) by A.ʼ GL read ἐν σαρκὶ γενόμενος θεός "God become incarnate."

[3] A Σg read ἐπιθυμία, "lust," which Lightfoot accepts.

business ought we to receive as him who sent him.
Therefore it is clear that we must regard the bishop
as the Lord himself.   2. Indeed Onesimus himself
gives great praise to your good order in God, for you
all live according to truth, and no heresy dwells
among you; nay, you do not even listen to any
unless he speak concerning Jesus Christ in truth.

VII

1. For there are some who make a practice of Warning
carrying about the Name with wicked guile, and do against
heretical
certain other things unworthy of God; these you preachers
must shun as wild beasts, for they are ravening
dogs, who bite secretly, and you must be upon your
guard against them, for they are scarcely to be
cured.   2. There is one Physician, who is both flesh
and spirit, born and yet not born, who is God in
man, true life in death, both of Mary and of God,
first passible and then impassible, Jesus Christ our
Lord.

VIII

1. Let none therefore deceive you, and indeed you Praise of the
have not been deceived, but belong wholly to God. Ephesians
For since no strife is fixed among you which might

σαι, ἄρα κατὰ θεὸν ζῆτε. περίψημα ὑμῶν καὶ
ἁγνίζομαι ὑμῶν Ἐφεσίων, ἐκκλησίας τῆς διαβοή-
Rom. 8, 5. 8 του τοῖς αἰῶσιν. 2. οἱ σαρκικοὶ τὰ πνευματικὰ
πράσσειν οὐ δύνανται, οὐδὲ οἱ πνευματικοὶ τὰ
σαρκικά, ὥσπερ οὐδὲ ἡ πίστις τὰ τῆς ἀπιστίας
οὐδὲ ἡ ἀπιστία τὰ τῆς πίστεως. ἃ δὲ καὶ κατὰ
σάρκα πράσσετε, ταῦτα πνευματικά ἐστιν· ἐν
Ἰησοῦ γὰρ Χριστῷ πάντα πράσσετε.

IX

1. Ἔγνων δὲ παροδεύσαντάς τινας ἐκεῖθεν, ἔχοντας κακὴν διδαχήν· οὓς οὐκ εἰάσατε σπεῖραι εἰς
ὑμᾶς, βύσαντες τὰ ὦτα, εἰς τὸ μὴ παραδέξασθαι
τὰ σπειρόμενα ὑπ' αὐτῶν, ὡς ὄντες λίθοι ναοῦ
πατρός, ἡτοιμασμένοι [1] εἰς οἰκοδομὴν θεοῦ πατρός,
ἀναφερόμενοι εἰς τὰ ὕψη διὰ τῆς μηχανῆς Ἰησοῦ
Χριστοῦ, ὅς ἐστιν σταυρός, σχοινίῳ χρώμενοι τῷ
πνεύματι τῷ ἁγίῳ· ἡ δὲ πίστις ὑμῶν ἀναγωγεὺς
ὑμῶν, ἡ δὲ ἀγάπη ὁδὸς ἡ ἀναφέρουσα εἰς θεόν.
2. ἐστὲ οὖν καὶ σύνοδοι πάντες, θεοφόροι καὶ
ναοφόροι, χριστοφόροι, ἁγιοφόροι, κατὰ πάντα
κεκοσμημένοι ἐντολαῖς Ἰησοῦ Χριστοῦ· οἷς

---

[1] Lightfoot emends πατρὸς (written π̄ρ̄ς̄) ἡτοιμασμένοι into
προητοιμασμένοι.

torture you, you do indeed live according to God. I am dedicated [1] and devoted to you Ephesians, and your Church, which is famous to eternity. 2. They who are carnal cannot do spiritual things, neither can they who are spiritual do carnal things, just as faith is incapable of the deeds of infidelity, and infidelity of the deeds of faith. But even what you do according to the flesh is spiritual, for you do all things in Jesus Christ.

IX

1. I HAVE learnt, however, that some from else-where have stayed with you, who have evil doctrine; but you did not suffer them to sow it among you, and stopped your ears, so that you might not receive what they sow, seeing that you are as stones of the temple of the Father, made ready for the building of God our Father, carried up to the heights by the engine of Jesus Christ, that is the cross, and using as a rope the Holy Spirit. And your faith is your windlass and love is the road which leads up to God. 2. You are then all fellow travellers, and carry with you God, and the Temple, and Christ, and holiness, and are in all ways adorned by commandments of Jesus Christ. And I

Their abstinence from heresy

---

[1] Lit. "The refuse of": the word was used of criminals and others whose death was regarded as a piacular sacrifice, and so it came to mean a sacrifice of this kind. Ultimately it lost its meaning so far as to become merely a form of epistolary politeness.

καὶ ἀγαλλιώμενος ἠξιώθην δι᾽ ὧν γράφω προσομιλῆσαι ὑμῖν καὶ συγχαρῆναι, ὅτι κατ᾽ ἀνθρώπων[1] βίον οὐδὲν ἀγαπᾶτε εἰ μὴ μόνον τὸν θεόν.

X

Thess. 5, 17

1. Καὶ ὑπὲρ τῶν ἄλλων δὲ ἀνθρώπων ἀδιαλείπτως προσεύχεσθε, ἔστιν γὰρ ἐν αὐτοῖς ἐλπὶς μετανοίας, ἵνα θεοῦ τύχωσιν. ἐπιτρέψατε οὖν αὐτοῖς κἂν ἐκ τῶν ἔργων ὑμῖν μαθητευθῆναι. 2. πρὸς τὰς ὀργὰς αὐτῶν ὑμεῖς πραεῖς, πρὸς τὰς μεγαλορημοσύνας αὐτῶν ὑμεῖς ταπεινόφρονες, πρὸς τὰς βλασφημίας αὐτῶν ὑμεῖς τὰς προσευχάς, πρὸς

Col. 1, 23; cf. Rom. 4, 20; I Cor. 16, 13

τὴν πλάνην αὐτῶν ὑμεῖς ἑδραῖοι τῇ πίστει, πρὸς τὸ ἄγριον αὐτῶν ὑμεῖς ἥμεροι, μὴ σπουδάζοντες ἀντιμιμήσασθαι αὐτούς. 3. ἀδελφοὶ αὐτῶν εὑρεθῶμεν τῇ ἐπιεικείᾳ· μιμηταὶ δὲ τοῦ κυρίου σπουδάζωμεν εἶναι, τίς πλέον ἀδικηθῇ, τίς ἀποστερηθῇ, τίς ἀθετηθῇ· ἵνα μὴ τοῦ διαβόλου βοτάνη τις εὑρεθῇ ἐν ὑμῖν, ἀλλ᾽ ἐν πάσῃ ἁγνείᾳ καὶ σωφροσύνῃ μένητε[2] ἐν Ἰησοῦ Χριστῷ σαρκικῶς καὶ πνευματικῶς.

XI

1. Ἔσχατοι καιροί. λοιπὸν αἰσχυνθῶμεν, φοβηθῶμεν τὴν μακροθυμίαν τοῦ θεοῦ, ἵνα μὴ ἡμῖν εἰς

[1] This is Lightfoot's emendation : GL read κατ᾽ ἄλλον βίον. A seems to imply the same reading, but it gives no good meaning and g reads οὐδὲ κατὰ σάρκα ἀγαπᾶτε ἀλλὰ κατὰ θεόν (you do not love according to the flesh but according to God), a paraphrase which may be taken to imply Lightfoot's reading.

[2] G reads μένετε, "but remain."

share in this joy, for it has been granted to me to speak to you through my writing, and to rejoice with you, that you love nothing, according to human life, but God alone.

X

1. Now for other men "pray unceasingly," for there is in them a hope of repentance, that they may find God. Suffer them therefore to become your disciples, at least through your deeds. 2. Be yourselves gentle in answer to their wrath; be humble minded in answer to their proud speaking; offer prayer for their blasphemy; be stedfast in the faith for their error; be gentle for their cruelty, and do not seek to retaliate. 3. Let us be proved their brothers by our gentleness and let us be imitators of the Lord, and seek who may suffer the more wrong, be the more destitute, the more despised; that no plant of the devil be found in you but that you may remain in all purity and sobriety in Jesus Christ, both in the flesh and in the Spirit.

Exhortation to prayer and lowliness

XI

1. THESE are the last times. Therefore let us be modest, let us fear the long-suffering of God, that it

The approach of the end: the fear of God

THE APOSTOLIC FATHERS

κρίμα γένηται. ἢ γὰρ τὴν μέλλουσαν ὀργὴν φοβηθῶμεν, ἢ τὴν ἐνεστῶσαν χάριν ἀγαπήσωμεν, ἓν
τῶν δύο· μόνον ἐν Χριστῷ Ἰησοῦ εὑρεθῆναι εἰς τὸ
ἀληθινὸν ζῆν. 2. χωρὶς τούτου μηδὲν ὑμῖν πρε-
πέτω, ἐν ᾧ τὰ δεσμὰ περιφέρω, τοὺς πνευματικοὺς
μαργαρίτας, ἐν οἷς γένοιτό μοι ἀναστῆναι τῇ προσευχῇ ὑμῶν, ἧς γένοιτό μοι ἀεὶ μέτοχον εἶναι, ἵνα
ἐν κλήρῳ Ἐφεσίων εὑρεθῶ τῶν Χριστιανῶν, οἳ
καὶ τοῖς ἀποστόλοις πάντοτε συνῄνεσαν ἐν δυνάμει
Ἰησοῦ Χριστοῦ.

XII

1. Οἶδα, τίς εἰμι καὶ τίσιν γράφω. ἐγὼ κατάκριτος, ὑμεῖς ἠλεημένοι· ἐγὼ ὑπὸ κίνδυνον, ὑμεῖς
ἐστηριγμένοι· 2. πάροδός ἐστε τῶν εἰς θεὸν ἀναι-
ρουμένων, Παύλου συμμύσται τοῦ ἡγιασμένου.
τοῦ μεμαρτυρημένου, ἀξιομακαρίστου, οὗ γένοιτό
μοι ὑπὸ τὰ ἴχνη εὑρεθῆναι, ὅταν θεοῦ ἐπιτύχω,
ὃς ἐν πάσῃ ἐπιστολῇ μνημονεύει ὑμῶν ἐν Χριστῷ
Ἰησοῦ.

XIII

1. Σπουδάζετε οὖν πυκνότερον συνέρχεσθαι εἰς
εὐχαριστίαν θεοῦ καὶ εἰς δόξαν. ὅταν γὰρ πυκνῶς
ἐπὶ τὸ αὐτὸ γίνεσθε, καθαιροῦνται αἱ δυνάμεις τοῦ
Σατανᾶ, καὶ λύεται ὁ ὄλεθρος αὐτοῦ ἐν τῇ ὁμονοίᾳ
ὑμῶν τῆς πίστεως. 2. οὐδέν ἐστιν ἄμεινον εἰρήνης,
ἐν ᾗ πᾶς πόλεμος καταργεῖται ἐπουρανίων καὶ
ἐπιγείων.

may not become our judgment. For let us either
fear the wrath to come, or love the grace which is
present,—one of the two,—only let us be found in
Christ Jesus unto true life. 2. Without him let
nothing seem comely to you, for in him I carry
about my chains, the spiritual pearls in which may
it be granted me to rise again through your prayers,
which I beg that I may ever share, that I be found
in the lot of the Christians of Ephesus, who also
were ever of one mind with the Apostles in the
power of Jesus Christ.

XII

1. I ᴋɴᴏᴡ who I am and to whom I write. I am Contrast
condemned, you have obtained mercy; I am in himself
danger, you are established in safety ; 2. you are the and his
passage for those who are being slain for the sake of readers
God, fellow-initiates with Paul, who was sanctified,
who gained a good report, who was right blessed, in
whose footsteps may I be found when I shall attain
to God, who in every Epistle makes mention of
you in Christ Jesus.

XIII

1. Sᴇᴇᴋ, then, to come together more frequently Exhortation
to give thanks[1] and glory to God. For when you to more
gather together frequently the powers of Satan are assemblies
destroyed, and his mischief is brought to nothing,
by the concord of your faith. 2. There is nothing
better than peace, by which every war in heaven
and on earth is abolished.

[1] It is probable that there is here an allusion to the
Eucharist.

XIV

1. Ὧν οὐδὲν λανθάνει ὑμᾶς, ἐὰν τελείως εἰς
Ἰησοῦν Χριστὸν ἔχητε τὴν πίστιν καὶ τὴν ἀγάπην,
ἥτις ἐστὶν ἀρχὴ ζωῆς καὶ τέλος· ἀρχὴ μὲν πίστις,
τέλος δὲ ἀγάπη. τὰ δὲ δύο ἐν ἑνότητι γενόμενα
θεός ἐστιν, τὰ δὲ ἄλλα πάντα εἰς καλοκἀγαθίαν
ἀκόλουθά ἐστιν. 2. οὐδεὶς πίστιν ἐπαγγελλόμενος
ἁμαρτάνει, οὐδὲ ἀγάπην κεκτημένος μισεῖ. φανερὸν
τὸ δένδρον ἀπὸ τοῦ καρποῦ αὐτοῦ. οὕτως οἱ ἐπαγ-
γελλόμενοι Χριστοῦ εἶναι δι᾽ ὧν πράσσουσιν
ὀφθήσονται. οὐ γὰρ νῦν ἐπαγγελίας τὸ ἔργον,
ἀλλ᾽ ἐν δυνάμει πίστεως ἐάν τις εὑρεθῇ εἰς τέλος.

I Tim. 1, 5

Mt. 12, 33

XV

1. Ἄμεινόν ἐστιν σιωπᾶν καὶ εἶναι, ἢ λαλοῦντα
μὴ εἶναι. καλὸν τὸ διδάσκειν, ἐὰν ὁ λέγων ποιῇ. εἷς
οὖν διδάσκαλος, ὃς εἶπεν, καὶ ἐγένετο· καὶ ἃ σιγῶν
δὲ πεποίηκεν ἄξια τοῦ πατρός ἐστιν. 2. ὁ λόγον
Ἰησοῦ κεκτημένος ἀληθῶς δύναται καὶ τῆς ἡσυ-
χίας αὐτοῦ ἀκούειν, ἵνα τέλειος ᾖ, ἵνα δι᾽ ὧν λαλεῖ
πράσσῃ καὶ δι᾽ ὧν σιγᾷ γινώσκηται. 3. οὐδὲν
λανθάνει τὸν κύριον, ἀλλὰ καὶ τὰ κρυπτὰ ἡμῶν
ἐγγὺς αὐτῷ ἐστιν. πάντα οὖν ποιῶμεν ὡς αὐτοῦ ἐν
ἡμῖν κατοικοῦντος, ἵνα ὦμεν αὐτοῦ ναοὶ καὶ αὐτὸς
ἐν ἡμῖν θεὸς ἡμῶν·[1] ὅπερ καὶ ἔστιν καὶ φανήσεται
πρὸ προσώπου ἡμῶν, ἐξ ὧν δικαίως ἀγαπῶμεν
αὐτόν.

Ps. 33, 9;
148, 5;
Judith 16, 14

I Cor. 3, 16

---

[1] ἐν ἡμῖν θεὸς ἡμῶν GL, ἐν ἡμῖν θεός Sg, θεὸς ἡμῶν A.

XIV

1. None of these things are unknown to you if Faith and Love you possess perfect faith towards Jesus Christ, and love, which are the beginning and end of life ; for the beginning is faith and the end is love, and when the two are joined together in unity it is God, and all other noble things follow after them. 2. No man who professes faith sins, nor does he hate who has obtained love. "The tree is known by its fruits " : so they who profess to be of Christ shall be seen by their deeds. For the " deed " is not in present profession, but is shown by the power of faith, if a man continue to the end.

XV

1. It is better to be silent and be real, than to Speech and silence talk and to be unreal. Teaching is good, if the teacher does what he says. There is then one teacher who "spoke and it came to pass," and what he has done even in silence is worthy of the Father. 2. He who has the word of Jesus for a true possession can also hear his silence, that he may be perfect, that he may act through his speech, and be understood through his silence. 3. Nothing is hid from the Lord, but even our secret things are near him. Let us therefore do all things as though he were dwelling in us, that we may be his temples, and that he may be our God in us.   This indeed is so, and will appear clearly before our face by the love which we justly have to him.

XVI

I Cor. 6, 9.
10;
cf. Eph. 5, 5

1. Μὴ πλανᾶσθε, ἀδελφοί μου· οἱ οἰκοφθόροι βασιλείαν θεοῦ οὐ κληρονομήσουσιν. 2. εἰ οὖν οἱ κατὰ σάρκα ταῦτα πράσσοντες ἀπέθανον, πόσῳ μᾶλλον, ἐὰν πίστιν θεοῦ ἐν κακῇ διδασκαλίᾳ φθείρῃ, ὑπὲρ ἧς Ἰησοῦς Χριστὸς ἐσταυρώθη; ὁ τοιοῦτος ῥυπαρὸς γενόμενος, εἰς τὸ πῦρ τὸ ἄσβεστον χωρήσει, ὁμοίως καὶ ὁ ἀκούων αὐτοῦ.

XVII

Mt. 26, 7;
Joh. 12, 3

1. Διὰ τοῦτο μύρον ἔλαβεν ἐπὶ τῆς κεφαλῆς αὐτοῦ ὁ κύριος, ἵνα πνέῃ τῇ ἐκκλησίᾳ ἀφθαρσίαν. μὴ ἀλείφεσθε δυσωδίαν τῆς διδασκαλίας τοῦ ἄρχοντος τοῦ αἰῶνος τούτου, μὴ αἰχμαλωτίσῃ ὑμᾶς ἐκ τοῦ προκειμένου ζῆν. 2. διὰ τί δὲ οὐ πάντες φρόνιμοι γινόμεθα λαβόντες θεοῦ γνῶσιν, ὅ ἐστιν Ἰησοῦς Χριστός; τί μωρῶς ἀπολλύμεθα, ἀγνοοῦντες τὸ χάρισμα, ὃ πέπομφεν ἀληθῶς ὁ κύριος;

XVIII

Gal. 5. 11
I Cor. 1, 20

1. Περίψημα τὸ ἐμὸν πνεῦμα τοῦ σταυροῦ, ὅ ἐστιν σκάνδαλον τοῖς ἀπιστοῦσιν, ἡμῖν δὲ σωτηρία καὶ ζωὴ αἰώνιος. ποῦ σοφός; ποῦ συζητητής; ποῦ καύχησις τῶν λεγομένων συνετῶν; 2. ὁ γὰρ θεὸς ἡμῶν Ἰησοῦς ὁ Χριστὸς ἐκυοφορήθη ὑπὸ

XVI

1. Do not err, my brethren ; they who corrupt Warning against false teachers families shall not inherit the kingdom of God. 2. If then those who do this according to the flesh suffer death, how much more if a man corrupt by false teaching the faith of God for the sake of which Jesus Christ was crucified ? Such a one shall go in his foulness to the unquenchable fire, as also shall he who listens to him.

XVII

1. For this end did the Lord receive ointment on his head that he might breathe immortality on the Church. Be not anointed with the evil odour of the doctrine of the Prince of this world, lest he lead you away captive from the life which is set before you. 2. But why are we not all prudent seeing that we have received knowledge of God, that is, Jesus Christ? Why are we perishing in our folly, ignoring the gift which the Lord has truly sent ?

XVIII

1. My spirit is devoted[1] to the cross, which is an True doctrine offence to unbelievers, but to us salvation and eternal life. " Where is the wise ? Where is the disputer ? " Where is the boasting of those who are called prudent ? 2. For our God, Jesus the Christ,

[1] See note on viii. 1, p. 183.

THE APOSTOLIC FATHERS

Joh. 7, 42 ;
Rom. 1, 3 ;
II Tim. 2, 8
Μαρίας κατ' οἰκονομίαν θεοῦ[1] ἐκ σπέρματος μὲν
Δαυείδ, πνεύματος δὲ ἁγίου· ὃς ἐγεννήθη καὶ
ἐβαπτίσθη, ἵνα τῷ πάθει τὸ ὕδωρ καθαρίσῃ.

XIX

1. Καὶ ἔλαθεν τὸν ἄρχοντα τοῦ αἰῶνος τούτου
ἡ παρθενία Μαρίας καὶ ὁ τοκετὸς αὐτῆς, ὁμοίως
καὶ ὁ θάνατος τοῦ κυρίου· τρία μυστήρια κραυγῆς,
ἅτινα ἐν ἡσυχίᾳ θεοῦ ἐπράχθη. 2. πῶς οὖν
ἐφανερώθη τοῖς αἰῶσιν; ἀστὴρ ἐν οὐρανῷ ἔλαμψεν
ὑπὲρ πάντας τοὺς ἀστέρας, καὶ τὸ φῶς αὐτοῦ
ἀνεκλάλητον ἦν καὶ ξενισμὸν παρεῖχεν ἡ καινότης
αὐτοῦ, τὰ δὲ λοιπὰ πάντα ἄστρα ἅμα ἡλίῳ καὶ
σελήνῃ χορὸς ἐγένετο τῷ ἀστέρι, αὐτὸς δὲ ἦν
ὑπερβάλλων τὸ φῶς αὐτοῦ ὑπὲρ πάντα· ταραχή
τε ἦν, πόθεν ἡ καινότης ἡ ἀνόμοιος αὐτοῖς.
3. ὅθεν ἐλύετο πᾶσα μαγεία καὶ πᾶς δεσμὸς
ἠφανίζετο κακίας· ἄγνοια καθῃρεῖτο, παλαιὰ βασιλεία διεφθείρετο[2] θεοῦ ἀνθρωπίνως φανερουμένου
Rom. 6, 4
εἰς καινότητα ἀιδίου ζωῆς· ἀρχὴν δὲ ἐλάμβανεν
τὸ παρὰ θεῷ ἀπηρτισμένον. ἔνθεν τὰ πάντα
συνεκινεῖτο διὰ τὸ μελετᾶσθαι θανάτου κατά-
λυσιν.

---

[1] Lightfoot omits θεοῦ on the authority of g and transcriptional probability.

[2] Lightfoot omits διεφθείρετο, and readjusts the punctuation,
on the authority of ΑΣ.

was conceived by Mary by the dispensation of God, "as well of the seed of David" as of the Holy Spirit: he was born, and was baptized, that by himself submitting [1] he might purify the water.

XIX

1. AND the virginity of Mary, and her giving birth were hidden from the Prince of this world, as was also the death of the Lord. Three mysteries of a cry which were wrought in the stillness of God. 2. How then was he manifested to the world? A star shone in heaven beyond all the stars, and its light was unspeakable, and its newness caused astonishment, and all the other stars, with the sun and moon, gathered in chorus [2] round this star, and it far exceeded them all in its light; and there was perplexity, whence came this new thing, so unlike them. 3. By this all magic was dissolved and every bond of wickedness vanished away, ignorance was removed, and the old kingdom was destroyed, for God was manifest as man for the "newness" of eternal life, and that which had been prepared by God received its beginning. Hence all things were disturbed, because the abolition of death was being planned.

The mystery of the Nativity and its manifestation

---

[1] Or perhaps "by his suffering"; but the allusion seems to be to the Baptism, not to the Passion.
[2] Cf. Ign. Rom. ii. The metaphor is probably from the chorus or choir which gathered round the altar in heathen ceremonial, and sang a sacrificial hymn.

XX

1. Ἐάν με καταξιώσῃ Ἰησοῦς Χριστὸς ἐν τῇ προσευχῇ ὑμῶν καὶ θέλημα ᾖ, ἐν τῷ δευτέρῳ βιβλιδίῳ, ὃ μέλλω γράφειν ὑμῖν, προσδηλώσω ὑμῖν, ἧς ἠρξάμην οἰκονομίας εἰς τὸν καινὸν ἄνθρωπον Ἰησοῦν Χριστόν, ἐν τῇ αὐτοῦ πίστει καὶ ἐν τῇ αὐτοῦ ἀγάπῃ, ἐν πάθει αὐτοῦ καὶ ἀναστάσει· 2. μάλιστα ἐὰν ὁ κύριός μοι ἀποκαλύψῃ, ὅτι[1] οἱ κατ᾽ ἄνδρα κοινῇ πάντες ἐν χάριτι ἐξ ὀνόματος συνέρχεσθε ἐν μιᾷ πίστει καὶ ἐν[2] Ἰησοῦ Χριστῷ,

Rom. 1, 3

τῷ κατὰ σάρκα ἐκ γένους Δαυείδ, τῷ υἱῷ ἀνθρώπου καὶ υἱῷ θεοῦ, εἰς τὸ ὑπακούειν ὑμᾶς τῷ ἐπισκόπῳ καὶ τῷ πρεσβυτερίῳ ἀπερισπάστῳ διανοίᾳ, ἕνα ἄρτον κλῶντες, ὅς ἐστιν φάρμακον ἀθανασίας, ἀντίδοτος τοῦ μὴ ἀποθανεῖν, ἀλλὰ ζῆν ἐν Ἰησοῦ Χριστῷ διὰ παντός.

XXI

1. Ἀντίψυχον ὑμῶν ἐγὼ καὶ ὧν ἐπέμψατε εἰς θεοῦ τιμὴν εἰς Σμύρναν, ὅθεν καὶ γράφω ὑμῖν, εὐχαριστῶν τῷ κυρίῳ, ἀγαπῶν Πολύκαρπον ὡς καὶ ὑμᾶς· μνημονεύετέ μου, ὡς καὶ ὑμῶν Ἰησοῦς Χριστός. 2. προσεύχεσθε ὑπὲρ τῆς ἐκκλησίας

---

[1] Zahn and, with some hesitation, Lightfoot emend ὅτι to τι, connecting it with ἀποκαλύψῃ. If so the translation would be "if the Lord reveal anything to me. Join in the common meeting, etc."

[2] Theodoret quotes this as ἑνὶ I. X. "one Jesus Christ," and Lightfoot accepts this reading.

XX

1. IF Jesus Christ permit me through your prayers, and it be his will, in the second book,[1] which I propose to write to you, I will show you concerning the dispensation of the new man Jesus Christ, which I have begun to discuss, dealing with his faith and his love, his suffering and his resurrection ; 2. especially if the Lord reveal[2] to me that you all severally join in the common meeting in grace from his name,[3] in one faith and in Jesus Christ, "who was of the family of David according to the flesh," the Son of Man and the Son of God, so that you obey the bishop and the presbytery with an undisturbed mind, breaking one bread, which is the medicine of immortality, the antidote that we should not die, but live for ever in Jesus Christ.

Promise of future doctrinal exposition

XXI

1. MAY my soul be given for yours, and for them whom you sent in the honour of God to Smyrna, whence I also write to you, thanking the Lord and loving Polycarp as I do also you. Remember me as Jesus Christ also remembers you. 2. Pray for the

Final greetings

---

[1] This second book was either never written, or at all events is not extant in the genuine recension : but a later editor has supplied a "second epistle to the Ephesians" which is undoubtedly not genuine.

[2] This appears to be the only possible translation. But the text is not improbably corrupt.

[3] Or possibly, as Lightfoot thinks, ἐξ ὀνόματος means "every individual of you." It is in any case a strange phrase.

τῆς ἐν Συρίᾳ, ὅθεν δεδεμένος εἰς Ῥώμην ἀπάγομαι, ἔσχατος ὢν τῶν ἐκεῖ πιστῶν, ὥσπερ ἠξιώθην εἰς τιμὴν θεοῦ εὑρεθῆναι. ἔρρωσθε ἐν θεῷ πατρὶ καὶ ἐν Ἰησοῦ Χριστῷ, τῇ κοινῇ ἐλπίδι ἡμῶν.

ΜΑΓΝΗΣΙΕΥΣΙΝ ΙΓΝΑΤΙΟΣ

Ἰγνάτιος, ὁ καὶ Θεοφόρος, τῇ εὐλογημένῃ ἐν χάριτι θεοῦ πατρὸς ἐν Χριστῷ Ἰησοῦ τῷ σωτῆρι ἡμῶν, ἐν ᾧ ἀσπάζομαι τὴν ἐκκλησίαν τὴν οὖσαν ἐν Μαγνησίᾳ τῇ πρὸς Μαιάνδρῳ καὶ εὔχομαι ἐν θεῷ πατρὶ καὶ ἐν Ἰησοῦ Χριστῷ πλεῖστα χαίρειν.

I

1. Γνοὺς ὑμῶν τὸ πολυεύτακτον τῆς κατὰ θεὸν ἀγάπης, ἀγαλλιώμενος προειλόμην ἐν πίστει Ἰησοῦ Χριστοῦ προσλαλῆσαι ὑμῖν. 2. καταξιωθεὶς γὰρ ὀνόματος θεοπρεπεστάτου, ἐν οἷς περιφέρω δεσμοῖς ᾄδω τὰς ἐκκλησίας, ἐν αἷς ἕνωσιν εὔχομαι σαρκὸς καὶ πνεύματος Ἰησοῦ Χριστοῦ, τοῦ διὰ παντὸς ἡμῶν ζῆν, πίστεώς τε καὶ ἀγάπης, ἧς οὐδὲν προκέκριται, τὸ δὲ κυριώτερον Ἰησοῦ καὶ πατρός· ἐν ᾧ ὑπομένοντες τὴν πᾶσαν ἐπήρειαν τοῦ ἄρχοντος τοῦ αἰῶνος τούτου καὶ διαφυγόντες θεοῦ τευξόμεθα.

Church in Syria, whence I am led a prisoner to
Rome, being the least of the faithful who are there,
even as I was thought worthy to show the honour of
God. Farewell in God our Father and in Jesus
Christ, our common hope.

———————

II.—IGNATIUS TO THE MAGNESIANS.

Ignatius, who is also called Theophorus, to her[1] Greetings
who is blessed in the Grace of God the
Father by Christ Jesus, our Saviour, in whom
I greet the Church which is in Magnesia on
the Maeander, and bid it in God the Father
and in Christ Jesus abundant greeting.

I

1. Knowing the great orderliness of your love Prayer
towards God I gladly determined to address you in the for the
faith of Jesus Christ. 2. For being counted worthy church
to bear a most godly name I sing the praise of the
Churches in the bonds which I carry about, and pray
that in them there may be a union of the flesh and
spirit of Jesus Christ, who is our everlasting life, a
union of faith and love, to which is nothing preferable,
and (what is more than all) a union of Jesus and the
Father. If we endure in him all the evil treatment
of the Prince of this world and escape, we shall
attain unto God.

[1] *i.e.* the Church.

II

1. Ἐπεὶ οὖν ἠξιώθην ἰδεῖν ὑμᾶς διὰ Δαμᾶ τοῦ ἀξιοθέου ὑμῶν ἐπισκόπου καὶ πρεσβυτέρων ἀξίων Βάσσου καὶ Ἀπολλωνίου καὶ τοῦ συνδούλου μου διακόνου Ζωτίωνος, οὗ ἐγὼ ὀναίμην, ὅτι ὑποτάσσεται τῷ ἐπισκόπῳ ὡς χάριτι θεοῦ καὶ τῷ πρεσβυτερίῳ ὡς νόμῳ Ἰησοῦ Χριστοῦ.'

III

1. Καὶ ὑμῖν δὲ πρέπει μὴ συγχρᾶσθαι τῇ ἡλικίᾳ τοῦ ἐπισκόπου, ἀλλὰ κατὰ δύναμιν θεοῦ πατρὸς πᾶσαν ἐντροπὴν αὐτῷ ἀπονέμειν, καθὼς ἔγνων καὶ τοὺς ἁγίους πρεσβυτέρους οὐ προσειληφότας τὴν φαινομένην νεωτερικὴν τάξιν, ἀλλ' ὡς φρονίμους [1] ἐν θεῷ συγχωροῦντας αὐτῷ, οὐκ αὐτῷ δέ, ἀλλὰ τῷ πατρὶ Ἰησοῦ Χριστοῦ, τῷ πάντων ἐπισκόπῳ. 2. εἰς τιμὴν οὖν ἐκείνου τοῦ θελήσαντος ἡμᾶς [2] πρέπον ἐστὶν ἐπακούειν κατὰ μηδεμίαν ὑπόκρισιν· ἐπεὶ οὐχ ὅτι τὸν ἐπίσκοπον τοῦτον τὸν βλεπόμενον πλανᾷ τις, ἀλλὰ τὸν ἀόρατον παραλογίζεται. τὸ δὲ τοιοῦτον οὐ πρὸς σάρκα ὁ λόγος, ἀλλὰ πρὸς θεὸν τὸν τὰ κρύφια εἰδότα.

[1] Lightfoot reads φρονίμῳ "as to one prudent in God" with Ag.: it certainly gives a better sense, but for that reason may be a correction.
[2] ἡμᾶς GL, ὑμᾶς Ag.

II

1. FORASMUCH then as I was permitted to see you in the person of Damas, your godly bishop, and the worthy presbyters Bassus and Apollonius, and my fellow servant the deacon Zotion, whose friendship I would enjoy because he is subject to the bishop as to the grace of God, and to the presbytery as to the law of Jesus Christ,——[1]

The representatives of the Magnesians

III

1. Now it becomes you not to presume on the youth of the bishop, but to render him all respect according to the power of God the Father, as I have heard that even the holy presbyters have not taken advantage of his outwardly youthful appearance, but yield to him in their godly prudence, yet not to him, but to the Father of Jesus Christ, to the bishop of all. 2. For the honour therefore of him who desired us, it is right that we yield obedience without hypocrisy, for a man does not merely deceive this bishop who is seen, but is dealing wrongly with him who is invisible. And in this matter his reckoning is not with flesh, but with God, who knows the secret things.

The bishop of Magnesia

---

[1] The sentence is unfinished : possibly the text is corrupt.

IV

1. Πρέπον οὖν ἐστιν μὴ μόνον καλεῖσθαι Χρισ-
τιανούς, ἀλλὰ καὶ εἶναι· ὥσπερ καί τινες ἐπίσκοπον μὲν καλοῦσιν, χωρὶς δὲ αὐτοῦ πάντα
πράσσουσιν. οἱ τοιοῦτοι δὲ οὐκ εὐσυνείδητοί μοι
εἶναι φαίνονται διὰ τὸ μὴ βεβαίως κατ᾽ ἐντολὴν
συναθροίζεσθαι.

V

1. Ἐπεὶ οὖν τέλος τὰ πράγματα ἔχει καὶ πρόκειται τὰ δύο ὁμοῦ, ὅ τε θάνατος καὶ ἡ ζωή, καὶ
Acts. 1, 25 ἕκαστος εἰς τὸν ἴδιον τόπον μέλλει χωρεῖν·
2. ὥσπερ γάρ ἐστιν νομίσματα δύο, ὃ μὲν θεοῦ,
ὃ δὲ κόσμου, καὶ ἕκαστον αὐτῶν ἴδιον χαρακτῆρα
ἐπικείμενον ἔχει, οἱ ἄπιστοι τοῦ κόσμου τούτου,
οἱ δὲ πιστοὶ ἐν ἀγάπῃ χαρακτῆρα θεοῦ πατρὸς διὰ
Ἰησοῦ Χριστοῦ, δι᾽ οὗ ἐὰν μὴ αὐθαιρέτως ἔχωμεν
τὸ ἀποθανεῖν εἰς τὸ αὐτοῦ πάθος, τὸ ζῆν αὐτοῦ
οὐκ ἔστιν ἐν ἡμῖν.

VI

1. Ἐπεὶ οὖν ἐν τοῖς προγεγραμμένοις προσώ-
ποις τὸ πᾶν πλῆθος ἐθεώρησα ἐν πίστει καὶ ἠγάπ-
ησα, παραινῶ, ἐν ὁμονοίᾳ θεοῦ σπουδάζετε πάντα
πράσσειν, προκαθημένου τοῦ ἐπισκόπου εἰς τόπον[1]

---

[1] τόπον GLg, τύπον SA, and so also in the next line. Cf.
Trall. iii. Lightfoot prefers τύπον, but it seems to be more
probably a softening of the rather startling τόπον by the
Syriac translator.

IV

1. It is right, then, that we should be really
Christians, and not merely have the name; even as
there are some who recognize the bishop in their
words, but disregard him in all their actions. Such
men seem to me not to act in good faith, since they
do not hold valid meetings according to the commandment.

V

1. Seeing then that there is an end to all, that the
choice is between two things, death and life, and that
each is to go to his own place; 2. for, just as there
are two coinages,[1] the one of God, the other of the
world, and each has its own stamp impressed on it, so
the unbelievers bear the stamp of this world, and the
believers the stamp of God the Father in love
through Jesus Christ, and unless we willingly choose
to die through him in his passion, his life is not
in us.

VI

1. Seeing then that I have looked on the whole congregation in faith in the persons mentioned above,
and have embraced them, I exhort you :—Be zealous
to do all things in harmony with God, with the bishop

---

[1] This is perhaps a reference to Mt. xxii. 19.

θεοῦ καὶ τῶν πρεσβυτέρων εἰς τόπον συνεδρίου
τῶν ἀποστόλων, καὶ τῶν διακόνων τῶν ἐμοὶ γλυ-
κυτάτων πεπιστευμένων διακονίαν Ἰησοῦ Χριστοῦ,
ὃς πρὸ αἰώνων παρὰ πατρὶ ἦν καὶ ἐν τέλει ἐφάνη.
2. πάντες οὖν ὁμοήθειαν θεοῦ λαβόντες ἐντρέπεσθε ἀλλήλους καὶ μηδεὶς κατὰ σάρκα βλεπέτω
τὸν πλησίον, ἀλλ᾽ ἐν Ἰησοῦ Χριστῷ ἀλλήλους διὰ
παντὸς ἀγαπᾶτε. μηδὲν ἔστω ἐν ὑμῖν, ὃ δυνήσεται ὑμᾶς μερίσαι ἀλλ᾽ ἑνώθητε τῷ ἐπισκόπῳ
καὶ τοῖς προκαθημένοις εἰς τύπον καὶ διδαχὴν
ἀφθαρσίας.

VII

Joh. 5, 19.
30 ; 8, 28

1. Ὥσπερ οὖν ὁ κύριος ἄνευ τοῦ πατρὸς οὐδὲν
ἐποίησεν, ἡνωμένος ὤν, οὔτε δι᾽ ἑαυτοῦ οὔτε διὰ
τῶν ἀποστόλων · οὕτως μηδὲ ὑμεῖς ἄνευ τοῦ ἐπισκόπου καὶ τῶν πρεσβυτέρων μηδὲν πράσσετε·
μηδὲ πειράσητε εὔλογόν τι φαίνεσθαι ἰδίᾳ ὑμῖν,
ἀλλ᾽ ἐπὶ τὸ αὐτὸ μία προσευχή, μία δέησις, εἷς
νοῦς, μία ἐλπὶς ἐν ἀγάπῃ, ἐν τῇ χαρᾷ τῇ ἀμώμῳ,
ὅ ἐστιν Ἰησοῦς Χριστός, οὗ ἄμεινον οὐδέν ἐστιν.
2. πάντες ὡς εἰς ἕνα ναὸν συντρέχετε θεοῦ, ὡς
ἐπὶ ἓν θυσιαστήριον, ἐπὶ ἕνα Ἰησοῦν Χριστόν, τὸν
ἀφ᾽ ἑνὸς πατρὸς προελθόντα καὶ εἰς ἕνα ὄντα καὶ
χωρήσαντα.

presiding in the place of God and the presbyters in the place of the Council of the Apostles, and the deacons,[1] who are most dear to me, entrusted with the service of Jesus Christ, who was from eternity with the Father and was made manifest at the end of time. 2. Be then all in conformity with God, and respect one another, and let no man regard his neighbour according to the flesh, but in everything love one another in Jesus Christ. Let there be nothing in you which can divide you, but be united with the bishop and with those who preside over you as an example and lesson of immortality.

VII

1. As then the Lord was united to the Father and did nothing without him, neither by himself nor through the Apostles, so do you do nothing without the bishop and the presbyters. Do not attempt to make anything appear right for you by yourselves, but let there be in common one prayer, one supplication, one mind, one hope in love, in the joy which is without fault, that is Jesus Christ, than whom there is nothing better. 2. Hasten all to come together as to one temple of God, as to one altar, to one Jesus Christ, who came forth from the one Father, and is with one, and departed to one.

Obedience to the bishop and presbyters

---

[1] The sentences seem to be unfinished: the Apostolic Constitutions ii. 26 say " Let the Deacon be honoured as a type of Holy Spirit."

VIII

1. Μὴ πλανᾶσθε ταῖς ἑτεροδοξίαις μηδὲ μυθεύμασιν τοῖς παλαιοῖς ἀνωφελέσιν οὖσιν. εἰ γὰρ μέχρι νῦν κατὰ Ἰουδαϊσμὸν ζῶμεν, ὁμολογοῦμεν χάριν μὴ εἰληφέναι. 2. οἱ γὰρ θειότατοι προφῆται κατὰ Χριστὸν Ἰησοῦν ἔζησαν. διὰ τοῦτο καὶ ἐδιώχθησαν, ἐμπνεόμενοι ὑπὸ τῆς χάριτος αὐτοῦ, εἰς τὸ πληροφορηθῆναι τοὺς ἀπειθοῦντας, ὅτι εἷς θεός ἐστιν, ὁ φανερώσας ἑαυτὸν διὰ Ἰησοῦ Χριστοῦ τοῦ υἱοῦ αὐτοῦ, ὅς ἐστιν αὐτοῦ λόγος ἀπὸ σιγῆς προελθών,[1] ὃς κατὰ πάντα εὐηρέστησεν τῷ πέμψαντι αὐτόν.

IX

1. Εἰ οὖν οἱ ἐν παλαιοῖς πράγμασιν ἀναστραφέντες εἰς καινότητα ἐλπίδος ἦλθον, μηκέτι σαββατίζοντες, ἀλλὰ κατὰ κυριακὴν ζῶντες, ἐν ᾗ καὶ ἡ ζωὴ ἡμῶν ἀνέτειλεν δι᾽ αὐτοῦ καὶ τοῦ θανάτου αὐτοῦ, ὅν τινες[2] ἀρνοῦνται, δι᾽ οὗ μυστηρίου ἐλάβομεν τὸ πιστεύειν, καὶ διὰ τοῦτο ὑπομένομεν, ἵνα εὑρεθῶμεν μαθηταὶ Ἰησοῦ Χριστοῦ τοῦ μόνου διδασκάλου ἡμῶν· 2. πῶς ἡμεῖς δυνησόμεθα ζῆσαι χωρὶς αὐτοῦ, οὗ καὶ οἱ προφῆται μαθηταὶ

---

[1] So A and a quotation in Severus. GL read λόγος ἀΐδιος οὐκ ἀπὸ σιγῆς προελθών, but this is rightly regarded by recent editors as a doctrinal emendation due to fear of Gnostic theories in which Σιγή and Θεός were the original pair from which Λόγος emanated, cf. Clem. Alex. *Ecl. Theol.* ii. 9.

[2] ὅ τινες L, οἵ τινες G, g paraphrases but has ὅν not ὅ, A is ambiguous. There is thus a slight balance in favour of ὅν τινες.

VIII

1. BE not led astray by strange doctrines or by old Warning fables which are profitless. For if we are living against Judaism until now according to Judaism, we confess that we have not received grace. 2. For the divine prophets lived according to Jesus Christ. Therefore they were also persecuted, being inspired by his grace, to convince the disobedient that there is one God, who manifested himself through Jesus Christ his son, who is his Word proceeding from silence, who in all respects was well-pleasing to him that sent him.

IX

1. IF then they who walked in ancient customs Life with came to a new hope, no longer living for the Christ Sabbath, but for the Lord's Day, on which also our life sprang up through him and his death,—though some deny him,—and by this mystery we received faith, and for this reason also we suffer, that we may be found disciples of Jesus Christ our only teacher ; 2. if these things be so, how then shall we be able to live without him of whom even the prophets were disciples in the Spirit and to whom they looked

ὄντες τῷ πνεύματι ὡς διδάσκαλον αὐτὸν προσε-
δόκων; καὶ διὰ τοῦτο, ὃν δικαίως ἀνέμενον, παρὼν
Mt. 27, 52   ἤγειρεν αὐτοὺς ἐκ νεκρῶν.

X

1. Μὴ οὖν ἀναισθητῶμεν τῆς χρηστότητος
αὐτοῦ. ἐὰν γὰρ ἡμᾶς μιμήσηται καθὰ πράσ-
σομεν, οὐκέτι ἐσμέν. διὰ τοῦτο, μαθηταὶ αὐτοῦ
γενόμενοι, μάθωμεν κατὰ Χριστιανισμὸν ζῆν. ὃς
γὰρ ἄλλῳ ὀνόματι καλεῖται πλέον τούτου, οὐκ
ἔστιν τοῦ θεοῦ. 2. ὑπέρθεσθε οὖν τὴν κακὴν
I Cor. 5, 7   ζύμην, τὴν παλαιωθεῖσαν καὶ ἐνοξίσασαν, καὶ
μεταβάλεσθε εἰς νέαν ζύμην, ὅ ἐστιν Ἰησοῦς
Χριστός. ἁλίσθητε ἐν αὐτῷ, ἵνα μὴ διαφθαρῇ τις
ἐν ὑμῖν, ἐπεὶ ἀπὸ τῆς ὀσμῆς ἐλεγχθήσεσθε.
3. ἄτοπόν ἐστιν, Ἰησοῦν Χριστὸν λαλεῖν καὶ
ἰουδαΐζειν. ὁ γὰρ Χριστιανισμὸς οὐκ εἰς Ἰουδαϊσμὸν ἐπίστευσεν, ἀλλ' Ἰουδαϊσμὸς εἰς Χρισ-
Is. 66, 18   τιανισμόν, ᾧ[1] πᾶσα γλῶσσα πιστεύσασα εἰς
θεὸν συνήχθη.

---

[1] ᾧ S, ὡς GL, εἰς ὅν g (A).

forward as their teacher? And for this reason he whom they waited for in righteousness, when he came raised them from the dead.[1]

X

1. LET us then not be insensible to his goodness, for if he should imitate us in our actions we are lost.[2] For this cause let us be his disciples, and let us learn to lead Christian lives. For whoever is called by any name other than this is not of God. 2. Put aside then the evil leaven, which has grown old and sour, and turn to the new leaven, which is Jesus Christ. Be salted in him, that none among you may be corrupted, since by your savour you shall be tested. 3. It is monstrous to talk of Jesus Christ and to practise Judaism. For Christianity did not base its faith on Judaism, but Judaism on Christianity, and every tongue believing on God was brought together in it.

Christianity and Judaism

[1] This is possibly a proleptic reference to final resurrection, but more probably to the belief, found in many documents of a later date, that Jesus by the descent into Hades set free, and took into Paradise, the righteous dead. Cf. especially the *Gospel of Nicodemus* or *Acta Pilati*.

[2] The meaning appears to be "if God should treat us according to human standards none of us should see salvation."

XI

1. Ταῦτα δέ, ἀγαπητοί μου, οὐκ ἐπεὶ ἔγνων τινὰς ἐξ ὑμῶν οὕτως ἔχοντας, ἀλλ' ὡς μικρότερος ὑμῶν θέλω προφυλάσσεσθαι ὑμᾶς, μὴ ἐμπεσεῖν εἰς τὰ ἄγκιστρα τῆς κενοδοξίας, ἀλλὰ πεπληροφορῆσθαι ἐν τῇ γεννήσει καὶ τῷ πάθει καὶ τῇ ἀναστάσει τῇ γενομένῃ ἐν καιρῷ τῆς ἡγεμονίας Ποντίου Πιλάτου· πραχθέντα ἀληθῶς καὶ βεβαίως ὑπὸ Ἰησοῦ Χριστοῦ, τῆς ἐλπίδος ἡμῶν, ἧς ἐκτραπῆναι μηδενὶ ὑμῶν γένοιτο.

XII

1. Ὀναίμην ὑμῶν κατὰ πάντα, ἐάνπερ ἄξιος ὦ. εἰ γὰρ καὶ δέδεμαι, πρὸς ἕνα τῶν λελυμένων ὑμῶν οὐκ εἰμί. οἶδα ὅτι οὐ φυσιοῦσθε· Ἰησοῦν γὰρ Χριστὸν ἔχετε ἐν ἑαυτοῖς· καὶ μᾶλλον, ὅταν ἐπαινῶ ὑμᾶς, οἶδα, ὅτι ἐντρέπεσθε, ὡς γέγραπται, Prov. 18, 17 ὅτι ὁ δίκαιος ἑαυτοῦ κατήγορος.

XIII

1. Σπουδάζετε οὖν βεβαιωθῆναι ἐν τοῖς δόγμασιν τοῦ κυρίου καὶ τῶν ἀποστόλων, ἵνα πάντα, ὅσα Ps. 1, 3 ποιεῖτε, κατευοδωθῆτε σαρκὶ καὶ πνεύματι, πίστει καὶ ἀγάπῃ, ἐν υἱῷ καὶ πατρὶ καὶ ἐν πνεύματι, ἐν ἀρχῇ καὶ ἐν τέλει, μετὰ τοῦ ἀξιοπρεπεστάτου ἐπισκόπου ὑμῶν καὶ ἀξιοπλόκου πνευματικοῦ στεφάνου τοῦ πρεσβυτερίου ὑμῶν καὶ τῶν κατὰ θεὸν διακόνων. 2. ὑποτάγητε τῷ ἐπισκόπῳ καὶ

XI

1. Now I say this, beloved, not because I know that there are any of you that are thus, but because I wish to warn you, though I am less than you, not to fall into the snare of vain doctrine, but to be convinced of the birth and passion and resurrection which took place at the time of the procuratorship of Pontius Pilate ; for these things were truly and certainly done by Jesus Christ, our hope, from which God grant that none of you be turned aside.

Warning as to the true faith

XII

1. Let me have joy of you in all things, if I be but worthy. For even though I am in bonds I am not to be compared to one of you that have been set free. I know that you are not puffed up; for you have Jesus Christ in yourselves. And I know that when I praise you your modesty increases the more, as it is written, "The righteous man is his own accuser."

Praise of the Magnesians

XIII

1. Be diligent therefore to be confirmed in the ordinances of the Lord and the Apostles, in order that "you may prosper in all things whatsoever ye do" in the flesh and in the spirit, in faith and love, in the Son and the Father and the Spirit, at the beginning and at the end, together with your revered bishop and with your presbytery, that aptly woven spiritual crown, and with the godly deacons. 2. Be subject to the bishop and to one another, even

Firmness in the faith

209

ἀλλήλοις, ὡς Ἰησοῦς Χριστὸς τῷ πατρὶ[1] καὶ
οἱ ἀπόστολοι τῷ Χριστῷ καὶ τῷ πατρὶ[2] ἵνα
ἕνωσις ᾖ σαρκική τε καὶ πνευματική.

XIV

1. Εἰδώς, ὅτι θεοῦ γέμετε, συντόμως παρεκέλευσα[3]
ὑμᾶς. μνημονεύετέ μοῦ ἐν ταῖς προσευχαῖς ὑμῶν,
ἵνα θεοῦ ἐπιτύχω, καὶ τῆς ἐν Συρίᾳ ἐκκλησίας,
ὅθεν οὐκ ἄξιός εἰμι καλεῖσθαι· ἐπιδέομαι γὰρ τῆς
ἡνωμένης ὑμῶν ἐν θεῷ προσευχῆς καὶ ἀγάπης, εἰς
τὸ ἀξιωθῆναι τὴν ἐν Συρίᾳ ἐκκλησίαν διὰ τῆς
ἐκκλησίας[4] ὑμῶν δροσισθῆναι.

XV

1. Ἀσπάζονται ὑμᾶς Ἐφέσιοι ἀπὸ Σμύρνης, ὅθεν
καὶ γράφω ὑμῖν, παρόντες εἰς δόξαν θεοῦ, ὥσπερ
καὶ ὑμεῖς οἳ κατὰ πάντα με ἀνέπαυσαν ἅμα
Πολυκάρπῳ, ἐπισκόπῳ Σμυρναίων. καὶ αἱ λοιπαὶ
δὲ ἐκκλησίαι ἐν τιμῇ Ἰησοῦ Χριστοῦ ἀσπάζονται
ὑμᾶς. ἔρρωσθε ἐν ὁμονοίᾳ θεοῦ, κεκτημένοι ἀδιάκριτον πνεῦμα, ὅς ἐστιν Ἰησοῦς Χριστός.

---

[1] πατρί A(g), add κατὰ σάρκα " according to the flesh " GL.
[2] πατρί A, add καὶ τῷ πνεύματι, " and the spirit " GL.
[3] παρεκέλευσα G, παρεκάλεσα g which Lightfoot adopts on
the ground that it is a common Ignatian word, while παρα-
κελεύειν is not found elsewhere in the Epistles.
[4] Lightfoot reads ἐκτενείας " of your fervent supplication "
on the authority of A.

as Jesus Christ was subject to the Father, and the Apostles were subject to Christ and to the Father, in order that there may be a union both of flesh and of spirit.

XIV

1. I ᴋɴᴏᴡ that you are full of God, and I have exhorted you briefly. Remember me in your prayers, that I may attain to God, and remember the Church in Syria, of which I am not worthy to be called a member. For I need your united prayer in God and your love, that the Church which is in Syria may be granted refreshment from the dew of your Church.

Request for the prayers of the Magnesians

XV

1. Tʜᴇ Ephesians greet you from Smyrna, whence also I am writing to you; they, like yourselves, are here for the glory of God and have in all things given me comfort, together with Polycarp the bishop of the Smyrnaeans. And the other Churches also greet you in honour of Jesus Christ. Farewell in godly concord and may you possess an unhesitating[1] spirit, for this is Jesus Christ.

Final greetings

[1] The translation "a spirit that knows no division" is possible, and perhaps suits the context here better than "unhesitating," but the latter rendering seems to be justified by Trallians i, 1. A somewhat different shade of meaning is found in Ignatius, Ephesians iii, 2.

THE APOSTOLIC FATHERS

ΤΡΑΛΛΙΑΝΟΙΣ ΙΓΝΑΤΙΟΣ

Ἰγνάτιος, ὁ καὶ Θεοφόρος, ἠγαπημένῃ θεῷ, πατρὶ Ἰησοῦ Χριστοῦ, ἐκκλησίᾳ ἁγίᾳ τῇ οὔσῃ ἐν Τράλλεσιν τῆς Ἀσίας, ἐκλεκτῇ καὶ ἀξιοθέῳ, εἰρηνευούσῃ ἐν σαρκὶ καὶ πνεύματι τῷ πάθει Ἰησοῦ Χριστοῦ, τῆς ἐλπίδος ἡμῶν ἐν τῇ εἰς αὐτὸν ἀναστάσει· ἣν καὶ ἀσπάζομαι ἐν τῷ πληρώματι ἐν ἀποστολικῷ χαρακτῆρι καὶ εὔχομαι πλεῖστα χαίρειν.

I

1. Ἄμωμον διάνοιαν καὶ ἀδιάκριτον ἐν ὑπομονῇ ἔγνων ὑμᾶς ἔχοντας, οὐ κατὰ χρῆσιν ἀλλὰ κατὰ φύσιν, καθὼς ἐδήλωσέν μοι Πολύβιος, ὁ ἐπίσκοπος ὑμῶν, ὃς παρεγένετο θελήματι θεοῦ καὶ Ἰησοῦ Χριστοῦ ἐν Σμύρνῃ καὶ οὕτως μοι συνεχάρη δεδεμένῳ ἐν Χριστῷ Ἰησοῦ, ὥστε με τὸ πᾶν πλῆθος ὑμῶν ἐν αὐτῷ θεωρεῖσθαι.[1] 2. ἀποδεξάμενος οὖν τὴν κατὰ θεὸν εὔνοιαν δι᾽ αὐτοῦ ἐδόξασα, εὑρὼν ὑμᾶς, ὡς ἔγνων, μιμητὰς ὄντας θεοῦ.

II

1. Ὅταν γὰρ τῷ ἐπισκόπῳ ὑποτάσσησθε ὡς Ἰησοῦ Χριστῷ, φαίνεσθέ μοι οὐ κατὰ ἄνθρωπον ζῶντες, ἀλλὰ κατὰ Ἰησοῦν Χριστὸν τὸν δι᾽ ἡμᾶς

---

[1] θεωρεῖσθαι G, θεωρῆσαι g.

III.—IGNATIUS TO THE TRALLIANS.

IGNATIUS, who is also called Theophorus, to the Holy Church which is at Tralles in Asia, beloved of God the Father of Jesus Christ, elect and worthy of God, having peace in the flesh and in the Spirit through the passion of Jesus Christ, who is our hope through our resurrection unto him. Which Church I also greet in the Divine fulness after the apostolic fashion, and I bid her abundant greeting. *Greetings*

I

1. I HAVE learned that you possess a mind free from blame and unhesitating in endurance, not from habit, but by nature, as Polybius your bishop showed me, when he visited me in Smyrna by the will of God and of Jesus Christ, and so greatly rejoiced with me, prisoner for Jesus Christ as I was, that I saw your whole congregation in his person. 2. I received therefore your godly benevolence through him, and gave God glory that I found you, as I had learnt, imitators of God. *The virtue of the Trallians*

II

1. FOR when you are in subjection to the bishop as to Jesus Christ it is clear to me that you are living not after men, but after Jesus Christ, who died for *Submission to the bishop, presbyters and deacons*

213

ἀποθανόντα, ἵνα πιστεύσαντες εἰς τὸν θάνατον αὐτοῦ τὸ ἀποθανεῖν ἐκφύγητε. 2. ἀναγκαῖον οὖν ἐστίν, ὥσπερ ποιεῖτε, ἄνευ τοῦ ἐπισκόπου μηδὲν πράσσειν ὑμᾶς, ἀλλ' ὑποτάσσεσθαι καὶ τῷ πρεσβυτερίῳ ὡς τοῖς ἀποστόλοις Ἰησοῦ Χριστοῦ τῆς ἐλπίδος ἡμῶν, ἐν ᾧ διάγοντες εὑρεθησόμεθα.[1] 3. δεῖ δὲ καὶ τοὺς διακόνους ὄντας μυστηρίων Ἰησοῦ Χριστοῦ κατὰ πάντα τρόπον πᾶσιν ἀρέσκειν. οὐ γὰρ βρωμάτων καὶ ποτῶν εἰσιν διάκονοι, ἀλλ' ἐκκλησίας θεοῦ ὑπηρέται· δέον οὖν αὐτοὺς φυλάσσεσθαι τὰ ἐγκλήματα ὡς πῦρ.

1 Cor. 4, 1

III

1. Ὁμοίως πάντες ἐντρεπέσθωσαν τοὺς διακόνους ὡς Ἰησοῦν Χριστόν, ὡς καὶ τὸν ἐπίσκοπον ὄντα τύπον τοῦ πατρός, τοὺς δὲ πρεσβυτέρους ὡς συνέδριον θεοῦ καὶ ὡς σύνδεσμον ἀποστόλων. χωρὶς τούτων ἐκκλησία οὐ καλεῖται. 2. περὶ ὧν πέπεισμαι ὑμᾶς οὕτως ἔχειν. τὸ γὰρ ἐξεμπλάριον τῆς ἀγάπης ὑμῶν ἔλαβον καὶ ἔχω μεθ' ἑαυτοῦ ἐν τῷ ἐπισκόπῳ ὑμῶν, οὗ αὐτὸ τὸ κατάστημα μεγάλη μαθητεία, ἡ δὲ πραότης αὐτοῦ δύναμις· ὃν λογίζομαι καὶ τοὺς ἀθέους ἐντρέπεσθαι. 3. ἀγαπῶν ὑμᾶς φείδομαι, συντονώτερον δυνάμενος γράφειν ὑπὲρ τούτου.[2] οὐκ εἰς τοῦτο ᾠήθην, ἵνα ὢν κατάκριτος ὡς ἀπόστολος ὑμῖν διατάσσωμαι.

---

[1] εὑρεθησόμεθα GL, ἐν αὐτῷ εὑρεθ. S g.
[2] The text is here confused and corrupt in all the authorities. Lightfoot prefers to read οὕτως φείδομαι, and adds [ἀλλ' οὐχ ἱκανὸν ἑαυτόν] εἰς τοῦτο κ.τ.λ.

our sake, that by believing on his death you may escape death. 2. Therefore it is necessary (as is your practice) that you should do nothing without the bishop, but be also in subjection to the presbytery, as to the Apostles of Jesus Christ our hope, for if we live in him we shall be found in him. 3. And they also who are deacons of the mysteries of Jesus Christ must be in every way pleasing to all men. For they are not the ministers of food and drink, but servants of the Church of God; they must therefore guard against blame as against fire.

III

1. LIKEWISE let all respect the deacons as Jesus Christ, even as the bishop is also a type of the Father, and the presbyters as the council of God and the college of Apostles. Without these the name of "Church" is not given. 2. I am confident that you accept this. For I have received the example of your love, and I have it with me in the person of your bishop, whose very demeanour is a great lesson, and whose meekness is a miracle,[1] and I believe that even the godless pay respect to him. 3. I am sparing you in my love, though I might write more sharply on his behalf: I did not think myself competent, as a convict, to give you orders like an Apostle.

The reverence due to them

---

[1] Or, possibly, "is his power."

IV

1. Πολλὰ φρονῶ ἐν θεῷ, ἀλλ' ἐμαυτὸν μετρῶ,
ἵνα μὴ ἐν καυχήσει ἀπόλωμαι. νῦν γάρ με δεῖ
πλέον φοβεῖσθαι καὶ μὴ προσέχειν τοῖς φυσιοῦσίν
με. οἱ γὰρ λέγοντές μοι μαστιγοῦσίν με. 2.
ἀγαπῶ μὲν γὰρ τὸ παθεῖν, ἀλλ' οὐκ οἶδα, εἰ ἄξιός
εἰμι. τὸ γὰρ ζῆλος πολλοῖς μὲν οὐ φαίνεται, ἐμὲ
δὲ πλέον πολεμεῖ. χρῄζω οὖν πραότητος, ἐν ᾗ
καταλύεται ὁ ἄρχων τοῦ αἰῶνος τούτου.

V

1. Μὴ οὐ δύναμαι ὑμῖν τὰ ἐπουράνια γράψαι ;
Cor. 3, 1. 2 ἀλλὰ φοβοῦμαι, μὴ νηπίοις οὖσιν ὑμῖν βλάβην
παραθῶ· καὶ συγγνωμονεῖτέ μοι, μήποτε οὐ
δυνηθέντες χωρῆσαι στραγγαλωθῆτε. 2. καὶ γὰρ
ἐγώ, οὐ καθότι δέδεμαι καὶ δύναμαι νοεῖν τὰ ἐπουράνια καὶ τὰς τοποθεσίας τὰς ἀγγελικὰς καὶ τὰς
Col. 1, 16 συστάσεις τὰς ἀρχοντικάς, ὁρατά τε καὶ ἀόρατα,
παρὰ τοῦτο ἤδη καὶ μαθητής εἰμι. πολλὰ γὰρ
ἡμῖν λείπει, ἵνα θεοῦ μὴ λειπώμεθα.

VI

1. Παρακαλῶ οὖν ὑμᾶς, οὐκ ἐγώ, ἀλλ' ἡ ἀγάπη
Ἰησοῦ Χριστοῦ· μόνῃ τῇ χριστιανῇ τροφῇ χρῆσθε,
ἀλλοτρίας δὲ βοτάνης ἀπέχεσθε, ἥτις ἐστὶν

IV

1. I HAVE many thoughts in God, but I take the measure of myself that I perish not through boasting, for at present it is far better for me to be timid, and not to give heed to them who puff me up. For they who speak thus are a scourge to me. 2. For I desire to suffer, but I know not if I am worthy, for the jealousy of the devil[1] is to many not obvious, but against me it fights the more. I have need therefore of meekness, by which the prince of this world is brought to nothing.

Ignatius' need of humility

V

1. AM I not able to write to you heavenly things? Yes, but I am afraid that I should do you harm "seeing you are babes." Pardon me, for I refrain lest you be choked by what you cannot receive. 2. For I myself, though I am in bonds and can understand heavenly things, and the places of the angels and the gatherings of principalities, and "things seen and unseen," not for this am I a disciple even now, for much is lacking to us, that we may not lack God.

Reason for simple teaching

VI

1. I BESEECH you therefore (yet not I but the love of Jesus Christ) live only on Christian fare, and refrain from strange food, which is heresy. 2. For

Warning against heresy

---

[1] This is probably the meaning: an alternative translation would be: "Ambition is not obvious, etc." But cf. the letter to the Romans v. 3.

αἵρεσις· 2. οἳ ἑαυτοῖς[1] παρεμπλέκουσιν Ἰησοῦν
Χριστὸν καταξιοπιστευόμενοι, ὥσπερ θανάσιμον
φάρμακον διδόντες μετὰ οἰνομέλιτος, ὅπερ ὁ
ἀγνοῶν ἡδέως λαμβάνει ἐν ἡδονῇ κακῇ[2] τὸ ἀποθανεῖν.

VII

1. Φυλάττεσθε οὖν τοὺς τοιούτους. τοῦτο δὲ
ἔσται ὑμῖν μὴ φυσιουμένοις καὶ οὖσιν ἀχωρίστοις
θεοῦ[3] Ἰησοῦ Χριστοῦ καὶ τοῦ ἐπισκόπου καὶ τῶν
διαταγμάτων τῶν ἀποστόλων. 2. ὁ ἐντὸς θυσιαστηρίου ὢν καθαρός ἐστιν· ὁ δὲ ἐκτὸς θυσιαστηρίου
ὢν οὐ καθαρός ἐστιν· τοῦτ’ ἔστιν, ὁ χωρὶς ἐπισκόπου καὶ πρεσβυτερίου καὶ διακόνων πράσσων
τι, οὗτος οὐ καθαρός ἐστιν τῇ συνειδήσει.

VIII

1. Οὐκ ἐπεὶ ἔγνων τοιοῦτόν τι ἐν ὑμῖν, ἀλλὰ
προφυλάσσω ὑμᾶς ὄντας μου ἀγαπητούς, προορῶν
τὰς ἐνέδρας τοῦ διαβόλου. ὑμεῖς οὖν τὴν πραϋπά-
θειαν ἀναλαβόντες ἀνακτήσασθε ἑαυτοὺς ἐν πίστει
ὅ ἐστιν σὰρξ τοῦ κυρίου, καὶ ἐν ἀγάπῃ, ὅ ἐστιν
αἷμα Ἰησοῦ Χριστοῦ. 2. μηδεὶς ὑμῶν κατὰ τοῦ

---

[1] οἳ ἑαυτοῖς παρεμπλέκουσιν seems to be the text implied by
the translations of SA, but G(L) read οἱ καιροὶ παρεμπλέκουσιν
and g has καὶ τὸν ἰὸν προσπλέκοντες. The text is clearly corrupt,
and Lightfoot suggests καὶ ἰῷ παρεμπλέκουσιν κ.τ.λ. "for they
even mingle poison with Jesus Christ."

[2] κακῇ L, om. SA, κἀκεῖ τὸ ἀποθανεῖν "and therein is
death" G.

[3] The text is doubtful. A omits θεοῦ: probably there is
some corruption though it is impossible to be sure what it is,

these men mingle Jesus Christ with themselves in specious honesty, mixing as it were a deadly poison with honeyed wine, which the ignorant takes gladly in his baneful pleasure, and it is his death.

VII

1. BEWARE therefore of such men ; and this will be possible for you, if you are not puffed up, and are inseparable from God, from Jesus Christ[1] and from the bishop and the ordinances of the Apostles. 2. He who is within the sanctuary is pure, but he who is without the sanctuary is not pure ; that is to say whoever does anything apart from the bishop and the presbytery and the deacons is not pure in his conscience.

The need of remaining loyal to the bishop

VIII

I. IT is not that I know that there is anything of this kind among you, but I warn you because you are dear to me, and I foresee the snares of the devil. Therefore adopt meekness and be renewed in faith, which is the flesh of the Lord, and in love, which is the blood of Jesus Christ. 2. Let none of you have a

Warning against the snares of the devil

---

[1] Or possibly "from our God Jesus Christ."

πλησίον ἐχέτω. μὴ ἀφορμὰς δίδοτε τοῖς ἔθνεσιν,
ἵνα μὴ δι’ ὀλίγους ἄφρονας τὸ ἐν θεῷ πλῆθος
Is. 52, 5 βλασφημῆται. Οὐαὶ γάρ, δι’ οὗ ἐπὶ ματαιότητι
τὸ ὄνομά μου ἐπί τινων βλασφημεῖται.

IX

1. Κωφώθητε οὖν, ὅταν ὑμῖν χωρὶς Ἰησοῦ
Χριστοῦ λαλῇ τις, τοῦ ἐκ γένους Δαυείδ, τοῦ
ἐκ Μαρίας, ὃς ἀληθῶς ἐγεννήθη, ἔφαγέν τε καὶ
ἔπιεν, ἀληθῶς ἐδιώχθη ἐπὶ Ποντίου Πιλάτου,
ἀληθῶς ἐσταυρώθη καὶ ἀπέθανεν, βλεπόντων
τῶν ἐπουρανίων καὶ ἐπιγείων καὶ ὑποχθονίων.
2. ὃς καὶ ἀληθῶς ἠγέρθη ἀπὸ νεκρῶν, ἐγείραντος
I Cor. 15, αὐτὸν τοῦ πατρὸς αὐτοῦ, κατὰ τὸ ὁμοίωμα ὃς καὶ[1]
12 ff. ἡμᾶς τοὺς πιστεύοντας αὐτῷ οὕτως ἐγερεῖ ὁ πατὴρ
αὐτοῦ ἐν Χριστῷ Ἰησοῦ, οὗ χωρὶς τὸ ἀληθινὸν ζῆν
οὐκ ἔχομεν.

X

1. Εἰ δέ, ὥσπερ τινὲς ἄθεοι ὄντες, τουτέστιν
ἄπιστοί, λέγουσιν, τὸ δοκεῖν πεπονθέναι αὐτόν,
αὐτοὶ ὄντες τὸ δοκεῖν, ἐγὼ τί δέδεμαι, τί δὲ καὶ
εὔχομαι θηριομαχῆσαι ; δωρεὰν οὖν ἀποθνήσκω.
ἄρα οὖν καταψεύδομαι τοῦ κυρίου.

---

[1] κατὰ τὸ ὁμοίωμα ὃς καί G, qui et secundum similitudinem
L.   SA perhaps imply ὡς καὶ κατὰ τὸ ὁμοίωμα.

grudge against his neighbour. Give no occasion to the heathen, in order that the congregation of God may not be blasphemed for a few foolish persons. For " Woe unto him through whom my name is vainly blasphemed among any."

IX

1. Be deaf therefore when anyone speaks to you apart from Jesus Christ, who was of the family of David, and of Mary, who was truly born, both ate and drank, was truly persecuted under Pontius Pilate, was truly crucified and died in the sight of those in heaven and on earth and under the earth ; 2. who also was truly raised from the dead, when his Father raised him up, as in the same manner his Father shall raise up in Christ Jesus us who believe in him, without whom we have no true life.

The history of Jesus Christ

X

1. But if, as some affirm who are without God, —that is, are unbelievers—his suffering was only a semblance (but it is they who are merely a semblance), why am I a prisoner, and why do I even long to fight with the beasts ? In that case I am dying in vain. Then indeed am I lying concerning the Lord.

Against docetism

XI

1. Φεύγετε οὖν τὰς κακὰς παραφυάδας τὰς γεννώσας καρπὸν θανατηφόρον, οὗ ἐὰν γεύσηταί τις, παρ' αὐτὰ ἀποθνήσκει. οὗτοι γὰρ οὔκ εἰσιν φυτεία πατρός. 2. εἰ γὰρ ἦσαν, ἐφαίνοντο ἂν κλάδοι τοῦ σταυροῦ, καὶ ἦν ἂν ὁ καρπὸς αὐτῶν ἄφθαρτος· δι' οὗ ἐν τῷ πάθει αὐτοῦ προσκαλεῖται ὑμᾶς ὄντας μέλη αὐτοῦ. οὐ δύναται οὖν κεφαλὴ χωρὶς γεννηθῆναι ἄνευ μελῶν, τοῦ θεοῦ ἕνωσιν ἐπαγγελλομένου, ὅ ἐστιν αὐτός.

Mt. 15, 13

XII

1. Ἀσπάζομαι ὑμᾶς ἀπὸ Σμύρνης ἅμα ταῖς συμπαρούσαις μοι ἐκκλησίαις τοῦ θεοῦ, οἳ κατὰ πάντα με ἀνέπαυσαν σαρκί τε καὶ πνεύματι. 2. παρακαλεῖ ὑμᾶς τὰ δεσμά μου, ἃ ἕνεκεν Ἰησοῦ Χριστοῦ περιφέρω, αἰτούμενος θεοῦ ἐπιτυχεῖν· διαμένετε ἐν τῇ ὁμονοίᾳ ὑμῶν καὶ τῇ μετ' ἀλλήλων προσευχῇ. πρέπει γὰρ ὑμῖν τοῖς καθ' ἕνα, ἐξαιρέτως καὶ τοῖς πρεσβυτέροις, ἀναψύχειν τὸν ἐπίσκοπον εἰς τιμὴν πατρός, Ἰησοῦ Χριστοῦ καὶ τῶν ἀποστόλων. 3. εὔχομαι ὑμᾶς ἐν ἀγάπῃ ἀκοῦσαί μου, ἵνα μὴ εἰς μαρτύριον ὦ ἐν ὑμῖν γράψας. καὶ περὶ ἐμοῦ δὲ προσεύχεσθε, τῆς ἀφ' ὑμῶν ἀγάπης χρῄζοντος ἐν τῷ ἐλέει τοῦ θεοῦ, εἰς τὸ καταξιωθῆναί με τοῦ κλήρου, οὗ περίκειμαι[1] ἐπιτυχεῖν, ἵνα μὴ ἀδόκιμος εὑρεθῶ.

I Cor. 9, 27

[1] Lightfoot thinks περίκειμαι impossible and accepts Bunsen's emendation οὗπερ ἔγκειμαι.

222

XI

1. FLY from these wicked offshoots, which bear deadly fruit, which if a man eat he presently dies. For these are not the planting of the Father. 2. For if they were they would appear as branches of the Cross (and their fruit would be incorruptible) by which through his Passion he calls you who are his members. The head therefore cannot be borne without limbs, since God promises union, that is himself.

Against heresy

XII

1. I GREET you from Smyrna together with the Churches of God that are present with me, men who in all things have given me rest in the flesh and in the spirit. 2. My bonds exhort you, which I carry about for the sake of Jesus Christ, praying that I may attain to God; continue in your present harmony and in prayer with one another. For it is right that each of you, and especially the presbyters, should refresh the bishop, to the honour of the Father, of Jesus Christ, and of the Apostles. 3. I entreat you to listen to me in love, that I become not by my writing a witness against you. And pray for me also, for I have need of your love in the mercy of God, that I may be granted the lot which I am set to obtain, that I be not found reprobate.

Exhortation to unity and love

XIII

1. Ἀσπάζεται ὑμᾶς ἡ ἀγάπη Σμυρναίων καὶ Ἐφεσίων. μνημονεύετε ἐν ταῖς προσευχαῖς ὑμῶν τῆς ἐν Συρίᾳ ἐκκλησίας, ὅθεν καὶ οὐκ ἄξιός εἰμι λέγεσθαι, ὧν ἔσχατος ἐκείνων. 2. ἔρρωσθε ἐν Ἰησοῦ Χριστῷ, ὑποτασσόμενοι τῷ ἐπισκόπῳ ὡς τῇ ἐντολῇ, ὁμοίως καὶ τῷ πρεσβυτερίῳ. καὶ οἱ κατ᾽ ἄνδρα ἀλλήλους ἀγαπᾶτε ἐν ἀμερίστῳ καρδίᾳ. 3. ἁγνίζεται ὑμῶν τὸ ἐμὸν πνεῦμα οὐ μόνον νῦν, ἀλλὰ καὶ ὅταν θεοῦ ἐπιτύχω. ἔτι γὰρ ὑπὸ κίνδυνόν εἰμι· ἀλλὰ πιστὸς ὁ πατὴρ ἐν Ἰησοῦ Χριστῷ πληρῶσαί μου τὴν αἴτησιν καὶ ὑμῶν, ἐν ᾧ εὑρεθείητε[1] ἄμωμοι.

ΡΩΜΑΙΟΙΣ ΙΓΝΑΤΙΟΣ

Ἰγνάτιος, ὁ καὶ Θεοφόρος, τῇ ἠλεημένῃ ἐν μεγαλειότητι πατρὸς ὑψίστου καὶ Ἰησοῦ Χριστοῦ τοῦ μόνου υἱοῦ αὐτοῦ ἐκκλησίᾳ ἠγαπημένῃ καὶ πεφωτισμένῃ ἐν θελήματι τοῦ θελήσαντος τὰ πάντα, ἃ ἔστιν, κατὰ ἀγάπην Ἰησοῦ Χριστοῦ, τοῦ θεοῦ ἡμῶν, ἥτις καὶ προκάθηται ἐν τόπῳ χωρίου Ῥωμαίων, ἀξιόθεος, ἀξιοπρεπής, ἀξιομακάριστος, ἀξιέπαινος, ἀξιεπίτευκτος, ἀξίαγνος καὶ προκαθημένη τῆς ἀγάπης, χριστώνυμος,[2] πατρώνυμος, ἣν καὶ ἀσπάζομαι ἐν

---

[1] The Armenian and g read εὑρεθείημεν "may we be found."

[2] ALS read χριστόνομος "having the law of Christ."

XIiI

1. The love of the Smyrnaeans and Ephesians greet Final greetings you : remember in your prayers the Church in Syria, in which I am not worthy to be reckoned, being the least of its members. 2. Farewell in Jesus Christ. Submit yourselves to the bishop as to the commandment, and likewise to the presbytery. Let each of you individually love one another with an undivided heart. 3. My spirit is consecrated to you not only now, but also when I attain to God. For I am still in peril, but the Father is faithful in Jesus Christ to fulfil both your and my prayer, in which may you be found blameless.

IV.—IGNATIUS TO THE ROMANS.

Ignatius, who is also called Theophorus, to her who Greeting has obtained mercy in the greatness of the Most High Father, and of Jesus Christ his only Son ; to the Church beloved and enlightened by the will of him who has willed all things which are, according to the love of Jesus Christ, our God, which also has the presidency in the country of the land of the Romans, worthy of God, worthy of honour, worthy of blessing, worthy of praise, worthy of success, worthy in its holiness, and pre-eminent in love, named after Christ, named after the Father, which also I greet in the name of

225

ὀνόματι Ἰησοῦ Χριστοῦ, υἱοῦ πατρός· κατὰ
σάρκα καὶ πνεῦμα ἡνωμένοις πάσῃ ἐντολῇ
αὐτοῦ, πεπληρωμένοις χάριτος θεοῦ ἀδιακρίτως καὶ ἀποδιϋλισμένοις ἀπὸ παντὸς ἀλ-
λοτρίου χρώματος πλεῖστα ἐν Ἰησοῦ Χριστῷ,
τῷ θεῷ ἡμῶν, ἀμώμως χαίρειν.

I

1. Ἐπεὶ εὐξάμενος θεῷ ἐπέτυχον ἰδεῖν ὑμῶν τὰ
ἀξιόθεα πρόσωπα, ὡς καὶ πλέον ἡτούμην λαβεῖν·
δεδεμένος γὰρ ἐν Χριστῷ Ἰησοῦ ἐλπίζω ὑμᾶς
ἀσπάσασθαι, ἐάνπερ θέλημα ᾖ τοῦ ἀξιωθῆναί με
εἰς τέλος εἶναι.   2. ἡ μὲν γὰρ ἀρχὴ εὐοικονόμητός
ἐστιν, ἐάνπερ χάριτος [1] ἐπιτύχω εἰς τὸ τὸν κλῆρόν
μου ἀνεμποδίστως ἀπολαβεῖν.   φοβοῦμαι γὰρ
τὴν ὑμῶν ἀγάπην, μὴ αὐτή με ἀδικήσῃ. ὑμῖν γὰρ
εὐχερές ἐστιν, ὃ θέλετε, ποιῆσαι· ἐμοὶ δὲ δύσκολόν
ἐστιν τοῦ θεοῦ ἐπιτυχεῖν, ἐάνπερ ὑμεῖς μὴ φεί-
σησθέ μου.

II

I Thess. 2, 4   1. Οὐ γὰρ θέλω ὑμᾶς ἀνθρωπαρεσκῆσαι, ἀλλὰ
θεῷ ἀρέσαι, ὥσπερ καὶ ἀρέσκετε. οὔτε γὰρ ἐγώ
ποτε ἕξω καιρὸν τοιοῦτον θεοῦ ἐπιτυχεῖν, οὔτε
ὑμεῖς, ἐὰν σιωπήσητε, κρείττονι ἔργῳ ἔχετε
ἐπιγραφῆναι. ἐὰν γὰρ σιωπήσητε ἀπ᾽ ἐμοῦ, ἐγὼ
λόγος θεοῦ· ἐὰν δὲ ἐρασθῆτε τῆς σαρκός μου,

---

[1] A, with partial support in other authorities, reads
πέρατος " may reach the goal."

Jesus Christ, the Son of the Father; to those who are united in flesh and spirit in every one of his commandments, filled with the grace of God without wavering, and filtered clear from every foreign stain, abundant greeting in Jesus Christ, our God, in blamelessness.

I

1. FORASMUCH as I have gained my prayer to God to see your godly faces, so that I have obtained more than I asked,—for in bondage in Christ Jesus I hope to greet you if it be his will that I be found worthy to the end. 2. For the beginning has been well ordered, if I may obtain grace to come unhindered to my lot. For I am afraid of your love, lest even that do me wrong. For it is easy for you to do what you will, but it is difficult for me to attain to God, if you do not spare me.

Hope of seeing the Romans

II

1. FOR I would not have you " men-pleasers " but " God-pleasers," even as you do indeed please him. For neither shall I ever have such an opportunity of attaining to God, nor can you, if you be but silent, have any better deed ascribed to you. For if you are silent concerning me, I am a word of God; but if

His desire not to be saved from the beasts

πάλιν ἔσομαι φωνή. 2. πλέον μοι μὴ παρά-
σχησθε τοῦ σπονδισθῆναι θεῷ, ὡς ἔτι θυσιαστήριον ἔτοιμόν ἐστιν, ἵνα ἐν ἀγάπῃ χορὸς γενόμενοι
ᾄσητε τῷ πατρὶ ἐν Χριστῷ Ἰησοῦ, ὅτι τὸν ἐπίσκοπον Συρίας ὁ θεὸς κατηξίωσεν εὑρεθῆναι εἰς
δύσιν ἀπὸ ἀνατολῆς μεταπεμψάμενος. καλὸν τὸ
δῦναι ἀπὸ κόσμου πρὸς θεόν, ἵνα εἰς αὐτὸν ἀνα-
τείλω.

III

1. Οὐδέποτε ἐβασκάνατε οὐδενί, ἄλλους ἐδιδά-
ξατε. ἐγὼ δὲ θέλω, ἵνα κἀκεῖνα βέβαια ᾖ ἃ
μαθητεύοντες ἐντέλλεσθε. 2. μόνον μοι δύναμιν
αἰτεῖσθε ἔσωθέν τε καὶ ἔξωθεν, ἵνα μὴ μόνον
λέγω ἀλλὰ καὶ θέλω, ἵνα μὴ μόνον λέγωμαι
Χριστιανὸς ἀλλὰ καὶ εὑρεθῶ. ἐὰν γὰρ εὑρεθῶ,
καὶ λέγεσθαι δύναμαι, καὶ τότε πιστὸς εἶναι, ὅταν
κόσμῳ μὴ φαίνωμαι. 3. οὐδὲν φαινόμενον καλόν·
ὁ γὰρ θεὸς ἡμῶν Ἰησοῦς Χριστὸς ἐν πατρὶ ὢν
μᾶλλον φαίνεται. οὐ πεισμονῆς τὸ ἔργον, ἀλλὰ
μεγέθους ἐστὶν ὁ Χριστιανισμός, ὅταν μισῆται
ὑπὸ κόσμου.

you love my flesh, I shall again be only a cry.
2. Grant me nothing more than that I be poured out
to God, while an altar is still ready, that forming
yourselves into a chorus[1] of love, you may sing to the
Father in Christ Jesus, that God has vouchsafed that
the bishop of Syria shall be found at the setting of
the sun, having fetched him from the sun's rising.
It is good to set to the world towards God, that I
may rise to him.

III

1. You never have envied anyone, you taught
others. But I desire that those things may stand
fast which you enjoin in your instructions. 2. Only
pray for me for strength, both inward and outward,
that I may not merely speak, but also have the will,
that I may not only be called a Christian, but may also
be found to be one. For if I be found to be one, I can
also be called one, and then be deemed faithful
when I no longer am visible in the world.
3. Nothing visible is good, for our God, Jesus Christ,
being now in the Father, is the more plainly visible.[2]
Christianity is not the work of persuasiveness,
but of greatness, when it is hated by the world.

Request that they should pray for him

---

[1] Cf. note on Eph. xix., p. 193.
[2] The sentence is clumsily expressed: apparently Ignatius
means "nothing directly visible is good, and Jesus Christ,
who is no longer visible, being in the Father, is more clearly
perceived by the eye of faith," but he has sacrificed clearness
to a paradoxical playing with the words.

IV

1. Ἐγὼ γράφω πάσαις ταῖς ἐκκλησίαις, καὶ ἐντέλλομαι πᾶσιν, ὅτι ἐγὼ ἑκὼν ὑπὲρ θεοῦ ἀποθνήσκω, ἐάνπερ ὑμεῖς μὴ κωλύσητε. παρακαλῶ ὑμᾶς, μὴ εὔνοια ἄκαιρος γένησθέ μοι. ἄφετέ με θηρίων εἶναι βοράν, δι’ ὧν ἔνεστιν θεοῦ ἐπιτυχεῖν. σῖτός εἰμι θεοῦ καὶ δι’ ὀδόντων θηρίων ἀλήθομαι, ἵνα καθαρὸς ἄρτος εὑρεθῶ τοῦ Χριστοῦ.[1] 2. μᾶλλον κολακεύσατε τὰ θηρία, ἵνα μοι τάφος γένωνται καὶ μηθὲν καταλίπωσι τῶν τοῦ σώματός μου, ἵνα μὴ κοιμηθεὶς βαρύς τινι γένωμαι. τότε ἔσομαι μαθητὴς ἀληθῶς Ἰησοῦ Χριστοῦ, ὅτε οὐδὲ τὸ σῶμά μου ὁ κόσμος ὄψεται. λιτανεύσατε τὸν Χριστὸν[2] ὑπὲρ ἐμοῦ, ἵνα διὰ τῶν ὀργάνων τούτων θυσία[3] εὑρεθῶ. 3. οὐχ ὡς Πέτρος καὶ Παῦλος διατάσσομαι ὑμῖν. ἐκεῖνοι ἀπόστολοι, ἐγὼ κατάκριτος· ἐκεῖνοι ἐλεύθεροι, ἐγὼ δὲ μέχρι νῦν δοῦλος. ἀλλ’ ἐὰν πάθω, ἀπελεύθερος γενήσομαι Ἰησοῦ Χριστοῦ καὶ ἀναστήσομαι ἐν αὐτῷ ἐλεύθερος. νῦν μανθάνω δεδεμένος μηδὲν ἐπιθυμεῖν.

Cf. Zenobius *Paroem.* i. 50

I Cor. 7, 22

V

1. Ἀπὸ Συρίας μέχρι Ῥώμης θηριομαχῶ, διὰ γῆς καὶ θαλάσσης, νυκτὸς καὶ ἡμέρας, δεδεμένος

---

[1] τοῦ Χριστοῦ GL, θεοῦ Sg Iren.^lat·, om. Iren.^gr· Hieron.
[2] τὸν Χριστόν GL, τὸν Κύριον SA.
[3] θεῷ (θεοῦ) θυσία LSA.

IV

1. I AM writing to all the Churches, and I give injunctions to all men, that I am dying willingly for God's sake, if you do not hinder it. I beseech you, be not "an unseasonable kindness"[1] to me. Suffer me to be eaten by the beasts, through whom I can attain to God. I am God's wheat, and I am ground by the teeth of wild beasts that I may be found pure bread of Christ. 2. Rather entice the wild beasts that they may become my tomb, and leave no trace of my body, that when I fall asleep I be not burdensome to any. Then shall I be truly a disciple of Jesus Christ, when the world shall not even see my body. Beseech Christ on my behalf, that I may be found a sacrifice through these instruments.[2] 3. I do not order you as did Peter and Paul; they were Apostles, I am a convict; they were free, I am even until now a slave. But if I suffer I shall be Jesus Christ's freedman, and in him I shall rise free. Now I am learning in my bonds to give up all desires.

His desire to suffer

V

1. FROM Syria to Rome I am fighting with wild beasts, by land and sea, by night and day, bound to

His journey, and expectation of martyrdom

---

[1] Apparently a partial quotation from the proverb preserved by Zenobius ἄκαιρος εὔνοι· οὐδὲν ἔχθρας διαφέρει "an unseasonable kindness is nothing different from hostility."

[2] I.e. the wild beasts.

δέκα λεοπάρδοις, ὅ ἐστιν στρατιωτικὸν τάγμα· οἳ
καὶ εὐεργετούμενοι χείρους γίνονται. ἐν δὲ τοῖς
Cor. 4, 4 ἀδικήμασιν αὐτῶν μᾶλλον μαθητεύομαι, ἀλλ' οὐ
παρὰ τοῦτο δεδικαίωμαι. 2. ὀναίμην τῶν θηρίων
τῶν ἐμοὶ ἡτοιμασμένων καὶ εὔχομαι σύντομά μοι
εὑρεθῆναι· ἃ καὶ κολακεύσω, συντόμως με κατα-
φαγεῖν, οὐχ ὥσπερ τινῶν δειλαινόμενα οὐχ ἥψαντο.
κἂν αὐτὰ δὲ ἄκοντα[1] μὴ θελήσῃ, ἐγὼ προσβιά-
σομαι. 3. συγγνώμην μοι ἔχετε· τί μοι συμφέρει,
ἐγὼ γινώσκω, νῦν ἄρχομαι μαθητὴς εἶναι. μηθέν
με ζηλώσαι τῶν ὁρατῶν καὶ ἀοράτων, ἵνα Ἰησοῦ
Χριστοῦ ἐπιτύχω. πῦρ καὶ σταυρὸς θηρίων τε
συστάσεις, ἀνατομαί, διαιρέσεις, σκορπισμοὶ
ὀστέων, συγκοπὴ μελῶν, ἀλεσμοὶ ὅλου τοῦ σώματος, κακαὶ κολάσεις τοῦ διαβόλου ἐπ' ἐμὲ ἐρχέ-
σθωσαν, μόνον ἵνα Ἰησοῦ Χριστοῦ ἐπιτύχω.

VI

Cor. 9, 15 1. Οὐδέν μοι ὠφελήσει τὰ πέρατα τοῦ κόσμου
οὐδὲ αἱ βασιλεῖαι τοῦ αἰῶνος τούτου. καλόν μοι
ἀποθανεῖν εἰς Χριστὸν Ἰησοῦν, ἢ βασιλεύειν τῶν
περάτων τῆς γῆς. ἐκεῖνον ζητῶ, τὸν ὑπὲρ ἡμῶν
ἀποθανόντα· ἐκεῖνον θέλω, τὸν δι' ἡμᾶς ἀναστάντα.
ὁ δὲ τοκετός μοι ἐπίκειται. 2. σύγγνωτέ μοι,

[1] ἄκοντα G Euseb, ἑκόντα Lg, (*om.* SA ?). Lightfoot prefers ἑκόντα "willing," which must be an accusative referring to Ignatius.

ten "leopards" (that is, a company of soldiers [1]), and they become worse for kind treatment. Now I become the more a disciple for their ill deeds, "but not by this am I justified." 2. I long for the beasts that are prepared for me; and I pray that they may be found prompt for me; I will even entice them to devour me promptly; not as has happened to some whom they have not touched from fear; even if they be unwilling of themselves, I will force them to it. 3. Grant me this favour. I know what is expedient for me; now I am beginning to be a disciple. May nothing of things seen or unseen envy me my attaining to Jesus Christ. Let there come on me fire, and cross, and struggles with wild beasts, cutting, and tearing asunder, rackings of bones, mangling of limbs, crushing of my whole body, cruel tortures of the devil, may I but attain to Jesus Christ!

VI

1. THE ends of the earth and the kingdoms of this world shall profit me nothing. It is better for me to die in Christ Jesus than to be king over the ends of the earth. I seek Him who died for our sake. I desire Him who rose for us. The pains of birth are upon me. 2. Suffer me, my brethren; hinder me

The glory of martyrdom

---

[1] The first impression made by this passage is that "leopards" was the name of some regiment, and that the following words are an explanatory gloss; but there is no evidence for this use of "leopard." Τάγμα is perhaps the equivalent of "manipulus" in the later sense of "ten men." The whole passage is rendered stranger still by the fact that it is the first instance of the word "leopard" in Greek or Latin literature.

ἀδελφοί· μὴ ἐμποδίσητέ μοι ζῆσαι, μὴ θελήσητέ
με ἀποθανεῖν· τὸν τοῦ θεοῦ θέλοντα εἶναι κόσμῳ
μὴ χαρίσησθε, μηδὲ ὕλῃ ἐξαπατήσητε·[1] ἄφετέ με
καθαρὸν φῶς λαβεῖν· ἐκεῖ παραγενόμενος ἄνθρωπος ἔσομαι. 3. ἐπιτρέψατέ μοι μιμητὴν εἶναι
τοῦ πάθους τοῦ θεοῦ μου. εἴ τις αὐτὸν ἐν ἑαυτῷ
ἔχει, νοησάτω ὃ θέλω, καὶ συμπαθείτω μοι
εἰδὼς τὰ συνέχοντά με.

VII

1. Ὁ ἄρχων τοῦ αἰῶνος τούτου διαρπάσαι με
βούλεται καὶ τὴν εἰς θεόν μου γνώμην διαφθεῖραι.
μηδεὶς οὖν τῶν παρόντων ὑμῶν βοηθείτω αὐτῷ
μᾶλλον ἐμοῦ γίνεσθε, τουτέστιν τοῦ θεοῦ. μὴ
λαλεῖτε Ἰησοῦν Χριστόν, κόσμον δὲ ἐπιθυμεῖτε.
2. βασκανία ἐν ὑμῖν μὴ κατοικείτω. μηδ᾽ ἂν ἐγὼ
παρὼν παρακαλῶ ὑμᾶς, πείσθητέ μοι· τούτοις δὲ
μᾶλλον πείσθητε, οἷς γράφω ὑμῖν. ζῶν γὰρ
γράφω ὑμῖν, ἐρῶν τοῦ ἀποθανεῖν. ὁ ἐμὸς ἔρως
ἐσταύρωται, καὶ οὐκ ἔστιν ἐν ἐμοὶ πῦρ φιλόϋλον·
Joh. 4, 10; ὕδωρ δὲ ζῶν καὶ λαλοῦν[2] ἐν ἐμοί, ἔσωθέν μοι λέγον·
7, 38   Δεῦρο πρὸς τὸν πατέρα. 3. οὐχ ἥδομαι τροφῇ
Joh. 6, 33   φθορᾶς οὐδὲ ἡδοναῖς τοῦ βίου τούτου. ἄρτον θεοῦ
Joh. 7, 42; θέλω, ὅ ἐστιν σὰρξ Ἰησοῦ[3] Χριστοῦ, τοῦ ἐκ
Rom. 1, 3;
II Tim. 2, 8 σπέρματος Δαυείδ, καὶ πόμα θέλω τὸ αἷμα αὐτοῦ,
ὅ ἐστιν ἀγάπη ἄφθαρτος.

[1] μηδὲ ὕλῃ ἐξαπατήσητε is omitted in Gg ; Lightfoot thinks
that LSA imply κολακεύσητε rather than ἐξαπατήσητε.
[2] The text is much expanded in the later authorities :
Lightfoot is inclined to emend καὶ λαλοῦν to ἁλλόμενον, which
is found in g, as a reference to Joh. 4, 14.
[3] Ἰησοῦ GLA, om. Σg.

not from living, do not wish me to die. Do not give
to the world one who desires to belong to God, nor
deceive him with material things. Suffer me to
receive the pure light; when I have come thither I
shall become a man. 3. Suffer me to follow the
example of the Passion of my God. If any man
have him within himself, let him understand what I
wish, and let him sympathise with me, knowing the
things which constrain me.

VII

1. THE Prince of this world wishes to tear me in
pieces, and to corrupt my mind towards God. Let
none of you who are present help him. Be rather
on my side, that is on God's. Do not speak of
Jesus Christ, and yet desire the world. 2. Let no
envy dwell among you. Even though when I come
I beseech you myself, do not be persuaded by me,
but rather obey this, which I write to you: for in
the midst of life I write to you desiring death. My
lust has been crucified, and there is in me no fire of
love for material things; but only water living and
speaking in me, and saying to me from within,
"Come to the Father." 3. I have no pleasure in
the food of corruption or in the delights of this life.
I desire the " bread of God," which is the flesh of
Jesus Christ, who was " of the seed of David," and for
drink I desire his blood, which is incorruptible love.[1]

The tempt-
ations of
the devil,
and his own
feelings

---

[1] There is here perhaps a play on the words : the word
translated " love " was also used either as a synonym for the
Eucharist, or, as some think, as the name of a religious
meal originally connected with the Eucharist.

VIII

1. Οὐκέτι θέλω κατὰ ἀνθρώπους ζῆν. τοῦτο δὲ ἔσται, ἐὰν ὑμεῖς θελήσητε. θελήσατε, ἵνα καὶ ὑμεῖς θεληθῆτε. 2. δι' ὀλίγων γραμμάτων αἰτοῦμαι ὑμᾶς· πιστεύσατέ μοι. Ἰησοῦς δὲ Χριστὸς ὑμῖν ταῦτα φανερώσει, ὅτι ἀληθῶς λέγω· τὸ ἀψευδὲς στόμα, ἐν ᾧ ὁ πατὴρ ἐλάλησεν ἀληθῶς. 3. αἰτήσασθε περὶ ἐμοῦ, ἵνα ἐπιτύχω. οὐ κατὰ σάρκα ὑμῖν ἔγραψα, ἀλλὰ κατὰ γνώμην θεοῦ. ἐὰν πάθω, ἠθελήσατε· ἐὰν ἀποδοκιμασθῶ, ἐμισήσατε.

IX

1. Μνημονεύετε ἐν τῇ προσευχῇ ὑμῶν τῆς ἐν Συρίᾳ ἐκκλησίας, ἥτις ἀντὶ ἐμοῦ ποιμένι τῷ θεῷ χρῆται. μόνος αὐτὴν Ἰησοῦς Χριστὸς ἐπισκοπήσει καὶ ἡ ὑμῶν ἀγάπη. 2. ἐγὼ δὲ αἰσχύνομαι I Cor. 15, 8. 9 ἐξ αὐτῶν λέγεσθαι· οὐδὲ γὰρ ἄξιός εἰμι, ὢν ἔσχατος αὐτῶν καὶ ἔκτρωμα· ἀλλ' ἠλέημαί τις εἶναι, ἐὰν θεοῦ ἐπιτύχω. 3. ἀσπάζεται ὑμᾶς τὸ ἐμὸν πνεῦμα καὶ ἡ ἀγάπη τῶν ἐκκλησιῶν τῶν δεξαμένων με εἰς ὄνομα Ἰησοῦ Χριστοῦ, οὐχ ὡς παροδεύοντα. καὶ γὰρ αἱ μὴ προσήκουσαί μοι τῇ ὁδῷ τῇ κατὰ σάρκα, κατὰ πόλιν με προῆγον.

X

1. Γράφω δὲ ὑμῖν ταῦτα ἀπὸ Σμύρνης δι' Ἐφεσίων τῶν ἀξιομακαρίστων. ἔστιν δὲ καὶ ἅμα ἐμοὶ σὺν ἄλλοις πολλοῖς καὶ Κρόκος, τὸ ποθητόν

VIII

1. I no longer desire to live after the manner of men, and this shall be, if you desire it. Desire it, in order that you also may be desired. 2. I beg you by this short letter; believe me. And Jesus Christ shall make this plain to you, that I am speaking the truth. He is the mouth which cannot lie, by which the Father has spoken truly. 3. Pray for me that I may attain. I write to you not according to the flesh, but according to the mind of God. If I suffer, it was your favour: if I be rejected, it was your hatred.

Desire of martyrdom

IX

1. Remember in your prayers the Church in Syria which has God for its Shepherd in my room. Its bishop shall be Jesus Christ alone,—and your love. 2. But for myself I am ashamed to be called one of them, for I am not worthy; for I am the least of them, and "born out of time;" but I have obtained mercy to be someone, if I may attain to God. 3. My spirit greets you, and the love of the Churches which have received me in the Name of Jesus Christ, not as a mere passer by, for even those which did not lie on my road according to the flesh went before me from city to city.

The Church in Syria

X

1. Now I am writing these things to you from Smyrna by the blessed Ephesians, and Crocus, a name very dear to me, is also with me, and many

Final greetings

μοι ὄνομα. 2. περὶ τῶν προελθόντων με ἀπὸ
Συρίας εἰς 'Ρώμην εἰς δόξαν τοῦ θεοῦ πιστεύω
ὑμᾶς ἐπεγνωκέναι, οἷς καὶ δηλώσατε ἐγγύς με ὄντα.
πάντες γάρ εἰσιν ἄξιοι τοῦ θεοῦ καὶ ὑμῶν· οὓς
πρέπον ὑμῖν ἐστιν κατὰ πάντα ἀναπαῦσαι.   3.
ἔγραψα δὲ ὑμῖν ταῦτα τῇ πρὸ ἐννέα καλανδῶν
Σεπτεμβρίων. ἔρρωσθε εἰς τέλος ἐν ὑπομονῇ
II Thess 3, 5 'Ιησοῦ Χριστοῦ.

ΦΙΛΑΔΕΛΦΕΥΣΙΝ ΙΓΝΑΤΙΟΣ

'Ιγνάτιος, ὁ καὶ Θεοφόρος, ἐκκλησίᾳ θεοῦ
πατρὸς καὶ κυρίου 'Ιησοῦ Χριστοῦ τῇ οὔσῃ
ἐν Φιλαδελφίᾳ τῆς 'Ασίας, ἠλεημένῃ καὶ
ἡδρασμένῃ ἐν ὁμονοίᾳ θεοῦ καὶ ἀγαλλιωμένῃ
ἐν τῷ πάθει τοῦ κυρίου ἡμῶν ἀδιακρίτως καὶ
ἐν τῇ ἀναστάσει αὐτοῦ πεπληροφορημένῃ ἐν
παντὶ ἐλέει, ἣν ἀσπάζομαι ἐν αἵματι 'Ιησοῦ
Χριστοῦ, ἥτις ἐστὶν χαρὰ αἰώνιος καὶ παρά-
μονος, μάλιστα ἐὰν ἐν ἑνὶ ὦσιν σὺν τῷ
ἐπισκόπῳ καὶ τοῖς σὺν αὐτῷ πρεσβυτέροις
καὶ διακόνοις ἀποδεδειγμένοις ἐν γνώμῃ
'Ιησοῦ Χριστοῦ, οὓς κατὰ τὸ ἴδιον θέλημα
ἐστήριξεν ἐν βεβαιωσύνῃ τῷ ἁγίῳ αὐτοῦ
πνεύματι.

I

1. °Ον ἐπίσκοπον ἔγνων οὐκ ἀφ' ἑαυτοῦ οὐδὲ δι'
ἀνθρώπων κεκτῆσθαι τὴν διακονίαν τὴν εἰς τὸ
238

others. 2. Concerning those who have preceded me from Syria to Rome to the glory of God, I believe that you have received information; tell them that I am close at hand; for they are all worthy of God and of you, and it is right for you to refresh them in every way. 3. I write this to you on the 24th of August. Farewell unto the end, in the endurance of Jesus Christ.

V.—IGNATIUS TO THE PHILADELPHIANS.

IGNATIUS, who is also called Theophorus, to the Church of God the Father and of the Lord Jesus Christ, which is in Philadelphia in Asia, which has obtained mercy, and is established in the harmony of God, and rejoices in the Passion of our Lord without doubting, and is fully assured in all mercy in his resurrection; I greet her in the blood of Jesus Christ, which is eternal and abiding joy, especially if men be at one with the bishop, and with the presbyters and deacons, who together with him have been appointed according to the mind of Jesus Christ, and he established them in security according to his own will by his Holy Spirit. *Greetings*

I

1. I KNOW that your bishop obtained the ministry, which makes for the common good, neither from *The Bishop of Philadelphia*

239

THE APOSTOLIC FATHERS

κοινὸν ἀνήκουσαν οὐδὲ κατὰ κενοδοξίαν, ἀλλ' ἐν
ἀγάπῃ θεοῦ πατρὸς καὶ κυρίου Ἰησοῦ Χριστοῦ·
οὗ καταπέπληγμαι τὴν ἐπιείκειαν, ὃς σιγῶν πλείονα δύναται τῶν μάταια¹ λαλούντων. 2. συνευρύθ-
μισται γὰρ ταῖς ἐντολαῖς ὡς χορδαῖς κιθάρα.
διὸ μακαρίζει μου ἡ ψυχὴ τὴν εἰς θεὸν αὐτοῦ
γνώμην, ἐπιγνοὺς ἐνάρετον καὶ τέλειον οὖσαν, τὸ
ἀκίνητον αὐτοῦ καὶ τὸ ἀόργητον αὐτοῦ ἐν πάσῃ
ἐπιεικείᾳ θεοῦ ζῶντος.

II

1. Τέκνα οὖν φωτὸς ἀληθείας,² φεύγετε τὸν
μερισμὸν καὶ τὰς κακοδιδασκαλίας· ὅπου δὲ ὁ
ποιμήν ἐστιν, ἐκεῖ ὡς πρόβατα ἀκολουθεῖτε. 2.
πολλοὶ γὰρ λύκοι ἀξιόπιστοι ἡδονῇ κακῇ αἰχ-
μαλωτίζουσιν τοὺς θεοδρόμους· ἀλλ' ἐν τῇ ἑνότητι
ὑμῶν οὐχ ἕξουσιν τόπον.

III

1. Ἀπέχεσθε τῶν κακῶν βοτανῶν, ἅστινας οὐ
γεωργεῖ Ἰησοῦς Χριστός, διὰ τὸ μὴ εἶναι αὐτοὺς
Mt. 15, 13 φυτείαν πατρός· οὐχ ὅτι παρ' ὑμῖν μερισμὸν
εὗρον, ἀλλ' ἀποδιϋλισμόν. 2. ὅσοι γὰρ θεοῦ εἰσιν
καὶ Ἰησοῦ Χριστοῦ, οὗτοι μετὰ τοῦ ἐπισκόπου
εἰσίν. καὶ ὅσοι ἂν μετανοήσαντες ἔλθωσιν ἐπὶ τὴν
ἑνότητα τῆς ἐκκλησίας, καὶ οὗτοι θεοῦ ἔσονται,

---

¹ μάταια GL, om. A, πλέον g. Lightfoot favours the
reading of A.
² φωτὸς καὶ ἀληθείας A " light and truth "; Lightfoot thinks
that φωτός is an early gloss.

himself nor through men, nor for vain-glory, but in the love of God the Father and the Lord Jesus Christ. And I was amazed at his gentleness, and at his ability to do more by silence than those who use vain words. 2. For he is attuned to the commandments as a harp to its strings. Therefore my soul blesses his godly mind, recognising its virtue and perfection, and the unmoveable and passionless temper by which he lives in all godly gentleness.

II

1. THEREFORE as children of the light of truth flee from division and wrong doctrine. And follow as sheep where the shepherd is. 2. For there are many specious wolves who lead captive with evil pleasures the runners in God's race, but they will find no place if you are in unity.

Warning against heresy

III

1. ABSTAIN from evil growths, which Jesus Christ does not tend, because they are not the planting of the Father. Not that I have found division among you but 'filtering.'[1] 2. For as many as belong to God and Jesus Christ,—these are with the bishop. And as many as repent and come to the unity of the Church, —these also shall be of God, to be living according to

Warning against schism

---

[1] The meaning is that the Christians at Philadelphia had "filtered out" the impurity of heresy from their church.

241

I Cor. 6, 9. 10 ἵνα ὦσιν κατὰ Ἰησοῦν Χριστὸν ζῶντες. 3. μὴ πλανᾶσθε, ἀδελφοί μου· εἴ τις σχίζοντι ἀκολουθεῖ, βασιλείαν θεοῦ οὐ κληρονομεῖ· εἴ τις ἐν ἀλλοτρίᾳ γνώμῃ περιπατεῖ, οὗτος τῷ πάθει οὐ συγκατατίθεται.

IV

I Cor. 10, 16, 17   Σπουδάσατε οὖν μιᾷ εὐχαριστίᾳ χρῆσθαι· μία γὰρ σὰρξ τοῦ κυρίου ἡμῶν Ἰησοῦ Χριστοῦ καὶ ἓν ποτήριον εἰς ἕνωσιν τοῦ αἵματος αὐτοῦ, ἓν θυσιαστήριον, ὡς εἷς ἐπίσκοπος ἅμα τῷ πρεσβυτερίῳ καὶ διακόνοις τοῖς συνδούλοις μου· ἵνα, ὃ ἐὰν πράσσητε, κατὰ θεὸν πράσσητε.

V

1. Ἀδελφοί μου, λίαν ἐκκέχυμαι ἀγαπῶν ὑμᾶς καὶ ὑπεραγαλλόμενος ἀσφαλίζομαι ὑμᾶς· οὐκ ἐγὼ δέ, ἀλλ' Ἰησοῦς Χριστός, ἐν ᾧ δεδεμένος φοβοῦμαι μᾶλλον, ὡς ἔτι ὢν ἀναπάρτιστος· ἀλλ' ἡ προσευχὴ ὑμῶν εἰς θεόν[1] με ἀπαρτίσει, ἵνα ἐν ᾧ κλήρῳ ἠλεήθην ἐπιτύχω, προσφυγὼν τῷ εὐαγγελίῳ ὡς σαρκὶ Ἰησοῦ, καὶ τοῖς ἀποστόλοις ὡς πρεσβυτερίῳ ἐκκλησίας. 2. καὶ τοὺς προφήτας δὲ ἀγαπῶμεν, διὰ τὸ καὶ αὐτοὺς εἰς τὸ εὐαγγέλιον κατηγγελκέναι καὶ εἰς αὐτὸν ἐλπίζειν καὶ αὐτὸν ἀναμένειν, ἐν ᾧ καὶ πιστεύσαντες ἐσώθησαν, ἐν ἑνότητι Ἰησοῦ

---

[1] εἰς θεόν Gg, om. L(A).

Jesus Christ.   3. " Be not deceived," my brethren,
if any one follow a maker of schism, " he does not
inherit the kingdom of God ; " if any man walk in
strange doctrine he has no part in the Passion.

IV

1. Be careful therefore to use one Eucharist (for
there is one flesh of our Lord Jesus Christ, and one
cup for union with his blood, one altar, as there is
one bishop with the presbytery and the deacons my
fellow servants), in order that whatever you do you
may do it according unto God.

The one Eucharist

V

1. Brethren, I am overflowing with love to you,
and exceedingly joyful in watching over your safety.
Yet not I, but Jesus Christ, whose bonds I bear, but
am the more fearful in that I am not yet perfected ;
but your prayer will make me perfect for God, that
I may attain the lot wherein I found mercy, making
the Gospel my refuge as the flesh of Jesus, and the
Apostles as the presbytery of the Church.   2. And
the prophets [1] also do we love,[2] because they also
have announced the Gospel, and are hoping in him
and waiting for him, by faith in whom they also
obtain salvation, being united with Jesus Christ, for

Petition for their prayers

The Christian prophets

---

[1] He probably means the Christian prophets : cf. the
Didache and Hermas.

[2] An alternative translation is "let us love."

THE APOSTOLIC FATHERS

Χριστοῦ ὄντες, ἀξιαγάπητοι καὶ ἀξιοθαύμαστοι
ἅγιοι, ὑπὸ Ἰησοῦ Χριστοῦ μεμαρτυρημένοι καὶ
συνηριθμημένοι ἐν τῷ εὐαγγελίῳ τῆς κοινῆς
ἐλπίδος.

VI

1. Ἐὰν δέ τις ἰουδαϊσμὸν ἑρμηνεύῃ ὑμῖν, μὴ
ἀκούετε αὐτοῦ. ἄμεινον γάρ ἐστιν παρὰ ἀνδρὸς
περιτομὴν ἔχοντος χριστιανισμὸν ἀκούειν, ἢ παρὰ
ἀκροβύστου ἰουδαϊσμόν. ἐὰν δὲ ἀμφότεροι περὶ
Ἰησοῦ Χριστοῦ μὴ λαλῶσιν, οὗτοι ἐμοὶ στῆλαί
εἰσιν καὶ τάφοι νεκρῶν, ἐφ᾽ οἷς γέγραπται μόνον
ὀνόματα ἀνθρώπων. 2. φεύγετε οὖν τὰς κακοτεχνίας καὶ ἐνέδρας τοῦ ἄρχοντος τοῦ αἰῶνος
τούτου, μήποτε θλιβέντες τῇ γνώμῃ αὐτοῦ ἐξα-
σθενήσετε ἐν τῇ ἀγάπῃ· ἀλλὰ πάντες ἐπὶ τὸ αὐτὸ
γίνεσθε ἐν ἀμερίστῳ καρδίᾳ. 3. εὐχαριστῶ δὲ
τῷ θεῷ μου, ὅτι εὐσυνείδητός εἰμι ἐν ὑμῖν καὶ οὐκ
ἔχει τις καυχήσασθαι οὔτε λάθρα οὔτε φανερῶς,
ὅτι ἐβάρησά τινα ἐν μικρῷ ἢ ἐν μεγάλῳ. καὶ
πᾶσι δέ, ἐν οἷς ἐλάλησα, εὔχομαι, ἵνα μὴ εἰς
μαρτύριον αὐτὸ κτήσωνται.

VII

Joh. 3, 8
I Cor. 2, 10
1. Εἰ γὰρ καὶ κατὰ σάρκα μέ τινες ἠθέλησαν
πλανῆσαι, ἀλλὰ τὸ πνεῦμα οὐ πλανᾶται ἀπὸ
θεοῦ ὄν. οἶδεν γάρ, πόθεν ἔρχεται καὶ ποῦ ὑπάγει,
καὶ τὰ κρυπτὰ ἐλέγχει. ἐκραύγασα μεταξὺ ὤν,
ἐλάλουν μεγάλῃ φωνῇ, θεοῦ φωνῇ· Τῷ ἐπισκόπῳ
προσέχετε καὶ τῷ πρεσβυτερίῳ καὶ διακόνοις.

they are worthy of love and saints worthy of admiration, approved by Jesus Christ, and numbered together in the Gospel of the common hope.

VI

1. But if anyone interpret Judaism to you do not listen to him ; for it is better to hear Christianity from the circumcised than Judaism from the uncircumcised. But both of them, unless they speak of Jesus Christ, are to me tombstones and sepulchres of the dead, on whom only the names of men are written. 2. Flee then from the wicked arts and snares of the prince of this world, lest you be afflicted by his device, and grow weak in love ; but come all together with undivided heart. 3. But I thank my God that I have a good conscience towards you, and that no one can boast either secretly or openly that I was a burden to anyone in small or in great matters. And I pray for all among whom I spoke, that they may not turn it to a testimony against themselves.

Against Judaism

VII

1. For even if some desired to deceive me after the flesh, the spirit is not deceived, for it is from God. For it "knoweth whence it comes and whither it goes" and tests secret things. I cried out while I was with you, I spoke with a great voice,— with God's own voice,—" Give heed to the bishop,

His conduct in Philadelphia

THE APOSTOLIC FATHERS

2. οἱ δὲ ὑποπτεύσαντές με ὡς προειδότα τὸν
μερισμόν τινων λέγειν ταῦτα· μάρτυς δέ μοι,
ἐν ᾧ δέδεμαι, ὅτι ἀπὸ σαρκὸς ἀνθρωπίνης οὐκ
ἔγνων. τὸ δὲ πνεῦμα ἐκήρυσσεν λέγον τάδε·
Χωρὶς τοῦ ἐπισκόπου μηδὲν ποιεῖτε, τὴν σάρκα
ὑμῶν ὡς ναὸν θεοῦ τηρεῖτε, τὴν ἕνωσιν ἀγαπᾶτε,
τοὺς μερισμοὺς φεύγετε, μιμηταὶ γίνεσθε Ἰησοῦ
Χριστοῦ, ὡς καὶ αὐτὸς τοῦ πατρὸς αὐτοῦ.

VIII

1. Ἐγὼ μὲν οὖν τὸ ἴδιον ἐποίουν ὡς ἄνθρωπος
εἰς ἕνωσιν κατηρτισμένος. οὗ δὲ μερισμός ἐστιν
καὶ ὀργή, θεὸς οὐ κατοικεῖ. πᾶσιν οὖν μετανο-
οῦσιν ἀφίει ὁ κύριος, ἐὰν μετανοήσωσιν εἰς
ἑνότητα θεοῦ καὶ συνέδριον τοῦ ἐπισκόπου. πιστεύω τῇ χάριτι Ἰησοῦ Χριστοῦ, ὃς λύσει ἀφ᾽
ὑμῶν πάντα δεσμόν. 2. παρακαλῶ δὲ ὑμᾶς μηδὲν
κατ᾽ ἐριθείαν πράσσειν,[1] ἀλλὰ κατὰ χριστομαθίαν.
ἐπεὶ ἤκουσά τινων λεγόντων, ὅτι ἐὰν μὴ ἐν τοῖς
ἀρχείοις εὕρω ἐν τῷ εὐαγγελίῳ οὐ πιστεύω· καὶ
λέγοντός μου αὐτοῖς ὅτι γέγραπται, ἀπεκρίθησάν
μοι ὅτι πρόκειται. ἐμοὶ δὲ ἀρχεῖά ἐστιν Ἰησοῦς
Χριστός, τὰ ἄθικτα ἀρχεῖα ὁ σταυρὸς αὐτοῦ καὶ
ὁ θάνατος καὶ ἡ ἀνάστασις αὐτοῦ καὶ ἡ πίστις
ἡ δι᾽ αὐτοῦ, ἐν οἷς θέλω ἐν τῇ προσευχῇ ὑμῶν
δικαιωθῆναι.

[1] Πράσσειν GL, πράσσετε GA.

and to the presbytery and deacons." 2. But some suspected me of saying this because I had previous knowledge of the division of some persons: but he in whom I am bound is my witness that I had no knowledge of this from any human being, but the Spirit was preaching, and saying this, " Do nothing without the bishop, keep your flesh as the temple of God, love unity, flee from divisions, be imitators of Jesus Christ, as was he also of his Father."

VIII

1. I THEN did my best as a man who was set on unity. But where there is division and anger God does not dwell. The Lord then forgives all who repent, if their repentance lead to the unity of God and the council of the bishop. I have faith in the grace of Jesus Christ, and he shall loose every bond from you. 2. But I beseech you to do nothing in factiousness, but after the teaching of Christ. For I heard some men saying, " if I find it not in the charters in the Gospel I do not believe,"[1] and when I said to them that it is in the Scripture, they answered me, " that is exactly the question." But to me the charters are Jesus Christ, the inviolable charter is his cross, and death, and resurrection, and the faith which is through him ;—in these I desire to be justified by your prayers.

Exhorta-tion to unity

---

[1] The Greek, without punctuation, is as ambiguous as the English : " If I find it not in the charters,—in the Gospel I do not believe," or " If I find it not in the charters, in the Gospel, I do not believe." Probably the former should be preferred on the ground that " the charters " probably means the Old Testament.

THE APOSTOLIC FATHERS

IX

1. Καλοὶ καὶ οἱ ἱερεῖς, κρεῖσσον δὲ ὁ ἀρχιερεὺς ὁ πεπιστευμένος τὰ ἅγια τῶν ἁγίων, ὃς μόνος πεπίστευται τὰ κρυπτὰ τοῦ θεοῦ· αὐτὸς ὢν θύρα τοῦ πατρός, δι’ ἧς εἰσέρχονται Ἀβραὰμ καὶ Ἰσαὰκ καὶ Ἰακὼβ καὶ οἱ προφῆται καὶ ἀπόστολοι καὶ ἡ ἐκκλησία. πάντα ταῦτα εἰς ἑνότητα θεοῦ. 2. ἐξαίρετον δέ τι ἔχει τὸ εὐαγγέλιον, τὴν παρουσίαν τοῦ σωτῆρος, κυρίου ἡμῶν Ἰησοῦ Χριστοῦ, τὸ πάθος αὐτοῦ, καὶ τὴν ἀνάστασιν. οἱ γὰρ ἀγαπητοὶ προφῆται κατήγγειλαν εἰς αὐτόν· τὸ δὲ εὐαγγέλιον ἀπάρτισμά ἐστιν ἀφθαρσίας. πάντα ὁμοῦ καλά ἐστιν, ἐὰν ἐν ἀγάπῃ πιστεύητε.

X

1. Ἐπειδὴ κατὰ τὴν προσευχὴν ὑμῶν καὶ κατὰ τὰ σπλάγχνα, ἃ ἔχετε ἐν Χριστῷ Ἰησοῦ, ἀπηγγέλη μοι εἰρηνεύειν τὴν ἐκκλησίαν τὴν ἐν Ἀντιοχείᾳ τῆς Συρίας, πρέπον ἐστὶν ὑμῖν ὡς ἐκκλησίᾳ θεοῦ, χειροτονῆσαι διάκονον εἰς τὸ πρεσβεῦσαι ἐκεῖ θεοῦ πρεσβείαν, εἰς τὸ συγχαρῆναι αὐτοῖς ἐπὶ τὸ αὐτὸ γενομένοις καὶ δοξάσαι τὸ ὄνομα. 2. μακάριος ἐν Ἰησοῦ Χριστῷ, ὃς καταξιωθήσεται τῆς τοιαύτης διακονίας, καὶ ὑμεῖς δοξασθήσεσθε. θέλουσιν δὲ ὑμῖν οὐκ ἔστιν ἀδύνατον ὑπὲρ ὀνόματος θεοῦ, ὡς καὶ αἱ ἔγγιστα ἐκκλησίαι ἔπεμψαν ἐπισκόπους, αἱ δὲ πρεσβυτέρους καὶ διακόνους.

IX

1. THE priests likewise are noble, but the High
Priest who has been entrusted with the Holy of Holies
is greater, and only to him have the secret things
of God been entrusted. He is the door of the
Father, through which enter Abraham and Isaac and
Jacob and the Prophets and the Apostles and the
Church. All these things are joined in the unity of
God. 2. But the Gospel has somewhat of pre-
eminence, the coming of the Saviour, our Lord Jesus
Christ, his passion, and the resurrection. For the
beloved prophets had a message pointing to him, but
the Gospel is the perfection of incorruption. All
things together are good if you hold the faith in love.

The old and new Dispensations

X

1. SINCE it was reported to me that the Church
which is in Antioch in Syria is in peace, in accordance
with your prayers, and the compassion which you
have in Christ Jesus, it is proper for you, as a Church
of God, to appoint a deacon to go as the ambassador
of God to it, to congratulate those who are gathered
together, and to glorify the Name. 2. Blessed in Jesus
Christ is he who shall be found worthy of such a
ministry, and you yourselves shall be glorified. And
if you have the will it is not impossible for you to do
this for the sake of the Name of God, even as the
neighbouring Churches have sent bishops, and others
presbyters and deacons.

The Church in Syria

XI

1. Περὶ δὲ Φίλωνος τοῦ διακόνου ἀπὸ Κιλικίας, ἀνδρὸς μεμαρτυρημένου, ὃς καὶ νῦν ἐν λόγῳ θεοῦ ὑπηρετεῖ μοι ἅμα ῾Ρέῳ[1] ᾽Αγαθόποδι, ἀνδρὶ ἐκλεκτῷ, ὃς ἀπὸ Συρίας μοι ἀκολουθεῖ ἀποταξάμενος τῷ βίῳ, οἳ καὶ μαρτυροῦσιν ὑμῖν, κἀγὼ τῷ θεῷ εὐχαριστῶ ὑπὲρ ὑμῶν, ὅτι ἐδέξασθε αὐτούς, ὡς καὶ ὑμᾶς ὁ κύριος· οἱ δὲ ἀτιμάσαντες αὐτοὺς λυτρωθείησαν ἐν τῇ χάριτι τοῦ ᾽Ιησοῦ Χριστοῦ. 2. ἀσπάζεται ὑμᾶς ἡ ἀγάπη τῶν ἀδελφῶν τῶν ἐν Τρωάδι· ὅθεν καὶ γράφω ὑμῖν διὰ Βούρρου πεμφθέντος ἅμα ἐμοὶ ἀπὸ ᾽Εφεσίων καὶ Σμυρναίων εἰς λόγον τιμῆς. τιμήσει αὐτοὺς ὁ κύριος ᾽Ιησοῦς Χριστός, εἰς ὃν ἐλπίζουσιν σαρκί, ψυχῇ, πνεύματι, πίστει, ἀγάπῃ, ὁμονοίᾳ. ἔρρωσθε ἐν Χριστῷ ᾽Ιησοῦ, τῇ κοινῇ ἐλπίδι ἡμῶν.

ΣΜΥΡΝΑΙΟΙΣ ΙΓΝΑΤΙΟΣ

I Cor. 1, 7

᾽Ιγνάτιος, ὁ · καὶ Θεοφόρος, ἐκκλησίᾳ θεοῦ πατρὸς καὶ τοῦ ἠγαπημένου ᾽Ιησοῦ Χριστοῦ, ἠλεημένῃ ἐν παντὶ χαρίσματι, πεπληρωμένῃ ἐν πίστει καὶ ἀγάπῃ, ἀνυστερήτῳ οὔσῃ παντὸς χαρίσματος, θεοπρεπεστάτῃ καὶ ἁγιο-

---

[1] Lighfoot emends to ῾Ραίῳ on the grounds that this form is justified by inscriptions, while ῾Ρέῳ is unknown, and g which has Γαίῳ implies this reading.

IGNATIUS TO THE SMYRNAEANS

XI

1. But concerning Philo, the deacon from Cilicia, Thanks and final greetings a man of good report, who is at present serving me in the word of God, with Rheus Agathopous, an elect man who is following me from Syria, and has renounced this life;—these bear you witness (and I also thank God on your behalf) that you received them even as the Lord received you;[1] but may those who treated them with disrespect be redeemed by the grace of Jesus Christ. 2. The love of the brethren at Troas salutes you; and I am writing thence to you by the hand of Burrhus, who was sent with me by the Ephesians and Smyrnaeans as a mark of honour. The Lord Jesus Christ shall reward them, on whom they hope in flesh and soul and spirit, in faith, in love and in harmony. Farewell in Christ Jesus, our common hope.

VI.—IGNATIUS TO THE SMYRNAEANS.

Ignatius, who is also called Theophorus, to the Greeting Church of God the Father and the Beloved Jesus Christ, which has obtained mercy in every gift, and is filled with faith and love, and comes behind in no gift, most worthy of God, and

---

[1] Or possibly "even as may the Lord receive you."

φόρῳ, τῇ οὔσῃ ἐν Σμύρνῃ τῆς Ἀσίας, ἐν
ἀμώμῳ πνεύματι καὶ λόγῳ θεοῦ πλεῖστα
χαίρειν.

I

1. Δοξάζω Ἰησοῦν Χριστὸν τὸν θεὸν τὸν οὕτως
ὑμᾶς σοφίσαντα· ἐνόησα γὰρ ὑμᾶς κατηρτισ-
μένους ἐν ἀκινήτῳ πίστει, ὥσπερ καθηλωμένους
ἐν τῷ σταυρῷ τοῦ κυρίου Ἰησοῦ Χριστοῦ σαρκί
τε καὶ πνεύματι καὶ ἡδρασμένους ἐν ἀγάπῃ ἐν τῷ
αἵματι Χριστοῦ, πεπληροφορημένους εἰς τὸν
κύριον ἡμῶν, ἀληθῶς ὄντα ἐκ γένους Δανεὶδ κατὰ
σάρκα, υἱὸν θεοῦ κατὰ θέλημα καὶ δύναμιν θεοῦ,[1]
γεγεννημένον ἀληθῶς ἐκ παρθένου, βεβαπτισμένον
ὑπὸ Ἰωάννου, ἵνα πληρωθῇ πᾶσα δικαιοσύνη ὑπ᾽
αὐτοῦ· 2. ἀληθῶς ἐπὶ Ποντίου Πιλάτου καὶ
Ἡρώδου τετράρχου καθηλωμένον ὑπὲρ ἡμῶν ἐν
σαρκί, ἀφ᾽ οὗ καρποῦ ἡμεῖς ἀπὸ τοῦ θεομακα-
ρίστου αὐτοῦ πάθους, ἵνα ἄρῃ σύσσημον εἰς τοὺς
αἰῶνας διὰ τῆς ἀναστάσεως εἰς τοὺς ἁγίους καὶ
πιστοὺς αὐτοῦ, εἴτε ἐν Ἰουδαίοις εἴτε ἐν ἔθνεσιν,
ἐν ἑνὶ σώματι τῆς ἐκκλησίας αὐτοῦ.

Rom. 1, 3

Mt. 3, 15

Is. 5, 26 (11,
12 ; 49, 22 ;
62, 10)

Eph. 2, 16

II

1. Ταῦτα γὰρ πάντα ἔπαθεν δι᾽ ἡμᾶς, ἵνα
σωθῶμεν[2] καὶ ἀληθῶς ἔπαθεν, ὡς καὶ ἀληθῶς
ἀνέστησεν ἑαυτόν, οὐχ ὥσπερ ἄπιστοί τινες

---

[1] A Theodoret omit θεοῦ and are followed by Lightfoot.
[2] ἵνα σωθῶμεν om. C.

gifted with holiness,—the Church which is in Smyrna in Asia—abundant greeting in a blameless spirit and in the Word of God.

I

1. I GIVE glory to Jesus Christ, the God who has thus given you wisdom; for I have observed that you are established in immoveable faith, as if nailed to the cross of the Lord Jesus Christ, both in flesh and spirit, and confirmed in love by the blood of Christ, being fully persuaded as touching our Lord, that he is in truth of the family of David according to the flesh, God's son by the will and power of God, truly born of a Virgin, baptised by John that "all righteousness might be fulfilled by him," 2. truly nailed to a tree[1] in the flesh for our sakes under Pontius Pilate and Herod the Tetrarch, (and of its fruit are we from his divinely blessed Passion) that "he might set up an ensign" for all ages through his Resurrection, for his saints and believers, whether among the Jews, or among the heathen, in one body of his Church.

The faith of the Smyrnaeans

II

1. FOR he suffered all these things for us that we might attain salvation, and he truly suffered even as he also truly raised himself, not as some unbelievers

Against Docetism

---

[1] "Tree" is not expressed in the Greek: but seems to be implied by the "fruit" in the next sentence, though the exact meaning of the passage is obscure.

λέγουσιν, τὸ δοκεῖν αὐτὸν πεπονθέναι, αὐτοὶ τὸ
δοκεῖν ὄντες· καὶ καθὼς φρονοῦσιν, καὶ συμβή-
σεται αὐτοῖς, οὖσιν ἀσωμάτοις καὶ δαιμονικοῖς.

III

1. Ἐγὼ γὰρ καὶ μετὰ τὴν ἀνάστασιν ἐν σαρκὶ
αὐτὸν οἶδα καὶ πιστεύω ὄντα. 2. καὶ ὅτε πρὸς
τοὺς περὶ Πέτρον ἦλθεν, ἔφη αὐτοῖς· Λάβετε,
ψηλαφήσατέ με καὶ ἴδετε, ὅτι οὐκ εἰμὶ δαιμόνιον
ἀσώματον. καὶ εὐθὺς αὐτοῦ ἥψαντο καὶ ἐπί-
στευσαν, κραθέντες τῇ σαρκὶ αὐτοῦ καὶ τῷ
πνεύματι.[1] διὰ τοῦτο καὶ θανάτου κατεφρόνησαν,
ηὑρέθησαν δὲ ὑπὲρ θάνατον. 3. μετὰ δὲ τὴν
ἀνάστασιν συνέφαγεν αὐτοῖς καὶ συνέπιεν ὡς
σαρκικός, καίπερ πνευματικῶς ἡνωμένος τῷ
πατρί.

Cf. Luke 24, 39

Acts 10, 41

IV

1. Ταῦτα δὲ παραινῶ ὑμῖν, ἀγαπητοί, εἰδὼς
ὅτι καὶ ὑμεῖς οὕτως ἔχετε. προφυλάσσω δὲ ὑμᾶς
ἀπὸ τῶν θηρίων τῶν ἀνθρωπομόρφων, οὓς οὐ
μόνον δεῖ ὑμᾶς μὴ παραδέχεσθαι, ἀλλ' εἰ δυνατὸν
μηδὲ συναντᾶν,[2] μόνον δὲ προσεύχεσθε[3] ὑπὲρ
αὐτῶν, ἐάν πως μετανοήσωσιν, ὅπερ δύσκολον,
τούτου δὲ ἔχει ἐξουσίαν Ἰησοῦς Χριστός, τὸ

---

[1] πνεύματι GLC, αἵματι A.
[2] συναντᾶν BG. συναντᾶν αὐτοῖς LAC.
[3] προσεύχεσθε BC(S), προσεύχεσθαι GLA.

254

say, that his Passion was merely in semblance,—but it is they who are merely in semblance, and even according to their opinions it shall happen to them, and they shall be without bodies and phantasmal.

III

1. For I know and believe that he was in the flesh even after the Resurrection. 2. And when he came to those with Peter he said to them : "Take, handle me and see that I am not a phantom without a body." And they immediately touched him and believed, being mingled both with his flesh and spirit. Therefore they despised even death, and were proved to be above death. 3. And after his Resurrection he ate and drank with them as a being of flesh, although he was united in spirit to the Father.

The Resurrection in the flesh

IV

1. Now I warn you of these things, beloved, knowing that you also are so minded. But I guard you in advance against beasts in the form of men, whom you must not only not receive, but if it is possible not even meet, but only pray for them, if perchance they may repent, difficult though that be,—but Jesus Christ who is our true life has the

Warning against heretical teachers

ἀληθινὸν ἡμῶν ζῆν. 2. εἰ γὰρ τὸ δοκεῖν[1] ταῦτα ἐπράχθη ὑπὸ τοῦ κυρίου ἡμῶν, κἀγὼ τὸ δοκεῖν δέδεμαι. τί δὲ καὶ ἑαυτὸν ἔκδοτον δέδωκα τῷ θανάτῳ, πρὸς πῦρ, πρὸς μάχαιραν, πρὸς θηρία; ἀλλ' ἐγγὺς μαχαίρας ἐγγὺς θεοῦ, μεταξὺ θηρίων μεταξὺ θεοῦ· μόνον ἐν τῷ ὀνόματι Ἰησοῦ Χριστοῦ

Phil. 4, 13 εἰς τὸ συμπαθεῖν αὐτῷ πάντα ὑπομένω, αὐτοῦ με ἐνδυναμοῦντος τοῦ τελείου ἀνθρώπου.[2]

V

1. Ὃν τινες ἀγνοοῦντες ἀρνοῦνται, μᾶλλον δὲ ἠρνήθησαν ὑπ' αὐτοῦ, ὄντες συνήγοροι τοῦ θανάτου μᾶλλον ἢ τῆς ἀληθείας· οὓς οὐκ ἔπεισαν αἱ προφητεῖαι οὐδὲ ὁ νόμος Μωύσεως, ἀλλ' οὐδὲ μέχρι νῦν τὸ εὐαγγέλιον, οὐδὲ τὰ ἡμέτερα τῶν κατ' ἄνδρα παθήματα. 2. καὶ γὰρ περὶ ἡμῶν τὸ αὐτὸ φρονοῦσιν. τί γάρ με ὠφελεῖ τις, εἰ ἐμὲ ἐπαινεῖ, τὸν δὲ κύριόν μου βλασφημεῖ, μὴ ὁμολογῶν αὐτὸν σαρκοφόρον; ὁ δὲ τοῦτο λέγων[3] τελείως αὐτὸν ἀπήρνηται, ὢν νεκροφόρος. 3. τὰ δὲ ὀνόματα αὐτῶν, ὄντα ἄπιστα, οὐκ ἔδοξέν μοι ἐγγράψαι. ἀλλὰ μηδὲ γένοιτό μοι αὐτῶν μνημονεύειν, μέχρις οὗ μετανοήσωσιν εἰς τὸ πάθος, ὅ ἐστιν ἡμῶν ἀνάστασις.

---

[1] Here and elsewhere Bg read τῷ δοκεῖν against G which has τὸ δοκεῖν.

[2] add. γενομένου GL.

[3] λέγον BC, μὴ λέγων GLA.

power over this. 2. For if it is merely in semblance that these things were done by our Lord I am also a prisoner in semblance. And why have I given myself up to death, to fire, to the sword, to wild beasts? Because near the sword is near to God; with the wild beasts is with God; in the name of Jesus Christ alone am I enduring all things, that I may suffer with him, and the perfect man himself gives me strength.

V

1. THERE are some who ignorantly deny him, but rather were denied by him, being advocates of death rather than of the truth. These are they whom neither the prophecies nor the law of Moses persuaded, nor the gospel even until now, nor our own individual sufferings. 2. For they have the same opinion concerning us. For what does anyone profit me if he praise me but blaspheme my Lord, and do not confess that he was clothed in flesh? But he who says this has denied him absolutely and is clothed with a corpse. 3. Now I have not thought right to put into writing their unbelieving names; but would that I might not even remember them, until they repent concerning the Passion, which is our resurrection.

Against Docetism

VI

1. Μηδεὶς πλανάσθω· καὶ τὰ ἐπουράνια καὶ ἡ δόξα τῶν ἀγγέλων καὶ οἱ ἄρχοντες ὁρατοί τε καὶ ἀόρατοι, ἐὰν μὴ πιστεύσωσιν εἰς τὸ αἷμα Χριστοῦ, κἀκείνοις κρίσις ἐστίν· ὁ χωρῶν χωρείτω. τόπος μηδένα φυσιούτω· τὸ γὰρ ὅλον ἐστὶν πίστις καὶ ἀγάπη, ὧν οὐδὲν προκέκριται. 2. καταμάθετε δὲ τοὺς ἑτεροδοξοῦντας εἰς τὴν χάριν Ἰησοῦ Χριστοῦ τὴν εἰς ἡμᾶς ἐλθοῦσαν, πῶς ἐναντίοι εἰσὶν τῇ γνώμῃ τοῦ θεοῦ. περὶ ἀγάπης οὐ μέλει αὐτοῖς, οὐ περὶ χήρας, οὐ περὶ ὀρφανοῦ, οὐ περὶ θλιβομένου, οὐ περὶ δεδεμένου ἢ λελυμένου,[1] οὐ περὶ πεινῶντος ἢ διψῶντος.

Mt. 19, 12

VII

1. Εὐχαριστίας καὶ προσευχῆς ἀπέχονται, διὰ τὸ μὴ ὁμολογεῖν τὴν εὐχαριστίαν σάρκα εἶναι τοῦ σωτῆρος ἡμῶν Ἰησοῦ Χριστοῦ τὴν ὑπὲρ τῶν ἁμαρτιῶν ἡμῶν παθοῦσαν, ἣν τῇ χρηστότητι ὁ πατὴρ ἤγειρεν. οἱ οὖν ἀντιλέγοντες τῇ δωρεᾷ τοῦ θεοῦ συζητοῦντες ἀποθνήσκουσιν· συνέφερεν δὲ αὐτοῖς ἀγαπᾶν, ἵνα καὶ ἀναστῶσιν. 2. πρέπον[2] ἐστὶν ἀπέχεσθαι τῶν τοιούτων καὶ μήτε κατ᾽ ἰδίαν περὶ αὐτῶν λαλεῖν μήτε κοινῇ, προσέχειν δὲ

---

[1] λελυμένου BGL, om. AC.
[2] πρέπον BA(L), πρέπον οὖν Gg.

VI.

1. LET no one be deceived; even things in heaven and the glory of the angels, and the rulers visible and invisible, even for them there is a judgment if they do not believe on the blood of Christ. "He that receiveth let him receive." Let not office exalt anyone, for faith and love is everything, and nothing has been preferred to them. 2. But mark those who have strange opinions concerning the grace of Jesus Christ which has come to us, and see how contrary they are to the mind of God. For love they have no care, none for the widow, none for the orphan, none for the distressed, none for the afflicted, none for the prisoner, or for him released from prison, none for the hungry or thirsty. *The universal judgment*

The unchristian behaviour of heretics

VII

1. THEY abstain from Eucharist and prayer, because they do not confess that the Eucharist is the flesh of our Saviour Jesus Christ who suffered for our sins, which the Father raised up by his goodness. They then who deny the gift of God are perishing in their disputes; but it were better for them to have love, that they also may attain to the Resurrection. 2. It is right to refrain from such men and not even to speak about them in private or in public, but to give heed to the prophets and especially to the *Heretics and the Eucharist*

τοῖς προφήταις, ἐξαιρέτως δὲ τῷ εὐαγγελίῳ, ἐν
ᾧ τὸ πάθος ἡμῖν δεδήλωται καὶ ἡ ἀνάστασις
τετελείωται. τοὺς δὲ μερισμοὺς φεύγετε ὡς ἀρχὴν
κακῶν.

VIII

1. Πάντες τῷ ἐπισκόπῳ ἀκολουθεῖτε, ὡς Ἰησοῦς
Χριστὸς τῷ πατρί, καὶ τῷ πρεσβυτερίῳ ὡς τοῖς
ἀποστόλοις. τοὺς δὲ διακόνους ἐντρέπεσθε ὡς
θεοῦ ἐντολήν. μηδεὶς χωρὶς τοῦ ἐπισκόπου τι
πρασσέτω τῶν ἀνηκόντων εἰς τὴν ἐκκλησίαν.
ἐκείνη βεβαία εὐχαριστία ἡγείσθω, ἡ ὑπὸ ἐπίσκοπον οὖσα ἢ ᾧ ἂν αὐτὸς ἐπιτρέψῃ. 2. ὅπου ἂν
φανῇ ὁ ἐπίσκοπος, ἐκεῖ τὸ πλῆθος ἤτω,[1] ὥσπερ
ὅπου ἂν ᾖ Ἰησοῦς Χριστός,[2] ἐκεῖ ἡ καθολικὴ
ἐκκλησία. οὐκ ἐξόν ἐστιν χωρὶς τοῦ ἐπισκόπου οὔτε
βαπτίζειν οὔτε ἀγάπην ποιεῖν· ἀλλ᾽ ὃ ἂν ἐκεῖνος
δοκιμάσῃ, τοῦτο καὶ τῷ θεῷ εὐάρεστον, ἵνα
ἀσφαλὲς ᾖ καὶ βέβαιον πᾶν ὃ πράσσετε.[3]

IX

1. Εὔλογόν ἐστιν λοιπὸν ἀνανῆψαι ἡμᾶς,[4] ὡς ἔτι
καιρὸν ἔχομεν εἰς θεὸν μετανοεῖν. καλῶς ἔχει,
θεὸν καὶ ἐπίσκοπον εἰδέναι. ὁ τιμῶν ἐπίσκοπον ὑπὸ
θεοῦ τετίμηται· ὁ λάθρα ἐπισκόπου τι πράσσων

---

[1] ἤτω B, ἔστω Gg.
[2] Ἰησ. Χρ. BA, Χρ. Ἰησ. GL.
[3] πράσσετε BSA(g), πράσσεται GL.
[4] ἡμᾶς Bg(SA) καί GL, " it is reasonable to return to soberness, and . . . to repent."

Gospel, in which the Passion has been revealed to us and the Resurrection has been accomplished. But flee from divisions as the beginning of evils.

VIII

1. SEE that you all follow the bishop, as Jesus Christ follows the Father, and the presbytery as if it were the Apostles. And reverence the deacons as the command of God. Let no one do any of the things appertaining to the Church without the bishop. Let that be considered a valid Eucharist which is celebrated by the bishop, or by one whom he appoints. 2. Wherever the bishop appears let the congregation be present; just as wherever Jesus Christ is, there is the Catholic Church. It is not lawful either to baptise or to hold an "agapé"[1] without the bishop; but whatever he approve, this is also pleasing to God, that everything which you do may be secure and valid.

Submission to the Bishop and the Presbyters

IX

1. MOREOVER it is reasonable for us to return to soberness, while we still have time to repent towards God. It is good to know God and the bishop. He who honours the bishop has been honoured by God; he who does anything without the knowledge of the

Honour due to the Bishop

---

[1] Agapé means "love": the name was given to some kind of religious meal. The context here suggests that it is a synonym for the Eucharist, but the point is doubted by some scholars. In the A.V. of Jud. 12 it is translated "Love feasts."

τῷ διαβόλῳ λατρεύει. 2. πάντα οὖν ὑμῖν ἐν
χάριτι περισσευέτω· ἄξιοι γάρ ἐστε. κατὰ πάντα
με ἀνεπαύσατε, καὶ ὑμᾶς Ἰησοῦς Χριστός. ἀπόντα
με καὶ παρόντα ἠγαπήσατε. ἀμοιβὴ[1] ὑμῖν ὁ θεός,
δι’ ὃν πάντα ὑπομένοντες αὐτοῦ τεύξεσθε.

X

1. Φίλωνα καὶ Ῥέον[2] Ἀγαθόπουν, οἳ ἐπηκολού-
θησάν μοι εἰς λόγον θεοῦ, καλῶς ἐποιήσατε
ὑποδεξάμενοι ὡς διακόνους θεοῦ·[3] οἳ καὶ εὐχαρισ-
τοῦσιν τῷ κυρίῳ ὑπὲρ ὑμῶν, ὅτι αὐτοὺς ἀνεπαύσατε
κατὰ πάντα τρόπον. οὐδὲν ὑμῖν οὐ μὴ ἀπολεῖται.
II Tim. 1, 16   2. ἀντίψυχον ὑμῶν τὸ πνεῦμά μου καὶ τὰ δεσμά
μου, ἃ οὐχ ὑπερηφανήσατε οὐδὲ ἐπῃσχύνθητε.
οὐδὲ ὑμᾶς ἐπαισχυνθήσεται ἡ τελεία ἐλπίς,[4]
Ἰησοῦς Χριστός.

XI

1. Ἡ προσευχὴ ὑμῶν ἀπῆλθεν ἐπὶ τὴν ἐκκλησίαν τὴν ἐν Ἀντιοχείᾳ τῆς Συρίας, ὅθεν δεδεμένος θεοπρεπεστάτοις δεσμοῖς πάντας ἀσπάζομαι, οὐκ ὢν ἄξιος ἐκεῖθεν εἶναι, ἔσχατος αὐτῶν
ὤν· κατὰ θέλημα δὲ κατηξιώθην, οὐκ ἐκ συνειδότος
ἀλλ’ ἐκ χάριτος θεοῦ· ἣν εὔχομαι τελείαν μοι

---

[1] ἀμοιβή B, ἀμοιβει G, ἀμείψεται g(A), *retribuat* (= ἀμείβοι?) L.
[2] B has Γάϊον and it is possible that this, also found in g, is
right, but Ῥέον is transcriptionally more probable.
[3] θεοῦ BA, Χριστοῦ θεοῦ G(L).
[4] ἐλπίς BAg, πίστις GIʟ.

bishop is serving the devil. 2. Let all things then abound to you in grace, for you are worthy. In all respects you have refreshed me, and may Jesus Christ give refreshment to you. You have loved me in my absence, and in my presence. God is your reward, and if for his sake you endure all things, you shall attain to him.

X

1. You did well to receive as deacons of God, Philo and Rheus Agathopous, who followed me in the cause of God; and they also give thanks to the Lord for your sake that you refreshed them in every way. Assuredly shall nothing be lost for you. 2. May my spirit be for your life, and my bonds, which you treated neither with haughtiness nor shame. And he who is perfect hope, Jesus Christ, shall not be ashamed of you.

Thanks to the Smyrnaeans

XI

1. Your prayer reached the Church which is in Antioch in Syria, and I greet all men as one who comes thence in bonds which are most seemly in God's sight, though I am not worthy to be from thence, for I am the least of them; but by the will of God I have been thought worthy, not that I am conscious of deserts,[1] but by the grace of God, and

The Church in Syria

---

[1] Or, possibly, "by my own complicity"

δοθῆναι, ἵνα ἐν τῇ προσευχῇ ὑμῶν θεοῦ ἐπιτύχω.
2. ἵνα οὖν ὑμῶν τέλειον γένηται τὸ ἔργον καὶ ἐπὶ
γῆς καὶ ἐν οὐρανῷ, πρέπει εἰς τιμὴν θεοῦ χειροτονῆσαι τὴν ἐκκλησίαν ὑμῶν θεοπρεσβεύτην, εἰς τὸ
γενόμενον ἐν Συρίᾳ[1] συγχαρῆναι αὐτοῖς, ὅτι
εἰρηνεύουσιν καὶ ἀπέλαβον τὸ ἴδιον μέγεθος καὶ
ἀπεκατεστάθη αὐτοῖς τὸ ἴδιον σωματεῖον. 3.
ἐφάνη μοι οὖν θεοῦ[2] ἄξιον πρᾶγμα, πέμψαι τινὰ
τῶν ὑμετέρων μετ' ἐπιστολῆς, ἵνα συνδοξάσῃ τὴν
κατὰ θεὸν αὐτοῖς γενομένην εὐδίαν, καὶ ὅτι λιμένος
ἤδη ἐτύγχανον[3] τῇ προσευχῇ ὑμῶν. τέλειοι
ὄντες τέλεια καὶ φρονεῖτε. θέλουσιν γὰρ ὑμῖν
εὖ πράσσειν θεὸς ἕτοιμος εἰς τὸ παρέχειν.[4]

Phil. 3, 15

XII

1. Ἀσπάζεται ὑμᾶς ἡ ἀγάπη τῶν ἀδελφῶν τῶν
ἐν Τρωάδι, ὅθεν καὶ γράφω ὑμῖν διὰ Βούρρου,[5] ὃν
ἀπεστείλατε μετ' ἐμοῦ ἅμα Ἐφεσίοις, τοῖς ἀδελφοῖς ὑμῶν, ὃς κατὰ πάντα με ἀνέπαυσεν. καὶ
ὄφελον πάντες αὐτὸν ἐμιμοῦντο, ὄντα ἐξεμπλάριον
θεοῦ διακονίας. ἀμείψεται αὐτὸν ἡ χάρις κατὰ
πάντα. 2. ἀσπάζομαι τὸν ἀξιόθεον ἐπίσκοπον
καὶ θεοπρεπὲς πρεσβυτέριον καὶ τοὺς συνδούλους
μου διακόνους καὶ τοὺς κατ' ἄνδρα καὶ κοινῇ
πάντας ἐν ὀνόματι Ἰησοῦ Χριστοῦ καὶ τῇ σαρκὶ

---

[1] ἐν Συρίᾳ B(A)g, ἕως Συρίας GL.   [2] θεοῦ BLA, om. Gg.
[3] ἔτυχον B.   [4] παρέχειν B, παρασχεῖν Gg.
[5] Βόρρου B; the spelling of this varies considerably both
here and in Eph. ii, 1, and Philad. xi, 2. It is possible that
Βόρρος, which has some support in L is really right.

I pray that this may be given to me to the end, and that by your prayers I may attain to God. 2. In order then that your work may be perfect both on earth and in heaven, your Church ought to appoint for the honour of God a delegate of God to go to Syria, and congratulate them that they have gained peace, and have recovered their proper greatness, and that their proper constitution has been restored. 3. It appeared to me therefore a deed worthy of God for you to send one of your number with a letter to join in extolling the tranquillity which they have obtained from God, and that through your prayers they were now gaining a haven. As you are perfect, so also may your counsel be perfect. For if you desire to do well God is ready to help you.

XII

1. THE love of the brethren who are at Troas salutes you, whence I am writing to you by Burrhus, whom you together with the Ephesians your brothers sent with me, and he has in every way refreshed me. Would that all imitated him, for he is a pattern of the ministry of God. In all things grace shall reward him. 2. I salute the godly bishop, and the revered presbytery, and the deacons my fellow-servants, and you all, individually and together, in the name of Jesus Christ, and in his flesh and blood,

Greetings from Troas

αὐτοῦ καὶ τῷ αἵματι, πάθει τε καὶ ἀναστάσει
σαρκικῇ τε καὶ πνευματικῇ, ἐν ἑνότητι θεοῦ καὶ
ὑμῶν. χάρις ὑμῖν, ἔλεος, εἰρήνη, ὑπομονὴ διὰ
παντός.

XIII

1. Ἀσπάζομαι τοὺς οἴκους τῶν ἀδελφῶν μου σὺν
γυναιξὶ καὶ τέκνοις καὶ τὰς παρθένους τὰς λεγο-
μένας χήρας. ἔρρωσθέ μοι ἐν δυνάμει πατρός.[1]
ἀσπάζεται ὑμᾶς Φίλων σὺν ἐμοὶ ὤν. 2. ἀσπάζομαι τὸν οἶκον Ταουΐας,[2] ἣν εὔχομαι ἑδρᾶσθαι
πίστει καὶ ἀγάπῃ σαρκικῇ τε καὶ πνευματικῇ.
ἀσπάζομαι Ἄλκην, τὸ ποθητόν μοι ὄνομα, καὶ
Δάφνον τὸν ἀσύγκριτον καὶ Εὔτεκνον καὶ πάντας
κατ᾽ ὄνομα. ἔρρωσθε ἐν χάριτι θεοῦ.

ΠΡΟΣ ΠΟΛΥΚΑΡΠΟΝ ΙΓΝΑΤΙΟΣ.

Ἰγνάτιος, ὁ καὶ Θεοφόρος, Πολυκάρπῳ ἐπισκόπῳ ἐκκλησίας Σμυρναίων, μᾶλλον ἐπι-
σκοπημένῳ ὑπὸ θεοῦ πατρὸς καὶ κυρίου Ἰησοῦ
Χριστοῦ, πλεῖστα χαίρειν.

[1] πατρός LA, πνεύματος G(g) "spirit." The difference in
MSS would be between πρς and πνς.
[2] Ταουΐας GL, Γαουΐας Ag.

by his Passion and Resurrection both of flesh and
spirit, in union with God and with you. Grace be
to you, mercy, peace and endurance for ever.

XIII

1. I SALUTE the families of my brethren with their
wives and children, and the maidens who are called
widows. Farewell in the power of the Father.
Philo who is with me greets you. 2. I salute the
house of Tavia, and pray that she be confirmed in
faith and love, both of the flesh and spirit. I salute
Alce, a name most dear to me, and the incomparable
Daphnus, and Eutecnus,[1] and all others by their
several names. Farewell in the grace of God.

Final greetings

VII.—IGNATIUS TO POLYCARP.

Ignatius, who is also called Theophorus, to Polycarp,
who is bishop of the Church of the Smyrnaeans,
or rather has for his bishop God the Father and
the Lord Jesus Christ, abundant greeting.

Greeting

---

[1] It is not impossible that εὔτεκνον is an adjective meaning
"with good children," and referring to Daphnus. Zahn
takes this view.

I

1. Ἀποδεχόμενός σου τὴν ἐν θεῷ γνώμην ἡδρασ-
μένην ὡς ἐπὶ πέτραν ἀκίνητον, ὑπερδοξάζω, καταξιωθεὶς τοῦ προσώπου σου τοῦ ἀμώμου, οὗ
ὀναίμην ἐν θεῷ. 2. παρακαλῶ σε ἐν χάριτι ᾗ
ἐνδέδυσαι, προσθεῖναι τῷ δρόμῳ σου καὶ πάντας
παρακαλεῖν, ἵνα σώζωνται. ἐκδίκει σου τὸν
τόπον ἐν πάσῃ ἐπιμελείᾳ σαρκικῇ τε καὶ πνευμα-
τικῇ· τῆς ἑνώσεως φρόντιζε, ἧς οὐδὲν ἄμεινον.
πάντας βάσταζε, ὡς καὶ σὲ ὁ κύριος· πάντων
ἀνέχου ἐν ἀγάπῃ, ὥσπερ καὶ ποιεῖς. 3. προσευχαῖς σχόλαζε ἀδιαλείπτοις· αἰτοῦ σύνεσιν
πλείονα ἧς ἔχεις· γρηγόρει ἀκοίμητον πνεῦμα
κεκτημένος. τοῖς κατ' ἄνδρα κατὰ ὁμοήθειαν
θεοῦ λάλει· πάντων τὰς νόσους βάσταζε ὡς
τέλειος ἀθλητής. ὅπου πλείων κόπος, πολὺ
κέρδος.

Eph. 4, 2

Mt. 8, 17

II

1. Καλοὺς μαθητὰς ἐὰν φιλῇς, χάρις σοι οὐκ
ἔστιν· μᾶλλον τοὺς λοιμοτέρους ἐν πραότητι
ὑπότασσε. οὐ πᾶν τραῦμα τῇ αὐτῇ ἐμπλάστρῳ
θεραπεύεται. τοὺς παροξυσμοὺς ἐμβροχαῖς παῦε.
2. φρόνιμος γίνου ὡς ὁ[1] ὄφις ἐν ἅπασιν καὶ ἀκέραιος
εἰς ἀεὶ ὡς ἡ περιστερά. διὰ τοῦτο σαρκικὸς εἶ
καὶ πνευματικός, ἵνα τὰ φαινόμενά σου εἰς πρόσ-

Mt. 10, 16

---

[1] ὁ om. G, but the parallelism with ἡ περιστερά shows that
this is only an accident.

I

1. WELCOMING your godly mind which is fixed as if on immovable rock, I glory exceedingly that it was granted me to see your blameless face wherein I would fain have pleasure in God. 2. I exhort you to press forward on your course, in the grace wherewith you are endued, and to exhort all men to gain salvation. Vindicate your office with all diligence, both of the flesh and spirit. Care for unity, for there is nothing better. Help all men, as the Lord also helps you ; suffer all men in love, as you indeed do. 3. Be diligent with unceasing prayer. Entreat for wisdom greater than you have, be watchful and keep the spirit from slumbering. Speak to each individually after the manner of God. "Bear the sicknesses" of all as a perfect athlete.[1] Where the toil is greatest, is the gain great.

Salutation and exhortation to diligence

II

1. IF you love good disciples, it is no credit to you ; rather bring to subjection by your gentleness the more troublesome. Not all wounds are healed by the same plaster. Relieve convulsions by fomentations. 2. "Be prudent as the serpent" in all things "and pure as the dove" for ever. For this reason you consist of flesh and spirit, that you may deal tenderly

The need of caring for the weaker brethren

---

[1] No other translation is possible : "athlete" was, both then and later, a favourite name for Christians who strove to excel in virtue, especially in ascetic practices.

269

ωπον κολακεύῃς· τὰ δὲ ἀόρατα αἴτει ἵνα σοι
φανερωθῇ, ὅπως μηδενὸς λείπῃ καὶ παντὸς χαρίσματος περισσεύῃς. 3. ὁ καιρὸς ἀπαιτεῖ σε, ὡς
κυβερνῆται ἀνέμους καὶ ὡς χειμαζόμενος λιμένα,
εἰς τὸ θεοῦ ἐπιτυχεῖν. νῆφε, ὡς θεοῦ ἀθλητής·
τὸ θέμα ἀφθαρσία καὶ ζωὴ αἰώνιος, περὶ ἧς καὶ
σὺ πέπεισαι. κατὰ πάντα σου ἀντίψυχον ἐγὼ
καὶ τὰ δεσμά μου, ἃ ἠγάπησας.

III

1. Οἱ δοκοῦντες ἀξιόπιστοι εἶναι καὶ ἑτεροδι-
δασκαλοῦντες μή σε καταπλησσέτωσαν. στῆθι
ἑδραῖος ὡς ἄκμων τυπτόμενος. μεγάλου ἐστιν
ἀθλητοῦ τὸ δέρεσθαι καὶ νικᾶν. μάλιστα δὲ
ἕνεκεν θεοῦ πάντα ὑπομένειν ἡμᾶς δεῖ, ἵνα καὶ
αὐτὸς ἡμᾶς ὑπομείνῃ. 2. πλέον σπουδαῖος γίνου
οὗ εἶ. τοὺς καιροὺς καταμάνθανε. τὸν ὑπὲρ
καιρὸν προσδόκα, τὸν ἄχρονον, τὸν ἀόρατον, τὸν
δι᾽ ἡμᾶς ὁρατόν, τὸν ἀψηλάφητον, τὸν ἀπαθῆ, τὸν
δι᾽ ἡμᾶς παθητόν, τὸν κατὰ πάντα τρόπον δι᾽
ἡμᾶς ὑπομείναντα.

IV

1. Χῆραι μὴ ἀμελείσθωσαν· μετὰ τὸν κύριον
σὺ αὐτῶν φροντιστὴς ἔσο. μηδὲν ἄνευ γνώμης

with the things which appear visibly; but pray that
the invisible things may be revealed to you, that you
may lack nothing and abound in every gift.   3. The
time calls on you to attain unto God, just as pilots
require wind, and the storm-tossed sailor seeks a
harbour.[1]   Be sober as God's athlete.   The prize[2] is
immortality and eternal life, of which you have been
persuaded.   In all things I am devoted to you,—I
and my bonds, which you loved.

III

1. LET not those that appear to be plausible, but Against
teach strange doctrine, overthrow you.   Stand firm as heretics
an anvil which is smitten.   The task of great
athletes is to suffer punishment and yet conquer.
But especially must we endure all things for the
sake of God, that he also may endure us.   2. Be
more diligent than you are.   Mark the seasons.
Wait for him who is above seasons, timeless, invisible,
who for our sakes became visible, who cannot be
touched, who cannot suffer, who for our sakes
accepted suffering, who in every way endured for our
sakes.

IV

1. LET not the widows be neglected.   Be yourself His duty to
their protector after the Lord.   Let nothing be done members of
the church

---

[1] The general meaning of this passage is fairly clear, but
the details are hopelessly obscure.   Possibly something has
dropped out of the text.

[2] $\theta\acute{\epsilon}\mu\alpha$ means a "money-prize," which was given in some of
the Greek games instead of the $\sigma\tau\acute{\epsilon}\phi\alpha\nu\sigma$ or crown.

σου γινέσθω μηδὲ σὺ ἄνευ θεοῦ τι πρᾶσσε, ὅπερ
οὐδὲ πράσσεις· εὐστάθει. 2. πυκνότερον συναγωγαὶ γινέσθωσαν· ἐξ ὀνόματος πάντας ζήτει.

I Tim. 6, 2   3. δούλους καὶ δούλας μὴ ὑπερηφάνει· ἀλλὰ μηδὲ
αὐτοὶ φυσιούσθωσαν, ἀλλ' εἰς δόξαν θεοῦ πλέον
δουλευέτωσαν, ἵνα κρείττονος ἐλευθερίας ἀπὸ θεοῦ
τύχωσιν. μὴ ἐράτωσαν ἀπὸ τοῦ κοινοῦ ἐλευθε-
ροῦσθαι, ἵνα μὴ δοῦλοι εὑρεθῶσιν ἐπιθυμίας.

V

1. Τὰς κακοτεχνίας φεῦγε, μᾶλλον δὲ περὶ
τούτων ὁμιλίαν ποιοῦ. ταῖς ἀδελφαῖς μου προσ-
λάλει, ἀγαπᾶν τὸν κύριον καὶ τοῖς συμβίοις
ἀρκεῖσθαι σαρκὶ καὶ πνεύματι. ὁμοίως καὶ τοῖς
ἀδελφοῖς μου παράγγελλε ἐν ὀνόματι Ἰησοῦ

Eph. 5 25. 29   Χριστοῦ, ἀγαπᾶν τὰς συμβίους ὡς ὁ κύριος τὴν
ἐκκλησίαν. 2. εἴ τις δύναται ἐν ἁγνείᾳ μένειν εἰς
τιμὴν τῆς σαρκὸς τοῦ κυρίου, ἐν ἀκαυχησίᾳ
μενέτω. ἐὰν καυχήσηται, ἀπώλετο, καὶ ἐὰν
γνωσθῇ πλέον τοῦ ἐπισκόπου, ἔφθαρται. πρέπει
δὲ τοῖς γαμοῦσι καὶ ταῖς γαμουμέναις μετὰ γνώμης
τοῦ ἐπισκόπου τὴν ἔνωσιν ποιεῖσθαι, ἵνα ὁ γάμος
ᾖ κατὰ κύριον καὶ μὴ κατ' ἐπιθυμίαν. πάντα εἰς
τιμὴν θεοῦ γινέσθω.

VI

1. Τῷ ἐπισκόπῳ προσέχετε, ἵνα καὶ ὁ θεὸς
ὑμῖν. ἀντίψυχον ἐγὼ τῶν ὑποτασσομένων τῷ
ἐπισκόπῳ, πρεσβυτέροις, διακόνοις· καὶ μετ'

272

without your approval, and do nothing yourself without God, as indeed you do nothing; stand fast. 2. Let the meetings be more numerous. Seek all by their name. 3. Do not be haughty to slaves, either men or women; yet do not let them be puffed up, but let them rather endure slavery to the glory of God, that they may obtain a better freedom from God. Let them not desire to be set free at the Church's expense, that they be not found the slaves of lust.

V

1. FLEE from evil arts, but rather preach against them. Speak to my sisters that they love the Lord, and be content with their husbands in flesh and in spirit. In the same way enjoin on my brothers in the name of Jesus Christ " to love their wives as the Lord loved the Church." 2. If any man can remain in continence to the honour of the flesh of the Lord let him do so without boasting. If he boast he is lost, and if it be made known except to the bishop, he is polluted. But it is right for men and women who marry to be united with the consent of the bishop, that the marriage be according to the Lord and not according to lust. Let all things be done to the honour of God.

The need of purity and of abstinence from boasting

VI

1. GIVE heed to the bishop, that God may also give heed to you. I am devoted to those who are subject to the bishop, presbyters, and deacons; and may it be

Advice to the community

αὐτῶν μοι τὸ μέρος γένοιτο σχεῖν ἐν θεῷ. συγκοπιᾶτε ἀλλήλοις, συναθλεῖτε, συντρέχετε, συμπάσχετε, συγκοιμᾶσθε, συνεγείρεσθε ὡς θεοῦ οἰκονόμοι καὶ πάρεδροι καὶ ὑπηρέται. 2. ἀρέσκετε ᾧ στρατεύεσθε, ἀφ᾽ οὗ καὶ τὰ ὀψώνια κομίζεσθε· μή τις ὑμῶν δεσέρτωρ εὑρεθῇ. τὸ βάπτισμα ὑμῶν μενέτω ὡς ὅπλα, ἡ πίστις ὡς περικεφαλαία, ἡ ἀγάπη ὡς δόρυ, ἡ ὑπομονὴ ὡς πανοπλία. τὰ δεπόσιτα ὑμῶν τὰ ἔργα ὑμῶν, ἵνα τὰ ἄκκεπτα[1] ὑμῶν ἄξια κομίσησθε. μακροθυμήσατε οὖν μετ᾽ ἀλλήλων ἐν πραότητι, ὡς ὁ θεὸς μεθ᾽ ὑμῶν. ὀναίμην ὑμῶν διὰ παντός.

II Tim. 2, 4

VII

1. Ἐπειδὴ ἡ ἐκκλησία ἡ ἐν Ἀντιοχείᾳ τῆς Συρίας εἰρηνεύει, ὡς ἐδηλώθη μοι, διὰ τὴν προσευχὴν ὑμῶν,[2] κἀγὼ εὐθυμότερος ἐγενόμην ἐν ἀμεριμνίᾳ θεοῦ, ἐάνπερ διὰ τοῦ παθεῖν θεοῦ ἐπιτύχω, εἰς τὸ εὑρεθῆναί με ἐν τῇ ἀναστάσει[3] ὑμῶν μαθητήν. 2. πρέπει, Πολύκαρπε θεομακαριστότατε, συμβούλιον ἀγαγεῖν θεοπρεπέστατον καὶ χειροτονῆσαί τινα, ὃν ἀγαπητὸν λίαν ἔχετε καὶ ἄοκνον, ὃς δυνήσεται θεοδρόμος καλεῖσθαι· τοῦτον καταξιῶσαι, ἵνα πορευθεὶς εἰς Συρίαν δοξάσῃ ὑμῶν τὴν ἄοκνον ἀγάπην εἰς δόξαν θεοῦ· 3. Χριστιανὸς

---

[1] The use of the Latin words is remarkable : δεσέρτωρ = deſertor, δεπόσιτα = depoſita, and ἄκκεπτα = accepta.

[2] διὰ τὴν προσευχήν G, διὰ τῆς προσευχῆς Lg.

[3] ἀναστάσει GL, αἰτήσει "through your intercession" gA.

mine to have my lot with them in God. Labour with one another, struggle together, run together, suffer together, rest together, rise up together as God's stewards and assessors and servants. 2. Be pleasing to him in whose ranks you serve, from whom you receive your pay,—let none of you be found a deserter. Let your baptism remain as your arms, your faith as a helmet, your love as a spear, your endurance as your panoply, let your works be your deposits that you may receive the back-pay[1] due to you. Be therefore long-suffering with one another in gentleness, as God is with you. May I have joy in you always.

VII

1. SINCE the Church which is in Antioch has peace through your prayers, as it has been reported to me, I was myself the more encouraged in the freedom from care given by God, if I may but attain to God through my sufferings, that I may be found your disciple at the resurrection.[2] 2. You ought, O Polycarp, most blessed of God, to summon a godly council, and elect someone who is very dear to you and is zealous, who can be called God's courier; appoint him to go to Syria to glorify your zealous love to the glory of God. 3. A Christian has no power over himself, but

The Church in Antioch

---

[1] It was the custom in the Roman army to pay to the soldiers only the half of any gratuities allowed them. The other half was "deposited" in a regimental savings bank, and was paid out to each soldier, when, and if, he was honourably discharged from the service.

[2] Or perhaps "a disciple at your resurrection."

ἑαυτοῦ ἐξουσίαν οὐκ ἔχει, ἀλλὰ θεῷ σχολάζει.
τοῦτο τὸ ἔργον θεοῦ ἐστιν καὶ ὑμῶν, ὅταν αὐτὸ
ἀπαρτίσητε. πιστεύω γὰρ τῇ χάριτι, ὅτι ἕτοιμοί
ἐστε εἰς εὐποιΐαν θεῷ ἀνήκουσαν. εἰδὼς ὑμῶν τὸ
σύντονον τῆς ἀληθείας, δι᾽ ὀλίγων ὑμᾶς γραμμάτων παρεκάλεσα.

VIII

1. Ἐπεὶ[1] πάσαις ταῖς ἐκκλησίαις οὐκ ἠδυνήθην
γράψαι διὰ τὸ ἐξαίφνης πλεῖν με ἀπὸ Τρωάδος
εἰς Νεάπολιν, ὡς τὸ θέλημα προστάσσει, γράψεις
ταῖς ἔμπροσθεν ἐκκλησίαις, ὡς θεοῦ γνώμην
κεκτημένος, εἰς τὸ καὶ αὐτοὺς τὸ αὐτὸ ποιῆσαι,
(οἱ μὲν δυνάμενοι πεζοὺς πέμψαι, οἱ δὲ ἐπιστολὰς διὰ τῶν ὑπό σου πεμπομένων, ἵνα δοξασ-
θῆτε αἰωνίῳ ἔργῳ,)[2] ὡς ἄξιος ὤν. 2. ἀσπάζομαι
πάντας ἐξ ὀνόματος καὶ τὴν τοῦ Ἐπιτρόπου
σὺν ὅλῳ τῷ οἴκῳ αὐτῆς καὶ τῶν τέκνων. ἀσπάζομαι Ἄτταλον τὸν ἀγαπητόν μου. ἀσπάζομαι
τὸν μέλλοντα καταξιοῦσθαι τοῦ εἰς Συρίαν
πορεύεσθαι. ἔσται ἡ χάρις μετ᾽ αὐτοῦ διὰ
παντὸς καὶ τοῦ πέμποντος αὐτὸν Πολυκάρπου.
3. ἐρρῶσθαι ὑμᾶς διὰ παντὸς ἐν θεῷ ἡμῶν Ἰησοῦ
Χριστῷ εὔχομαι, ἐν ᾧ διαμείνητε ἐν ἑνότητι θεοῦ
καὶ ἐπισκοπῇ. ἀσπάζομαι Ἄλκην, τὸ ποθητόν
μοι ὄνομα. ἔρρωσθε ἐν κυρίῳ.

---

[1] ἐπεί GA, ἐπεὶ οὖν Lg.
[2] The combination of singular and plural is very strange.
L makes all singular, A all plural. The punctuation given
is in the main Lightfoot's, but even so the sentence is
unsatisfactory.

gives his time to God. This is the work of God and of yourselves, when you complete it. For I believe in the grace of God, that you are ready to do the good deeds which are proper for God. I exhort you by no more than these few lines, for I recognise your fervour for the truth.

VIII

1. SINCE I could not write to all the Churches because of my sudden sailing from Troas to Neapolis[1] as the will of God enjoins, you shall write as one possessing the mind of God to the Churches on the road in front of me, that they also shall treat me in the same way (let those who can send messengers, and the others send letters through those whom you send, that you[2] may be glorified by a memorable deed), as is worthy of you. 2. I greet all by name, and the wife of the Procurator[3] with the whole house of herself and her children. I greet my beloved Attalus. I greet him who shall be appointed to go to Syria. Grace will be with him through all, and with Polycarp, who sends him. 3. I bid you farewell always in our God, Jesus Christ; may you remain in him in the unity and care of God. I greet Alce, a name very dear to me. Farewell in the Lord.

Request for Polycarp to write to other Churches

Final greetings

---

[1] The modern Cavalla, on the coast of Macedonia, between Constantinople and Salonica; the Roman road comes down to the sea there, and is still in fair preservation.

[2] Modern English obscures the fact that this "you" is plural. The others are singular.

[3] Or, perhaps, "of Epitropus."

THE EPISTLE OF POLYCARP TO
THE PHILIPPIANS

THE EPISTLE OF POLYCARP TO THE PHILIPPIANS.

Polycarp was the Bishop of Smyrna in the first half of the second century, and was martyred, in all probability, on February 23rd, 155 A.D., at the age of eighty-six. He had been a disciple of John, and opinions differ as to whether this John was the son of Zebedee, or John the Presbyter.

According to Irenaeus[1] Polycarp wrote several epistles, but only one is extant. This is the epistle sent to the Philippians in connection with Ignatius.

The object of the epistle is apparently partly to warn the Philippians against certain disorders in the Church at Philippi, and especially against apostasy; but it appears to have been immediately called for by the desire of the Philippians to make a collection of the letters of Ignatius. They had written to Polycarp to help him in this task, and the letter to the Philippians is, as we should say, a "covering letter" for the copies which Polycarp sends of all the Ignatian epistles to which he had access. It is interesting to notice that the one epistle which neither Polycarp nor the Philippians could easily obtain would be that to the Romans, and that it is

[1] Adv. Haer. v. 33. 4.

this letter which in the Ignatian MSS. seems to have had a different textual history from that of the other six.

The epistle is preserved in eight defective Greek MSS., representing a single archetype, in two long quotations in Eusebius, and in a Latin version contained in the Latin version of the *Corpus Ignatianum* (see p. 171). The reconstructed archetype of the Greek MSS. is quoted as G, that of the Latin MSS, as L, and Eusebius as Eus. A full collation of the individual Greek and Latin MSS. is given by Lightfoot.

ΤΟΥ ΑΓΙΟΥ ΠΟΛΥΚΑΡΠΟΥ

ΕΠΙΣΚΟΠΟΥ ΣΜΥΡΝΗΣ ΚΑΙ ΙΕΡΟΜΑΡΤΥΡΟΣ

ΠΡΟΣ ΦΙΛΙΠΠΗΣΙΟΥΣ ΕΠΙΣΤΟΛΗ

Πολύκαρπος καὶ οἱ σὺν αὐτῷ πρεσβύτεροι
τῇ ἐκκλησίᾳ τοῦ θεοῦ τῇ παροικούσῃ
Φιλίππους· ἔλεος ὑμῖν καὶ εἰρήνη παρὰ
θεοῦ παντοκράτορος καὶ Ἰησοῦ Χριστοῦ
τοῦ σωτῆρος ἡμῶν πληθυνθείη.

I

1. Συνεχάρην ὑμῖν μεγάλως ἐν τῷ κυρίῳ ἡμῶν
Ἰησοῦ Χριστῷ, δεξαμένοις τὰ μιμήματα τῆς
ἀληθοῦς ἀγάπης καὶ προπέμψασιν, ὡς ἐπέβαλεν
ὑμῖν, τοὺς ἐνειλημένους τοῖς ἁγιοπρεπέσιν δεσμοῖς,
ἅτινά ἐστιν διαδήματα τῶν ἀληθῶς ὑπὸ θεοῦ καὶ
τοῦ κυρίου ἡμῶν ἐκλελεγμένων· 2. καὶ ὅτι ἡ
βεβαία τῆς πίστεως ὑμῶν ῥίζα, ἐξ ἀρχαίων
καταγγελλομένη χρόνων, μέχρι νῦν διαμένει καὶ
καρποφορεῖ εἰς τὸν κύριον ἡμῶν Ἰησοῦν Χριστόν,
ὃς ὑπέμεινεν ὑπὲρ τῶν ἁμαρτιῶν ἡμῶν ἕως θανάτου
καταντῆσαι, ὃν ἤγειρεν ὁ θεός, λύσας τὰς ὠδῖνας
τοῦ ᾅδου· 3. εἰς ὃν οὐκ ἰδόντες πιστεύετε χαρᾷ

Acts. 2, 24
I Pet. 1, 8

EPISTLE TO THE PHILIPPIANS
OF SAINT POLYCARP
BISHOP OF SMYRNA AND HOLY MARTYR

POLYCARP and the Elders with him to the Church Greeting of God sojourning in Philippi; mercy and peace from God Almighty and Jesus Christ our Saviour be multiplied to you.

I

1. I REJOICE greatly with you in our Lord Jesus The hospitality of the Philippians Christ that you have followed the pattern of true love, and have helped on their way, as opportunity was given you, those who were bound in chains, which become the saints, and are the diadems of those who have been truly chosen by God and our Lord. 2. I rejoice also that your firmly Their faith rooted faith, which was famous in past years, still flourishes and bears fruit unto our Lord Jesus Christ, who endured for our sins, even to the suffering of death, "whom God raised up, having loosed the pangs of Hades, 3. in whom, though you did not see him, you believed in unspeakable and

Eph. 2, 5. 8. 9 ἀνεκλαλήτῳ καὶ δεδοξασμένῃ, εἰς ἣν πολλοὶ ἐπιθυμοῦσιν εἰσελθεῖν, εἰδότες, ὅτι χάριτί ἐστε σεσωσμένοι, οὐκ ἐξ ἔργων, ἀλλὰ θελήματι θεοῦ διὰ Ἰησοῦ Χριστοῦ.

II

1. Διὸ ἀναζωσάμενοι τὰς ὀσφύας ὑμῶν δουλεύ-σατε τῷ θεῷ ἐν φόβῳ καὶ ἀληθείᾳ, ἀπολιπόντες

I Pet. 1, 13 (Eph. 6, 14) ; τὴν κενὴν ματαιολογίαν καὶ τὴν τῶν πολλῶν
Ps. 2, 11 πλάνην, πιστεύσαντες εἰς τὸν ἐγείραντα τὸν κύριον
I Pet. 1, 21 ἡμῶν Ἰησοῦν Χριστὸν ἐκ νεκρῶν καὶ δόντα αὐτῷ

Phil. 3, 21 ; δόξαν καὶ θρόνον ἐκ δεξιῶν αὐτοῦ· ᾧ ὑπετάγη τὰ
2, 10 πάντα ἐπουράνια καὶ ἐπίγεια, ᾧ πᾶσα πνοὴ

Acts 10, 42 λατρεύει, ὃς ἔρχεται κριτὴς ζώντων καὶ νεκρῶν,
(II Tim. 4, 1; οὗ τὸ αἷμα ἐκζητήσει ὁ θεὸς ἀπὸ τῶν ἀπειθούντων
I Pet. 4, 5)
II Cor. 4, 14 αὐτῷ. 2. ὁ δὲ ἐγείρας αὐτὸν ἐκ νεκρῶν καὶ ἡμᾶς
(I Cor. 6, 14; ἐγερεῖ, ἐὰν ποιῶμεν αὐτοῦ τὸ θέλημα καὶ πορευώ-
Rom. 8, 11) μεθα ἐν ταῖς ἐντολαῖς αὐτοῦ καὶ ἀγαπῶμεν ἃ ἠγάπησεν, ἀπεχόμενοι πάσης ἀδικίας, πλεονεξίας,

I Pet. 3, 9 φιλαργυρίας, καταλαλιᾶς, ψευδομαρτυρίας· μὴ ἀποδιδόντες κακὸν ἀντὶ κακοῦ ἢ λοιδορίαν ἀντὶ λοιδορίας ἢ γρόνθον ἀντὶ γρόνθου ἢ κατάραν ἀντὶ κατάρας· 3. μνημονεύοντες δὲ ὧν εἶπεν ὁ κύριος

Mt. 7, 1, 2 ; διδάσκων· Μὴ κρίνετε, ἵνα μὴ κριθῆτε· ἀφίετε,
Luke 6, καὶ ἀφεθήσεται ὑμῖν· ἐλεᾶτε, ἵνα ἐλεηθῆτε· ᾧ
36-38
Luke 6, 20 ; μέτρῳ μετρεῖτε, ἀντιμετρηθήσεται ὑμῖν· καὶ ὅτι
Mt. 5, 3. 10 μακάριοι οἱ πτωχοὶ καὶ οἱ διωκόμενοι ἕνεκεν δικαιοσύνης, ὅτι αὐτῶν ἐστιν ἡ βασιλεία τοῦ θεοῦ.

glorified joy,"—into which joy many desire to come, knowing that " by grace ye are saved, not by works but by the will of God through Jesus Christ.

II

1. "WHEREFORE girding up your loins serve God in fear" and truth, putting aside empty vanity and vulgar error, " believing on him who raised up our Lord Jesus Christ from the dead and gave him glory," and a throne on his right hand, " to whom are subject all things in heaven and earth," whom all breath serves, who is coming as " the Judge of the living and of the dead," whose blood God will require from them who disobey him. 2. Now "he who raised him" from the dead " will also raise us up " if we do his will, and walk in his commandments and love the things which he loved, refraining from all unrighteousness, covetousness, love of money, evil speaking, false witness, " rendering not evil for evil, or railing for railing," or blow for blow, or curse for curse, 3. but remembering what the Lord taught when he said, " Judge not that ye be not judged, forgive and it shall be forgiven unto you, be merciful that ye may obtain mercy, with what measure ye mete, it shall be measured to you again," and, " Blessed are the poor, and they who are perse- cuted for righteousness' sake, for theirs is the Kingdom of God."

Exhorta-
tion to
virtue

The hope of
resurrection

The Lord's
teaching

III

1. Ταῦτα, ἀδελφοί, οὐκ ἐμαυτῷ ἐπιτρέψας γράφω ὑμῖν περὶ τῆς δικαιοσύνης, ἀλλ' ἐπεὶ ὑμεῖς προεπεκαλέσασθέ με. 2. οὔτε γὰρ ἐγὼ οὔτε ἄλλος ὅμοιος ἐμοὶ δύναται κατακολουθῆσαι τῇ σοφίᾳ τοῦ μακαρίου καὶ ἐνδόξου Παύλου, ὃς γενόμενος ἐν ὑμῖν κατὰ πρόσωπον τῶν τότε ἀνθρώπων ἐδίδαξεν ἀκριβῶς καὶ βεβαίως τὸν περὶ ἀληθείας λόγον, ὃς καὶ ἀπὼν ὑμῖν ἔγραψεν ἐπιστολάς, εἰς ἃς ἐὰν ἐγκύπτητε, δυνηθήσεσθε οἰκοδομεῖσθαι εἰς τὴν δοθεῖσαν ὑμῖν πίστιν·

Gal 4, 26

3. ἥτις ἐστὶν μήτηρ πάντων ἡμῶν, ἐπακολουθούσης τῆς ἐλπίδος, προαγούσης τῆς ἀγάπης τῆς εἰς θεὸν καὶ Χριστὸν καὶ εἰς τὸν πλησίον. ἐὰν γάρ τις τούτων ἐντὸς ᾖ, πεπλήρωκεν ἐντολὴν δικαιοσύνης· ὁ γὰρ ἔχων ἀγάπην μακράν ἐστιν πάσης ἁμαρτίας.

IV

1. Ἀρχὴ δὲ πάντων χαλεπῶν φιλαργυρία. εἰδότες οὖν ὅτι οὐδὲν εἰσηνέγκαμεν εἰς τὸν κόσμον,

I Tim. 6, 10
I Tim. 6, 7 ;
cf. Job. 1, 21
II Cor. 6, 7

ἀλλ' οὐδὲ ἐξενεγκεῖν τι ἔχομεν, ὁπλισώμεθα τοῖς ὅπλοις τῆς δικαιοσύνης καὶ διδάξωμεν ἑαυτοὺς πρῶτον πορεύεσθαι ἐν τῇ ἐντολῇ τοῦ κυρίου· 2. ἔπειτα καὶ τὰς γυναῖκας ἡμῶν [1] ἐν τῇ δοθείσῃ αὐταῖς πίστει καὶ ἀγάπῃ καὶ ἁγνείᾳ στεργούσας

---

[1] The MSS read ὑμῶν "your," but the confusion between ὑμῶν and ἡμῶν is so common that " our "may safely be restored.

III

1. THESE things, brethren, I write to you concerning righteousness, not at my own instance, but
because you first invited me. 2. For neither am I,
nor is any other like me, able to follow the wisdom
of the blessed and glorious Paul, who when he was
among you in the presence of the men of that time
taught accurately and stedfastly the word of truth,
and also when he was absent wrote letters to you,
from the study of which you will be able to build
yourselves up into the faith given you ; 3. " which
is the mother of us all" when faith follows, and love
of God and Christ and neighbour goes before. For
if one be in this company he has fulfilled the command of righteousness, for he who has love is far
from all sin.

Polycarp's reason for writing : the invitation of the Philippians

IV

1. " BUT the beginning of all evils is the love of
money." Knowing therefore that "we brought
nothing into the world and we can take nothing
out of it," let us arm ourselves with the armour of
righteousness, and let us first of all teach ourselves
to walk in the commandment of the Lord ; 2. next
teach our wives to remain in the faith given to
them, and in love and purity, tenderly loving their

Exhortations to virtue

287

τοὺς ἑαυτῶν ἄνδρας ἐν πάσῃ ἀληθείᾳ καὶ ἀγα-
πώσας πάντας ἐξ ἴσου ἐν πάσῃ ἐγκρατείᾳ, καὶ τὰ
τέκνα παιδεύειν τὴν παιδείαν τοῦ φόβου τοῦ θεοῦ·
3. τὰς χήρας σωφρονούσας περὶ τὴν τοῦ κυρίου

I Tim. 5, 5 πίστιν, ἐντυγχανούσας ἀδιαλείπτως περὶ πάντων,
μακρὰν οὔσας πάσης διαβολῆς, καταλαλιᾶς,
ψευδομαρτυρίας, φιλαργυρίας καὶ παντὸς κακοῦ,
γινωσκούσας ὅτι εἰσὶ θυσιαστήριον θεοῦ καὶ ὅτι
πάντα μωμοσκοπεῖται, καὶ λέληθεν αὐτὸν οὐδὲν

I Cor. 14, 25 οὔτε λογισμῶν οὔτε ἐννοιῶν οὔτε τι τῶν κρυπτῶν
τῆς καρδίας.

V

Gal. 6, 7   1. Εἰδότες, οὖν, ὅτι θεὸς οὐ μυκτηρίζεται,
ὀφείλομεν ἀξίως τῆς ἐντολῆς αὐτοῦ καὶ δόξης
περιπατεῖν. 2. ὁμοίως διάκονοι ἄμεμπτοι κατεν-
ώπιον αὐτοῦ τῆς δικαιοσύνης ὡς θεοῦ καὶ

I Tim. 3, 8 Χριστοῦ διάκονοι καὶ οὐκ ἀνθρώπων· μὴ διά-
βολοι, μὴ δίλογοι, ἀφιλάργυροι, ἐγκρατεῖς περὶ
πάντα, εὔσπλαγχνοι, ἐπιμελεῖς, πορευόμενοι κατὰ
τὴν ἀλήθειαν τοῦ κυρίου, ὃς ἐγένετο διάκονος
πάντων· ᾧ ἐὰν εὐαρεστήσωμεν ἐν τῷ νῦν αἰῶνι,
ἀποληψόμεθα καὶ τὸν μέλλοντα, καθὼς ὑπέσχετο

Joh. 5, 21 ἡμῖν ἐγεῖραι ἡμᾶς ἐκ νεκρῶν, καὶ ὅτι ἐὰν πολιτευ-
II Tim 2, 12 ; σώμεθα ἀξίως αὐτοῦ, καὶ συμβασιλεύσομεν αὐτῷ,
cf. Rom.8,17 εἴγε πιστεύομεν. 3. ὁμοίως καὶ νεώτεροι ἄμεμπτοι ἐν πᾶσιν, πρὸ παντὸς προνοοῦντες ἁγνείας
καὶ χαλιναγωγοῦντες ἑαυτοὺς ἀπὸ παντὸς κακοῦ.
καλὸν γὰρ τὸ ἀνακόπτεσθαι ἀπὸ τῶν ἐπιθυμιῶν

I Pet. 2, 11 ; ἐν τῷ κόσμῳ, ὅτι πᾶσα ἐπιθυμία κατὰ τοῦ
cf. Gal. 5, 17
I Cor. 6, 9. 10 πνεύματος στρατεύεται, καὶ οὔτε πόρνοι οὔτε

husbands in all truth, and loving all others equally in all chastity, and to educate their children in the fear of God. 3. Let us teach the widows to be discreet in the faith of the Lord, praying ceaselessly for all men, being far from all slander, evil speaking, false witness, love of money, and all evil, knowing that they are an altar of God, and that all offerings are tested, and that nothing escapes him of reasonings or thoughts, or of " the secret things of the heart."

V

1. KNOWING then that " God is not mocked " we ought to walk worthily of his commandment and glory. 2. Likewise must the deacons be blameless before his righteousness, as the servants of God and Christ and not of man, not slanderers, not double-tongued, not lovers of money, temperate in all things, compassionate, careful, walking according to the truth of the Lord, who was the " servant of all." For if we please him in this present world we shall receive from him that which is to come ; even as he promised us to raise us from the dead, and that if we are worthy citizens of his community, " we shall also reign with him," if we have but faith. 3. Likewise also let the younger men be blameless in all things ; caring above all for purity, and curbing themselves from all evil ; for it is good to be cut off from the lust of the things in the world, because " every lust warreth against the Spirit, and neither fornicators nor the effeminate nor sodomites shall

Christian obligations to a virtuous life

289

μαλακοὶ οὔτε ἀρσενοκοῖται βασιλείαν θεοῦ
κληρονομήσουσιν, οὔτε οἱ ποιοῦντες τὰ ἄτοπα.
διὸ δέον ἀπέχεσθαι ἀπὸ πάντων τούτων, ὑποτασ-
σομένους τοῖς πρεσβυτέροις καὶ διακόνοις ὡς θεῷ
καὶ Χριστῷ· τὰς παρθένους ἐν ἀμώμῳ καὶ ἁγνῇ
συνειδήσει περιπατεῖν.

VI

1. Καὶ οἱ πρεσβύτεροι δὲ εὔσπλαγχνοι, εἰς
πάντας ἐλεήμονες, ἐπιστρέφοντες τὰ ἀποπε-
πλανημένα, ἐπισκεπτόμενοι πάντας ἀσθενεῖς, μὴ
ἀμελοῦντες χήρας ἢ ὀρφανοῦ ἢ πένητος. ἀλλὰ
προνοοῦντες ἀεὶ τοῦ καλοῦ ἐνώπιον θεοῦ καὶ
ἀνθρώπων, ἀπεχόμενοι πάσης ὀργῆς, προσωπο-
λημψίας, κρίσεως ἀδίκου, μακρὰν ὄντες πάσης
φιλαργυρίας, μὴ ταχέως πιστεύοντες κατά τινος,
μὴ ἀπότομοι ἐν κρίσει, εἰδότες ὅτι πάντες ὀφει-
λέται ἐσμὲν ἁμαρτίας. 2. εἰ οὖν δεόμεθα τοῦ
κυρίου, ἵνα ἡμῖν ἀφῇ, ὀφείλομεν καὶ ἡμεῖς
ἀφιέναι· ἀπέναντι γὰρ τῶν τοῦ κυρίου καὶ θεοῦ
ἐσμὲν ὀφθαλμῶν, καὶ πάντας δεῖ παραστῆναι
τῷ βήματι τοῦ Χριστοῦ καὶ ἕκαστον ὑπὲρ αὐτοῦ
λόγον δοῦναι. 3. οὕτως οὖν δουλεύσωμεν αὐτῷ
μετὰ φόβου καὶ πάσης εὐλαβείας, καθὼς αὐτὸς
ἐνετείλατο καὶ οἱ εὐαγγελισάμενοι ἡμᾶς ἀπόστολοι
καὶ οἱ προφῆται, οἱ προκηρύξαντες τὴν ἔλευσιν τοῦ
κυρίου ἡμῶν· ζηλωταὶ περὶ τὸ καλόν, ἀπεχόμενοι
τῶν σκανδάλων καὶ τῶν ψευδαδέλφων καὶ τῶν
ἐν ὑποκρίσει φερόντων τὸ ὄνομα τοῦ κυρίου,
οἵτινες ἀποπλανῶσι κενοὺς ἀνθρώπους.

Prov. 3, 4
(II Cor. 8, 21;
Rom. 12, 17)

Rom. 14, 10.
12
cf. II Cor. 5
10
Ps. 2, 11;
Heb. 12, 28

inherit the Kingdom of God," nor they who do iniquitous things. Wherefore it is necessary to refrain from all these things, and to be subject to the presbyters and deacons as to God and Christ. The virgins must walk with a blameless and pure conscience.

VI

1. AND let the presbyters also be compassionate, merciful to all, bringing back those that have wandered, caring for all the weak, neglecting neither widow, nor orphan nor poor, but " ever providing for that which is good before God and man," refraining from all wrath, respect of persons, unjust judgment, being far from all love of money, not quickly believing evil of any, not hasty in judgment, knowing that " we all owe the debt of sin." [1] 2. If then we pray the Lord to forgive us, we also ought to forgive, for we stand before the eyes of the Lord and of God, and " we must all appear before the judgment seat of Christ, and each must give an account of himself." 3. So then "let us serve him with fear and all reverence," as he himself commanded us, and as did the Apostles, who brought us the Gospel, and the Prophets who foretold the coming of our Lord. Let us be zealous for good, refraining from offence, and from the false brethren, and from those who bear the name of the Lord in hypocrisy, who deceive empty-minded men.

The duties of the presbyters

Forgiveness

The service of God

---

[1] The introductory formula "knowing that" renders it probable that these words are a quotation, but the source is unknown.

VII

I Joh. 4, 2. 3;
II Joh. 7

1. Πᾶς γὰρ ὃς ἂν μὴ ὁμολογῇ Ἰησοῦν Χριστὸν ἐν σαρκὶ ἐληλυθέναι, ἀντίχριστός ἐστιν· καὶ ὃς ἂν μὴ ὁμολογῇ τὸ μαρτύριον τοῦ σταυροῦ, ἐκ τοῦ διαβόλου ἐστίν· καὶ ὃς ἂν μεθοδεύῃ τὰ λόγια τοῦ κυρίου πρὸς τὰς ἰδίας ἐπιθυμίας καὶ λέγῃ μήτε ἀνάστασιν μήτε κρίσιν, οὗτος πρωτότοκός ἐστι τοῦ σατανᾶ. 2. διὸ ἀπολιπόντες τὴν ματαιότητα τῶν πολλῶν καὶ τὰς ψευδοδιδασκαλίας ἐπὶ τὸν ἐξ ἀρχῆς ἡμῖν παραδοθέντα λόγον ἐπιστρέψωμεν, νήφοντες πρὸς τὰς εὐχὰς καὶ προσκαρτεροῦντες νηστείαις, δεήσεσιν αἰτούμενοι τὸν παντεπόπτην θεὸν μὴ εἰσενεγκεῖν ἡμᾶς εἰς πειρασμόν, καθὼς εἶπεν ὁ κύριος· Τὸ μὲν πνεῦμα πρόθυμον, ἡ δὲ σὰρξ ἀσθενής.

I Pet. 4, 7
Mt. 6, 13
Mt. 26. 41;
Mk. 14, 38

VIII

I Tim. 1, 1

1. Ἀδιαλείπτως οὖν προσκαρτερῶμεν τῇ ἐλπίδι ἡμῶν καὶ τῷ ἀρραβῶνι τῆς δικαιοσύνης ἡμῶν, ὅς ἐστι Χριστὸς Ἰησοῦς, ὃς ἀνήνεγκεν ἡμῶν τὰς ἁμαρτίας τῷ ἰδίῳ σώματι ἐπὶ τὸ ξύλον, ὃς ἁμαρτίαν οὐκ ἐποίησεν, οὐδὲ εὑρέθη δόλος ἐν τῷ στόματι αὐτοῦ· ἀλλὰ δι᾽ ἡμᾶς, ἵνα ζήσωμεν ἐν αὐτῷ, πάντα ὑπέμεινεν. 2. μιμηταὶ οὖν γενώμεθα τῆς ὑπομονῆς αὐτοῦ, καὶ ἐὰν πάσχωμεν διὰ τὸ ὄνομα αὐτοῦ, δοξάζωμεν αὐτόν. τοῦτον γὰρ ἡμῖν τὸν ὑπογραμμὸν ἔθηκε δι᾽ ἑαυτοῦ, καὶ ἡμεῖς τοῦτο ἐπιστεύσαμεν.

I Pet. 2, 24
I Pet. 2, 22

VII

1. "For everyone who does not confess that Jesus Christ has come in the flesh is an anti-Christ"; and whosoever does not confess the testimony of the Cross is of the devil: and whosoever perverts the oracles of the Lord for his own lusts, and says that there is neither resurrection nor judgment,—this man is the first-born of Satan.[1] 2. Wherefore, leaving the foolishness of the crowd, and their false teaching, let us turn back to the word which was delivered to us in the beginning, "watching unto prayer" and persevering in fasting, beseeching the all-seeing God in our supplications "to lead us not into temptation," even as the Lord said, "The spirit is willing, but the flesh is weak."

Warning against heresy

VIII

1. Let us then persevere unceasingly in our hope, and in the pledge of our righteousness, that is in Christ Jesus, "who bare our sins in his own body on the tree, who did no sin, neither was guile found in his mouth," but for our sakes, that we might live in him, he endured all things. 2. Let us then be imitators of his endurance, and if we suffer for his name's sake let us glorify him. For this is the example which he gave us in himself, and this is what we have believed.

Perseverance

---

[1] This phrase, according to Irenaeus (*Adv. Haer.* iii. 3, 4.) was applied, presumably later, by Polycarp to Marcion.

IX

1. Παρακαλῶ οὖν πάντας ὑμᾶς, πειθαρχεῖν τῷ λόγῳ τῆς δικαιοσύνης[1] καὶ ἀσκεῖν πᾶσαν ὑπομονήν, ἣν καὶ εἴδατε κατ' ὀφθαλμοὺς οὐ μόνον ἐν τοῖς μακαρίοις Ἰγνατίῳ καὶ Ζωσίμῳ καὶ Ῥούφῳ, ἀλλὰ καὶ ἐν ἄλλοις τοῖς ἐξ ὑμῶν καὶ ἐν αὐτῷ Παύλῳ καὶ τοῖς λοιποῖς ἀποστόλοις· 2. πεπεισ-

Phil. 2, 16 μένους ὅτι οὗτοι πάντες οὐκ εἰς κενὸν ἔδραμον, ἀλλ' ἐν πίστει καὶ δικαιοσύνῃ, καὶ ὅτι εἰς τὸν

I Clem. 5, 4 ὀφειλόμενον αὐτοῖς τόπον εἰσὶ παρὰ τῷ κυρίῳ, ᾧ

II Tim. 4, 10 καὶ συνέπαθον. οὐ γὰρ τὸν νῦν ἠγάπησαν αἰῶνα, ἀλλὰ τὸν ὑπὲρ ἡμῶν ἀποθανόντα καὶ δι' ἡμᾶς[2] ὑπὸ τοῦ θεοῦ ἀναστάντα.

X

Col. 1, 23;
I Cor. 15, 58   1. In his ergo state et domini exemplar sequimini,

I Pet. 3, 8 (2, firmi in fide et immutabiles, fraternitatis amatores,
17);
Joh. 13, 34; diligentes invicem, in veritate sociati, mansuetudine
15, 12. 17;
Rom. 13, 8 domini alterutri praestolantes, nullum despicientes.
etc.
Tob. 4, 10; 2. Cum possitis benefacere, nolite differre, quia
12, 9
I Pet. 5, 5; eleëmosyna de morte liberat.   Omnes vobis invicem
Eph. 5, 21
subiecti estote, conversationem vestram irreprensi-
bilem habentes in gentibus, ut ex bonis operibus

I Pet. 2, 12 vestris et vos laudem accipiatis et dominus in vobis

---

[1] τῷ λόγῳ τῆς δικαιοσύνης GL, om. Eus.
[2] Here G breaks off, but the rest of the sentence is given by L Eus.

IX

1. Now I beseech you all to obey the word of righteousness, and to endure with all the endurance which you also saw before your eyes, not only in the blessed Ignatius, and Zosimus, and Rufus, but also in others among yourselves, and in Paul himself, and in the other Apostles; 2. being persuaded that all of these "ran not in vain," but in faith and righteousness, and that they are with the Lord in the " place which is their due," with whom they also suffered. For they did not " love this present world " but him who died on our behalf, and was raised by God for our sakes. *The examples of the martyrs*

X

1. STAND fast therefore in these things and follow the example of the Lord, "firm and unchangeable in faith, loving the brotherhood, affectionate to one another," joined together in the truth, forestalling one another in the gentleness of the Lord, despising no man. 2. When you can do good defer it not, " for almsgiving sets free from death; be ye all subject one to the other, having your conversation blameless among the Gentiles," that you may receive praise " for your good works " and that the Lord be not blasphemed in you. 3. " But woe to him *Persever-ance in philanthro-py and good works.*

THE APOSTOLIC FATHERS

Is. 52, non blasphemetur. 3. Vae autem, per quem nomen domini blasphematur. Sobrietatem ergo docete omnes, in qua et vos conversamini.

XI

1. Nimis contristatus sum pro Valente, qui presbyter factus est aliquando apud vos, quod sic ignoret is locum qui datus est ei. Moneo itaque ut abstineatis vos ab avaritia et sitis casti[1] veraces. Abstinete vos ab omni malo. 2. Qui autem non potest se in his gubernare, quomodo alii pronuntiat Eph. 5, 5 ; hoc ? Si quis non se abstinuerit ab avaritia, ab
Col. 3, 5
Jer. 5, 4 idololatria coinquinabitur et tamquam inter gentes
I Cor. 6, 2 iudicabitur, qui ignorant iudicium domini. Aut nescimus, quia sancti mundum iudicabunt ? sicut Paulus docet. 3. Ego autem nihil tale sensi in vobis vel audivi, in quibus laboravit beatus Paulus, qui
Cf. Phil. estis in principio epistulae eius. De vobis etenim
4, 15
II Thess. 1, 4 gloriatur in omnibus ecclesiis, quae dominum[2] solae tunc cognoverant ; nos autem nondum cognoveramus. 4. Valde ergo, fratres, contristor pro illo et
II Tim. 2, 25 pro coniuge eius, quibus det dominus paenitentiam veram. Sobrii ergo estote et vos in hoc ; et non
II Thess. 3, sicut inimicos tales existimetis, sed sicut passibilia
15
membra et errantia eos revocate, ut omnium vestrum corpus salvetis. Hoc enim agentes vos ipsos aedificatis.

---

[1] An *et* after *casti* would be natural, but it is only found in two of the MSS of L.
[2] Some MSS. of L read *deum* instead of *dominum*.

through whom the name of the Lord is blasphemed."
Therefore teach sobriety to all and show it forth in
your own lives.

XI

1. I AM deeply sorry for Valens, who was once Valens
made a presbyter among you, that he so little under-
stands the place which was given to him. I advise,
therefore, that you keep from avarice, and be pure
and truthful. Keep yourselves from all evil. 2. For Against
how may he who cannot attain self-control in these avarice
matters enjoin it on another? If any man does not
abstain from avarice he will be defiled by idolatry,
and shall be judged as if he were among the Gentiles
who " know not the judgment of God." Or do we
" not know that the saints shall judge the world?" as
Paul teaches. 3. But I have neither perceived nor
heard any such thing among you, among whom the·
blessed Paul laboured, who are praised in the
beginning of his Epistle.[1] For concerning you he
boasts in all the Churches who then alone had known
the Lord, for we had not yet known him. 4. There- The
fore, brethren, I am deeply sorry for him [i.e. Valens] treatment
and for his wife, and " may the Lord grant them
true repentance." Therefore be yourselves also
moderate in this matter, and " do not regard such
men as enemies," but call them back as fallible and
straying members, that you may make whole the
body of you all. For in doing this you edify
yourselves.

[1] The Greek was perhaps τοῖς οὖσιν ἐν ἀρχῇ ἐπιστολαῖς
αὐτοῦ, and ought to be rendered " who were his epistles in
the beginning," with a reference to II Cor. 3, 2.

XII

1. Confido enim vos bene exercitatos esse in sacris
literis et nihil vos latet; mihi autem non est con-
cessum. Modo, ut his scripturis dictum est, irascim-
ini et nolite peccare, et sol non occidat super
iracundiam vestram. Beatus, qui meminerit; quod
ego credo esse in vobis. 2. Deus autem et pater
domini nostri Iesu Christi, et ipse sempiternus
pontifex, dei filius Iesus Christus, aedificet vos in fide
et veritate et in omni mansuetudine et sine iracundia
et in patientia et in longanimitate et tolerantia et
castitate ; et det vobis sortem et partem inter
sanctos suos et nobis vobiscum et omnibus, qui sunt
sub caelo, qui credituri sunt in dominum nostrum et
deum [1] Iesum Christum et in ipsius patrem, qui
resuscitavit eum a mortuis. 3. Pro omnibus sanctis
orate. Orate etiam pro regibus et potestatibus et
principibus atque pro persequentibus et odientibus
vos et pro inimicis crucis, ut fructus vester manifestus
sit in omnibus, ut sitis in illo perfecti.

Ps. 4, 5 ;
Eph. 4, 26

Heb. 6, 20 ;
7, 3

Gal. 1, 1
I Tim. 2, 1. 2
Mt. 5, 44 ;
Luke 6, 27
Phil. 3, 18
Joh. 15, 16 ;
I Tim. 4, 15
James 1, 4

XIII

1. Ἐγράψατέ [2] μοι καὶ ὑμεῖς καὶ Ἰγνάτιος, ἵν',
ἐάν τις ἀπέρχηται εἰς Συρίαν, καὶ τὰ παρ' ὑμῶν

---

[1] *Et deum* is omitted by some of the MSS of L.
[2] The Greek is here again available from the quotation in
Eusebius.

XII

1. For I am confident that you are well versed in the Scriptures,[1] and from you nothing is hid ; but to me this is not granted. Only, as it is said in these Scriptures, "Be ye angry and sin not," and "Let not the sun go down upon your wrath." Blessed is the man who remembers this, and I believe that it is so with you. 2. Now may God and the Father of our Lord Jesus Christ, and the "eternal Priest" himself, Jesus Christ, the Son of God, build you up in faith and truth, and in all gentleness, and without wrath, and in patience, and in longsuffering, and endurance, and purity, and may he give you lot and part with his saints, and to us with you, and to all under heaven who shall believe in our Lord and God Jesus Christ and in his "Father who raised him from the dead." 3. "Pray for all the saints. Pray also for the Emperors,"[2] and for potentates, and princes, and for "those who persecute you and hate you," and for "the enemies of the Cross" that "your fruit may be manifest among all men, that you may be perfected" in him.

The need of forgiveness

Prayer for blessing

XIII

1. Both you and Ignatius wrote to me that if anyone was going to Syria he should also take your

[1] Probably this ought to be regarded as a quotation from the letter of the Philippians to Polycarp.

[2] *Pro regibus* is no doubt a translation of ὑπὲρ βασιλέων and βασιλεύς is regularly used as the title of the Emperor.

ἀποκομίσῃ γράμματα· ὅπερ ποιήσω, ἐὰν λάβω
καιρὸν εὔθετον, εἴτε ἐγώ, εἴτε ὃν πέμπω[1] πρε-
σβεύσοντα καὶ περὶ ὑμῶν.   2. τὰς ἐπιστολὰς
Ἰγνατίου τὰς πεμφθείσας ἡμῖν ὑπ᾽ αὐτοῦ καὶ
ἄλλας, ὅσας εἴχομεν παρ᾽ ἡμῖν, ἐπέμψαμεν ὑμῖν,
καθὼς ἐνετείλασθε· αἵτινες ὑποτεταγμέναι εἰσὶν
τῇ ἐπιστολῇ ταύτῃ, ἐξ ὧν μεγάλα ὠφεληθῆναι
δυνήσεσθε. περιέχουσι γὰρ πίστιν καὶ ὑπομονὴν
καὶ πᾶσαν οἰκοδομὴν τὴν εἰς τὸν κύριον ἡμῶν
ἀνήκουσαν. Et de ipso Ignatio et de his, qui cum
eo sunt, quod certius agnoveritis, significate.

XIV

Haec vobis scripsi per Crescentem, quem in
praesenti commendavi vobis et nunc commendo.
Conversatus est enim nobiscum inculpabiliter; credo
quia et vobiscum similiter.   Sororem autem eius
habebitis commendatam, cum venerit ad vos.   In-
columes estote in domino Iesu Christo in gratia cum
omnibus vestris.   Amen.

[1] πέμπω Eus. misero (= πέμψω) L.

letters. I will do this if I have a convenient opportunity, either myself or the man whom I am sending as a representative for you and me. 2. We send you, as you asked, the letters of Ignatius, which were sent to us by him, and others which we had by us. These are subjoined to this letter, and you will be able to benefit greatly from them. For they contain faith, patience, and all the edification which pertains to our Lord. Let us know anything further which you have heard about Ignatius himself and those who are with him. Ignatius and the Church in Syria

XIV

1. I HAVE written this to you by Crescens, whom I commended to you when I was present, and now commend again. For he has behaved blamelessly among us, and I believe that he will do the same with you. His sister shall be commended to you when she comes to you. Farewell in the Lord Jesus Christ in grace, with all who are yours. Amen. Final greetings

THE DIDACHE, OR TEACHING OF
THE TWELVE APOSTLES

THE DIDACHE, OR TEACHING OF THE TWELVE APOSTLES

The Didache, or Teaching of the Twelve Apostles, is one of the most important discoveries of the second half of the nineteenth century. There are several references in early Christian literature to a book with this or a similar title, and by applying the methods of comparative criticism to documents which had probably made use of it, especially the "Apostolic Constitutions" and the "Church Ordinances," a rough reconstruction of some of its features had been obtained; but it was not known to be extant until Bryennios in 1875 discovered it in the Patriarchal library of Jerusalem at Constantinople, in the manuscript which also contains I and II Clement and is quoted for them as C.

This is the document of which a text and translation is given in the following pages. But the question still remains open how far it truly represents the original "Teaching." Since Bryennios' discovery two copies of a Latin version either of a part of our Didache, or of a cognate document have been discovered, and it would now be possible to use

at least four authorities for the text of the original
"Teaching." These are :—

(1) Bryennios' Didache = C.
·(2) The Latin version.
(3) The "Church Ordinances" (usually quoted
as KO).
(4) The "Apostolic Constitutions," bk. vii.

All these authorities[1] have to be considered in any
attempt to reconstruct the original "Teaching."
Their mutual relations are not clear; it is possible
that Bryennios' Didache, and the Apostolic Constitutions represent a second recension of the
"Teaching" and that the Latin version, KO, and the
reconstructed "fifth source" represent, though not
in relatively so pure a form, the first recension.
The question may be best studied in Funk's edition
of the Didache, and in Harnack's *Geschichte der
altchristlichen Literatur.*
Besides this there is a further question : it is clear
that the Didache or "Teaching" was itself a com-
posite document, and the first part is always known
as "The Two Ways." A moment's comparison shows
that this part is closely connected with the last
chapters of the Epistle of Barnabas. The problem
therefore arises whether Barnabas used the Didache
(or the original "Teaching"), or the Didache used
Barnabas, or both used a common source. The
matter is not clear, but probably the majority of
scholars incline to the last view, and many think
that the common source,—the original "Two Ways"

[1] Harnack, probably rightly, suggests others as well. See
his *Geschichte der altchristlichen Literatur*, pp. 86 ff.

THE DIDACHE

—was a Jewish pre-Christian document, used for catechetical purposes, perhaps especially among Proselytes.

The chronology of this complex document is very obscure. The original "Two Ways" may be early first century or even earlier. The original "Teaching" is probably early second century, or possibly earlier, and the second recension of the "Teaching," represented by C, can scarcely be later than the second century, though it is possible that a few phrases in C may represent textual accretions.

As it stands the Didache may be described as a manual of Church instruction. The first part, "The Two Ways," is a statement of the principles of Christian conduct, which is to be taught to catechumens before their baptism (chaps. i–vi); then follows a series of instructions as to the practice of Christian worship, Baptism, Fasting, the Eucharist, the discrimination and treatment of Apostles[1] and Prophets, the Worship on Sunday, Bishops and Deacons (chaps. vii–xv); finally a short statement of the eschatological hope is appended for the warning and encouragement of Christians.

The text given in the following pages is that of C (published in photographic facsimile by Dr. Rendel Harris). The very few necessary corrections (except obvious mistakes) have been noted at the foot of the page.

[1] It should be noted that "Apostle" in the Didache does not mean a member of "the Twelve," but is merely an inspired teacher who is engaged in preaching, especially to those as yet unconverted,—very much what is now called a Missionary.

ΔΙΔΑΧΗ ΤΩΝ ΔΩΔΕΚΑ
ΑΠΟΣΤΟΛΩΝ

Διδαχὴ κυρίου διὰ τῶν δώδεκα ἀποστόλων
τοῖς ἔθνεσιν.

I

1. Ὁδοὶ δύο εἰσί, μία τῆς ζωῆς καὶ μία τοῦ
θανάτου, διαφορὰ δὲ πολλὴ μεταξὺ τῶν δύο ὁδῶν.

Mt. 22, 37–39 ; Mk. 12, 30–31 ; Lev. 19, 18 2. Ἡ μὲν οὖν ὁδὸς τῆς ζωῆς ἐστιν αὕτη· πρῶτον
ἀγαπήσεις τὸν θεὸν τὸν ποιήσαντά σε, δεύτερον
τὸν πλησίον σου ὡς σεαυτόν· πάντα δὲ ὅσα ἐὰν
θελήσῃς μὴ γίνεσθαί σοι, καὶ σὺ ἄλλῳ μὴ ποίει.

Mt. 7, 12 ; Luke 6, 31 Mt. 5, 44. 46. 47 ; Luke 6,32–33 3. Τούτων δὲ τῶν λόγων ἡ διδαχή ἐστιν αὕτη·
εὐλογεῖτε τοὺς καταρωμένους ὑμῖν καὶ προσεύ-
χεσθε ὑπὲρ τῶν ἐχθρῶν ὑμῶν, νηστεύετε δὲ ὑπὲρ
τῶν διωκόντων ὑμᾶς· ποία γὰρ χάρις, ἐὰν ἀγαπᾶτε
τοὺς ἀγαπῶντας ὑμᾶς; οὐχὶ καὶ τὰ ἔθνη τὸ αὐτὸ
ποιοῦσιν; ὑμεῖς δὲ ἀγαπᾶτε τοὺς μισοῦντας
I Pet. 2, 11 ; cf. Tit. 2, 12 ὑμᾶς, καὶ οὐχ ἕξετε ἐχθρόν. 4. ἀπέχου τῶν
σαρκικῶν καὶ σωματικῶν ἐπιθυμιῶν· ἐάν τίς

THE DIDACHE, OR TEACHING OF THE TWELVE APOSTLES

The Lord's teaching to the heathen by the Twelve
  Apostles.

I

1. THERE are two Ways, one of Life and one of Death, and there is a great difference between the two Ways. *The two Ways*

2. The Way of Life is this: "First, thou shalt love the God who made thee, secondly, thy neighbour as thyself; and whatsoever thou wouldst not have done to thyself, do not thou to another."[1] *The Way of Life*

3. Now, the teaching of these words is this: "Bless those that curse you, and pray for your enemies, and fast for those that persecute you. For what credit is it to you if you love those that love you? Do not even the heathen do the same?" But, for your part, "love those that hate you," and you will have no enemy. 4. "Abstain from carnal" and bodily "lusts." "If any man smite thee on the *The explanation*

---

[1] This is the so-called "negative form of the Golden Rule." It is found in some MSS. in the "Apostolic decrees" in Acts xv. 28, and is, in various forms, met with in Jewish and Early Christian literature.

THE APOSTOLIC FATHERS

Mt. 5, 39 48 σοὶ δῷ ῥάπισμα εἰς τὴν δεξιὰν σιαγόνα, στρέψον
Mt. 5, 41. 40 αὐτῷ καὶ τὴν ἄλλην, καὶ ἔσῃ τέλειος· ἐὰν ἀγγα-
ρεύσῃ σέ τις μίλιον ἕν, ὕπαγε μετ᾽ αὐτοῦ δύο· ἐὰν
Luke 6, 30 ἄρῃ τις τὸ ἱμάτιόν σου, δὸς αὐτῷ καὶ τὸν χιτῶνα·
ἐὰν λάβῃ τις ἀπὸ σοῦ τὸ σόν, μὴ ἀπαίτει· οὐδὲ
Luke 6, 30 γὰρ δύνασαι. 5. παντὶ τῷ αἰτοῦντί σε δίδου καὶ
μὴ ἀπαίτει· πᾶσι γὰρ θέλει δίδοσθαι ὁ πατὴρ ἐκ
τῶν ἰδίων χαρισμάτων. μακάριος ὁ διδοὺς κατὰ
τὴν ἐντολήν·[1] ἀθῷος γάρ ἐστιν. οὐαὶ τῷ λαμβά-
νοντι· εἰ μὲν γὰρ χρείαν ἔχων λαμβάνει τις, ἀθῷος
ἔσται· ὁ δὲ μὴ χρείαν ἔχων δώσει δίκην, ἱνατί
ἔλαβε καὶ εἰς τί· ἐν συνοχῇ δὲ γενόμενος ἐξετασ-
Mt. 5, 26 θήσεται περὶ ὧν ἔπραξε, καὶ οὐκ ἐξελεύσεται
ἐκεῖθεν, μέχρις οὗ ἀποδῷ τὸν ἔσχατον κοδράντην.
6. ἀλλὰ καὶ περὶ τούτου δὲ εἴρηται· Ἱδρωσάτω ἡ
ἐλεημοσύνη σου εἰς τὰς χεῖράς σου, μέχρις ἂν
γνῷς, τίνι δῷς.

II

Mt. 19, 18   1. Δευτέρα δὲ ἐντολὴ τῆς διδαχῆς· 2. οὐ
φονεύσεις, οὐ μοιχεύσεις, οὐ παιδοφθορήσεις, οὐ
πορνεύσεις, οὐ κλέψεις, οὐ μαγεύσεις, οὐ φαρ-
μακεύσεις, οὐ φονεύσεις τέκνον ἐν φθορᾷ, οὐδὲ

---

[1] This passage is found in the 4th mandate of Hermas, and suggests that this part of the Didache is later than Hermas (c. 140 A.D.).

319

right cheek, turn to him the other cheek also," and thou wilt be perfect. " If any man impress thee to go with him one mile, go with him two. If any man take thy coat, give him thy shirt also. If any man will take from thee what is thine, refuse it not"—not even if thou canst.[1] 5. Give to everyone Alms-giving that asks thee, and do not refuse, for the Father's will is that we give to all from the gifts we have received. Blessed is he that gives according to the mandate; for he is innocent. Woe to him who receives; for if any man receive alms under pressure of need he is innocent; but he who receives it without need shall be tried as to why he took and for what, and being in prison he shall be examined as to his deeds, and " he shall not come out thence until he pay the last farthing." 6. But concerning this it was also said, " Let thine alms sweat into thine hands until thou knowest to whom thou art giving."

II

1. But the second commandment of the teaching The second is this; 2. " Thou shalt do no murder; thou shalt not part of the commit adultery"; thou shalt not commit sodomy; thou shalt not commit fornication; thou shalt not steal; thou shalt not use magic; thou shalt not use philtres; thou shalt not procure abortion, nor

---

[1] The Greek is literally "for thou art not even able"; but this makes no sense, and though an emendation is difficult the sense must be something like that given by the translation—unless, indeed, the whole phrase be merely a flippant gloss, which has been erroneously taken into the text.

THE APOSTOLIC FATHERS

Exod. 20, 17
Mt. 5, 33;
19, 18

γεννηθὲν ἀποκτενεῖς, οὐκ ἐπιθυμήσεις τὰ τοῦ
πλησίον.   3. οὐκ ἐπιορκήσεις, οὐ ψευδομαρτυρή-
σεις, οὐ κακολογήσεις, οὐ μνησικακήσεις. ⸢4. οὐκ
ἔσῃ διγνώμων οὐδὲ δίγλωσσος· παγὶς γὰρ
θανάτου ἡ διγλωσσία.   5. οὐκ ἔσται ὁ λόγος σου
ψευδής, οὐ κενός, ἀλλὰ μεμεστωμένος πράξει.
6. οὐκ ἔσῃ πλεονέκτης οὐδὲ ἅρπαξ οὐδὲ ὑποκριτὴς
οὐδὲ κακοήθης οὐδὲ ὑπερήφανος. οὐ λήψῃ βουλὴν πονηρὰν κατὰ τοῦ πλησίον σου.   7. οὐ
μισήσεις πάντα ἄνθρωπον, ἀλλὰ οὓς μὲν ἐλέγξεις,
περὶ δὲ ὧν προσεύξῃ, οὓς δὲ ἀγαπήσεις ὑπὲρ τὴν
ψυχήν σου.

III

1. Τέκνον μου, φεῦγε ἀπὸ παντὸς πονηροῦ καὶ
ἀπὸ παντὸς ὁμοίου αὐτοῦ.   2. μὴ γίνου ὀργίλος,
ὁδηγεῖ γὰρ ἡ ὀργὴ πρὸς τὸν φόνον, μηδὲ ζηλω-
τὴς μηδὲ ἐριστικὸς μηδὲ θυμικός· ἐκ γὰρ τούτων
ἁπάντων φόνοι γεννῶνται.   3. τέκνον μου, μὴ
γίνου ἐπιθυμητής, ὁδηγεῖ γὰρ ἡ ἐπιθυμία πρὸς
τὴν πορνείαν, μηδὲ αἰσχρολόγος μηδὲ ὑψηλόφ-
θαλμος· ἐκ γὰρ τούτων ἁπάντων μοιχεῖαι γεννῶνται.   4. τέκνον μου, μὴ γίνου οἰωνοσκόπος,
ἐπειδὴ ὁδηγεῖ εἰς τὴν εἰδωλολατρίαν, μηδὲ ἐπαοι-
δὸς μηδὲ μαθηματικὸς μηδὲ περικαθαίρων, μηδὲ
θέλε αὐτὰ βλέπειν· ἐκ γὰρ τούτων ἁπάντων εἰδωλο-
λατρία γεννᾶται.   5. τέκνον μου, μὴ γίνου ψεύστης,
ἐπειδὴ ὁδηγεῖ τὸ ψεῦσμα εἰς τὴν κλοπήν, μηδὲ
φιλάργυρος μηδὲ κενόδοξος· ἐκ γὰρ τούτων ἁπάν-

312

commit infanticide; "thou shalt not covet thy neighbour's goods"; 3. thou shalt not commit perjury, "thou shalt not bear false witness"; thou shalt not speak evil; thou shalt not bear malice. 4. Thou shalt not be double-minded nor double-tongued, for to be double-tongued is the snare of death. 5. Thy speech shall not be false nor vain, but completed in action. 6. Thou shalt not be covetous nor extortionate, nor a hypocrite, nor malignant, nor proud, thou shalt make no evil plan against thy neighbour. 7. Thou shalt hate no man; but some thou shalt reprove,[1] and for some shalt thou pray, and some thou shalt love more than thine own life.

III

1. My child, flee from every evil man and from all like him. 2. Be not proud, for pride leads to murder, nor jealous, nor contentious, nor passionate, for from all these murders are engendered. 3. My child, be not lustful, for lust leads to fornication, nor a speaker of base words, nor a lifter up of the eyes, for from all these is adultery engendered. 4. My child, regard not omens, for this leads to idolatry; neither be an enchanter, nor an astrologer, nor a magician, neither wish to see these things, for from them all is idolatry engendered. 5. My child, be not a liar, for lying leads to theft, nor a lover of money, nor vain-glorious, for from all these things

Further advice to the catechumen

---

[1] On the ground of a comparison with Jude 22 f. etc., some think that "and some thou shalt pity" ought to be added.

τῶν κλοπαὶ γεννῶνται. 6. τέκνον μου, μὴ γίνου
γόγγυσος, ἐπειδὴ ὁδηγεῖ εἰς τὴν βλασφημίαν,
μηδὲ αὐθάδης μηδὲ πονηρόφρων· ἐκ γὰρ τούτων
ἁπάντων βλασφημίαι γεννῶνται. 7. ἴσθι δὲ
πραΰς, ἐπεὶ οἱ πραεῖς κληρονομήσουσι τὴν γῆν.
8. γίνου μακρόθυμος καὶ ἐλεήμων καὶ ἄκακος καὶ

Mt. 5, 5;
Ps. 36, 11

ἡσύχιος καὶ ἀγαθὸς καὶ τρέμων τοὺς λόγους διὰ
παντός, οὓς ἤκουσας. 9. οὐχ ὑψώσεις σεαυτὸν
οὐδὲ δώσεις τῇ ψυχῇ σου θράσος. οὐ κολληθή-
σεται ἡ ψυχή σου μετὰ ὑψηλῶν, ἀλλὰ μετὰ
δικαίων καὶ ταπεινῶν ἀναστραφήσῃ. 10. τὰ
συμβαίνοντά σοι ἐνεργήματα ὡς ἀγαθὰ προσδέξῃ,
εἰδὼς ὅτι ἄτερ θεοῦ οὐδὲν γίνεται.

IV

1. Τέκνον μου, τοῦ λαλοῦντός σοι τὸν λόγον
τοῦ θεοῦ μνησθήσῃ νυκτὸς καὶ ἡμέρας, τιμήσεις
δὲ αὐτὸν ὡς κύριον· ὅθεν γὰρ ἡ κυριότης λαλεῖται,
ἐκεῖ κύριός ἐστιν. 2. ἐκζητήσεις δὲ καθ' ἡμέραν
τὰ πρόσωπα τῶν ἁγίων, ἵνα ἐπαναπαῇς τοῖς
λόγοις αὐτῶν. 3. οὐ ποθήσεις[1] σχίσμα, εἰρηνεύ-

Deut. 1, 16;
Prov. 31, 9;
cf. Joh. 7, 24

σεις δὲ μαχομένους· κρινεῖς δικαίως, οὐ λήψῃ
πρόσωπον ἐλέγξαι ἐπὶ παραπτώμασιν. 4. οὐ
διψυχήσεις, πότερον ἔσται ἢ οὔ.

5. Μὴ γίνου πρὸς μὲν τὸ λαβεῖν ἐκτείνων τὰς
χεῖρας, πρὸς δὲ τὸ δοῦναι συσπῶν. 6. ἐὰν ἔχῃς

[1] The editors usually emend to ποιήσεις "make."

are thefts engendered. 6. My child, be not a grumbler, for this leads to blasphemy, nor stubborn, nor a thinker of evil, for from all these are blasphemies engendered, 7. but be thou "meek, for the meek shall inherit the earth;" 8. be thou long-suffering, and merciful and guileless, and quiet, and good, and ever fearing the words which thou hast heard. 9. Thou shalt not exalt thyself, nor let thy soul be presumptuous. Thy soul shall not consort with the lofty, but thou shalt walk with righteous and humble men. 10. Receive the accidents that befall to thee as good, knowing that nothing happens without God.

IV

1. My child, thou shalt remember, day and night, him who speaks the word of God to thee; and thou shalt honour him as the Lord, for where the Lord's nature is spoken of, there is he present. 2. And thou shalt seek daily the presence of the saints, that thou mayest find rest in their words. 3. Thou shalt not desire a schism, but shalt reconcile those that strive. Thou shalt give righteous judgment; thou shalt favour no man's person in reproving transgression. 4. Thou shalt not be of two minds whether it shall be or not. *The duty of the catechumen to the Church*

5. Be not one who stretches out his hands to receive, but shuts them when it comes to giving. 6. Of *Against meanness*

315

διὰ τῶν χειρῶν σου, δώσεις λύτρωσιν ἁμαρτιῶν
σου. 7. οὐ διστάσεις δοῦναι οὐδὲ διδοὺς γογγύ-
σεις· γνώσῃ γάρ, τίς ἐστιν ὁ τοῦ μισθοῦ καλὸς
ἀνταποδότης. 8. οὐκ ἀποστραφήσῃ τὸν ἐνδεόμενον, συγκοινωνήσεις δὲ πάντα τῷ ἀδελφῷ σοῦ
καὶ οὐκ ἐρεῖς ἴδια εἶναι· εἰ γὰρ ἐν τῷ ἀθανάτῳ
κοινωνοί ἐστε, πόσῳ μᾶλλον ἐν τοῖς θνητοῖς ;
9. Οὐκ ἀρεῖς τὴν χεῖρά σου ἀπὸ τοῦ υἱοῦ σου
ἢ ἀπὸ τῆς θυγατρός σου, ἀλλὰ ἀπὸ νεότητος
διδάξεις τὸν φόβον τοῦ θεοῦ. 10. οὐκ ἐπιτάξεις
δούλῳ σου ἢ παιδίσκῃ, τοῖς ἐπὶ τὸν αὐτὸν θεὸν
ἐλπίζουσιν, ἐν πικρίᾳ σου, μήποτε οὐ μὴ φοβηθήσονται τὸν ἐπ' ἀμφοτέροις θεόν· οὐ γὰρ ἔρχεται
κατὰ πρόσωπον καλέσαι, ἀλλ' ἐφ' οὓς τὸ πνεῦμα
ἡτοίμασεν. 11. ὑμεῖς δὲ οἱ δοῦλοι ὑποταγή-
σεσθε τοῖς κυρίοις ὑμῶν ὡς τύπῳ θεοῦ ἐν αἰσχύνῃ
καὶ φόβῳ.
12. Μισήσεις πᾶσαν ὑπόκρισιν καὶ πᾶν ὃ μὴ
ἀρεστὸν τῷ κυρίῳ. 13. οὐ μὴ ἐγκαταλίπῃς
ἐντολὰς κυρίου, φυλάξεις δὲ ἃ παρέλαβες, μήτε
προστιθεὶς μήτε ἀφαιρῶν. 14. ἐν ἐκκλησίᾳ ἐξομολογήσῃ τὰ παραπτώματά σου, καὶ οὐ προσελεύσῃ
ἐπὶ προσευχήν σου ἐν συνειδήσει πονηρᾷ· αὕτη
ἐστὶν ἡ ὁδὸς τῆς ζωῆς.

V

1. Ἡ δὲ τοῦ θανάτου ὁδός ἐστιν αὕτη· πρῶτον
πάντων πονηρά ἐστι καὶ κατάρας μεστή· φόνοι,
μοιχεῖαι, ἐπιθυμίαι, πορνεῖαι, κλοπαί, εἰδωλο-
316

whatsoever thou hast gained by thy hands thou shalt give a ransom for thy sins. 7. Thou shalt not hesitate to give, nor shalt thou grumble when thou givest, for thou shalt know who is the good Paymaster of the reward. 8. Thou shalt not turn away the needy, but shalt share everything with thy brother, and shalt not say that it is thine own, for if you are sharers in the imperishable, how much more in the things which perish?

9. Thou shalt not withhold thine hand from thy son or from thy daughter, but thou shalt teach them the fear of God from their youth up. 10. Thou shalt not command in thy bitterness thy slave or thine handmaid, who hope in the same God, lest they cease to fear the God who is over you both; for he comes not to call men with respect of persons, but those whom the Spirit has prepared. 11. But do you who are slaves be subject to your master, as to God's representative, in reverence and fear. Household duties

12. Thou shalt hate all hypocrisy, and everything that is not pleasing to the Lord. 13. Thou shalt not forsake the commandments of the Lord, but thou shalt keep what thou didst receive, "adding nothing to it and taking nothing away." 14. In the congregation thou shalt confess thy transgressions, and thou shalt not betake thyself to prayer with an evil conscience. This is the way of life. Against hypocrisy

V

1. But the Way of Death is this: First of all, it is wicked and full of cursing, murders, adulteries, lusts, fornications, thefts, idolatries, witchcrafts, charms, The Way of Death

Rom. 1, 29-30

λατρίαι, μαγεῖαι, φαρμακίαι, ἁρπαγαί, ψευδο-
μαρτυρίαι, ὑποκρίσεις, διπλοκαρδία, δόλος, ὑπερηφανία, κακία, αὐθάδεια, πλεονεξία, αἰσχρολογία,
ζηλοτυπία, θρασύτης, ὕψος, ἀλαζονεία. 2. διώκ-
ται ἀγαθῶν, μισοῦντες ἀλήθειαν, ἀγαπῶντες
ψεῦδος, οὐ γινώσκοντες μισθὸν δικαιοσύνης, οὐ

Rom. 12, 9

κολλώμενοι ἀγαθῷ οὐδὲ κρίσει δικαίᾳ, ἀγρυπνοῦντες οὐκ εἰς τὸ ἀγαθόν, ἀλλ' εἰς τὸ πονηρόν·

Ps. 4, 2
Is. 1, 23

ὧν μακρὰν πραΰτης καὶ ὑπομονή, μάταια ἀγαπῶντες, διώκοντες ἀνταπόδομα, οὐκ ἐλεοῦντες
πτωχόν, οὐ πονοῦντες ἐπὶ καταπονουμένῳ, οὐ

Wisd. 12, 7

γινώσκοντες τὸν ποιήσαντα αὐτούς, φονεῖς τέκνων,
φθορεῖς πλάσματος θεοῦ, ἀποστρεφόμενοι τὸν
ἐνδεόμενον, καταπονοῦντες τὸν θλιβόμενον, πλουσίων παράκλητοι, πενήτων ἄνομοι κριταί,
πανθαμάρτητοι· ῥυσθείητε, τέκνα, ἀπὸ τούτων
ἁπάντων.

VI

Mt. 24, 4

1. Ὅρα, μή τίς σε πλανήσῃ ἀπὸ ταύτης τῆς
ὁδοῦ τῆς διδαχῆς, ἐπεὶ παρεκτὸς θεοῦ σε διδάσκει.
2. εἰ μὲν γὰρ δύνασαι βαστάσαι ὅλον τὸν ζυγὸν
τοῦ κυρίου, τέλειος ἔσῃ· εἰ δ' οὐ δύνασαι, ὃ δύνῃ,
τοῦτο ποίει. 3. περὶ δὲ τῆς βρώσεως, ὃ δύνασαι
βάστασον· ἀπὸ δὲ τοῦ εἰδωλοθύτου λίαν πρόσεχε·
λατρεία γάρ ἐστι θεῶν νεκρῶν.

VII

1. Περὶ δὲ τοῦ βαπτίσματος, οὕτω βαπτίσατε·

Mt. 28, 19

ταῦτα πάντα προειπόντες, βαπτίσατε εἰς τὸ

318

robberies, false witness, hypocrisies, a double heart, fraud, pride, malice, stubbornness, covetousness, foul speech, jealousy, impudence, haughtiness, boastfulness. 2. Persecutors of the good, haters of truth, lovers of lies, knowing not the reward of righteousness, not cleaving to the good nor to righteous judgment, spending wakeful nights not for good but for wickedness, from whom meekness and patience is far, lovers of vanity, following after reward, unmerciful to the poor, not working for him who is oppressed with toil, without knowledge of him who made them, murderers of children, corrupters of God's creatures, turning away the needy, oppressing the distressed, advocates of the rich, unjust judges of the poor, altogether sinful ; may ye be delivered, my children, from all these.

VI

1. SEE "that no one make thee to err" from this Way of the teaching, for he teaches thee without God. 2. For if thou canst bear the whole yoke of the Lord, thou wilt be perfect, but if thou canst not, do what thou canst. 3. And concerning food, bear what thou canst, but keep strictly from that which is offered to idols, for it is the worship of dead gods. Final exhortation

Food, and 'things offered to idols.'

VII

1. CONCERNING baptism, baptise thus : Having first rehearsed all these things, "baptise, in the Name of Baptism

ὄνομα τοῦ πατρὸς καὶ τοῦ υἱοῦ καὶ τοῦ ἁγίου
πνεύματος ἐν ὕδατι ζῶντι. 2. ἐὰν δὲ μὴ ἔχῃς
ὕδωρ ζῶν, εἰς ἄλλο ὕδωρ βάπτισον· εἰ δ᾽ οὐ
δύνασαι ἐν ψυχρῷ, ἐν θερμῷ. 3. ἐὰν δὲ ἀμφότερα
μὴ ἔχῃς, ἔκχεον εἰς τὴν κεφαλὴν τρὶς ὕδωρ εἰς
ὄνομα πατρὸς καὶ υἱοῦ καὶ ἁγίου πνεύματος.
4. πρὸ δὲ τοῦ βαπτίσματος προνηστευσάτω ὁ
βαπτίζων καὶ ὁ βαπτιζόμενος καὶ εἴ τινες ἄλλοι
δύνανται· κελεύεις δὲ νηστεῦσαι τὸν βαπτιζόμενον
πρὸ μιᾶς ἢ δύο.

Mt. 28, 19

VIII

Mt. 6, 16

1. Αἱ δὲ νηστεῖαι ὑμῶν μὴ ἔστωσαν μετὰ τῶν
ὑποκριτῶν. νηστεύουσι γὰρ δευτέρᾳ σαββάτων
καὶ πέμπτῃ· ὑμεῖς δὲ νηστεύσατε τετράδα καὶ
παρασκευήν. 2. μηδὲ προσεύχεσθε ὡς οἱ ὑπο-
κριταί, ἀλλ᾽ ὡς ἐκέλευσεν ὁ κύριος ἐν τῷ εὐαγγελίῳ
αὐτοῦ, οὕτω προσεύχεσθε· Πάτερ ἡμῶν ὁ ἐν τῷ
οὐρανῷ, ἁγιασθήτω τὸ ὄνομά σου, ἐλθέτω ἡ
βασιλεία σου, γενηθήτω τὸ θέλημά σου ὡς ἐν
οὐρανῷ καὶ ἐπὶ γῆς· τὸν ἄρτον ἡμῶν τὸν ἐπιούσιον
δὸς ἡμῖν σήμερον, καὶ ἄφες ἡμῖν τὴν ὀφειλὴν
ἡμῶν, ὡς καὶ ἡμεῖς ἀφίεμεν τοῖς ὀφειλέταις ἡμῶν,
καὶ μὴ εἰσενέγκῃς ἡμᾶς εἰς πειρασμόν, ἀλλὰ
ῥῦσαι ἡμᾶς ἀπὸ τοῦ πονηροῦ· ὅτι σοῦ ἐστιν ἡ
δύναμις καὶ ἡ δόξα εἰς τοὺς αἰῶνας. 3. τρὶς τῆς
ἡμέρας οὕτω προσεύχεσθε.

Mt. 6, 5

Mt. 6, 9–13

the Father and of the Son and of the Holy Spirit," in running water; 2. but if thou hast no running water, baptise in other water, and if thou canst not in cold, then in warm.   3. But if thou hast neither, pour water three times on the head "in the Name of the Father, Son and Holy Spirit."   4. And before the baptism let the baptiser and him who is to be baptised fast, and any others who are able.   And thou shalt bid him who is to be baptised to fast one or two days before.

VIII

1. LET not your fasts be with the hypocrites, for they fast on Mondays and Thursdays, but do you fast on Wednesdays and Fridays.   2. And do not pray as the hypocrites, but as the Lord commanded in his Gospel, pray thus: "Our Father, who art in Heaven, hallowed be thy Name, thy Kingdom come, thy will be done, as in Heaven so also upon earth; give us to-day our daily [1] bread, and forgive us our debt as we forgive our debtors, and lead us not into trial, but deliver us from the Evil One, for thine is the power and the glory for ever."   3. Pray thus three times a day.

Fasting

Prayers

---

[1] This is the traditional translation of ἐπιούσιον, but it is by no means certain that it is correct.   The word has from the beginning been a puzzle, and its meaning is not clearly known.   See further any good commentary on the gospels.

IX

1. Περὶ δὲ τῆς εὐχαριστίας, οὕτως εὐχαριστή-
σατε· 2. πρῶτον περὶ τοῦ ποτηρίου·[1] Εὐχαριστοῦμέν σοι, πάτερ ἡμῶν, ὑπὲρ τῆς ἁγίας ἀμπέλου
Δαυεὶδ τοῦ παιδός σου, ἧς ἐγνώρισας ἡμῖν διὰ
Ἰησοῦ τοῦ παιδός σου· σοὶ ἡ δόξα εἰς τοὺς αἰῶνας.
3. περὶ δὲ τοῦ κλάσματος· Εὐχαριστοῦμέν σοι,
πάτερ ἡμῶν, ὑπὲρ τῆς ζωῆς καὶ γνώσεως, ἧς
ἐγνώρισας ἡμῖν διὰ Ἰησοῦ τοῦ παιδός σου· σοὶ ἡ
δόξα εἰς τοὺς αἰῶνας. 4. ὥσπερ ἦν τοῦτο τὸ[2]
κλάσμα διεσκορπισμένον ἐπάνω τῶν ὀρέων καὶ
συναχθὲν ἐγένετο ἕν, οὕτω συναχθήτω σου ἡ
ἐκκλησία ἀπὸ τῶν περάτων τῆς γῆς εἰς τὴν σὴν
βασιλείαν· ὅτι σοῦ ἐστιν ἡ δόξα καὶ ἡ δύναμις
διὰ Ἰησοῦ Χριστοῦ εἰς τοὺς αἰῶνας. 5. μηδεὶς δὲ
φαγέτω μηδὲ πιέτω ἀπὸ τῆς εὐχαριστίας ὑμῶν,
ἀλλ᾽ οἱ βαπτισθέντες εἰς ὄνομα κυρίου· καὶ γὰρ
Mt. 7, 6 περὶ τούτου εἴρηκεν ὁ κύριος· Μὴ δῶτε τὸ ἅγιον
τοῖς κυσί.

X

1. Μετὰ δὲ τὸ ἐμπλησθῆναι οὕτως εὐχαριστή-
σατε· 2. Εὐχαριστοῦμέν σοι, πάτερ ἅγιε, ὑπὲρ
τοῦ ἁγίου ὀνόματός σου, οὗ κατεσκήνωσας ἐν ταῖς

[1] It is noteworthy that this order "first the Cup" is only
found elsewhere in the earliest text of Lc. 22, 17 ff. (which
omits v. 20) and perhaps in I. Cor. 10, 16.
[2] τό om. C.

IX

1. And concerning the Eucharist, hold[1] Eucharist thus: 2. First concerning the Cup, "We give thanks to thee, our Father, for the Holy Vine of David thy child, which, thou didst make known to us through Jesus thy child; to thee be glory for ever." 3. And concerning the broken Bread: "We give thee thanks, our Father, for the life and knowledge which thou didst make known to us through Jesus thy child. To thee be glory for ever. 4. As this broken bread was scattered upon the mountains, but was brought together and became one, so let thy Church be gathered together from the ends of the earth into thy kingdom, for thine is the glory and the power through Jesus Christ for ever." 5. But let none eat or drink of your Eucharist except those who have been baptised in the Lord's Name. For concerning this also did the Lord say, "Give not that which is holy to the dogs."

The Eucharist

The Cup

The Bread

X

1. But after you are satisfied with food, thus give thanks: 2. "We give thanks to thee, O Holy Father, for thy Holy Name which thou didst make to taber-

The final prayer in the Eucharist

---

[1] The translation fails to preserve the play on the words, which might be rendered "concerning the giving of thanks, give thanks thus, etc." But this would obscure the fact that εὐχαριστία is here quite clearly "Eucharist" (cf. v. 5).

καρδίαις ἡμῶν, καὶ ὑπὲρ τῆς γνώσεως καὶ πίστεως
καὶ ἀθανασίας, ἧς ἐγνώρισας ἡμῖν διὰ Ἰησοῦ τοῦ
παιδός σου· σοὶ ἡ δόξα εἰς τοὺς αἰῶνας. 3. σύ,
δέσποτα παντοκράτορ, ἔκτισας τὰ πάντα ἕνεκεν
τοῦ ὀνόματός σου, τροφήν τε καὶ ποτὸν ἔδωκας
τοῖς ἀνθρώποις εἰς ἀπόλαυσιν, ἵνα σοι εὐχαριστή-
σωσιν, ἡμῖν δὲ ἐχαρίσω πνευματικὴν τροφὴν καὶ
ποτὸν καὶ ζωὴν αἰώνιον διὰ τοῦ παιδός σου.
4. πρὸ πάντων εὐχαριστοῦμέν σοι, ὅτι δυνατὸς εἶ·
σοὶ[1] ἡ δόξα εἰς τοὺς αἰῶνας. 5. μνήσθητι, κύριε,
τῆς ἐκκλησίας σου, τοῦ ῥύσασθαι αὐτὴν ἀπὸ
παντὸς πονηροῦ καὶ τελειῶσαι αὐτὴν ἐν τῇ ἀγάπῃ
σου, καὶ σύναξον αὐτὴν ἀπὸ τῶν τεσσάρων
ἀνέμων, τὴν ἁγιασθεῖσαν, εἰς τὴν σὴν βασιλείαν,
ἣν ἡτοίμασας αὐτῇ· ὅτι σοῦ ἐστιν ἡ δύναμις καὶ
ἡ δόξα εἰς τοὺς αἰῶνας. 6. ἐλθέτω χάρις καὶ
παρελθέτω ὁ κόσμος οὗτος. Ὡσαννὰ τῷ θεῷ
Δαυείδ. εἴ τις ἅγιός ἐστιν, ἐρχέσθω· εἴ τις οὐκ
ἔστι, μετανοείτω· μαρὰν ἀθά· ἀμήν. 7. τοῖς δὲ
προφήταις ἐπιτρέπετε εὐχαριστεῖν ὅσα θέλουσιν.

XI

1. Ὃς ἂν οὖν ἐλθὼν διδάξῃ ὑμᾶς ταῦτα πάντα
τὰ προειρημένα, δέξασθε αὐτόν· 2. ἐὰν δὲ αὐτὸς
ὁ διδάσκων στραφεὶς διδάσκῃ ἄλλην διδαχὴν εἰς
τὸ καταλῦσαι, μὴ αὐτοῦ ἀκούσητε· εἰς δὲ τὸ
προσθεῖναι δικαιοσύνην καὶ γνῶσιν κυρίου, δέξασθε
αὐτὸν ὡς κύριον.

---

[1] C reads σύ which is a common mistake for σοι, but
Harnack prefers to emend to ὅτι δυνατὸς εἶ σύ· σοὶ κ.τ.λ.

Margin references:
Wisd. 1, 14;
Ecclus. 18, 1;
24, 8;
Rev. 4, 11
Mt. 24, 31
Mt. 21, 9. 15
I Cor. 16, 22

nacle in our hearts, and for the knowledge and faith
and immortality which thou didst make known to us
through Jesus thy Child. To thee be glory for ever.
3. Thou, Lord Almighty, didst create all things for
thy Name's sake, and didst give food and drink to men
for their enjoyment, that they might give thanks to
thee, but us hast thou blessed with spiritual food and
drink and eternal light through thy Child. 4. Above
all we give thanks to thee for that thou art mighty.
To thee be glory for ever. 5. Remember, Lord, thy
Church, to deliver it from all evil and to make it
perfect in thy love, and gather it together in its
holiness from the four winds to thy kingdom which
thou hast prepared for it. For thine is the power
and the glory for ever. 6. Let grace come and let
this world pass away. Hosannah to the God of
David. If any man be holy, let him come! if any
man be not, let him repent: Maran atha,[1] Amen."

7. But suffer the prophets to hold Eucharist as
they will.

XI

1. Whosoever then comes and teaches you all ^Travelling
these things aforesaid, receive him. 2. But if the ^teachers
teacher himself be perverted and teach another
doctrine to destroy these things, do not listen to
him, but if his teaching be for the increase of
righteousness and knowledge of the Lord, receive
him as the Lord.

[1] A transliteration of Aramaic words meaning "Our Lord!
Come!"

3. Περὶ δὲ τῶν ἀποστόλων καὶ προφητῶν, κατὰ τὸ δόγμα τοῦ εὐαγγελίου οὕτω ποιήσατε. 4. πᾶς δὲ ἀπόστολος ἐρχόμενος πρὸς ὑμᾶς δεχθήτω ὡς κύριος· 5. οὐ μενεῖ δὲ εἰ μὴ[1] ἡμέραν μίαν· ἐὰν δὲ ᾖ χρεία, καὶ τὴν ἄλλην· τρεῖς δὲ ἐὰν μείνῃ, ψευδοπροφήτης ἐστίν. 6. ἐξερχόμενος δὲ ὁ ἀπόστολος μηδὲν λαμβανέτω εἰ μὴ ἄρτον, ἕως οὗ αὐλισθῇ· ἐὰν δὲ ἀργύριον αἰτῇ, ψευδοπροφήτης ἐστί.

Mt. 12, 31

7. Καὶ πάντα προφήτην λαλοῦντα ἐν πνεύματι οὐ πειράσετε οὐδὲ διακρινεῖτε· πᾶσα γὰρ ἁμαρτία ἀφεθήσεται, αὕτη δὲ ἡ ἁμαρτία οὐκ ἀφεθήσεται. 8. οὐ πᾶς δὲ ὁ λαλῶν ἐν πνεύματι προφήτης ἐστίν, ἀλλ᾽ ἐὰν ἔχῃ τοὺς τρόπους κυρίου. ἀπὸ οὖν τῶν τρόπων γνωσθήσεται ὁ ψευδοπροφήτης καὶ ὁ προφήτης. 9. καὶ πᾶς προφήτης ὁρίζων τράπεζαν ἐν πνεύματι οὐ φάγεται ἀπ᾽ αὐτῆς, εἰ δὲ μήγε ψευδοπροφήτης ἐστί. 10. πᾶς δὲ προφήτης διδάσκων τὴν ἀλήθειαν, εἰ ἃ διδάσκει οὐ ποιεῖ, ψευδοπροφήτης ἐστί. 11. πᾶς δὲ προφήτης δεδοκιμασμένος, ἀληθινός, ποιῶν εἰς μυστήριον κοσμικὸν ἐκκλησίας, μὴ διδάσκων δὲ ποιεῖν, ὅσα αὐτὸς ποιεῖ, οὐ κριθήσεται ἐφ᾽ ὑμῶν· μετὰ θεοῦ γὰρ ἔχει τὴν κρίσιν· ὡσαύτως γὰρ ἐποίησαν καὶ οἱ ἀρχαῖοι προφῆται. 12. ὃς δ᾽ ἂν εἴπῃ ἐν πνεύματι· δός μοι ἀργύρια ἢ ἕτερά τινα, οὐκ ἀκούσεσθε αὐτοῦ· ἐὰν δὲ περὶ ἄλλων ὑστερούντων εἴπῃ δοῦναι, μηδεὶς αὐτὸν κρινέτω.

---

[1] εἰ μή are omitted by C, but xii. 2 seems to make the correction quite certain.

3. And concerning the Apostles and Prophets, Apostles
act thus according to the ordinance of the Gospel.[1]
4. Let every Apostle who comes to you be received
as the Lord, **5.** but let him not stay more than one
day, or if need be a second as well; but if he stay
three days, he is a false prophet. **6.** And when an
Apostle goes forth let him accept nothing but
bread till he reach his night's lodging; but if he
ask for money, he is a false prophet.

7. Do not test or examine any prophet who is speak- Prophets
ing in a spirit, "for every sin shall be forgiven, but
this sin shall not be forgiven." **8.** But not everyone
who speaks in a spirit is a prophet, except he have the
behaviour of the Lord. From his behaviour, then,
the false prophet and the true prophet shall be
known. **9.** And no prophet who orders a meal in a
spirit shall eat of it: otherwise he is a false prophet.
10. And every prophet who teaches the truth, if he
do not what he teaches, is a false prophet. **11.** But
no prophet who has been tried and is genuine,
though he enact a worldly mystery[2] of the Church,
if he teach not others to do what he does himself,
shall be judged by you: for he has his judgment
with God, for so also did the prophets of old.
12. But whosoever shall say in a spirit 'Give me
money, or something else,' you shall not listen to
him; but if he tell you to give on behalf of others
in want, let none judge him.

---

[1] It is unknown to what ordinance the writer refers.
[2] This passage has never been satisfactorily explained: it
probably refers to a tendency among some prophets to intro-
duce forms of worship, or of illustration of their teaching, of
doubtful propriety, if so the reference below to the prophets
of old is perhaps an allusion to Hosea (Hos. 1, 2 ff.).

XII

Mt. 21, 9;
Ps. 118, 26,
cf. Joh. 5, 43
1. Πᾶς δὲ ὁ ἐρχόμενος ἐν ὀνόματι κυρίου δεχθήτω· ἔπειτα δὲ δοκιμάσαντες αὐτὸν γνώσεσθε, σύνεσιν γὰρ ἕξετε δεξιὰν καὶ ἀριστεράν. 2. εἰ μὲν παρόδιός ἐστιν ὁ ἐρχόμενος, βοηθεῖτε αὐτῷ, ὅσον δύνασθε· οὐ μενεῖ δὲ πρὸς ὑμᾶς εἰ μὴ δύο ἢ τρεῖς ἡμέρας, ἐὰν ᾖ ἀνάγκη. 3. εἰ δὲ θέλει πρὸς ὑμᾶς καθῆσθαι, τεχνίτης ὤν, ἐργαζέσθω καὶ φαγέτω. 4. εἰ δὲ οὐκ ἔχει τέχνην, κατὰ τὴν σύνεσιν ὑμῶν προνοήσατε, πῶς μὴ ἀργὸς μεθ' ὑμῶν ζήσεται Χριστιανός. 5. εἰ δ' οὐ θέλει οὕτω ποιεῖν, χριστέμπορός ἐστι· προσέχετε ἀπὸ τῶν τοιούτων.

XIII

Mt. 10, 10;
cf. Luke 10, 7;
I Cor. 9, 13,
14; I Tim. 5,
17, 18
1. Πᾶς δὲ προφήτης ἀληθινὸς θέλων καθῆσθαι πρὸς ὑμᾶς ἄξιός ἐστι τῆς τροφῆς αὐτοῦ. 2. ὡσαύτως διδάσκαλος ἀληθινός ἐστιν ἄξιος καὶ αὐτὸς ὥσπερ ὁ ἐργάτης τῆς τροφῆς αὐτοῦ. 3. πᾶσαν οὖν ἀπαρχὴν γεννημάτων ληνοῦ καὶ ἅλωνος, βοῶν τε καὶ προβάτων λαβὼν δώσεις τὴν ἀπαρχὴν τοῖς προφήταις· αὐτοὶ γάρ εἰσιν οἱ ἀρχιερεῖς ὑμῶν. 4. ἐὰν δὲ μὴ ἔχητε προφήτην, δότε τοῖς πτωχοῖς. 5. ἐὰν σιτίαν ποιῇς, τὴν ἀπαρχὴν λαβὼν δὸς κατὰ τὴν ἐντολήν. 6. ὡσαύτως κεράμιον οἴνου ἢ ἐλαίου ἀνοίξας, τὴν ἀπαρχὴν λαβὼν δὸς τοῖς προφήταις· 7. ἀργυρίου δὲ καὶ ἱματισμοῦ καὶ παντὸς κτήματος λαβὼν τὴν ἀπαρχήν, ὡς ἄν σοι δόξῃ, δὸς κατὰ τὴν ἐντολήν.

XII

1. LET everyone who "comes in the Name of the Lord" be received; but when you have tested him you shall know him, for you shall have understanding of true and false.[1] 2. If he who comes is a traveller, help him as much as you can, but he shall not remain with you more than two days, or, if need be, three. 3. And if he wishes to settle among you and has a craft, let him work for his bread. 4. But if he has no craft provide for him according to your understanding, so that no man shall live among you in idleness because he is a Christian. 5. But if he will not do so, he is making traffic of Christ; beware of such.

Travelling Christians

XIII

1. BUT every true prophet who wishes to settle among you is "worthy of his food." 2. Likewise a true teacher is himself worthy, like the workman, of his food. 3. Therefore thou shalt take the firstfruit of the produce of the winepress and of the threshing-floor and of oxen and sheep, and shalt give them as the firstfruits to the prophets, for they are your high priests. 4. But if you have not a prophet, give to the poor. 5. If thou makest bread, take the first-fruits, and give it according to the commandment. 6. Likewise when thou openest a jar of wine or oil, give the firstfruits to the prophets. 7. Of money also and clothes, and of all your possessions, take the firstfruits, as it seem best to you, and give according to the commandment.

Prophets who desire to remain

Their payment by firstfruits

[1] Literally, "right and left understanding."

XIV

1. Κατὰ κυριακὴν δὲ κυρίου συναχθέντες κλάσατε ἄρτον καὶ εὐχαριστήσατε, προεξομολογησάμενοι[1] τὰ παραπτώματα ὑμῶν, ὅπως καθαρὰ ἡ θυσία ὑμῶν[2] ᾖ.   2. πᾶς δὲ ἔχων τὴν ἀμφιβολίαν μετὰ τοῦ ἑταίρου αὐτοῦ μὴ συνελθέτω ὑμῖν, ἕως οὗ διαλλαγῶσιν, ἵνα μὴ κοινωθῇ ἡ θυσία ὑμῶν. 3. αὕτη γάρ ἐστιν ἡ ῥηθεῖσα ὑπὸ κυρίου· Ἐν παντὶ τόπῳ καὶ χρόνῳ προσφέρειν μοι θυσίαν καθαράν. ὅτι βασιλεὺς μέγας εἰμί, λέγει κύριος, καὶ τὸ ὄνομά μου θαυμαστὸν ἐν τοῖς ἔθνεσι.

cf. Mt. 5, 23. 24

Malach. 1, 11. 14

XV

1. Χειροτονήσατε οὖν ἑαυτοῖς ἐπισκόπους καὶ διακόνους ἀξίους τοῦ κυρίου, ἄνδρας πραεῖς καὶ ἀφιλαργύρους καὶ ἀληθεῖς καὶ δεδοκιμασμένους· ὑμῖν γὰρ λειτουργοῦσι καὶ αὐτοὶ τὴν λειτουργίαν τῶν προφητῶν καὶ διδασκάλων. 2. μὴ οὖν ὑπερίδητε αὐτούς· αὐτοὶ γάρ εἰσιν οἱ τετιμημένοι ὑμῶν μετὰ τῶν προφητῶν καὶ διδασκάλων. 3. Ἐλέγχετε δὲ ἀλλήλους μὴ ἐν ὀργῇ, ἀλλ' ἐν εἰρήνῃ ὡς ἔχετε ἐν τῷ εὐαγγελίῳ· καὶ παντὶ ἀστοχοῦντι κατὰ τοῦ ἑτέρου μηδεὶς λαλείτω μηδὲ παρ' ὑμῶν ἀκουέτω, ἕως οὗ μετανοήσῃ. 4. τὰς δὲ εὐχὰς ὑμῶν καὶ τὰς ἐλεημοσύνας καὶ πάσας τὰς πράξεις οὕτω ποιήσατε, ὡς ἔχετε ἐν τῷ εὐαγγελίῳ τοῦ κυρίου ἡμῶν.

Mt. 5, 22-26; 18, 15-35

---

[1] προσεξομολογησάμενοι. C.   [2] ἡμῶν C.

XIV

1. On the Lord's Day of the Lord come together, break bread and hold Eucharist, after confessing your transgressions that your offering may be pure; 2. but let none who has a quarrel with his fellow join in your meeting until they be reconciled, that your sacrifice be not defiled. 3. For this is that which was spoken by the Lord, " In every place and time offer me a pure sacrifice, for I am a great king," saith the Lord, " and my name is wonderful among the heathen."

XV

1. Appoint therefore for yourselves bishops and deacons worthy of the Lord, meek men, and not lovers of money, and truthful and approved, for they also minister to you the ministry of the prophets and teachers. 2. Therefore do not despise them, for they are your honourable men together with the prophets and teachers.

3. And reprove one another not in wrath but in peace as you find in the Gospel, and let none speak with any who has done a wrong to his neighbour, nor let him hear a word from you until he repents. 4. But your prayers and alms and all your acts perform as ye find in the Gospel of our Lord.

THE APOSTOLIC FATHERS

XVI

1. Γρηγορεῖτε ὑπὲρ τῆς ζωῆς ὑμῶν· οἱ λύχνοι ὑμῶν μὴ σβεσθήτωσαν, καὶ αἱ ὀσφύες ὑμῶν μὴ ἐκλυέσθωσαν, ἀλλὰ γίνεσθε ἕτοιμοι· οὐ γὰρ οἴδατε τὴν ὥραν, ἐν ᾗ ὁ κύριος ἡμῶν ἔρχεται. 2. πυκνῶς δὲ συναχθήσεσθε ζητοῦντες τὰ ἀνήκοντα ταῖς ψυχαῖς ὑμῶν· οὐ γὰρ ὠφελήσει ὑμᾶς ὁ πᾶς χρόνος τῆς πίστεως ὑμῶν, ἐὰν μὴ ἐν τῷ ἐσχάτῳ καιρῷ τελειωθῆτε. 3. ἐν γὰρ ταῖς ἐσχάταις ἡμέραις πληθυνθήσονται οἱ ψευδοπροφῆται καὶ οἱ φθορεῖς, καὶ στραφήσονται τὰ πρόβατα εἰς λύκους, καὶ ἡ ἀγάπη στραφήσεται εἰς μῖσος. 4. αὐξανούσης γὰρ τῆς ἀνομίας μισήσουσιν ἀλλήλους καὶ διώξουσι καὶ παραδώσουσι, καὶ τότε φανήσεται ὁ κοσμοπλανὴς ὡς υἱὸς θεοῦ, καὶ ποιήσει σημεῖα καὶ τέρατα, καὶ ἡ γῆ παραδοθήσεται εἰς χεῖρας αὐτοῦ, καὶ ποιήσει ἀθέμιτα, ἃ οὐδέποτε γέγονεν ἐξ αἰῶνος. 5. τότε ἥξει ἡ κτίσις τῶν ἀνθρώπων εἰς τὴν πύρωσιν τῆς δοκιμασίας, καὶ σκανδαλισθήσονται πολλοὶ καὶ ἀπολοῦνται, οἱ δὲ ὑπομείναντες ἐν τῇ πίστει αὐτῶν σωθήσονται ὑπ' αὐτοῦ τοῦ καταθέματος. 6. καὶ τότε φανήσεται τὰ σημεῖα τῆς ἀληθείας· πρῶτον σημεῖον ἐκπετάσεως ἐν οὐρανῷ, εἶτα σημεῖον φωνῆς σάλπιγγος, καὶ τὸ τρίτον ἀνάστασις νεκρῶν. 7. οὐ πάντων δέ, ἀλλ' ὡς ἐρρέθη· Ἥξει ὁ κύριος καὶ πάντες οἱ ἅγιοι μετ' αὐτοῦ. 8. τότε ὄψεται ὁ κόσμος τὸν κύριον ἐρχόμενον ἐπάνω τῶν νεφελῶν τοῦ οὐρανοῦ.

Marginalia: Mt. 24, 42; Luke 12, 35; Mt. 24, 44; Mt. 25, 13; Barnabas iv. 9; Mt. 24, 24; cf. II Thess. 2, 9; Apoc. 13, 2.13; Mt. 24, 10; Mt. 10, 22; 24, 13; Mt. 24, 30; Mt. 24, 31; cf. I Cor. 15, 22; I Thess. 4, 16; Zech. 14, 5; Mt. 24, 30; 26, 64

XVI

1. "WATCH" over your life: "let your lamps" be not quenched "and your loins" be not ungirded, but be "ready," for ye know not "the hour in which our Lord cometh." 2. But be frequently gathered together seeking the things which are profitable for your souls, for the whole time of your faith shall not profit you except ye be found perfect at the last time; 3. for in the last days the false prophets and the corrupters shall be multiplied, and the sheep shall be turned into wolves, and love shall change to hate; 4. for as lawlessness increaseth they shall hate one another and persecute and betray, and then shall appear the deceiver of the world as a Son of God, and shall do signs and wonders and the earth shall be given over into his hands and he shall commit iniquities which have never been since the world began. 5. Then shall the creation of mankind come to the fiery trial and "many shall be offended" and be lost, but "they who endure" in their faith "shall be saved" by the curse itself.[1] 6. And "then shall appear the signs" of the truth. First the sign spread out in Heaven, then the sign of the sound of the trumpet, and thirdly the resurrection of the dead: 7. but not of all the dead, but as it was said, "The Lord shall come and all his saints with him." 8. Then shall the world "see the Lord coming on the clouds of Heaven."

Warning that the end is at hand

[1] The meaning is obscure; but there seem to be other traces in early literature of a doctrine that each curse also contained the elements of a counterbalancing power to salvation. There is a valuable and long note on the subject in Rendel Harris's edition of the Didache.

THE EPISTLE OF BARNABAS

THE EPISTLE OF BARNABAS

THE document which is always known as the Epistle of Barnabas is, like I. Clement, really anonymous, and it is generally regarded as impossible to accept the tradition which ascribes it to the Barnabas who was a companion of S. Paul, though it is convenient to continue to use the title.

It is either a general treatise or was intended for some community in which Alexandrian ideas prevailed, though it is not possible to define either its destination, or the locality from which it was written, with any greater accuracy. Its main object is to warn Christians against a Judaistic conception of the Old Testament, and the writer carries a symbolical exegesis as far as did Philo; indeed he goes farther and apparently denies any literal significance at all to the commands of the Law. The literal exegesis of the ceremonial law is to him a device of an evil angel who deceived the Jews.

The date of Barnabas is doubtful. Two attempts have been made to fix it from internal evidence. In the first place, the ten kings in chap. vi. have been identified with the Roman Emperors, and thus a date well within the limits of the first century has been suggested, though there is no unanimity as to the exact manner in which the number of the ten Emperors is to be reached. In the second place attention has been drawn to the reference in chap. xvi. to the rebuilding of the Temple, and this is supposed to refer to the events of 132 A.D. Neither theory is quite satisfactory, but neither date is in itself impossible. The document no doubt belongs to the end of the first or beginning of the second century.

The text is found in the following authorities :—

(1) The *Codex Sinaiticus*, an uncial of the fourth century, now in the British Museum, and published in photographic facsimile by the Clarendon Press.

(2) The *Codex Constantinopolitanus*, found by Bryennios in 1875 and now at Jerusalem, the same MS. as that known as C in I. Clement and the Didache.

(3) In eight defective MSS., in which owing to some accident the ninth chapter of the epistle of Polycarp is continued without a break by the fifth chapter of Barnabas. These MSS. are clearly descended from a common archetype, copied from a MS. in which Barnabas followed Polycarp, but the pages containing the end of the latter and beginning of the former were lost, and a copyist who did not observe this merged the one into the other.

(4) A Latin version, extant in a single MS. at St. Petersburg, in which the text stops at the end of chap. xvii. It thus omits the "Two Ways," and the question (perhaps insoluble) arises whether the Latin has omitted it, or the Greek interpolated it. At present the general opinion is in favour of the former view.

THE EPISTLE OF BARNABAS

Barnabas, like I. Clement and Hermas, became canonical in some circles : it is quoted by Clement of Alexandria as Scripture, and is referred to by Origen as a Catholic Epistle, while it is included in the Codex Sinaiticus among the books of the New Testament, not, as is sometimes said, as an appendix, but following immediately after the Apocalypse, without any suggestion that it belonged to a different category of books.

The symbols employed in quoting the textual evidence are as follows :—

ℵ = Codex Sinaiticus.
C = Codex Constantinopolitanus.
G = the archetype of the eight Greek MSS.
L = the Latin version.

ΒΑΡΝΑΒΑ ΕΠΙΣΤΟΛΗ

I

1. Χαίρετε, υἱοὶ καὶ θυγατέρες, ἐν ὀνόματι κυρίου τοῦ ἀγαπήσαντος ἡμᾶς, ἐν εἰρήνῃ.

2. Μεγάλων μὲν ὄντων καὶ πλουσίων τῶν τοῦ θεοῦ δικαιωμάτων εἰς ὑμᾶς, ὑπέρ τι καὶ καθ' ὑπερβολὴν ὑπερευφραίνομαι ἐπὶ τοῖς μακαρίοις καὶ ἐνδόξοις ὑμῶν πνεύμασιν· οὕτως [1] ἔμφυτον τῆς δωρεᾶς πνευματικῆς χάριν εἰλήφατε. 3. διὸ καὶ μᾶλλον συγχαίρω ἐμαυτῷ ἐλπίζων σωθῆναι, ὅτι ἀληθῶς βλέπω ἐν ὑμῖν ἐκκεχυμένον ἀπὸ τοῦ πλουσίου τῆς πηγῆς κυρίου πνεῦμα ἐφ' ὑμᾶς. οὕτω με ἐξέπληξεν ἐπὶ ὑμῶν ἡ ἐμοὶ ἐπιποθήτη ὄψις ὑμῶν. 4. πεπεισμένος οὖν τοῦτο καὶ συνειδὼς ἐμαυτῷ, ὅτι ἐν ὑμῖν λαλήσας πολλὰ ἐπίσταμαι, ὅτι ἐμοὶ συνώδευσεν ἐν ὁδῷ δικαιοσύνης κύριος, καὶ πάντως ἀναγκάζομαι κἀγὼ εἰς τοῦτο, ἀγαπᾶν ὑμᾶς ὑπὲρ τὴν ψυχήν μου, ὅτι μεγάλη πίστις καὶ ἀγάπη ἐγκατοικεῖ ἐν ὑμῖν ἐπ' ἐλπίδι ζωῆς αὐτοῦ. 5. λογισάμενος οὖν τοῦτο, ὅτι ἐὰν μελήσῃ μοι περὶ ὑμῶν τοῦ μέρος τι μεταδοῦναι ἀφ' οὗ ἔλαβον, ὅτι ἔσται μοι τοιούτοις πνεύμασιν ὑπηρετήσαντι εἰς μισθόν, ἐσπούδασα κατὰ μικρὸν ὑμῖν πέμπειν,

Tit. 1, 1, 2; 3, 7

[1] οὕτω L, ουτο ℵ, οὗ τό C.

THE EPISTLE OF BARNABAS

I

1. HAIL, sons and daughters, in the name of the Lord who loved us, in peace. Greeting and introduction
2. Exceedingly and abundantly do I rejoice over your blessed and glorious spirit for the greatness and richness of God's ordinances towards you; so innate a grace of the gift of the spirit have you received.
3. Wherefore I congratulate myself the more in my hope of salvation, because I truly see in you that the Spirit has been poured out upon you from the Lord, who is rich in his bounty;[1] so that the sight of you, for which I longed, amazed me.
4. Being persuaded then of this, and being conscious that since I spoke among you I have much understanding because the Lord has travelled with me in the way of righteousness, I am above all constrained to this, to love you above my own life, because great faith and love dwell in you in the "hope of his life." 5. I have therefore reckoned that, if I make it my care in your behalf to communicate somewhat of that which I received, it shall bring me the reward of having ministered to such spirits, and I hasten to send you a short letter in order that

[1] Literally "spring."

ἵνα μετὰ τῆς πίστεως ὑμῶν τελείαν ἔχητε τὴν
γνῶσιν.

6. Τρία οὖν δόγματά ἐστιν κυρίου· ζωῆς ἐλπίς,
ἀρχὴ καὶ τέλος πίστεως ἡμῶν· καὶ δικαιοσύνη,
κρίσεως ἀρχὴ καὶ τέλος· ἀγάπη εὐφροσύνης
καὶ ἀγαλλιάσεως ἔργων δικαιοσύνης μαρτυρία.[1]
7. ἐγνώρισεν γὰρ ἡμῖν ὁ δεσπότης διὰ τῶν
προφητῶν τὰ παρεληλυθότα καὶ τὰ ἐνεστῶ-
τα, καὶ τῶν μελλόντων δοὺς ἀπαρχὰς ἡμῖν
γεύσεως, ὧν τὰ καθ' ἕκαστα βλέποντες ἐνεργού-
μενα, καθὼς ἐλάλησεν, ὀφείλομεν πλουσιώτερον
καὶ ὑψηλότερον προσάγειν τῷ φόβῳ αὐτοῦ.
8. ἐγὼ δὲ οὐχ ὡς διδάσκαλος, ἀλλ' ὡς εἷς ἐξ
ὑμῶν ὑποδείξω ὀλίγα, δι' ὧν ἐν τοῖς παροῦσιν
εὐφρανθήσεσθε.

II

1. Ἡμερῶν οὖν οὐσῶν πονηρῶν καὶ αὐτοῦ τοῦ
ἐνεργοῦντος ἔχοντος τὴν ἐξουσίαν, ὀφείλομεν
ἑαυτοῖς προσέχοντες ἐκζητεῖν τὰ δικαιώματα
κυρίου. 2. τῆς οὖν πίστεως ἡμῶν εἰσιν βοηθοὶ
φόβος καὶ ὑπομονή, τὰ δὲ συμμαχοῦντα ἡμῖν
μακροθυμία καὶ ἐγκράτεια· 3. τούτων οὖν μενόν-
των τὰ πρὸς κύριον ἁγνῶς, συνευφραίνονται

[1] The text of this whole passage is confused : *tres sunt
ergo constitutiones domini, vitae spes initium et consummatio*
L and no more ; τρία οὖν δόγματά ἐστιν κυρίου, ζωή, πίστις,
ἐλπίς, ἀρχὴ καὶ τέλος ἡμῶν, καὶ δικεοσύνη κρίσεως ἀρχή, καὶ τέλος
ἀγάπη, εὐφροσύνη, καὶ ἀγαλλιάσεως ἔργων ἐν δικαιοσύναις μαρτυρία ℵ The text printed is that of C, which gives the best
sense, though it is doubtful if it is more than the correction
of an early corruption.

your knowledge may be perfected along with your faith.

6. There are then three doctrines [1] of the Lord : The three doctrines " the hope of life " is the beginning and end of our faith ; and righteousness is the beginning and end of judgment ; love of joy and of gladness is the testimony of the works of righteousness.   7. For the Lord Prophecy made known to us through the prophets things past and things present and has given us the firstfruits of the taste of things to come ; and when we see these things coming to pass one by one, as he said, we ought to make a richer and deeper offering for fear of him.   8. But I will show you a few things, not as a teacher but as one of yourselves, in which you shall rejoice at this present time.

II

1. SEEING then that the days are evil, and that The need of virtue the worker of evil himself is in power, we ought to give heed to ourselves, and seek out the ordinances of the Lord.   2. Fear then, and patience are the helpers of our faith, and long-suffering and continence are our allies.   3. While then these things remain in holiness towards the Lord, wisdom, prudence, understanding, and knowledge rejoice

---

[1] Or possibly " ordinances " or " decrees."

αὐτοῖς σοφία, σύνεσις, ἐπιστήμη, γνῶσις. 4. πε-
φανέρωκεν γὰρ ἡμῖν διὰ πάντων τῶν προφητῶν,
ὅτι οὔτε θυσιῶν οὔτε ὁλοκαυτωμάτων οὔτε προσφορῶν χρῄζει, λέγων ὅτε μέν· 5. Τί μοι πλῆθος
τῶν θυσιῶν ὑμῶν; λέγει κύριος. πλήρης εἰμὶ
ὁλοκαυτωμάτων, καὶ στέαρ ἀρνῶν καὶ αἷμα ταύρων
καὶ τράγων οὐ βούλομαι, οὐδ᾽ ἂν ἔρχησθε ὀφθῆναί
μοι. τίς γὰρ ἐξεζήτησεν ταῦτα ἐκ τῶν χειρῶν
ὑμῶν; πατεῖν μου τὴν αὐλὴν οὐ προσθήσεσθε.
ἐὰν φέρητε σεμίδαλιν, μάταιον· θυμίαμα βδέλυγμά
μοί ἐστιν· τὰς νεομηνίας ὑμῶν καὶ τὰ σάββατα
οὐκ ἀνέχομαι. 6. ταῦτα οὖν κατήργησεν, ἵνα ὁ
καινὸς νόμος τοῦ κυρίου ἡμῶν Ἰησοῦ Χριστοῦ,
ἄνευ ζυγοῦ ἀνάγκης ὤν, μὴ ἀνθρωποποίητον ἔχῃ
τὴν προσφοράν. 7. λέγει δὲ πάλιν πρὸς αὐτούς·
Μὴ ἐγὼ ἐνετειλάμην τοῖς πατράσιν ὑμῶν ἐκπο-
ρευομένοις ἐκ γῆς Αἰγύπτου, προσενέγκαι μοι
ὁλοκαυτώματα καὶ θυσίας; 8. ἀλλ᾽ ἢ τοῦτο
ἐνετειλάμην αὐτοῖς· ἕκαστος ὑμῶν κατὰ τοῦ
πλησίον ἐν τῇ καρδίᾳ ἑαυτοῦ κακίαν μὴ μνησικα-
κείτω, καὶ ὅρκον ψευδῆ μὴ ἀγαπᾶτε. 9. αἰσθάνεσθαι οὖν ὀφείλομεν, μὴ ὄντες ἀσύνετοι, τὴν
γνώμην τῆς ἀγαθωσύνης τοῦ πατρὸς ἡμῶν, ὅτ᾽
ἡμῖν λέγει, θέλων ἡμᾶς μὴ ὁμοίως πλανωμένους
ἐκείνοις ζητεῖν, πῶς προσάγωμεν αὐτῷ. 10. ἡμῖν
οὖν οὕτως λέγει· Θυσία τῷ κυρίῳ[1] καρδία συντε-
τριμμένη, ὀσμὴ εὐωδίας τῷ κυρίῳ καρδία δοξά-
ζουσα τὸν πεπλακότα αὐτήν. ἀκριβεύεσθαι οὖν
ὀφείλομεν, ἀδελφοί, περὶ τῆς σωτηρίας ἡμῶν, ἵνα

Is. 1, 1-13

Jer. 7, 22, 23

Zech. 8, 17

Ps. 51, 19

---

[1] τω κυρίῳ CL, τῷ θεῷ ℵ (LXX).

with them. 4. For he has made plain to us through all the Prophets that he needs neither sacrifices nor burnt-offerings nor oblations, saying in one place, 5. " What is the multitude of your sacrifices unto me ? saith the Lord. I am full of burnt offerings and desire not the fat of lambs and the blood of bulls and goats, not even when ye come to appear before me. For who has required these things at your hands ? Henceforth shall ye tread my court no more. If ye bring flour, it is vain. Incense is an abomination to me. I cannot away with your new moons and sabbaths." 6. These things then he abolished in order that the new law of our Lord Jesus Christ, which is without the yoke of necessity, might have its oblation not made by man. 7. And again he says to them, " Did I command your fathers when they came out of the land of Egypt to offer me burnt offerings and sacrifices ? 8. Nay, but rather did I command them this : Let none of you cherish any evil in his heart against his neighbour, and love not a false oath." 9. We ought then to understand, if we are not foolish, the loving intention of our Father, for he speaks to us, wishing that we should not err like them, but seek how we may make our offering to him. 10. To us then he speaks thus : " Sacrifice for the Lord is a broken heart, a smell of sweet savour to the Lord is a heart that glorifieth him that made it." [1] We ought, therefore, brethren, carefully to enquire concerning our salvation, in

---

[1] The first part of this quotation is Ps. 51, 19 ; the second part according to a note in C is from the Apocalypse of Adam, which is no longer extant.

μὴ ὁ πονηρὸς παρείσδυσιν πλάνης ποιήσας ἐν ἡμῖν ἐκσφενδονήσῃ ἡμᾶς ἀπὸ τῆς ζωῆς ἡμῶν.

III

Is. 58, 4. 5   1. Λέγει οὖν πάλιν περὶ τούτων πρὸς αὐτούς· Ἰνατί μοι νηστεύετε, λέγει κύριος, ὡς σήμερον ἀκουσθῆναι ἐν κραυγῇ τὴν φωνὴν ὑμῶν; οὐ ταύτην τὴν νηστείαν ἐγὼ ἐξελεξάμην, λέγει κύριος, οὐκ ἄνθρωπον ταπεινοῦντα τὴν ψυχὴν αὐτοῦ, 2. οὐδ' ἂν κάμψητε ὡς κρίκον τὸν τράχηλον ὑμῶν καὶ σάκκον ἐνδύσησθε καὶ σποδὸν ὑποστρώσητε, οὐδ' οὕτως καλέσετε νηστείαν δεκτήν. 3. πρὸς ἡμᾶς

Is. 58, 6-10   δὲ λέγει· Ἰδοὺ αὕτη ἡ νηστεία, ἣν ἐγὼ ἐξελεξάμην, λέγει κύριος· λύε πάντα σύνδεσμον ἀδικίας, διάλυε στραγγαλιὰς βιαίων συναλλαγμάτων, ἀπόστελλε τεθραυσμένους ἐν ἀφέσει καὶ πᾶσαν ἄδικον συγγραφὴν διάσπα. διάθρυπτε πεινῶσιν τὸν ἄρτον σου, καὶ γυμνὸν ἐὰν ἴδῃς περίβαλε· ἀστέγους εἴσαγε εἰς τὸν οἶκόν σου, καὶ ἐὰν ἴδῃς ταπεινόν, οὐχ ὑπερόψῃ αὐτόν, οὐδὲ ἀπὸ τῶν οἰκείων τοῦ σπέρματός σου. 4. τότε ῥαγήσεται πρώϊμον τὸ φῶς σου, καὶ τὰ ἱμάτιά[1] σου ταχέως ἀνατελεῖ, καὶ προπορεύσεται ἔμπροσθέν σου ἡ δικαιοσύνη, καὶ ἡ δόξα τοῦ θεοῦ περιστελεῖ σε. 5. τότε βοήσεις, καὶ ὁ θεὸς ἐπακούσεταί σου, ἔτι λαλοῦντός σου ἐρεῖ· Ἰδοὺ πάρειμι· ἐὰν ἀφέλῃς

---

[1] ἱμάτια ℵ* CL, ἱάματα ℵ Corr. (healings) (LXX). This correction, which Lightfoot accepts, is no doubt what Barnabas meant, but the MSS. evidence suggests that it is not what he wrote.

order that the evil one may not achieve a deceitful entry into us and hurl us away from our life.

III

1. To them he says then again concerning these things, " Why do ye fast for me, saith the Lord, so that your voice is heard this day with a cry ! This is not the fast which I chose, saith the Lord, not a man humbling his soul; 2. nor though ye bend your neck as a hoop, and put on sackcloth, and make your bed of ashes, not even so shall ye call it an acceptable fast." 3. But to us he says, " Behold this is the fast which I chose," saith the Lord, " loose every bond of wickedness, set loose the fastenings of harsh agreements, send away the bruised in forgiveness, and tear up every unjust contract, give to the hungry thy bread, and if thou seest a naked man clothe him, bring the homeless into thy house, and if thou seest a humble man, despise him not, neither thou nor any of the household of thy seed. 4. Then shall thy light break forth as the dawn, and thy robes shall rise quickly, and thy righteousness shall go before thee, and the glory of God shall surround thee." 5. " Then thou shalt cry and God shall hear thee; while thou art still speaking He shall say, ' Lo I am here '; if thou puttest away from thee bondage, and

ἀπὸ σοῦ σύνδεσμον καὶ χειροτονίαν καὶ ῥῆμα γογ-
γυσμοῦ, καὶ δῷς πεινῶντι τὸν ἄρτον σου ἐκ ψυχῆς
σου καὶ ψυχὴν τεταπεινωμένην ἐλεήσῃς. 6. εἰς
τοῦτο οὖν, ἀδελφοί, ὁ μακρόθυμος προβλέψας, ὡς
ἐν ἀκεραιοσύνῃ πιστεύσει ὁ λαός, ὃν ἡτοίμασεν ἐν
τῷ ἠγαπημένῳ αὐτοῦ, προεφανέρωσεν ἡμῖν περὶ
πάντων, ἵνα μὴ προσρησσώμεθα ὡς ἐπήλυτοι[1] τῷ
ἐκείνων νόμῳ.

IV

1. Δεῖ οὖν ἡμᾶς περὶ τῶν ἐνεστώτων ἐπιπολὺ
ἐραυνῶντας[2] ἐκζητεῖν τὰ δυνάμενα ἡμᾶς σώζειν.
φύγωμεν οὖν τελείως ἀπὸ πάντων τῶν ἔργων τῆς
ἀνομίας, μήποτε καταλάβῃ ἡμᾶς τὰ ἔργα τῆς
ἀνομίας· καὶ μισήσωμεν τὴν πλάνην τοῦ νῦν
καιροῦ, ἵνα εἰς τὸν μέλλοντα ἀγαπηθῶμεν. 2. μὴ
δῶμεν τῇ ἑαυτῶν ψυχῇ ἄνεσιν, ὥστε ἔχειν αὐτὴν
ἐξουσίαν μετὰ ἁμαρτωλῶν καὶ πονηρῶν συντρέχειν, μήποτε ὁμοιωθῶμεν αὐτοῖς. 3. τὸ τέλειον
σκάνδαλον ἤγγικεν, περὶ οὗ γέγραπται, ὡς Ἐνὼχ

Enoch, 89,
61–64 ; 90, 17

λέγει. Εἰς τοῦτο γὰρ ὁ δεσπότης συντέτμηκεν
τοὺς καιροὺς καὶ τὰς ἡμέρας, ἵνα ταχύνῃ ὁ
ἠγαπημένος αὐτοῦ καὶ ἐπὶ τὴν κληρονομίαν ἥξῃ.

Dan. 7, 24

4. λέγει δὲ οὕτως καὶ ὁ προφήτης· Βασιλεῖαι
δέκα ἐπὶ τῆς γῆς βασιλεύσουσιν, καὶ ἐξαναστή-
σεται ὄπισθεν[3] μικρὸς βασιλεύς, ὃς ταπεινώσει
τρεῖς ὑφ᾽ ἓν τῶν βασιλέων. 5. ὁμοίως περὶ τοῦ

---

[1] ἐπήλυτοι ℵ, προσήλυτοι C, *proselytae* L; the use of the
words in Philo suggests that they both mean proselytes, so
that the evidence of L is ambiguous.

[2] ἐραυνῶντας ℵ, ἐρευνῶντας C.

[3] ὄπισθεν CL, ὄπισθεν αὐτῶν ℵ (Theod.).

violence, and the word of murmuring, and dost give to the poor thy bread with a cheerful heart, and dost pity the soul that is abased." 6. So then, brethren, the long-suffering one foresaw that the people whom He prepared in his Beloved should believe in guilelessness, and made all things plain to us beforehand that we should not be shipwrecked by conversion to their law.

IV

1. WE ought, then, to enquire earnestly into the things which now are, and to seek out those which are able to save us. Let us then utterly flee from all the works of lawlessness, lest the works of lawlessness overcome us, and let us hate the error of this present time, that we may be loved in that which is to come. 2. Let us give no freedom to our souls to have power to walk with sinners and wicked men, lest we be made like to them. 3. The final stumbling block is at hand of which it was written, as Enoch says, "For to this end the Lord has cut short the times and the days, that his beloved should make haste and come to his inheritance." 4. And the Prophet also says thus : "Ten kingdoms shall reign upon the earth and there shall rise up after them a little king, who shall subdue three of the kings under one." 5. Daniel says likewise concerning the same : "And I beheld

Warning that the final trial is at hand

Dan. 7, 7. 8 αὐτοῦ λέγει Δανιήλ· Καὶ εἶδον τὸ τέταρτον θηρίον τὸ πονηρὸν καὶ ἰσχυρὸν καὶ χαλεπώτερον παρὰ πάντα τὰ θηρία τῆς θαλάσσης,[1] καὶ ὡς ἐξ αὐτοῦ ἀνέτειλεν δέκα κέρατα, καὶ ἐξ αὐτῶν μικρὸν κέρας παραφυάδιον, καὶ ὡς ἐταπείνωσεν ὑφ' ἓν τρία τῶν μεγάλων κεράτων. 6. συνιέναι οὖν ὀφείλετε. ἔτι δὲ καὶ τοῦτο ἐρωτῶ ὑμᾶς ὡς εἷς ἐξ ὑμῶν ὤν,

Didache ii, 7 ἰδίως δὲ καὶ πάντας ἀγαπῶν ὑπὲρ τὴν ψυχήν μου, προσέχειν νῦν ἑαυτοῖς καὶ μὴ ὁμοιοῦσθαί τισιν ἐπισωρεύοντας ταῖς ἁμαρτίαις ὑμῶν λέγοντας, ὅτι ἡ διαθήκη ἐκείνων καὶ ἡμῶν. 7. ἡμῶν μέν· ἀλλ' ἐκεῖνοι οὕτως εἰς τέλος ἀπώλεσαν αὐτὴν λαβόντος

Exod. 34, 28 ἤδη τοῦ Μωϋσέως. λέγει γὰρ ἡ γραφή· Καὶ ἦν Μωϋσῆς ἐν τῷ ὄρει νηστεύων ἡμέρας τεσσαράκοντα καὶ νύκτας τεσσαράκοντα, καὶ ἔλαβεν τὴν

Exod. 32, 16 διαθήκην ἀπὸ τοῦ κυρίου, πλάκας λιθίνας γεγραμμένας τῷ δακτύλῳ τῆς χειρὸς τοῦ κυρίου. 8. ἀλλὰ ἐπιστραφέντες ἐπὶ τὰ εἴδωλα ἀπώλεσαν αὐτήν.

Exod. 32, 7
Deut. 9, 12 λέγει γὰρ οὕτως κύριος. Μωϋσῆ Μωϋσῆ, κατάβηθι τὸ τάχος, ὅτι ἠνόμησεν ὁ λαός σου, οὓς ἐξήγαγες ἐκ γῆς Αἰγύπτου, καὶ συνῆκεν Μωϋσῆς καὶ ἔριψεν τὰς δύο πλάκας ἐκ τῶν χειρῶν αὐτοῦ· καὶ συνετρίβη αὐτῶν ἡ διαθήκη, ἵνα ἡ τοῦ ἠγαπημένου Ἰησοῦ ἐγκατασφραγισθῇ εἰς τὴν καρδίαν ἡμῶν ἐν ἐλπίδι τῆς πίστεως αὐτοῦ. 9. πολλὰ δὲ θέλων γράφειν, οὐχ ὡς διδάσκαλος, ἀλλ' ὡς πρέπει ἀγαπῶντι ἀφ' ὧν ἔχομεν μὴ ἐλλείπειν, γράφειν ἐσπούδασα, περίψημα ὑμῶν. διὸ προσέχωμεν ἐν ταῖς ἐσχάταις ἡμέραις· οὐδὲν

---

[1] θαλάσσης CL, γῆς ℵ.

the fourth Beast, wicked and powerful and fiercer than all the beasts of the sea, and that ten horns sprang from it, and out of them a little excrescent horn, and that it subdued under one three of the great horns." 6. You ought then to understand. And this also I ask you, as being one of yourselves, and especially as loving you all above my own life ; take heed to yourselves now, and be not made like unto some, heaping up your sins and saying that the covenant is both theirs and ours. 7. It is ours: but in this way did they finally lose it when Moses had just received it, for the Scripture says : " And Moses was in the mount fasting forty days and forty nights, and he received the covenant from the Lord, tables of stone written with the finger of the hand of the Lord." 8. But they turned to idols and lost it. For thus saith the Lord: " Moses, Moses, go down quickly, for thy people, whom thou broughtest forth out of the land of Egypt, have broken the Law." And Moses understood and cast the two tables out of his hands, and their covenant was broken, in order that the covenant of Jesus the Beloved should be sealed in our hearts in hope of his faith. 9. (And though I wish to write much, I hasten to write in devotion to you, not as a teacher, but as it becomes one who loves to leave out nothing of that which we have.)[1] Wherefore let us pay heed in the last days, for the whole

The covenant. Christian or Jewish?

Admonition to stedfastness

---

[1] It is possible that the odd change of construction is due to some reference to a well known maxim : but the source of such quotation or reference has not been found.

Didache
xvi. 2

γὰρ ὠφελήσει ἡμᾶς ὁ πᾶς χρόνος τῆς πίστεως ἡμῶν,[1] ἐὰν μὴ νῦν ἐν τῷ ἀνόμῳ καιρῷ καὶ τοῖς μέλλουσιν σκανδάλοις, ὡς πρέπει υἱοῖς θεοῦ, ἀντιστῶμεν, ἵνα[2] μὴ σχῇ παρείσδυσιν ὁ μέλας. 10. φύγωμεν ἀπὸ πάσης ματαιότητος, μισήσωμεν τελείως τὰ ἔργα τῆς πονηρᾶς ὁδοῦ. μὴ καθ' ἑαυτοὺς ἐνδύνοντες μονάζετε ὡς ἤδη δεδικαιω μένοι, ἀλλ' ἐπὶ τὸ αὐτὸ συνερχόμενοι συνζητεῖτε περὶ τοῦ κοινῇ συμφέροντος. 11. λέγει γὰρ ἡ

Is. 5, 21

γραφή· Οὐαὶ οἱ συνετοὶ ἑαυτοῖς καὶ ἐνώπιον ἑαυτῶν ἐπιστήμονες. γενώμεθα πνευματικοί, γενώμεθα ναὸς τέλειος τῷ θεῷ. ἐφ' ὅσον ἐστὶν ἐν

Is. 33, 18

ἡμῖν, μελετῶμεν τὸν φόβον τοῦ θεοῦ καὶ φυλάσ σειν ἀγωνιζώμεθα τὰς ἐντολὰς αὐτοῦ, ἵνα ἐν τοῖς δικαιώμασιν αὐτοῦ εὐφρανθῶμεν. 12. ὁ κύριος ἀπροσωπολήμπτως κρινεῖ τὸν κόσμον. ἕκαστος

I. Pet. 1, 17,
cf. Rom. 2,
11;
Gal. 2, 6
II Cor. 5, 10

καθὼς ἐποίησεν κομιεῖται. ἐὰν ᾖ ἀγαθός, ἡ δικαιοσύνη αὐτοῦ προηγήσεται αὐτοῦ· ἐὰν ᾖ πονηρός, ὁ μισθὸς τῆς πονηρίας ἔμπροσθεν αὐτοῦ· 13. ἵνα μήποτε ἐπαναπαυόμενοι ὡς κλητοὶ ἐπικαθ υπνώσωμεν ταῖς ἁμαρτίαις ἡμῶν, καὶ ὁ πονηρὸς ἄρχων λαβὼν τὴν καθ' ἡμῶν ἐξουσίαν ἀπώσηται ἡμᾶς ἀπὸ τῆς βασιλείας τοῦ κυρίου. 14. ἔτι δὲ κἀκεῖνο, ἀδελφοί μου, νοεῖτε· ὅταν βλέπετε μετὰ τηλικαῦτα σημεῖα καὶ τέρατα γεγονότα ἐν τῷ Ἰσραήλ, καὶ οὕτως ἐγκαταλελεῖφθαι αὐτούς·

mt. 20, 16;
22, 14

προσέχωμεν, μήποτε, ὡς γέγραπται, πολλοὶ κλητοί, ὀλίγοι δὲ ἐκλεκτοὶ εὑρεθῶμεν.

---

[1] τῆς πίστεως ἡμῶν ℵ, τῆς ζωῆς ἡμῶν C, vitae nostrae et fidei L.

[2] ἵνα ℵ, ἵνα οὖν C, ἵνα ... μέλας om. L.

time of our life and faith will profit us nothing, unless we resist, as becomes the sons of God in this present evil time, against the offences which are to come, that the Black One may have no opportunity of entry. 10. Let us flee from all vanity, let us utterly hate the deeds of the path of wickedness. Do not by retiring apart live alone as if you were already made righteous, but come together and seek out the common good. 11. For the Scripture says : " Woe to them who are prudent for themselves and understanding in their own sight." Let us be spiritual, let us be a temple consecrated to God, so far as in us lies let us " exercise ourselves in the fear " of God, and let us strive to keep his commandments in order that we may rejoice in his ordinances. 12. The Lord will " judge " the world " without respect of persons." Each will receive according to his deeds. If he be good his righteousness will lead him, if he be evil the reward of iniquity is before him. 13. Let us never rest as though we were ' called '[1] and slumber in our sins, lest the wicked ruler gain power over us and thrust us out from the Kingdom of the Lord. 14. And consider this also, my brethren, when you see that after such great signs and wonders were wrought in Israel they were even then finally abandoned ;—let us take heed lest as it was written we be found " many called but few chosen."

---

[1] Apparently a loose expression = " confiding in our call."

V

1. Εἰς τοῦτο γὰρ ὑπέμεινεν ὁ κύριος παραδοῦναι τὴν σάρκα εἰς καταφθοράν, ἵνα τῇ ἀφέσει τῶν ἁμαρτιῶν ἁγνισθῶμεν, ὅ ἐστιν ἐν τῷ αἵματι τοῦ ῥαντίσματος αὐτοῦ.[1] 2. γέγραπται γὰρ περὶ αὐτοῦ ἃ μὲν πρὸς τὸν Ἰσραήλ, ἃ δὲ πρὸς Is. 53, 5. 7 ἡμᾶς, λέγει δὲ οὕτως· Ἐτραυματίσθη διὰ τὰς ἀνομίας ἡμῶν καὶ μεμαλάκισται διὰ τὰς ἁμαρτίας ἡμῶν· τῷ μώλωπι αὐτοῦ ἡμεῖς ἰάθημεν· ὡς πρόβατον ἐπὶ σφαγὴν ἤχθη, καὶ ὡς ἀμνὸς ἄφωνος ἐναντίον τοῦ κείραντος αὐτόν. 3. οὐκοῦν ὑπερευχαριστεῖν ὀφείλομεν τῷ κυρίῳ, ὅτι καὶ τὰ παρεληλυθότα ἡμῖν ἐγνώρισεν καὶ ἐν τοῖς ἐνεστῶσιν ἡμᾶς ἐσόφισεν, καὶ εἰς τὰ μέλλοντα οὐκ Prov. 1, 17 ἐσμὲν ἀσύνετοι. 4. λέγει δὲ ἡ γραφή· Οὐκ ἀδίκως ἐκτείνεται δίκτυα πτερωτοῖς. τοῦτο λέγει, ὅτι δικαίως ἀπολεῖται ἄνθρωπος, ὃς ἔχων ὁδοῦ δικαιοσύνης γνῶσιν ἑαυτὸν εἰς ὁδὸν σκότους ἀποσυνέχει. 5. ἔτι δὲ καὶ τοῦτο, ἀδελφοί μου· εἰ ὁ κύριος ὑπέμεινεν παθεῖν περὶ τῆς ψυχῆς ἡμῶν, ὢν παντὸς τοῦ κόσμου κύριος ᾧ εἶπεν ὁ Gen. 1, 26 θεὸς ἀπὸ καταβολῆς κόσμου· Ποιήσωμεν ἄνθρωπον κατ᾽ εἰκόνα καὶ καθ᾽ ὁμοίωσιν ἡμετέραν· πῶς οὖν ὑπέμεινεν ὑπὸ χειρὸς ἀνθρώπων παθεῖν; 6. μάθετε. οἱ προφῆται, ἀπ᾽ αὐτοῦ ἔχοντες τὴν χάριν, εἰς αὐτὸν ἐπροφήτευσαν· αὐτὸς δέ, ἵνα II Tim. 1, 10 καταργήσῃ τὸν θάνατον καὶ τὴν ἐκ νεκρῶν ἀνά I Tim. 3, 16 στασιν δείξῃ, ὅτι ἐν σαρκὶ ἔδει αὐτὸν φανερωθῆναι,

---

[1] αἵματι τοῦ ῥαντίσματος αὐτοῦ ℵ, ῥαντίσματι αὐτοῦ τοῦ αἵματος CL, a natural correction of the more difficult phrase.

V

1. FOR it was for this reason that the Lord endured to deliver up his flesh to corruption, that we should be sanctified by the remission of sin, that is, by his sprinkled blood. 2. For the scripture concerning him relates partly to Israel, partly to us, and it speaks thus: "He was wounded for our transgressions and bruised for our iniquities, by his stripes we were healed. He was brought as a sheep to the slaughter, and as a lamb dumb before its shearer." 3. Therefore we ought to give great thanks to the Lord that he has given us knowledge of the past, and wisdom for the present, and that we are not without understanding for the future. 4. And the Scripture says, "Not unjustly are the nets spread out for the birds." This means that a man deserves to perish who has a knowledge of the way of righteousness, but turns aside into the way of darkness. 5. Moreover, my brethren, if the Lord endured to suffer for our life, though he is the Lord of all the world, to whom God said before the foundation of the world, "Let us make man in our image and likeness," how, then, did he endure to suffer at the hand of man? 6. Learn:—The Prophets who received grace from him prophesied of him, and he, in order that he "might destroy death," and show forth the Resurrection from the dead, because he needs must be made "manifest in the

ὑπέμεινεν, 7. ἵνα τοῖς πατράσιν τὴν ἐπαγγελίαν
ἀποδῷ, καὶ αὐτὸς ἑαυτῷ τὸν λαὸν τὸν καινὸν
ἑτοιμάζων ἐπιδείξῃ ἐπὶ τῆς γῆς ὤν, ὅτι τὴν
ἀνάστασιν αὐτὸς ποιήσας κρινεῖ. 8. πέρας γέ
τοι διδάσκων τὸν Ἰσραὴλ καὶ τηλικαῦτα τέρατα
καὶ σημεῖα ποιῶν ἐκήρυσσεν, καὶ ὑπερηγάπησεν
αὐτόν. 9. ὅτε δὲ τοὺς ἰδίους ἀποστόλους τοὺς
μέλλοντας κηρύσσειν τὸ εὐαγγέλιον αὐτοῦ ἐξελέξ-
ατο, ὄντας ὑπὲρ πᾶσαν ἁμαρτίαν ἀνομωτέρους,
Mk. 2, 17 ἵνα δείξῃ, ὅτι οὐκ ἦλθεν καλέσαι δικαίους, ἀλλὰ
ἁμαρτωλούς, τότε ἐφανέρωσεν ἑαυτὸν εἶναι υἱὸν
θεοῦ. 10. εἰ γὰρ μὴ ἦλθεν ἐν σαρκί, οὐδ᾽ ἄν πως[1]
οἱ ἄνθρωποι ἐσώθησαν βλέποντες αὐτόν, ὅτε τὸν
μέλλοντα μὴ εἶναι ἥλιον, ἔργον τῶν χειρῶν αὐτοῦ
ὑπάρχοντα, ἐμβλέποντες οὐκ ἰσχύουσιν εἰς τὰς
ἀκτῖνας αὐτοῦ ἀντοφθαλμῆσαι; 11. οὐκοῦν ὁ
υἱὸς τοῦ θεοῦ εἰς τοῦτο ἐν σαρκὶ ἦλθεν, ἵνα τὸ
τέλειον τῶν ἁμαρτιῶν ἀνακεφαλαιώσῃ τοῖς διώξ-
ασιν ἐν θανάτῳ τοὺς προφήτας αὐτοῦ. 12. οὐκοῦν
εἰς τοῦτο ὑπέμεινεν. λέγει γὰρ ὁ θεὸς τὴν πληγὴν
Zach. 13, 6. 7;
cf. Mt. 26, 31 τῆς σαρκὸς αὐτοῦ ὅτι ἐξ αὐτῶν· Ὅταν πατάξ-
ωσιν τὸν ποιμένα ἑαυτῶν, τότε ἀπολεῖται τὰ
πρόβατα τῆς ποίμνης. 13. αὐτὸς δὲ ἠθέλησεν
οὕτω παθεῖν· ἔδει γάρ, ἵνα ἐπὶ ξύλου πάθῃ.
Ps. 22, 40 λέγει γὰρ ὁ προφητεύων ἐπ᾽ αὐτῷ. Φεῖσαί μου
Ps. 119, 120; τῆς ψυχῆς ἀπὸ ῥομφαίας, καί· Καθήλωσόν μου
τὰς σάρκας, ὅτι πονηρευομένων συναγωγαὶ ἐπα-
Is. 50, 6. 7 νέστησάν μοι. 14. καὶ πάλιν λέγει· Ἰδού, τέθεικά
μου τὸν νῶτον εἰς μάστιγας, τὰς δὲ σιαγόνας εἰς
ῥαπίσματα. τὸ δὲ πρόσωπόν μου ἔθηκα ὡς στερεὰν
πέτραν.

---

[1] οὐδ᾽ ἄν πως ℵ, οὐδ᾽ ἄν C, πῶς ἄν GL.

flesh," endured 7. in order to fulfil the promise made to the fathers, and himself prepare for himself the new people and show while he was on earth that he himself will raise the dead and judge the risen. 8. Furthermore, while teaching Israel and doing such great signs and wonders he preached to them and loved them greatly ; 9. but when he chose out his own Apostles who were to preach his Gospel, he chose those who were iniquitous above all sin to show that "he came not to call the righteous but sinners,"—then he manifested himself as God's Son. 10. For if he had not come in the flesh men could in no way have been saved by beholding him ; seeing that they have not the power when they look at the sun to gaze straight at its rays, though it is destined to perish, and is the work of his hands. 11. So then the Son of God came in the flesh for this reason, that he might complete the total of the sins of those who persecuted his prophets to death. 12. For this cause he endured. For God says of the chastisement of his flesh that it is from them : "When they shall smite their shepherd, then the sheep of the flock shall be destroyed." 13. And he was willing to suffer thus, for it was necessary that he should suffer on a tree, for the Prophet says of him, "Spare my soul from the sword" and, "Nail my flesh, for the synagogues of the wicked have risen against me." 14. And again he says : "Lo, I have given my back to scourges, and my cheeks to strokes, and I have set my face as a solid rock."

THE APOSTOLIC FATHERS

VI

Is. 50, 8, 9 1. Ὅτε οὖν ἐποίησεν τὴν ἐντολήν, τί λέγει; Τίς ὁ κρινόμενός μοι; ἀντιστήτω μοι· ἢ τίς ὁ δικαιούμενός μοι; ἐγγισάτω τῷ παιδὶ κυρίου. 2. οὐαὶ ὑμῖν, ὅτι ὑμεῖς πάντες ὡς ἱμάτιον παλαιωθήσεσθε, καὶ σὴς καταφάγεται ὑμᾶς. καὶ πάλιν λέγει ὁ προ-
Is. 28, 16,
cf. Rom.
9, 33 ;
I Pet. 2, 6 φήτης, ἐπεὶ ὡς λίθος ἰσχυρὸς ἐτέθη εἰς συντριβήν· Ἰδού, ἐμβαλῶ εἰς τὰ θεμέλια Σιὼν λίθον πολυτελῆ, ἐκλεκτόν, ἀκρογωνιαῖον, ἔντιμον. 3. εἶτα τί
Is. 28, 16 λέγει; Καὶ ὃς ἐλπίσει ἐπ᾽ αὐτὸν[1] ζήσεται εἰς τὸν αἰῶνα. ἐπὶ λίθον οὖν ἡμῶν ἡ ἐλπίς; μὴ γένοιτο· ἀλλ᾽ ἐπεὶ ἐν ἰσχύϊ τέθεικεν τὴν σάρκα αὐτοῦ
Is. 50, 7 κύριος. λέγει γάρ· Καὶ ἔθηκέ με ὡς στερεὰν
Ps. 117
22. 24 πέτραν. 4. λέγει δὲ πάλιν ὁ προφήτης· Λίθον ὃν ἀπεδοκίμασαν οἱ οἰκοδομοῦντες, οὗτος ἐγενήθη εἰς κεφαλὴν γωνίας. καὶ πάλιν λέγει· Αὕτη ἐστὶν ἡ ἡμέρα ἡ μεγάλη καὶ θαυμαστή, ἣν ἐποίησεν ὁ κύριος. 5. ἁπλούστερον ὑμῖν γράφω, ἵνα συνιῆτε· ἐγὼ περίψημα τῆς ἀγάπης ὑμῶν.
Ps. 22, 18 ;
118, 12 6. τί οὖν λέγει πάλιν ὁ προφήτης; Περιέσχεν με συναγωγὴ πονηρευομένων, ἐκύκλωσάν με ὡσεὶ
Ps. 21, 19 μέλισσαι κηρίον, καί· Ἐπὶ τὸν ἱματισμόν μου ἔβαλον κλῆρον. 7. ἐν σαρκὶ οὖν αὐτοῦ μέλλοντος φανεροῦσθαι καὶ πάσχειν, προεφανερώθη τὸ πάθος. λέγει γὰρ ὁ προφήτης ἐπὶ τὸν Ἰσραήλ·
Is. 3, 9, 10,
cf. Wisd.
2, 12 Οὐαὶ τῇ ψυχῇ αὐτῶν, ὅτι βεβούλευνται βουλὴν πονηρὰν καθ᾽ ἑαυτῶν, εἰπόντες· Δήσωμεν τὸν

---

[1] ὃς ἐλπίσει ἐπ᾽ αὐτόν G, ὁ πιστεύων εἰς αὐτόν אCL, probably owing to the influence of the LXX. ἐλπίσει is covered by the following ἐλπίς.

VI

1. WHEN therefore he made the commandment what does he say ? " Who is he that comes into court with me? Let him oppose me; or, who is he that seeks justice against me ? Let him draw near to the Lord's servant. 2. Woe unto you, for ye shall all wax old as a garment and the moth shall eat you up." And again the Prophet says that he was placed as a strong stone for crushing, " Lo, I will place for the foundations of Sion a precious stone, chosen out, a chief corner stone, honourable." 3. Then what does he say? "And he that hopeth on it shall live for ever." Is then our hope on a stone ? God forbid. But he means that the Lord placed his flesh in strength. For he says, "And he placed me as a solid rock." 4. And again the Prophet says, " The stone which the builders rejected, this is become the head of the corner," and again he says, " This is the great and wonderful day which the Lord made." 5. I write to you more simply that you may understand : I am devoted to your love. 6. What then does the Prophet say again ? " The synagogue of the sinners compassed me around, they surrounded me as bees round the honeycomb " and, " They cast lots for my clothing." 7. Since therefore he was destined to be manifest and to suffer in the flesh his Passion was foretold. For the Prophet says concerning Israel, "Woe unto their soul, for they have plotted an evil plot against themselves, saying, ' Let us

THE APOSTOLIC FATHERS

δίκαιόν, ὅτι δύσχρηστος ἡμῖν ἐστίν. 8. τί λέγει
ὁ ἄλλος προφήτης Μωϋσῆς αὐτοῖς; Ἰδού, τάδε
λέγει κύριος ὁ θεός· Εἰσέλθατε εἰς τὴν γῆν τὴν
ἀγαθήν, ἣν ὤμοσεν κύριος τῷ Ἀβραὰμ καὶ
Ἰσαὰκ καὶ Ἰακώβ, καὶ κατακληρονομήσατε
αὐτήν, γῆν ῥέουσαν γάλα καὶ μέλι. 9. τί δὲ
λέγει ἡ γνῶσις; μάθετε. ἐλπίσατε, φησίν,[1] ἐπὶ
τὸν ἐν σαρκὶ μέλλοντα φανεροῦσθαι ὑμῖν Ἰησοῦν.
ἄνθρωπος γὰρ γῆ ἐστιν πάσχουσα· ἀπὸ προσώπου γὰρ τῆς γῆς ἡ πλάσις τοῦ Ἀδὰμ ἐγένετο.
10. τί οὖν λέγει· Εἰς τὴν γῆν τὴν ἀγαθήν, γῆν
ῥέουσαν γάλα καὶ μέλι; εὐλογητὸς ὁ κύριος ἡμῶν,
ἀδελφοί, ὁ σοφίαν καὶ νοῦν θέμενος ἐν ἡμῖν τῶν
κρυφίων αὐτοῦ· λέγει γὰρ ὁ προφήτης παρα-
βολὴν κυρίου· τίς νοήσει, εἰ μὴ σοφὸς καὶ ἐπισ-
τήμων καὶ ἀγαπῶν τὸν κύριον αὐτοῦ; 11. ἐπεὶ
οὖν ἀνακαινίσας ἡμᾶς ἐν τῇ ἀφέσει τῶν ἁμαρτιῶν, ἐποίησεν ἡμᾶς ἄλλον τύπον, ὡς παιδίων
ἔχειν τὴν ψυχήν, ὡς ἂν δὴ ἀναπλάσσοντος αὐτοῦ
ἡμᾶς. 12. λέγει γὰρ ἡ γραφὴ περὶ ἡμῶν, ὡς
λέγει τῷ υἱῷ· Ποιήσωμεν κατ᾽ εἰκόνα καὶ καθ᾽
ὁμοίωσιν ἡμῶν τὸν ἄνθρωπον, καὶ ἀρχέτωσαν
τῶν θηρίων τῆς γῆς καὶ τῶν πετεινῶν τοῦ οὐρανοῦ
καὶ τῶν ἰχθύων τῆς θαλάσσης. καὶ εἶπεν κύριος,
ἰδὼν τὸ καλὸν πλάσμα ἡμῶν· Αὐξάνεσθε καὶ
πληθύνεσθε καὶ πληρώσατε τὴν γῆν. ταῦτα
πρὸς τὸν υἱόν. 13. πάλιν σοι ἐπιδείξω, πῶς
πρὸς ἡμᾶς λέγει.[2] δευτέραν πλάσιν ἐπ᾽ ἐσχάτων

Exod. 33,
1. 3;
Lev. 20, 24

Exod. 33,
1. 3

Eph. 2. 10;
4, 22–24

Gen. 1, 26

Gen. 1, 28

---

[1] φησίν ℵC CL Clem. Alex. om. ℵ*G.
[2] λέγει CL(g), λέγει κύριος ℵ.

bind the Just one, for he is unprofitable to us.'"
8. What does the other Prophet, Moses, say to them?
"Lo, thus saith the Lord God, enter into the good
land which the Lord sware that he would give to
Abraham, Isaac, and Jacob, and inherit it, a land
flowing with milk and honey." 9. But learn what
knowledge says. Hope, it says, on that Jesus[1]
who will be manifested to you in the flesh. For
man is earth which suffers, for the creation of Adam
was from the face of the earth. 10. What then is
the meaning of "into the good land, a land flowing
with milk and honey"? Blessed be our Lord,
brethren, who has placed in us wisdom and understanding of his secrets. For the prophet speaks a
parable of the Lord: "Who shall understand save
he who is wise, and learned, and a lover of his Lord?"
11. Since then he made us new by the remission of
sins he made us another type, that we should have
the soul of children, as though he were creating us
afresh. 12. For it is concerning us that the scripture
says that he says to the Son, "Let us make man after
our image and likeness, and let them rule the beasts
of the earth, and the birds of heaven, and the fishes of
the sea." And the Lord said, when he saw our fair
creation, "Increase and multiply and fill the earth";
these things were spoken to the Son. 13. Again I
will show you how he speaks to us. In the last

---

[1] A contrast is here no doubt implied between "that
Jesus who will be manifested" and the Jesus, or Joshua (the
two names are the same in Greek) who led the Israelites over
the Jordan.

Cf. Mt.
19, 30;
20, 16
Exod. 33, 3

Ezek.
11, 19; 36, 26

Ps. 43, 4

Ps. 22, 23

Gen. 1,
26, 28

ἐποίησεν. λέγει δὲ κύριος· Ἰδού, ποιῶ τὰ ἔσχατα
ὡς τὰ πρῶτα. εἰς τοῦτο οὖν ἐκήρυξεν ὁ προ-
φήτης· Εἰσέλθατε εἰς γῆν ῥέουσαν γάλα καὶ μέλι
καὶ κατακυριεύσατε αὐτῆς. 14. ἴδε οὖν, ἡμεῖς
ἀναπεπλάσμεθα, καθὼς πάλιν ἐν ἑτέρῳ προφήτῃ
λέγει· Ἰδού, λέγει κύριος, ἐξελῶ τούτων, τουτέστιν ὧν προέβλεπεν τὸ πνεῦμα κυρίου, τὰς
λιθίνας καρδίας καὶ ἐμβαλῶ σαρκίνας· ὅτι αὐτὸς
ἐν σαρκὶ ἔμελλεν φανεροῦσθαι καὶ ἐν ἡμῖν
κατοικεῖν. 15. ναὸς γὰρ ἅγιος, ἀδελφοί μου,
τῷ κυρίῳ τὸ κατοικητήριον ἡμῶν τῆς καρδίας.
16. λέγει γὰρ κύριος πάλιν· Καὶ ἐν τίνι ὀφθή-
σομαι τῷ κυρίῳ τῷ θεῷ μου καὶ δοξασθήσομαι;
λέγει· Ἐξομολογήσομαί σοι ἐν ἐκκλησίᾳ ἀδελφῶν
μου, καὶ ψαλῶ σοι ἀνάμεσον ἐκκλησίας ἁγίων.
οὐκοῦν ἡμεῖς ἐσμέν, οὓς εἰσήγαγεν εἰς τὴν γῆν τὴν
ἀγαθήν. 17. τί οὖν τὸ γάλα καὶ τὸ μέλι; ὅτι
πρῶτον τὸ παιδίον μέλιτι, εἶτα γάλακτι ζωοποι-
εῖται· οὕτως οὖν καὶ ἡμεῖς τῇ πίστει τῆς ἐπαγγελίας καὶ τῷ λόγῳ ζωοποιούμενοι ζήσομεν κατα-
κυριεύοντες τῆς γῆς. 18. προειρήκαμεν¹ δὲ
ἐπάνω. Καὶ αὐξανέσθωσαν καὶ πληθυνέσθωσαν
καὶ ἀρχέτωσαν τῶν ἰχθύων. τίς οὖν ὁ δυνάμενος
νῦν ἄρχειν θηρίων ἢ ἰχθύων ἢ πετεινῶν τοῦ
οὐρανοῦ; αἰσθάνεσθαι γὰρ ὀφείλομεν, ὅτι τὸ
ἄρχειν ἐξουσίας ἐστίν, ἵνα τις ἐπιτάξας κυριεύσῃ.
19. εἰ οὖν οὐ γίνεται τοῦτο νῦν, ἄρα ἡμῖν εἴρηκεν,
πότε· ὅταν καὶ αὐτοὶ τελειωθῶμεν κληρονόμοι
τῆς διαθήκης κυρίου γενέσθαι.

¹ προειρήκαμεν ℵ, προείρηκε CG, L omits the whole sentence.

days he made a second creation; and the Lord says, "See, I make the last things as the first." To this then the Prophet referred when he proclaimed, "Enter into a land flowing with milk and honey, and rule over it." 14. See then, we have been created afresh, as he says again in another Prophet, "See," saith the Lord, "I will take out from them" (that is those whom the Spirit of the Lord foresaw) "the hearts of stone and I will put in hearts of flesh." Because he himself was going to be manifest in the flesh and to dwell among us. 15. For, my brethren, the habitation of our hearts is a shrine holy to the Lord. 16. For the Lord says again, "And wherewith shall I appear before the Lord my God and be glorified?" He says, "I will confess to thee in the assembly of my brethren, and will sing to thee in the midst of the assembly of saints." We then are they whom he brought into the good land. 17. What then is the milk and the honey? Because a child is first nourished with honey, and afterwards with milk. Thus therefore we also, being nourished on the faith of the promise and by the word, shall live and possess the earth. 18. And we have said above, "And let them increase and multiply and rule over the fishes." Who then is it who is now able to rule over beasts or fishes or the birds of heaven? For we ought to understand that to rule implies authority, so that one may give commandments and have domination. 19. If then this does not happen at present he has told us the time when it will;—when we ourselves also have been made perfect as heirs of the covenant of the Lord.

THE APOSTOLIC FATHERS

VII

1. Οὐκοῦν νοεῖτε, τέκνα εὐφροσύνης, ὅτι πάντα ὁ καλὸς κύριος προεφανέρωσεν ἡμῖν, ἵνα γνῶμεν, ᾧ κατὰ πάντα εὐχαριστοῦντες ὀφείλομεν αἰνεῖν. 2. εἰ οὖν ὁ υἱὸς τοῦ θεοῦ, ὢν κύριος καὶ μέλλων κρίνειν ζῶντας καὶ νεκρούς, ἔπαθεν, ἵνα ἡ πληγὴ αὐτοῦ ζωοποιήσῃ ἡμᾶς· πιστεύσωμεν, ὅτι ὁ υἱὸς τοῦ θεοῦ οὐκ ἠδύνατο παθεῖν εἰ μὴ δι᾽ ἡμᾶς. 3. ἀλλὰ καὶ σταυρωθεὶς ἐποτίζετο ὄξει καὶ χολῇ. ἀκούσατε, πῶς περὶ τούτου πεφανέρωκαν οἱ ἱερεῖς τοῦ ναοῦ. γεγραμμένης ἐντολῆς· Ὃς ἂν μὴ νηστεύσῃ τὴν νηστείαν, θανάτῳ ἐξολεθρευθή-σεται, ἐνετείλατο κύριος, ἐπεὶ καὶ αὐτὸς ὑπὲρ τῶν ἡμετέρων ἁμαρτιῶν ἔμελλεν τὸ σκεῦος τοῦ πνεύ-ματος προσφέρειν θυσίαν, ἵνα καὶ ὁ τύπος ὁ γενόμενος ἐπὶ Ἰσαὰκ τοῦ προσενεχθέντος ἐπὶ τὸ θυσιαστήριον τελεσθῇ. 4. τί οὖν λέγει ἐν τῷ προφήτῃ; Καὶ φαγέτωσαν ἐκ τοῦ τράγου τοῦ προσφερομένου τῇ νηστείᾳ ὑπὲρ πασῶν τῶν ἁμαρτιῶν. προσέχετε ἀκριβῶς· Καὶ φαγέτωσαν οἱ ἱερεῖς μόνοι πάντες τὸ ἔντερον ἄπλυτον μετὰ ὄξους. 5. πρὸς τί; ἐπειδὴ ἐμὲ ὑπὲρ ἁμαρτιῶν μέλλοντα τοῦ λαοῦ μου τοῦ καινοῦ προσφέρειν τὴν σάρκα μου μέλλετε ποτίζειν χολὴν μετὰ ὄξους, φάγετε ὑμεῖς μόνοι, τοῦ λαοῦ νηστεύοντος καὶ κοπτομένου ἐπὶ σάκκου καὶ σποδοῦ. ἵνα δείξῃ, ὅτι δεῖ αὐτὸν παθεῖν ὑπ᾽ αὐτῶν. 6. ἃ ἐνετείλατο, προσέχετε· Λάβετε δύο τράγους καλοὺς καὶ ὁμοίους καὶ προσενέγκατε, καὶ λαβέτω ὁ ἱερεὺς τὸν ἕνα εἰς ὁλοκαύτωμα ὑπὲρ ἁμαρτιῶν. 7. τὸν

II Tim. 4, 1
(I. Pet. 4, 5)

Mt. 27,
34. 48

Lev. 23, 29

Mt. 27,
34. 48

Lev. 16, 7. 9

VII

1. UNDERSTAND therefore, children of gladness, that the good Lord made all things plain beforehand to us, that we should know him to whom we ought to give thanks and praise for everything. 2. If then the Son of God, though he was the Lord and was "destined to judge the living and the dead" suffered in order that his wounding might make us alive, let us believe that the Son of God could not suffer except for our sakes. 3. But moreover when he was crucified "he was given to drink vinegar and gall." Listen how the priests of the Temple foretold this. The commandment was written, "Whosoever does not keep the fast shall die the death," and the Lord commanded this because he himself was going to offer the vessel of the spirit as a sacrifice for our sins, in order that the type established in Isaac, who was offered upon the altar, might be fulfilled. 4. What then does he say in the Prophet? "And let them eat of the goat which is offered in the fast for all their sins." Attend carefully,—"and let all the priests alone eat the entrails unwashed with vinegar." 5. Why? Because you are going "to give to me gall and vinegar to drink" when I am on the point of offering my flesh for my new people, therefore you alone shall eat, while the people fast and mourn in sackcloth and ashes. To show that he must suffer for them. 6. Note what was commanded: "Take two goats, goodly and alike, and offer them, and let the priest take the one as a burnt offering for sins." 7. But what are they to do with the other? "The

Fasting and the scape-goat

Lev. 16, 8. 10 δὲ ἕνα τί ποιήσωσιν; [1] Ἐπικατάρατος, φησίν, ὁ εἷς. προσέχετε, πῶς ὁ τύπος τοῦ Ἰησοῦ φανεροῦται· 8. Καὶ ἐμπτύσατε πάντες καὶ κατακεντήσατε καὶ περίθετε τὸ ἔριον τὸ κόκκινον περὶ τὴν κεφαλὴν αὐτοῦ, καὶ οὕτως εἰς ἔρημον βληθήτω. καὶ ὅταν γένηται οὕτως, ἄγει ὁ βαστάζων τὸν τράγον εἰς τὴν ἔρημον καὶ ἀφαιρεῖ τὸ ἔριον καὶ ἐπιτίθησιν αὐτὸ ἐπὶ φρύγανον τὸ λεγόμενον ῥαχήλ,[2] οὗ καὶ τοὺς βλαστοὺς εἰώθαμεν τρώγειν ἐν τῇ χώρᾳ εὑρίσκοντες· οὕτω μόνης τῆς ῥαχοῦς[3] οἱ καρποὶ γλυκεῖς εἰσιν. 9. τί οὖν τοῦτό ἐστιν; Lev. 16, 8 προσέχετε· Τὸν μὲν ἕνα ἐπὶ τὸ θυσιαστήριον, τὸν δὲ ἕνα ἐπικατάρατον, καὶ ὅτι τὸν ἐπικατάρατον ἐστεφανωμένον; ἐπειδὴ ὄψονται αὐτὸν τότε τῇ Rev. 1, 7. 13 ἡμέρᾳ τὸν ποδήρη ἔχοντα τὸν κόκκινον περὶ τὴν σάρκα καὶ ἐροῦσιν· Οὐχ οὗτός ἐστιν, ὅν ποτε ἡμεῖς ἐσταυρώσαμεν ἐξουθενήσαντες καὶ κατακεντήσαντες καὶ ἐμπτύσαντες;[4] ἀληθῶς οὗτος ἦν, ὁ τότε λέγων ἑαυτὸν υἱὸν θεοῦ εἶναι. 10. πῶς Lev. 16. 7 γὰρ ὅμοιος ἐκείνῳ; εἰς τοῦτο ὁμοίους τοὺς τράγους, καλούς, ἴσους, ἵνα, ὅταν ἴδωσιν αὐτὸν τότε ἐρχόμενον, ἐκπλαγῶσιν ἐπὶ τῇ ὁμοιότητι τοῦ τράγου. οὐκοῦν ἴδε τὸν τύπον τοῦ μέλλοντος πάσχειν Ἰησοῦ. 11. τί δέ, ὅτι τὸ ἔριον μέσον τῶν ἀκανθῶν τιθέασιν; τύπος ἐστὶν τοῦ Ἰησοῦ τῇ ἐκκλησίᾳ θέμενος, ὅτι ὃς ἐὰν θέλῃ τὸ ἔριον ἆραι τὸ κόκκινον, δεῖ αὐτὸν πολλὰ παθεῖν διὰ τὸ εἶναι

---

[1] ποιήσωσιν ℵ, ποιήσουσιν CG.
[2] ῥαχήλ ℵ, ῥαχίλ G, ῥαχή C.
[3] ῥαχοῦς ℵG, ῥαχῆς C. τῆς ῥαχοῦς can scarcely be right, but in face of the evidence can hardly be rejected.
[4] ἐξουθενήσαμεν ἐμπτύσαντες ℵ.

other," he says, "is accursed." Notice how the type
of Jesus is manifested : 8. "And do ye all spit on it,
and goad it, and bind the scarlet wool about its head,
and so let it be cast into the desert." And when it
is so done, he who takes the goat into the wilderness
drives it forth, and takes away the wool, and puts it
upon a shrub which is called Rachél,[1] of which we are
accustomed to eat the shoots when we find them in
the country : thus of Rachél alone is the fruit sweet.
9. What does this mean ? Listen: "the first goat is
for the altar, but the other is accursed," and note
that the one that is accursed is crowned, because
then " they will see him " on that day with the long
scarlet robe " down to the feet " on his body, and they
will say, " Is not this he whom we once crucified and
rejected and pierced and spat upon ? Of a truth it
was he who then said that he was the Son of God."
10. But how is he like to the goat? For this
reason: "the goats shall be alike, beautiful, and a
pair," in order that when they see him come at that
time they may be astonished at the likeness of the
goat. See then the type of Jesus destined to suffer.
11. But why is it that they put the wool in the
middle of the thorns ? It is a type of Jesus placed
in the Church, because whoever wishes to take away
the scarlet wool must suffer much because the thorns

---

[1] It is probable that Barnabas has mistaken a word
meaning a hill for the name of a herb with which he was
familiar ; but it is not clear whether the confusion was made
in Hebrew or in Greek (ῥαχός = a brier, and sometimes a wild-
olive, and ῥάχις = a mountain ridge, seems to suggest some
such possibility). But the identity of the herb is unknown.
There is an interesting article on it in the *Journal of Biblical
Literature*, 1890, by Rendel Harris.

φοβερὰν τὴν ἄκανθαν, καὶ θλιβέντα κυριεῦσαι
αὐτοῦ. οὕτω, φησίν, οἱ θέλοντές με ἰδεῖν καὶ
ἅψασθαί μου τῆς βασιλείας ὀφείλουσιν θλιβέντες
καὶ παθόντες λαβεῖν με.

VIII

Num. 19
1. Τίνα δὲ δοκεῖτε τύπον εἶναι, ὅτι ἐντέταλται
τῷ Ἰσραὴλ προσφέρειν δάμαλιν τοὺς ἄνδρας, ἐν
οἷς εἰσιν ἁμαρτίαι τέλειαι, καὶ σφάξαντας κατα-
καίειν, καὶ αἴρειν τότε τὴν σποδὸν παιδία καὶ
βάλλειν εἰς ἄγγη καὶ περιτιθέναι τὸ ἔριον τὸ
κόκκινον ἐπὶ ξύλον (ἴδε πάλιν ὁ τύπος ὁ τοῦ
σταυροῦ καὶ τὸ ἔριον τὸ κόκκινον) καὶ τὸ ὕσσωπον,
καὶ οὕτως ῥαντίζειν τὰ παιδία καθ’ ἕνα τὸν λαόν,
ἵνα ἁγνίζωνται ἀπὸ τῶν ἁμαρτιῶν ; 2. νοεῖτε,
πῶς ἐν ἁπλότητι λέγει ὑμῖν. ὁ μόσχος ὁ Ἰησοῦς
ἐστίν, οἱ προσφέροντες ἄνδρες ἁμαρτωλοὶ οἱ
προσενέγκαντες αὐτὸν ἐπὶ τὴν σφαγήν. εἶτα
οὐκέτι ἄνδρες, οὐκέτι ἁμαρτωλῶν ἡ δόξα.[1] 3. οἱ
ῥαντίζοντες παῖδες οἱ εὐαγγελισάμενοι ἡμῖν τὴν
ἄφεσιν τῶν ἁμαρτιῶν καὶ τὸν ἁγνισμὸν τῆς καρδίας, οἷς ἔδωκεν τοῦ εὐαγγελίου τὴν ἐξουσίαν
(οὖσιν δεκάδυο εἰς μαρτύριον τῶν φυλῶν ὅτι δεκάδυο φυλαὶ τοῦ Ἰσραήλ), εἰς τὸ κηρύσσειν. 4. διὰ
τί δὲ τρεῖς παῖδες οἱ ῥαντίζοντες ; εἰς μαρτύριον
Ἀβραάμ, Ἰσαάκ, Ἰακώβ, ὅτι οὗτοι μεγάλοι τῷ
θεῷ. 5. ὅτι δὲ τὸ ἔριον ἐπὶ τὸ ξύλον ; ὅτι ἡ

---

[1] εἶτα . . . δόξα om. L.

are terrible and he can gain it only through pain. Thus he says, "those who will see me, and attain to my kingdom must lay hold of me through pain and suffering."

VIII

1. But what do you think that it typifies, that the commandment has been given to Israel that the men in whom sin is complete offer a heifer and slay it and burn it, and that boys then take the ashes and put them into vessels and bind scarlet wool on sticks (see again the type of the Cross and the scarlet wool) and hyssop, and that the boys all sprinkle the people thus one by one in order that they all be purified from their sins? 2. Observe how plainly he speaks to you. The calf is Jesus; the sinful men offering it are those who brought him to be slain. Then there are no longer men, no longer the glory [1] of sinners. 3. The boys who sprinkle are they who preached to us the forgiveness of sins, and the purification of the heart, to whom he gave the power of the Gospel to preach, and there are twelve as a testimony to the tribes, because there are twelve tribes of Israel. 4. But why are there three boys who sprinkle? As a testimony to Abraham, Isaac, and Jacob, for these are great before God. 5. And why was the wool put on the wood? Because the king-

The sacrifice of a heifer

---

[1] This seems to be the only possible translation, but the text must surely be corrupt.

369

βασιλεία Ἰησοῦ ἐπὶ ξύλου,[1] καὶ ὅτι οἱ ἐλπίζοντες
ἐπ᾽ αὐτὸν ζήσονται εἰς τὸν αἰῶνα· 6. διὰ τί δὲ
ἅμα τὸ ἔριον καὶ τὸ ὕσσωπον; ὅτι ἐν τῇ βασιλείᾳ
αὐτοῦ ἡμέραι ἔσονται πονηραὶ καὶ ῥυπαραί, ἐν αἷς
ἡμεῖς σωθησόμεθα· ὅτι καὶ ὁ ἀλγῶν σάρκα διὰ
τοῦ ῥύπου τοῦ ὑσσύπου ἰᾶται. 7. καὶ διὰ τοῦτο
οὕτως γενόμενα ἡμῖν μέν ἐστιν φανερά, ἐκείνοις δὲ
σκοτεινά, ὅτι οὐκ ἤκουσαν φωνῆς κυρίου.

IX

1. Λέγει γὰρ πάλιν περὶ τῶν ὠτίων, πῶς περιέτεμεν ἡμῶν τὴν καρδίαν. λέγει κύριος ἐν τῷ
προφήτῃ· Εἰς ἀκοὴν ὠτίου ὑπήκουσάν μου. καὶ
πάλιν λέγει· Ἀκοῇ ἀκούσονται οἱ πόρρωθεν,
ἃ ἐποίησα γνώσονται. καί· Περιτμήθητε, λέγει
κύριος, τὰς καρδίας ὑμῶν. 2. καὶ πάλιν λέγει·
Ἄκουε Ἰσραήλ, ὅτι τάδε λέγει κύριος ὁ θεός σου.
καὶ πάλιν τὸ πνεῦμα κυρίου προφητεύει·[2] Τίς
ἐστιν ὁ θέλων ζῆσαι εἰς τὸν αἰῶνα; ἀκοῇ ἀκου-
σάτω τῆς φωνῆς τοῦ παιδός μου. 3. καὶ πάλιν
λέγει· Ἄκουε οὐρανέ, καὶ ἐνωτίζου γῆ, ὅτι κύριος
ἐλάλησεν ταῦτα εἰς μαρτύριον. καὶ πάλιν λέγει·
Ἀκούσατε λόγον κυρίου, ἄρχοντες τοῦ λαοῦ τούτου. καὶ πάλιν λέγει· Ἀκούσατε, τέκνα, φωνῆς
βοῶντος ἐν τῇ ἐρήμῳ. οὐκοῦν περιέτεμεν ἡμῶν
τὰς ἀκοάς, ἵνα ἀκούσαντες λόγον πιστεύσωμεν
ἡμεῖς. 4. ἀλλὰ καὶ ἡ περιτομή, ἐφ᾽ ᾗ πεποίθασιν,
κατήργηται. περιτομὴν γὰρ εἴρηκεν οὐ σαρκὸς
γενηθῆναι· ἀλλὰ παρέβησαν, ὅτι ἄγγελος πονηρὸς

Ps. 18, 44
Is. 33, 13
Jer. 4, 4

Jer. 7, 2. 3
Ps.33(34),13;
Exod, 15, 26

Is. 1, 2

Is. 1, 10
Is. 40, 3

---

[1] ξύλου ℵ, ξύλῳ CS. [2] καὶ πάλιν ... προφητεύει GL, om. ℵC.

dom of Jesus is on the wood,[1] and because those who hope on him shall live for ever. 6. But why are the wool and the hyssop together? Because in his kingdom there shall be evil and foul days, in which we shall be saved, for he also who has pain in his flesh is cured by the foulness of the hyssop. 7. And for this reason the things which were thus done are plain to us, but obscure to them, because they did not hear the Lord's voice.

IX

1. FOR he speaks again concerning the ears, how he circumcised our hearts; for the Lord says in the Prophet: " In the hearing of the ear they obey me." And again he says, " They who are afar off shall hear clearly, they shall know the things that I have done," and " Circumcise your hearts, saith the Lord." 2. And again he says, "Hear, O Israel, thus saith the Lord thy God," and again the Spirit of the Lord prophesies, " Who is he that will live for ever? Let him hear the voice of my servant." 3. And again he says, " Hear, O heaven, and give ear, O earth, for the Lord hath spoken these things for a testimony." And again he says, " Hear the word of the Lord, ye rulers of this people." And again he says, " Hear, O children, a voice of one crying in the wilderness." So then he circumcised our hearing in order that we should hear the word and believe. 4. But moreover the circumcision in which they trusted has been abolished. For he declared that circumcision was not of the flesh, but they erred because an evil angel

The circumcision

---

[1] Or "on the tree."

Jer. 4, 3. 4 ἐσόφιζεν αὐτούς. 5. λέγει πρὸς αὐτούς· Τάδε
λέγει κύριος ὁ θεὸς ὑμῶν (ὧδε εὑρίσκω ἐντολήν)·
Μὴ σπείρητε ἐπ᾽ ἀκάνθαις, περιτμήθητε τῷ κυρίῳ
Deut. 10, 16 ὑμῶν. καὶ τί λέγει; Περιτμήθητε τὴν σκληρο-
καρδίαν ὑμῶν, καὶ τὸν τράχηλον ὑμῶν οὐ σκλη-
Jer. 9, 25. 26 ρυνεῖτε. λάβε πάλιν· Ἰδού, λέγει κύριος, πάντα
τὰ ἔθνη ἀπερίτμητα ἀκροβυστίαν, ὁ δὲ λαὸς οὗτος
ἀπερίτμητος καρδίας. 6. ἀλλ᾽ ἐρεῖς· Καὶ μὴν
περιτέτμηται ὁ λαὸς εἰς σφραγῖδα. ἀλλὰ καὶ
πᾶς Σύρος καὶ Ἄραψ καὶ πάντες οἱ ἱερεῖς τῶν
εἰδώλων. ἄρα οὖν κἀκεῖνοι ἐκ τῆς διαθήκης
αὐτῶν εἰσίν; ἀλλὰ καὶ οἱ Αἰγύπτιοι ἐν περιτομῇ
εἰσίν. 7. μάθετε οὖν, τέκνα ἀγάπης, περὶ πάντων
πλουσίως, ὅτι Ἀβραάμ, πρῶτος περιτομὴν δούς,
ἐν πνεύματι προβλέψας εἰς τὸν Ἰησοῦν περιέτεμεν, λαβὼν τριῶν γραμμάτων δόγματα. 8. λέγει
Gen. 17, γάρ· Καὶ περιέτεμεν Ἀβραὰμ ἐκ τοῦ οἴκου
23. 27 ; 14. 14 αὐτοῦ ἄνδρας δεκαοκτὼ καὶ τριακοσίους. τίς οὖν
ἡ δοθεῖσα αὐτῷ γνῶσις; μάθετε, ὅτι τοὺς δεκα-
οκτὼ πρώτους, καὶ διάστημα ποιήσας λέγει
τριακοσίους. τὸ δεκαοκτὼ ι᾽ δέκα, ἡ ὀκτώ· ἔχεις
Ἰησοῦν. ὅτι δὲ ὁ σταυρὸς ἐν τῷ ταῦ ἤμελλεν
ἔχειν τὴν χάριν, λέγει καὶ τοὺς τριακοσίους.
δηλοῖ οὖν τὸν μὲν Ἰησοῦν ἐν τοῖς δυσὶν γράμ-
μασιν, καὶ ἐν τῷ ἑνὶ τὸν σταυρόν. 9. οἶδεν ὁ τὴν
ἔμφυτον δωρεὰν τῆς διδαχῆς αὐτοῦ θέμενος ἐν
ἡμῖν. οὐδεὶς γνησιώτερον ἔμαθεν ἀπ᾽ ἐμοῦ λόγον·
ἀλλὰ οἶδα, ὅτι ἄξιοί ἐστε ὑμεῖς.

was misleading them. 5. He says to them, " Thus saith the Lord your God" (here I find a commandment), " Sow not among thorns, be circumcised to your Lord." And what does he say? " Circumcise the hardness of your heart, and stiffen not your neck." Take it again : " Behold, saith the Lord, all the heathen are uncircumcised in the foreskin, but this people is uncircumcised in heart." 6. But you will say, surely the people has received circumcision as a seal? Yes, but every Syrian and Arab and all priests of the idols have been circumcised ; are then these also within their [1] covenant?— indeed even the Egyptians belong to the circumcision. 7. Learn fully then, children of love, concerning all things, for Abraham, who first circumcised, did so looking forward in the spirit to Jesus, and had received the doctrines of three letters. 8. For it says, " And Abraham circumcised from his household eighteen men and three hundred." [2] What then was the knowledge that was given to him? Notice that he first mentions the eighteen, and after a pause the three hundred. The eighteen is I (= ten) and H (= 8)—you have Jesus [3]—and because the cross was destined to have grace in the T he says " and three hundred." [4] So he indicates Jesus in the two letters and the cross in the other. 9. He knows this who placed the gift of his teaching in our hearts. No one has heard a more excellent lesson from me, but I know that you are worthy.

[1] *I.e.* of the Jews.
[2] In Greek, which expresses numerals by letters, this is TIH.
[3] Because IH are in Greek the first letters of the word Jesus. [4] The Greek symbol for 300 is T.

X

1. "Ὅτι δὲ Μωϋσῆς εἶπεν· Οὐ φάγεσθε χοῖρον οὔτε ἀετὸν οὔτε ὀξύπτερον οὔτε κόρακα οὔτε πάντα ἰχθύν, ὃς οὐκ ἔχει λεπίδα ἐν ἑαυτῷ, τρία ἔλαβεν ἐν τῇ συνέσει δόγματα. 2. πέρας γέ τοι

λέγει αὐτοῖς ἐν τῷ Δευτερονομίῳ· Καὶ διαθήσομαι πρὸς τὸν λαὸν τοῦτον τὰ δικαιώματά μου. ἄρα οὖν οὐκ ἔστιν ἐντολὴ θεοῦ τὸ μὴ τρώγειν, Μωϋσῆς δὲ ἐν πνεύματι ἐλάλησεν. 3. τὸ οὖν χοιρίον πρὸς τοῦτο εἶπεν· οὐ κολληθήσῃ, φησίν, ἀνθρώποις τοιούτοις, οἵτινές εἰσιν ὅμοιοι χοίρων·[1] τουτέστιν ὅταν σπαταλῶσιν, ἐπιλανθάνονται τοῦ κυρίου, ὅταν δὲ ὑστεροῦνται, ἐπιγινώσκουσιν τὸν κύριον, ὡς καὶ ὁ χοῖρος ὅταν τρώγει τὸν κύριον οὐκ οἶδεν, ὅταν δὲ πεινᾷ κραυγάζει, καὶ λαβὼν πάλιν

σιωπᾷ. 4. Οὐδὲ φάγῃ τὸν ἀετὸν οὐδὲ τὸν ὀξύπτερον οὐδὲ τὸν ἰκτῖνα οὐδὲ τὸν κόρακα· οὐ μή, φησίν, κολληθήσῃ οὐδὲ ὁμοιωθήσῃ ἀνθρώποις τοιούτοις, οἵτινες οὐκ οἴδασιν διὰ κόπου καὶ ἱδρῶτος πορίζειν ἑαυτοῖς τὴν τροφήν, ἀλλὰ ἁρπάζουσιν τὰ ἀλλότρια ἐν ἀνομίᾳ αὐτῶν καὶ ἐπιτηροῦσιν ὡς ἐν ἀκεραιοσύνῃ περιπατοῦντες καὶ περιβλέπονται, τίνα ἐκδύσωσιν διὰ τὴν πλεονεξίαν, ὡς καὶ τὰ ὄρνεα ταῦτα μόνα ἑαυτοῖς οὐ προΐζει τὴν τροφήν, ἀλλὰ ἀργὰ καθήμενα ἐκζητεῖ, πῶς ἀλλοτρίας σάρκας καταφάγῃ, ὄντα λοιμὰ τῇ πονηρίᾳ αὐτῶν.

5. Καὶ οὐ φάγῃ, φησίν, σμύραιναν οὐδὲ πολύποδα οὐδὲ σηπίαν· οὐ μή, φησίν, ὁμοιωθήσῃ κολλώμενος[2] ἀνθρώποις τοιούτοις, οἵτινες εἰς τέλος

---

[1] χοίρων ℵ, χοίροις ϹG.   [2] κολλώμενος GL, om. ℵ C.

374

X

1. Now, in that Moses said, " Ye shall not eat swine, nor an eagle, nor a hawk, nor a crow, nor any fish which has no scales on itself," he included three doctrines in his understanding. 2. Moreover he says to them in Deuteronomy, " And I will make a covenant of my ordinances with this people." So then the ordinance of God is not abstinence from eating, but Moses spoke in the spirit. 3. He mentioned the swine for this reason : you shall not consort, he means, with men who are like swine, that is to say, when they have plenty they forget the Lord, but when they are in want they recognise the Lord, just as the swine when it eats does not know its master, but when it is hungry it cries out, and after receiving food is again silent. 4. " Neither shalt thou eat the eagle nor the hawk nor the kite nor the crow." Thou shalt not, he means, join thyself or make thyself like to such men, as do not know how to gain their food by their labour and sweat, but plunder other people's property in their iniquity, and lay wait for it, though they seem to walk in innocence, and look round to see whom they may plunder in their covetousness, just as these birds alone provide no food for themselves, but sit idle, and seek how they may devour the flesh of others, and become pestilent in their iniquity. 5. " Thou shalt not eat," he says, " the lamprey nor the polypus nor the cuttlefish." Thou shalt not, he means, consort with or become like such men who are utterly ungodly and who are already condemned

The Food-law of the Jews

375

εἰσὶν ἀσεβεῖς καὶ κεκριμένοι ἤδη τῷ θανάτῳ, ὡς καὶ ταῦτα τὰ ἰχθύδια μόνα ἐπικατάρατα ἐν τῷ βυθῷ νήχεται, μὴ κολυμβῶντα ὡς τὰ λοιπά, ἀλλ᾽ ἐν τῇ γῇ κάτω τοῦ βυθοῦ κατοικεῖ. 6. ἀλλὰ

Lev. 11, 5 καὶ τὸν δασύποδα οὐ φάγῃ. πρὸς τί; οὐ μὴ γένῃ, φησίν, παιδοφθόρος οὐδὲ ὁμοιωθήσῃ τοῖς τοιούτοις, ὅτι ὁ λαγωὸς κατ᾽ ἐνιαυτὸν πλεονεκτεῖ τὴν ἀφόδευσιν· ὅσα γὰρ ἔτη ζῇ, τοσαύτας ἔχει τρύπας. 7. ἀλλὰ οὐδὲ τὴν ὕαιναν φάγῃ· οὐ μή, φησίν, γένῃ μοιχὸς οὐδὲ φθορεὺς οὐδὲ ὁμοιωθήσῃ τοῖς τοιούτοις. πρὸς τί; ὅτι τὸ ζῷον τοῦτο παρ᾽ ἐνιαυτὸν ἀλλάσσει τὴν φύσιν καὶ ποτὲ μὲν ἄρρεν,

Lev. 11. 29 ποτὲ δὲ θῆλυ γίνεται. 8. ἀλλὰ καὶ τὴν γαλῆν ἐμίσησεν καλῶς. οὐ μή, φησίν, γενηθῇς τοιοῦτος, οἵους ἀκούομεν ἀνομίαν ποιοῦντας ἐν τῷ στόματι δι᾽ ἀκαθαρσίαν, οὐδὲ κολληθήσῃ ταῖς ἀκαθάρτοις ταῖς τὴν ἀνομίαν ποιούσαις ἐν τῷ στόματι. τὸ γὰρ ζῷον τοῦτο τῷ στόματι κύει. 9. περὶ μὲν τῶν βρωμάτων λαβὼν Μωϋσῆς τρία δόγματα οὕτως ἐν πνεύματι ἐλάλησεν· οἱ δὲ κατ᾽ ἐπιθυμίαν τῆς σαρκὸς ὡς περὶ βρώσεως προσεδέξαντο. 10. λαμβάνει δὲ τῶν αὐτῶν τριῶν δογμάτων γνῶσιν

Ps. 1, 1 Δαυείδ καὶ λέγει· Μακάριος ἀνήρ, ὃς οὐκ ἐπορεύθη ἐν βουλῇ ἀσεβῶν, καθὼς καὶ οἱ ἰχθύες πορεύονται ἐν σκότει εἰς τὰ βάθη· καὶ ἐν ὁδῷ ἁμαρτωλῶν οὐκ ἔστη, καθὼς οἱ δοκοῦντες φοβεῖσθαι τὸν κύριον ἁμαρτάνουσιν ὡς ὁ χοῖρος, καὶ ἐπὶ καθέδραν λοιμῶν οὐκ ἐκάθισεν, καθὼς τὰ πετεινὰ καθήμενα εἰς ἁρπαγήν. ἔχετε τελείως

to death, just as these fish alone are accursed, and float in the deep water, not swimming like the others but living on the ground at the bottom of the sea. 6. Moreover,[1] thou shalt not eat the rabbit. For what reason? Because thou shalt not, he means, become a corruptor of the young, or become like such men; for the rabbit multiplies during every year its retirements by the way; for it has as many burrow-holes as it lives years. 7. Moreover thou shalt not eat the hyaena.[2] Thou shalt not, he means, become an adulterer or a corruptor nor shalt thou become like such men. For what reason? Because this animal in every other year changes its nature and becomes now male now female. 8. Moreover Moses abhors the weasel rightly. Thou shalt not, he says, become such a person—such men as we hear committing lawlessness in their mouths because of uncleanliness; nor shalt thou cleave to women who are unclean and who commit lawlessness in their mouths. For this animal gives birth with its mouth. 9. Moses received three doctrines concerning food and thus spoke of them in the Spirit; but they received them as really referring to food, owing to the lust of their flesh. 10. But David received knowledge concerning the same three doctrines, and says: " Blessed is the man who has not gone in the counsel of the ungodly " as the fishes go in darkness in the deep waters, " and has not stood in the way of sinners " like those who seem to fear the Lord, but sin like the swine, " and has not sat in the seat of the scorners " like the birds who sit and wait for their prey. Grasp fully

The explanation in the Psalter

---

[1] The translation of sections 6–5 is editorial. Lake gave the Old Latin version. [2] This prohibition is not in the O.T.

καὶ περὶ τῆς βρώσεως. 11. πάλιν λέγει Μωϋσῆς·
Φάγεσθε πᾶν διχηλοῦν καὶ μαρυκώμενον. τί λέγει ;
ὅτι τὴν τροφὴν λαμβάνων οἶδεν τὸν τρέφοντα αὐτὸν
καὶ ἐπ᾽ αὐτῷ ἀναπαυόμενος εὐφραίνεσθαι δοκεῖ.
καλῶς εἶπεν βλέπων τὴν ἐντολήν. τί οὖν λέγει;
κολλᾶσθε μετὰ τῶν φοβουμένων τὸν κύριον, μετὰ
τῶν μελετώντων ὃ ἔλαβον διάσταλμα ῥήματος ἐν
τῇ καρδίᾳ, μετὰ τῶν λαλούντων τὰ διδαιώματα
κυρίου καὶ τηρούντων, μετὰ τῶν εἰδότων, ὅτι ἡ
μελέτη ἐστὶν ἔργον εὐφροσύνης, καὶ ἀναμαρυκω-
μένων τὸν λόγον κυρίου. τί δὲ τὸ διχηλοῦν; ὅτι
ὁ δίκαιος καὶ ἐν τούτῳ τῷ κόσμῳ περιπατεῖ καὶ
τὸν ἅγιον αἰῶνα ἐκδέχεται. βλέπετε, πῶς ἐνομο-
θέτησεν Μωϋσῆς καλῶς. 12. ἀλλὰ πόθεν ἐκείνοις
ταῦτα νοῆσαι ἢ συνιέναι; ἡμεῖς δὲ δικαίως νοήσαντες τὰς ἐντολὰς λαλοῦμεν, ὡς ἠθέλησεν ὁ
κύριος. διὰ τοῦτο περιέτεμεν τὰς ἀκοὰς ἡμῶν καὶ
τὰς καρδίας, ἵνα συνιῶμεν ταῦτα.

Lev. 11, 3 ;
Deut. 14, 6

XI

1. Ζητήσωμεν δέ, εἰ ἐμέλησεν τῷ κυρίῳ προ-
φανερῶσαι περὶ τοῦ ὕδατος καὶ περὶ τοῦ σταυροῦ.
περὶ μὲν τοῦ ὕδατος γέγραπται ἐπὶ τὸν Ἰσραήλ,
πῶς τὸ βάπτισμα τὸ φέρον ἄφεσιν ἁμαρτιῶν οὐ
μὴ προσδέξονται, ἀλλ᾽ ἑαυτοῖς οἰκοδομήσουσιν.
2. λέγει γὰρ ὁ προφήτης· Ἔκστηθι οὐρανέ, καὶ
ἐπὶ τούτῳ πλεῖον φριξάτω ἡ γῆ, ὅτι δύο καὶ
πονηρὰ ἐποίησεν ὁ λαὸς οὗτος· ἐμὲ ἐγκατέλιπον,

Jer. 2, 12. 13

the doctrines concerning food. 11. Moses says
again, "Eat of every animal that is cloven hoofed
and ruminant." What does he mean? That he
who receives food knows him who feeds him, and
rests on him and seems to rejoice. Well did he
speak with regard to the commandment. What
then does he mean? Consort with those who fear
the Lord, with those who meditate in their heart on
the meaning of the word which they have received,
with those who speak of and observe the ordinances
of the Lord, with those who know that meditation
is a work of gladness, and who ruminate on the
word of the Lord. But what does "the cloven
hoofed" mean? That the righteous both walks in
this world and looks forward to the holy age. See
how well Moses legislated. 12. But how was it
possible for them to understand or comprehend
these things? But we having a righteous understanding of them announce the commandments as
the Lord wished. For this cause he circumcised
our hearing and our hearts that we should
comprehend these things.

XI

1. But let us enquire if the Lord took pains to Baptism
foretell the water of baptism and the cross. Concerning the water it has been written with regard to
Israel that they will not receive the baptism that
brings the remission of sins, but will build for themselves. 2. For the Prophet says, "Be astonished O
heaven, and let the earth tremble the more at this,
that this people hath committed two evils: they
have deserted me, the spring of life, and they have

πηγὴν ζωῆς, καὶ ἑαυτοῖς ὤρυξαν βόθρον θανάτου.

Is. 16, 1. 2 — 3. Μὴ πέτρα ἔρημός ἐστιν τὸ ὄρος τὸ ἅγιόν μου Σινᾶ; ἔσεσθε γὰρ ὡς πετεινοῦ νοσσοὶ ἀνιπτάμενοι νοσσιᾶς ἀφῃρημένοι. 4. καὶ πάλιν λέγει ὁ προ-

Is. 45, 2. 3 — φήτης· Ἐγὼ πορεύσομαι ἔμπροσθέν σου καὶ ὄρη ὁμαλιῶ καὶ πύλας χαλκᾶς συντρίψω καὶ μοχλοὺς σιδηροῦς συγκλάσω, καὶ δώσω σοι θησαυροὺς σκοτεινούς, ἀποκρύφους, ἀοράτους, ἵνα γνῶσιν

Is. 33, 16–18 — ὅτι ἐγὼ κύριος ὁ θεός. 5. καί· Κατοικήσεις ἐν ὑψηλῷ σπηλαίῳ πέτρας ἰσχυρᾶς. καί· τὸ ὕδωρ αὐτοῦ πιστόν· βασιλέα μετὰ δόξης ὄψεσθε, καὶ ἡ ψυχὴ ὑμῶν μελετήσει φόβον κυρίου. 6. καὶ

Ps. 1, 3–6 — πάλιν ἐν ἄλλῳ προφήτῃ λέγει· Καὶ ἔσται ὁ ταῦτα ποιῶν ὡς τὸ ξύλον τὸ πεφυτευμένον παρὰ τὰς διεξόδους τῶν ὑδάτων, ὃ τὸν καρπὸν αὐτοῦ δώσει ἐν καιρῷ αὐτοῦ, καὶ τὸ φύλλον αὐτοῦ οὐκ ἀπορυήσεται, καὶ πάντα, ὅσα ἂν ποιῇ, κατευοδω-θήσεται. 7. οὐχ οὕτως οἱ ἀσεβεῖς, οὐχ οὕτως, ἀλλ' ἢ ὡς ὁ χνοῦς, ὃν ἐκρίπτει ὁ ἄνεμος ἀπὸ προσώπου τῆς γῆς. διὰ τοῦτο οὐκ ἀναστήσονται ἀσεβεῖς ἐν κρίσει οὐδὲ ἁμαρτωλοὶ ἐν βουλῇ δικαίων, ὅτι γινώσκει κύριος ὁδὸν δικαίων, καὶ ὁδὸς ἀσεβῶν ἀπολεῖται. 8. αἰσθάνεσθε, πῶς τὸ ὕδωρ καὶ τὸν σταυρὸν ἐπὶ τὸ αὐτὸ ὥρισεν. τοῦτο γὰρ λέγει· μακάριοι, οἱ ἐπὶ τὸν σταυρὸν ἐλπίσαντες κατέ-βησαν εἰς τὸ ὕδωρ, ὅτι τὸν μὲν μισθὸν λέγει ἐν καιρῷ αὐτοῦ· τότε, φησίν, ἀποδώσω. νῦν δὲ ὃ λέγει· τὰ φύλλα οὐκ ἀπορυήσεται, τοῦτο λέγει· ὅτι πᾶν ῥῆμα, ὃ ἐὰν ἐξελεύσεται ἐξ ὑμῶν διὰ τοῦ

Ps. 1, 3 — στόματος ὑμῶν ἐν πίστει καὶ ἀγάπῃ, ἔσται εἰς ἐπιστροφὴν καὶ ἐλπίδα πολλοῖς. 9. καὶ πάλιν ἕτερος προφήτης λέγει. Καὶ ἦν ἡ γῆ τοῦ Ἰακὼβ

dug for themselves a cistern of death. 3. Is my
holy mountain Sinai a desert rock? For ye shall
be as the fledgling birds, fluttering about when they
are taken away from the nest." 4. And again the
Prophet says, " I will go before you and I will make
mountains level, and I will break gates of brass, and
I will shatter bars of iron, and I will give thee trea-
sures of darkness, secret, invisible, that they may
know that I am the Lord God." 5. And, " Thou
shalt dwell in a lofty cave of a strong rock.'' And,
" His water is sure, ye shall see the King in his glory,
and your soul shall meditate on the fear of the
Lord." 6. And again he says in another Prophet,
" And he who does these things shall be as
the tree, which is planted at the partings of the
waters, which shall give its fruit in its season, and
its leaf shall not fade, and all things, whatsoever he doeth, shall prosper. 7. It is not so
with the wicked, it is not so; but they are even
as the chaff which the wind driveth away from
the face of the earth. Therefore the wicked shall
not rise up in judgment, nor sinners in the counsel
of the righteous, for the Lord knoweth the way
of the righteous, and the way of the ungodly
shall perish." 8. Mark how he described the water The Cross
and the cross together. For he means this : blessed
are those who hoped on the cross, and descended
into the water. For he speaks of their reward " in
his season"; at that time, he says, I will repay.
But now when he says, " Their leaves shall not fade,"
he means that every word which shall come forth
from your mouth in faith and love, shall be for conversion and hope for many. 9. And again another
Prophet says, " And the land of Jacob was praised

ἐπαινουμένη παρὰ πᾶσαν τὴν γῆν. τοῦτο λέγει·

Cf.Wisd.3,19 τὸ σκεῦος τοῦ πνεύματος αὐτοῦ δοξάζει. 10. εἶτα

Ezek. 47, 1-12 τί λέγει ; Καὶ ἦν ποταμὸς ἕλκων ἐκ δεξιῶν, καὶ ἀνέβαινεν ἐξ αὐτοῦ δένδρα ὡραῖα· καὶ ὃς ἂν φάγῃ ἐξ αὐτῶν, ζήσεται εἰς τὸν αἰῶνα. 11. τοῦτο λέγει ὅτι ἡμεῖς μὲν καταβαίνομεν εἰς τὸ ὕδωρ γέμοντες ἁμαρτιῶν καὶ ῥύπου, καὶ ἀναβαίνομεν καρποφο-ροῦντες ἐν τῇ καρδίᾳ τὸν φόβον καὶ τὴν ἐλπίδα

Ezek. 47, 9 εἰς τὸν Ἰησοῦν ἐν τῷ πνεύματι ἔχοντες. Καὶ ὃς ἂν φάγῃ ἀπὸ τούτων, ζήσεται εἰς τὸν αἰῶνα, τοῦτο λέγει· ὃς ἄν, φησίν, ἀκούσῃ τούτων λαλου-μένων καὶ πιστεύσῃ, ζήσεται εἰς τὸν αἰῶνα.

XII

IV Esr. 4, 33 ; 5, 5 1. Ὁμοίως πάλιν περὶ τοῦ σταυροῦ ὁρίζει ἐν ἄλλῳ προφήτῃ λέγοντι· Καὶ πότε ταῦτα συν-τελεσθήσεται ; λέγει κύριος· ὅταν ξύλον κλιθῇ καὶ ἀναστῇ, καὶ ὅταν ἐκ ξύλου αἷμα στάξῃ. ἔχεις πάλιν περὶ τοῦ σταυροῦ καὶ τοῦ σταυροῦ-

Exod. 17, 18 ff. σθαι μέλλοντος. 2. λέγει δὲ πάλιν τῷ Μωϋσῇ,[1] πολεμουμένου τοῦ Ἰσραὴλ ὑπὸ τῶν ἀλλοφύλων, καὶ ἵνα ὑπομνήσῃ αὐτοὺς πολεμουμένους, ὅτι διὰ τὰς ἁμαρτίας αὐτῶν παρεδόθησαν εἰς θάνατον· λέγει εἰς τὴν καρδίαν Μωϋσέως τὸ πνεῦμα, ἵνα ποιήσῃ τύπον σταυροῦ καὶ τοῦ μέλλοντος πάσ-χειν, ὅτι, ἐὰν μή, φησίν, ἐλπίσωσιν ἐπ' αὐτῷ, εἰς τὸν αἰῶνα πολεμηθήσονται. τίθησιν οὖν Μωϋσῆς ἓν ἐφ' ἓν ὅπλον ἐν μέσῳ τῆς πυγμῆς, καὶ ὑψηλό-τερος σταθεὶς πάντων ἐξέτεινεν τὰς χεῖρας, καὶ

---

[1] τῷ Μωϋσῇ אC, ἐν τῷ Μωϋσῇ GL " in Moses " i.e. in the " Pentateuch " which was spoken of as " Moses."

above every land." He means to say that he is glorifying the vessel of his Spirit. 10. What does he say next? "And there was a river flowing on the right hand, and beautiful trees grew out of it, and whosoever shall eat of them shall live for ever." 11. He means to say that we go down into the water full of sins and foulness, and we come up bearing the fruit of fear in our hearts, and having hope on Jesus in the Spirit. "And whosoever shall eat of them shall live for ever." He means that whosoever hears and believes these things spoken shall live for ever.

XII

1. SIMILARLY, again, he describes the cross in another Prophet, who says, "And when shall all these things be accomplished? saith the Lord. When the tree shall fall and rise, and when blood shall flow from the tree." Here again you have a reference to the cross, and to him who should be crucified. 2. And he says again to Moses, when Israel was warred upon by strangers, and in order to remind those who were warred upon that they were delivered unto death by reason of their sins—the Spirit speaks to the heart of Moses to make a representation of the cross, and of him who should suffer, because, he says, unless they put their trust in him, they shall suffer war for ever. Moses therefore placed one shield upon another in the midst of the fight, and standing there raised above them all kept stretching

The Cross

οὕτως πάλιν ἐνίκα ὁ Ἰσραήλ. εἶτα, ὁπόταν καθεῖλεν, ἐθανατοῦντο. 3. πρὸς τί; ἵνα γνῶσιν ὅτι οὐ δύνανται σωθῆναι, ἐὰν μὴ ἐπ' αὐτῷ ἐλπίσω-
Is. 65, 2 σιν. 4. καὶ πάλιν ἐν ἑτέρῳ προφήτῃ λέγει· Ὅλην τὴν ἡμέραν ἐξεπέτασα τὰς χεῖράς μου πρὸς λαὸν ἀπειθῆ[1] καὶ ἀντιλέγοντα ὁδῷ δικαίᾳ μου. 5. πάλιν Μωϋσῆς ποιεῖ τύπον τοῦ Ἰησοῦ, ὅτι δεῖ αὐτὸν παθεῖν, καὶ αὐτὸς ζωοποιήσει, ὃν δόξουσιν ἀπολωλεκέναι, ἐν σημείῳ πίπτοντος τοῦ Ἰσραήλ,
Num. 21, 6 ff. (ἐποίησεν γὰρ κύριος πάντα ὄφιν δάκνειν αὐτούς, καὶ ἀπέθνησκον ἐπειδὴ ἡ παράβασις διὰ τοῦ ὄφεως ἐν Εὔᾳ ἐγένετο), ἵνα ἐλέγξῃ αὐτούς, ὅτι διὰ τὴν παράβασιν αὐτῶν εἰς θλῖψιν θανάτου παρα-
Deut. 27, 15 δοθήσονται. 6. πέρας γέ τοι αὐτὸς Μωϋσῆς ἐντειλάμενος· Οὐκ ἔσται ὑμῖν οὔτε χωνευτὸν οὔτε γλυπτὸν εἰς θεὸν ὑμῖν, αὐτὸς ποιεῖ, ἵνα τύπον τοῦ Ἰησοῦ δείξῃ. ποιεῖ οὖν Μωϋσῆς χαλκοῦν ὄφιν καὶ τίθησιν ἐνδόξως καὶ κηρύγματι καλεῖ τὸν λαόν. 7. ἐλθόντες οὖν ἐπὶ τὸ αὐτὸ ἐδέοντο Μωϋσέως, ἵνα περὶ αὐτῶν ἀνενέγκῃ δέησιν περὶ τῆς ἰάσεως αὐτῶν. εἶπεν δὲ πρὸς αὐτοὺς Μωϋσῆς·
Num. 21, 8. 9 Ὅταν, φησίν, δηχθῇ τις ὑμῶν, ἐλθέτω ἐπὶ τὸν ὄφιν τὸν ἐπὶ τοῦ ξύλου ἐπικείμενον καὶ ἐλπισάτω πιστεύσας, ὅτι αὐτὸς ὢν νεκρὸς δύναται ζωοποιῆσαι, καὶ παραχρῆμα σωθήσεται. καὶ οὕτως ἐποίουν. ἔχεις πάλιν καὶ ἐν τούτοις τὴν δόξαν τοῦ Ἰησοῦ, ὅτι ἐν αὐτῷ πάντα καὶ εἰς αὐτόν.
Num. 13, 17 8. τί λέγει πάλιν Μωϋσῆς Ἰησοῦ, υἱῷ Ναυή, ἐπιθεὶς αὐτῷ τοῦτο τὸ ὄνομα, ὄντι προφήτῃ, ἵνα μόνον ἀκούσῃ πᾶς ὁ λαός; ὅτι πάντα ὁ πατὴρ

---

[1] ἀπειθῆ ℵ, ἀπειθοῦντα Cg (LXX).

out his hands, and so Israel again began to be victo-
rious : then, whenever he let them drop they began
to perish. 3. Why? That they may know that
they cannot be saved if they do not hope on him.
4. And again he says in another Prophet, " I
stretched out my hands the whole day to a disobedient people and one that refuses my righteous
way." 5. Again Moses makes a representation of
Jesus, showing that he must suffer, and shall himself
give life, though they will believe that he has been
put to death, by the sign given when Israel was falling
(for the Lord made every serpent bite them, and
they were perishing, for the fall[1] took place in Eve
through the serpent), in order to convince them that
they will be delivered over to the affliction of death
because of their transgression. 6. Moreover, though
Moses commanded them :—" You shall have neither
graven nor molten image for your God," yet he
makes one himself to show a type of Jesus. Moses
therefore makes a graven serpent, and places it in
honour and calls the people by a proclamation.
7. So they came together and besought Moses that
he would offer prayer on their behalf for their healing.
But Moses said to them, " Whenever one of you," he
said, " be bitten, let him come to the serpent that is
placed upon the tree, and let him hope, in faith that
it though dead is able to give life, and he shall
straightway be saved." And they did so. In this
also you have again the glory of Jesus, for all
things are in him and for him. 8. Again, why does Joshua
Moses say to Jesus, the son of Naue,[2] when he gives
him, prophet as he is, this name, that the whole

---

[1] Literally the "transgression."   [2] i.e. Joshua the son of
Nun, of which names Jesus and Naue are the Greek forms.

φανεροῖ περὶ τοῦ υἱοῦ Ἰησοῦ. 9. λέγει οὖν
Μωϋσῆς Ἰησοῦ, υἱῷ Ναυή, ἐπιθεὶς τοῦτο τὸ ὄνομα,
Exod. 17, 14 ὁπότε ἔπεμψεν αὐτὸν κατάσκοπον τῆς γῆς· Λάβε
βιβλίον εἰς τὰς χεῖράς σου καὶ γράψον, ἃ λέγει
κύριος, ὅτι ἐκκόψει ἐκ ῥιζῶν τὸν οἶκον πάντα τοῦ
Ἀμαλὴκ ὁ υἱὸς τοῦ θεοῦ ἐπ' ἐσχάτων τῶν ἡμερῶν.
10. ἴδε πάλιν Ἰησοῦς, οὐχὶ υἱὸς ἀνθρώπου, ἀλλὰ
Mt. 22, 42-44 υἱὸς τοῦ θεοῦ, τύπῳ δὲ ἐν σαρκὶ φανερωθείς. ἐπεὶ
οὖν μέλλουσιν λέγειν, ὅτι Χριστὸς υἱὸς Δαυεὶδ
ἐστιν,[1] αὐτὸς προφητεύει Δαυείδ, φοβούμενος καὶ
Ps. 110, 1 συνίων τὴν πλάνην τῶν ἁμαρτωλῶν· Εἶπεν
κύριος τῷ κυρίῳ μου· Κάθου ἐκ δεξιῶν μου, ἕως
ἂν θῶ τοὺς ἐχθρούς σου ὑποπόδιον τῶν ποδῶν σου.
Is. 45, 1 11. καὶ πάλιν λέγει οὕτως Ἡσαΐας· Εἶπεν κύριος
τῷ Χριστῷ μου κυρίῳ, οὗ ἐκράτησα τῆς δεξιᾶς
αὐτοῦ, ἐπακοῦσαι ἔμπροσθεν αὐτοῦ ἔθνη, καὶ
ἰσχὺν βασιλέων διαρρήξω. ἴδε, πῶς Δαυεὶδ λέγει
Mk. 12, 37
cf. Mt. 22, αὐτὸν κύριον, καὶ υἱὸν οὐ λέγει.
45; Luke, 20,
44

XIII

1. Ἴδωμεν δὲ εἰ οὗτος ὁ λαὸς κληρονομεῖ ἢ
ὁ πρῶτος, καὶ εἰ ἡ διαθήκη εἰς ἡμᾶς ἢ εἰς
ἐκείνους. 2. ἀκούσατε οὖν περὶ τοῦ λαοῦ τί λέγει
Gen. 25, 21 ἡ γραφή· Ἐδεῖτο δὲ Ἰσαὰκ περὶ Ῥεβέκκας τῆς
γυναικὸς αὐτοῦ, ὅτι στεῖρα ἦν· καὶ συνέλαβεν.
Gen. 25, εἶτα ἐξῆλθεν Ῥεβέκκα πυθέσθαι παρὰ κυρίου,
22-23
cf. Rom. 9, καὶ εἶπεν κύριος πρὸς αὐτήν· Δύο ἔθνη ἐν τῇ
10-12 γαστρί σου καὶ δύο λαοὶ ἐν τῇ κοιλίᾳ σου, καὶ

[1] Χριστὸς υἱὸς Δαυεὶδ ἐστιν ℵ, ὁ Χριστὸς υἱός ἐστιν Δαυεὶδ
CG.

people should listen to him alone? Because the Father was revealing everything concerning his Son Jesus. 9. Moses therefore says to Jesus the son of Naue, after giving him this name, when he sent him to spy out the land, "Take a book in thy hands and write what the Lord saith, that the Son of God shall in the last day tear up by the roots the whole house of Amalek." 10. See again Jesus, not as son of man, but as Son of God, but manifested in a type in the flesh. Since therefore they are going to say that the Christ is David's son, David himself prophesies, fearing and understanding the error of the sinners, "The Lord said to my Lord sit thou on my right hand until I make thy enemies thy footstool." 11. And again Isaiah speaks thus, "The Lord said to Christ my Lord, whose right hand I held, that the nations should obey before him, and I will shatter the strength of Kings." See how "David calls him Lord" and does not say Son.

XIII

1. Now let us see whether this people or the former people is the heir, and whether the covenant is for us or for them. 2. Hear then what the Scripture says concerning the people: "And Isaac prayed concerning Rebecca his wife, because she was barren, and she conceived. Then Rebecca went forth to enquire of the Lord and the Lord said to her: two nations are in thy womb, and two peoples in thy belly, and one people shall

Jews and Christians as heirs of the covenant

ὑπερέξει λαὸς λαοῦ καὶ ὁ μείζων δουλεύσει τῷ
ἐλάσσονι. 3. αἰσθάνεσθαι ὀφείλετε, τίς ὁ Ἰσαὰκ
καὶ τίς ἡ Ῥεβέκκα, καὶ ἐπὶ τίνων δέδειχεν, ὅτι
μείζων ὁ λαὸς οὗτος ἢ ἐκεῖνος.   4. καὶ ἐν ἄλλῃ
προφητείᾳ λέγει φανερώτερον ὁ Ἰακὼβ πρὸς

Gen. 48, 11   Ἰωσὴφ τὸν υἱὸν αὐτοῦ, λέγων· Ἰδού, οὐκ ἐστέ-
ρησέν με κύριος τοῦ προσώπου σου· προσάγαγέ
μοι τοὺς υἱούς σου, ἵνα εὐλογήσω αὐτούς. 5. καὶ

Gen. 48, 9   προσήγαγεν Ἐφραὶμ καὶ Μανασσῆ, τὸν Μανασσῆ
θέλων ἵνα εὐλογηθῇ, ὅτι πρεσβύτερος ἦν· ὁ γὰρ
Ἰωσὴφ προσήγαγεν εἰς τὴν δεξιὰν χεῖρα τοῦ
πατρὸς Ἰακώβ.   εἶδεν δὲ Ἰακὼβ τύπον τῷ πνεύ-

Gen. 48,   ματι τοῦ λαοῦ τοῦ μεταξύ· καὶ τί λέγει; Καὶ
13-19
ἐποίησεν Ἰακὼβ ἐναλλὰξ τὰς χεῖρας αὐτοῦ καὶ
ἐπέθηκεν τὴν δεξιὰν ἐπὶ τὴν κεφαλὴν Ἐφραίμ,
τοῦ δευτέρου καὶ νεωτέρου, καὶ εὐλόγησεν αὐτόν.
καὶ εἶπεν Ἰωσὴφ πρὸς Ἰακώβ· Μετάθες σου τὴν
δεξιὰν ἐπὶ τὴν κεφαλὴν Μανασσῆ, ὅτι πρωτότοκός μου υἱός ἐστιν. καὶ εἶπεν Ἰακὼβ πρὸς
Ἰωσήφ· Οἶδα, τέκνον, οἶδα· ἀλλ' ὁ μείζων δουλεύσει τῷ ἐλάσσονι, καὶ οὗτος δὲ εὐλογηθήσεται.
6. βλέπετε, ἐπὶ τίνων τέθεικεν, τὸν λαὸν τοῦτον
εἶναι πρῶτον καὶ τῆς διαθήκης κληρονόμον. 7. εἰ
οὖν ἔτι καὶ διὰ τοῦ Ἀβραὰμ ἐμνήσθη, ἀπέχομεν

Gen. 15, 6   τὸ τέλειον τῆς γνώσεως ἡμῶν. τί οὖν λέγει τῷ
Ἀβραάμ, ὅτε μόνος πιστεύσας ἐτέθη εἰς δικαιο-

Gen. 17, 4. 5,   σύνην; Ἰδού, τέθεικά σε, Ἀβραάμ, πατέρα
cf. Rom. 4
12-13   ἐθνῶν τῶν πιστευόντων δι' ἀκροβυστίας τῷ θεῷ.

overcome a people, and the greater shall serve the less." 3. You ought to understand who is Isaac and who is Rebecca, and of whom he has shown that this people is greater than that people. 4. And in another prophecy Jacob speaks more plainly to Joseph his son, saying, "Behold the Lord hath not deprived me of thy presence; bring me thy sons, that I may bless them." 5. And he brought Ephraim and Manasses, and wished that Manasses should be blessed, because he was the elder; for Joseph brought him to the right hand of his father Jacob. But Jacob saw in the spirit a type of the people of the future. And what does he say? "And Jacob crossed his hands, and placed his right hand on the head of Ephraim, the second and younger son, and blessed him; and Joseph said to Jacob, Change thy right hand on to the head of Manasses, for he is my first-born son. And Jacob said to Joseph, I know it, my child, I know it; but the greater shall serve the less, and this one shall indeed be blessed." 6. See who it is of whom he ordained that this people is the first and heir of the covenant. 7. If then besides this he remembered it also in the case of Abraham, we reach the perfection of our knowledge. What then does he say to Abraham, when he alone was faithful, and it was counted him for righteousness? "Behold I have made thee, Abraham, the father of the Gentiles who believe in God in uncircumcision."

XIV

1. Ναί. ἀλλὰ ἴδωμεν, εἰ ἡ διαθήκη, ἣν ὤμοσεν
τοῖς πατράσιν δοῦναι τῷ λαῷ, εἰ δέδωκεν.[1]
δέδωκεν· αὐτοὶ δὲ οὐκ ἐγένοντο ἄξιοι λαβεῖν διὰ
τὰς ἁμαρτίας αὐτῶν. 2. λέγει γὰρ ὁ προφήτης·
Exod. 24, 18 Καὶ ἦν Μωϋσῆς νηστεύων ἐν ὄρει Σινᾶ, τοῦ λαβεῖν
τὴν διαθήκην κυρίου πρὸς τὸν λαόν, ἡμέρας τεσ-
Exod. 31, 18 σεράκοντα καὶ νύκτας τεσσεράκοντα. καὶ ἔλαβεν
Μωϋσῆς παρὰ κυρίου τὰς δύο πλάκας τὰς
γεγραμμένας τῷ δακτύλῳ τῆς χειρὸς κυρίου ἐν
πνεύματι· καὶ λαβὼν Μωϋσῆς κατέφερεν πρὸς
τὸν λαὸν δοῦναι. 3. καὶ εἶπεν κύριος πρὸς
Exod. 32, Μωϋσῆν. Μωϋσῆ Μωϋσῆ, κατάβηθι τὸ τάχος,
7–19 ; ὅτι ὁ λαός σου, ὃν ἐξήγαγες ἐκ γῆς Αἰγύπτου,
Deut. 9, ἠνόμησεν. καὶ συνῆκεν Μωϋσῆς, ὅτι ἐποίησαν
12–17 ἑαυτοῖς πάλιν χωνεύματα, καὶ ἔρριψεν ἐκ τῶν
χειρῶν,[2] καὶ συνετρίβησαν αἱ πλάκες τῆς διαθήκης κυρίου. 4. Μωϋσῆς μὲν ἔλαβεν, αὐτοὶ
δὲ οὐκ ἐγένοντο ἄξιοι. πῶς δὲ ἡμεῖς ἐλάβομεν, μάθετε. Μωϋσῆς θεράπων ὢν ἔλαβεν,
αὐτὸς δὲ κύριος ἡμῖν ἔδωκεν εἰς λαὸν κληρονομίας, δι' ἡμᾶς ὑπομείνας. 5. ἐφανερώθη δέ,
ἵνα κἀκεῖνοι τελειωθῶσιν τοῖς ἁμαρτήμασιν, καὶ
ἡμεῖς διὰ τοῦ κληρονομοῦντος διαθήκην κυρίου
Tit. 2, 14 Ἰησοῦ λάβωμεν, ὃς εἰς τοῦτο ἡτοιμάσθη, ἵνα
αὐτὸς φανείς, τὰς ἤδη δεδαπανημένας ἡμῶν καρ-

---

[1] εἰ δέδωκεν אֹ, εἰ δέδωκεν ζητῶμεν C(GL) ; the grammar of
the sentence is emended by G to ἀλλὰ τὴν διαθήκην, ἥν . . .
λαῷ, εἰ δέδωκεν ζητῶμεν.

[2] χειρῶν אC, χειρῶν τὰς πλάκας GL.

XIV

1. So it is. But let us see whether the covenant which he sware to the fathers to give to the people—whether he has given it. He has given it. But they were not worthy to receive it because of their sins. 2. For the Prophet says, " And Moses was fasting on Mount Sinai, to receive the covenant of the Lord for the people, forty days and forty nights. And Moses received from the Lord the two tables, written by the finger of the hand of the Lord in the Spirit "; and Moses took them, and carried them down to give them to the people. 3. And the Lord said to Moses, " Moses, Moses, go down quickly, for thy people whom thou didst bring out of the land of Egypt have broken the Law. And Moses perceived that they had made themselves again molten images, and he cast them out of his hands, and the tables of the covenant of the Lord were broken." 4. Moses received it, but they were not worthy. But learn how we received it. Moses received it when he was a servant, but the Lord himself gave it to us, as the people of the inheritance, by suffering for our sakes. 5. And it was made manifest both that the tale of their sins should be completed in their sins, and that we through Jesus, the Lord who inherits the covenant, should receive it, for he was prepared for this purpose, that when he appeared he might redeem from darkness

δίας τῷ θανάτῳ καὶ παραδεδομένας τῇ τῆς πλάνης ἀνομίᾳ λυτρωσάμενος ἐκ τοῦ σκότους, διάθηται ἐν ἡμῖν διαθήκην λόγῳ. 6. γέγραπται γάρ, πῶς αὐτῷ ὁ πατὴρ ἐντέλλεται, λυτρωσάμενον ἡμᾶς ἐκ τοῦ σκότους ἑτοιμάσαι ἑαυτῷ λαὸν

Is. 42, 6. 7 ἅγιον. 7. λέγει οὖν ὁ προφήτης· Ἐγὼ κύριος, ὁ θεός σου, ἐκάλεσά σε ἐν δικαιοσύνῃ καὶ κρατήσω τῆς χειρός σου καὶ ἐνισχύσω σε, καὶ ἔδωκά σε εἰς διαθήκην γένους, εἰς φῶς ἐθνῶν ἀνοῖξαι ὀφθαλμοὺς τυφλῶν καὶ ἐξαγαγεῖν ἐκ δεσμῶν πεπεδημένους καὶ ἐξ οἴκου φυλακῆς καθημένους ἐν σκότει. γινώσκομεν οὖν, πόθεν ἐλυτρώθημεν.

Is. 49, 6. 7 8. πάλιν ὁ προφήτης λέγει· Ἰδού, τέθεικά σε εἰς φῶς ἐθνῶν, τοῦ εἶναί σε εἰς σωτηρίαν ἕως ἐσχάτου τῆς γῆς, οὕτως λέγει κύριος ὁ λυτρωσάμενός σε θεός.

Is. 61, 1. 2, cf. Luke, 4, 17. 19 9. καὶ πάλιν ὁ προφήτης λέγει· Πνεῦμα κυρίου ἐπ᾽ ἐμέ, οὗ εἵνεκεν ἔχρισέν με εὐαγγελίσασθαι ταπεινοῖς χάριν,[1] ἀπέσταλκέν με ἰάσασθαι τοὺς συντετριμμένους τὴν καρδίαν, κηρῦξαι αἰχμαλώτοις ἄφεσιν καὶ τυφλοῖς ἀνάβλεψιν, καλέσαι ἐνιαυτὸν κυρίου δεκτὸν καὶ ἡμέραν ἀνταποδόσεως, παρακαλέσαι πάντας τοὺς πενθοῦντας.

XV

1. Ἔτι οὖν καὶ περὶ τοῦ σαββάτου γέγραπται ἐν τοῖς δέκα λόγοις, ἐν οἷς ἐλάλησεν ἐν τῷ ὄρει

Exod. 20, 8; Deut. 5, 12, cf. Ps. 23, 4 Σινᾶ πρὸς Μωϋσῆν κατὰ πρόσωπον· Καὶ ἁγιάσατε τὸ σάββατον κυρίου χερσὶν καθαραῖς καὶ καρδίᾳ καθαρᾷ. 2. καὶ ἐν ἑτέρῳ λέγει· Ἐὰν

[1] ταπεινοῖς χάριν G, ταπεινοῖς L, πτωχοῖς א (LXX) om. C.

our hearts which were already paid over to death, and given over to the iniquity of error, and by his word might make a covenant with us. 6. For it is written that the Father enjoins on him that he should redeem us from darkness and prepare a holy people for himself. 7. The Prophet therefore says, "I the Lord thy God did call thee in righteousness, and I will hold thy hands, and I will give thee strength, and I have given thee for a covenant of the people, for a light to the Gentiles, to open the eyes of the blind, and to bring forth from their fetters those that are bound and those that sit in darkness out of the prison house." We know then whence we have been redeemed. 8. Again the Prophet says, "Lo, I have made thee a light for the Gentiles, to be for salvation unto the ends of the earth, thus saith the Lord the God who did redeem thee." 9. And again the Prophet saith, "The Spirit of the Lord is upon me, because he anointed me to preach the Gospel of grace to the humble, he sent me to heal the brokenhearted, to proclaim delivery to the captives, and sight to the blind, to announce a year acceptable to the Lord, and a day of recompense, to comfort all who mourn."

XV

1. FURTHERMORE it was written concerning the Sabbath in the ten words which he spake on Mount Sinai face to face to Moses. "Sanctify also the Sabbath of the Lord with pure hands and a pure heart." 2. And in another place he says, "If my

The Sabbath

THE APOSTOLIC FATHERS

φυλάξωσιν οἱ υἱοί μου τὸ σάββατον, τότε ἐπιθήσω
τὸ ἔλεός μου ἐπ᾽ αὐτούς. 3. τὸ σάββατον λέγει
ἐν ἀρχῇ τῆς κτίσεως· Καὶ ἐποίησεν ὁ θεὸς ἐν
ἓξ ἡμέραις τὰ ἔργα τῶν χειρῶν αὐτοῦ, καὶ συνετέλεσεν ἐν τῇ ἡμέρᾳ τῇ ἑβδόμῃ καὶ κατέπαυσεν ἐν
αὐτῇ καὶ ἡγίασεν αὐτήν. 4. προσέχετε, τέκνα, τί
λέγει τὸ συνετέλεσεν ἐν ἓξ ἡμέραις. τοῦτο λέγει,
ὅτι ἐν ἑξακισχιλίοις ἔτεσιν συντελέσει κύριος
τὰ σύμπαντα· ἡ γὰρ ἡμέρα παρ᾽ αὐτῷ σημαίνει
χίλια ἔτη. αὐτὸς δέ μοι μαρτυρεῖ λέγων· Ἰδού,
ἡμέρα κυρίου ἔσται ὡς χίλια ἔτη. οὐκοῦν, τέκνα,
ἐν ἓξ ἡμέραις, ἐν τοῖς ἑξακισχιλίοις ἔτεσιν συντε-
λεσθήσεται τὰ σύμπαντα. 5. Καὶ κατέπαυσεν
τῇ ἡμέρᾳ τῇ ἑβδόμῃ. τοῦτο λέγει· ὅταν ἐλθὼν
ὁ υἱὸς αὐτοῦ καταργήσει τὸν καιρὸν τοῦ ἀνόμου
καὶ κρινεῖ τοὺς ἀσεβεῖς καὶ ἀλλάξει τὸν ἥλιον
καὶ τὴν σελήνην καὶ τοὺς ἀστέρας, τότε καλῶς
καταπαύσεται ἐν τῇ ἡμέρᾳ τῇ ἑβδόμῃ. 6. πέρας
γέ τοι λέγει· Ἁγιάσεις αὐτὴν χερσὶν καθαραῖς
καὶ καρδίᾳ καθαρᾷ. εἰ οὖν ἦν ὁ θεὸς ἡμέραν
ἡγίασεν νῦν τις δύναται ἁγιάσαι καθαρὸς ὢν τῇ
καρδίᾳ, ἐν πᾶσιν πεπλανήμεθα. 7. ἴδε ὅτι ἄρα
τότε καλῶς καταπαυόμενοι ἁγιάσομεν αὐτήν, ὅτε
δυνησόμεθα αὐτοὶ δικαιωθέντες καὶ ἀπολαβόντες
τὴν ἐπαγγελίαν, μηκέτι οὔσης τῆς ἀνομίας, καινῶν
δὲ γεγονότων πάντων ὑπὸ κυρίου· τότε δυνησόμεθα αὐτὴν ἁγιάσαι, αὐτοὶ ἁγιασθέντες πρῶτον.
8. πέρας γέ τοι λέγει αὐτοῖς· Τὰς νεομηνίας ὑμῶν
καὶ τὰ σάββατα οὐκ ἀνέχομαι. ὁρᾶτε, πῶς λέγει;
οὐ τὰ νῦν σάββατα ἐμοὶ δεκτά, ἀλλὰ ὃ πεποίηκα,
ἐν ᾧ καταπαύσας τὰ πάντα ἀρχὴν ἡμέρας ὀγδόης

Jer.
17. 24. 25,
cf. Ex. 31,
13–17
Gen. 2, 2

Gen. 2, 2

Ps. 90, 4;
II Pet. 3, 8

Gen. 2, 2

Ex. 20, 8

Is. 1, 13

sons keep the Sabbath, then will I bestow my mercy upon them." 3. He speaks of the Sabbath at the beginning of the Creation, "And God made in six days the works of his hands and on the seventh day he made an end, and rested in it and sanctified it." 4. Notice, children, what is the meaning of "He made an end in six days"? He means this: that the Lord will make an end of everything in six thousand years, for a day with him means a thousand years. And he himself is my witness when he says, "Lo, the day of the Lord shall be as a thousand years." So then, children, in six days, that is in six thousand years, everything will be completed. 5. "And he rested on the seventh day." This means, when his Son comes he will destroy the time of the wicked one, and will judge the godless, and will change the sun and the moon and the stars, and then he will truly rest on the seventh day. 6. Furthermore he says, "Thou shalt sanctify it with clean hands and a pure heart." If, then, anyone has at present the power to keep holy the day which God made holy, by being pure in heart, we are altogether deceived. 7. See that we shall indeed keep it holy at that time, when we enjoy true rest, when we shall be able to do so because we have been made righteous ourselves and have received the promise, when there is no more sin, but all things have been made new by the Lord: then we shall be able to keep it holy because we ourselves have first been made holy. 8. Furthermore he says to them, "Your new moons and the sabbaths I cannot away with." Do you see what he means? The present sabbaths are not acceptable to me, but that which I have made, in which I will give rest to all things and make the beginning of an

ποιήσω, ὅ ἐστιν ἄλλου κόσμου ἀρχήν. 9. διὸ
καὶ ἄγομεν τὴν ἡμέραν τὴν ὀγδόην εἰς εὐφροσύνην, ἐν ᾗ καὶ ὁ Ἰησοῦς ἀνέστη ἐκ νεκρῶν καὶ
φανερωθεὶς ἀνέβη εἰς οὐρανούς.

XVI

1. Ἔτι δὲ καὶ περὶ τοῦ ναοῦ ἐρῶ ὑμῖν, ὡς
πλανώμενοι οἱ ταλαίπωροι εἰς τὴν οἰκοδομὴν
ἤλπισαν, καὶ οὐκ ἐπὶ τὸν θεὸν αὐτῶν τὸν ποιήσαντα αὐτούς, ὡς ὄντα οἶκον θεοῦ. 2. σχεδὸν
γὰρ ὡς τὰ ἔθνη ἀφιέρωσαν αὐτὸν ἐν τῷ ναῷ.
ἀλλὰ πῶς λέγει κύριος καταργῶν αὐτόν, μάθετε·
Is. 40, 12 Τίς ἐμέτρησεν τὸν οὐρανὸν σπιθαμῇ ἢ τὴν γῆν δρακί;
Is. 66, 1 οὐκ ἐγώ; λέγει κύριος· Ὁ οὐρανός μοι θρόνος, ἡ δὲ
γῆ ὑποπόδιον τῶν ποδῶν μου· ποῖον οἶκον οἰκο-
δομήσετέ μοι, ἢ τίς τόπος τῆς καταπαύσεώς μου ;
ἐγνώκατε, ὅτι ματαία ἡ ἐλπὶς αὐτῶν. 3. πέρας
Is. 49, 17 γέ τοι πάλιν λέγει· Ἰδού, οἱ καθελόντες τὸν ναὸν
τοῦτον αὐτοὶ αὐτὸν οἰκοδομήσουσιν. 4. γίνεται.
διὰ γὰρ τὸ πολεμεῖν αὐτοὺς καθῃρέθη ὑπὸ τῶν
ἐχθρῶν· νῦν καὶ αὐτοὶ οἱ τῶν ἐχθρῶν ὑπηρέται
ἀνοικοδομήσουσιν αὐτόν. 5. πάλιν ὡς ἔμελλεν
ἡ πόλις καὶ ὁ ναὸς καὶ ὁ λαὸς Ἰσραὴλ παραδίδο-
Enoch 89,
55. 66. 67 σθαι, ἐφανερώθη. λέγει γὰρ ἡ γραφή· Καὶ
ἔσται ἐπ᾽ ἐσχάτων τῶν ἡμερῶν, καὶ παραδώσει
κύριος τὰ πρόβατα τῆς νομῆς καὶ τὴν μάνδραν
καὶ τὸν πύργον αὐτῶν εἰς καταφθοράν. καὶ
ἐγένετο καθ᾽ ἃ ἐλάλησεν κύριος. 6. ζητήσωμεν
δέ, εἰ ἔστιν ναὸς θεοῦ. ἔστιν, ὅπου αὐτὸς λέγει
Dan. 9,
24–27 ? ποιεῖν καὶ καταρτίζειν. γέγραπται γάρ· Καὶ

eighth day, that is the beginning of another world.
9. Wherefore we also celebrate with gladness the
eighth day in which Jesus also rose from the dead,
and was made manifest, and ascended into Heaven.

XVI

1. I WILL also speak with you concerning the The Temple
Temple, and show how the wretched men erred by
putting their hope on the building, and not on the God
who made them, and is the true house of God. 2. For
they consecrated him in the Temple almost like the
heathen. But learn how the Lord speaks, in bringing it to naught, " Who has measured the heaven
with a span, or the earth with his outstretched hand ?
Have not I ? saith the Lord. Heaven is my throne,
and the earth is my footstool, what house will ye
build for me, or what is the place of my rest ? "
You know that their hope was vain. 3. Furthermore
he says again, " Lo, they who destroyed this temple
shall themselves build it." 4. That is happening now.
For owing to the war it was destroyed by the enemy ;
at present even the servants of the enemy will build
it up again. 5. Again, it was made manifest that
the city and the temple and the people of Israel
were to be delivered up. For the Scripture says,
" And it shall come to pass in the last days that the
Lord shall deliver the sheep of his pasture, and the
sheep-fold, and their tower to destruction." And it
took place according to what the Lord said. 6. But
let us inquire if a temple of God exists. Yes, it
exists, where he himself said that he makes and
perfects it. For it is written, " And it shall come to

ἔσται, τῆς ἑβδομάδος συντελουμένης οἰκοδομηθή-
σεται ναὸς θεοῦ ἐνδόξως ἐπὶ τῷ ὀνόματι κυρίου.
7. εὑρίσκω οὖν, ὅτι ἔστιν ναός. πῶς οὖν οἰκοδο-
μηθήσεται ἐπὶ τῷ ὀνόματι κυρίου, μάθετε. πρὸ
τοῦ ἡμᾶς πιστεῦσαι τῷ θεῷ ἦν ἡμῶν τὸ κατοικητήριον τῆς καρδίας φθαρτὸν καὶ ἀσθενές, ὡς
ἀληθῶς οἰκοδομητὸς ναὸς διὰ χειρός, ὅτι ἦν πλήρης
μὲν εἰδωλολατρείας καὶ ἦν οἶκος δαιμονίων διὰ τὸ

Dan. 9,
24–27 ?

ποιεῖν, ὅσα ἦν ἐναντία τῷ θεῷ. 8. Οἰκοδομηθή-
σεται δὲ ἐπὶ τῷ ὀνόματι κυρίου. προσέχετε δέ,
ἵνα ὁ ναὸς τοῦ κυρίου ἐνδόξως οἰκοδομηθῇ. πῶς,
μάθετε. λαβόντες τὴν ἄφεσιν τῶν ἁμαρτιῶν καὶ
ἐλπίσαντες ἐπὶ τὸ ὄνομα ἐγενόμεθα καινοί, πάλιν
ἐξ ἀρχῆς κτιζόμενοι· διὸ ἐν τῷ κατοικητηρίῳ ἡμῶν
ἀληθῶς ὁ θεὸς κατοικεῖ ἐν ἡμῖν. 9. πῶς; ὁ λόγος
αὐτοῦ τῆς πίστεως, ἡ κλῆσις αὐτοῦ τῆς ἐπαγγελίας, ἡ σοφία τῶν δικαιωμάτων, αἱ ἐντολαὶ τῆς
διδαχῆς, αὐτὸς ἐν ἡμῖν προφητεύων, αὐτὸς ἐν ἡμῖν
κατοικῶν, τοὺς τῷ θανάτῳ δεδουλωμένους[1] ἀνοίγων
ἡμῖν τὴν θύραν τοῦ ναοῦ, ὅ ἐστιν στόμα, μετάνοιαν
διδοὺς ἡμῖν, εἰσάγει εἰς τὸν ἄφθαρτον ναόν. 10. ὁ
γὰρ ποθῶν σωθῆναι βλέπει οὐκ εἰς τὸν ἄνθρωπον,
ἀλλ’ εἰς τὸν ἐν αὐτῷ κατοικοῦντα καὶ λαλοῦντα, ἐπ’
αὐτῷ ἐκπλησσόμενος, ἐπὶ τῷ μηδέποτε μήτε τοῦ
λέγοντος τὰ ῥήματα ἀκηκοέναι ἐκ τοῦ στόματος
μήτε αὐτός ποτε ἐπιτεθυμηκέναι ἀκούειν. τοῦτό
ἐστιν πνευματικὸς ναὸς οἰκοδομούμενος τῷ κυρίῳ.

[1] τοὺς . . . δεδουλωμένους CGL, τοῖς δεδουλωμένοις ℵ (probably
a correction of the unexpected accusative).

pass when the week is ended that a temple of ·God shall be built gloriously in the name of the Lord." 7. I find then that a temple exists. Learn then how it will be built in the name of the Lord. Before we believed in God the habitation of our heart was corrupt and weak, like a temple really built with hands, because it was full of idolatry, and was the house of demons through doing things which were contrary to God. 8. "But it shall be built in the name of the Lord." Now give heed, in order that the temple of the Lord may be built gloriously. Learn in what way. When we received the remission of sins, and put our hope on the Name, we became new, being created again from the beginning; wherefore God truly dwells in us, in the habitation which we are. 9. How? His word of faith, the calling of his promise, the wisdom of the ordinances, the commands of the teaching, himself prophesying in us, himself dwelling in us, by opening the door of the temple (that is the mouth) to us, giving repentance to us, and thus he leads us, who have been enslaved to death into the incorruptible temple. 10. For he who desires to be saved looks not at the man, but at him who dwells and speaks in him, and· is amazed at him, for he has never either heard him speak such words with his mouth, nor has he himself ever desired to hear them. This is a spiritual temple being built for the Lord.

XVII

1. Ἐφ’ ὅσον ἦν ἐν δυνατῷ καὶ ἁπλότητι δηλῶσαι ὑμῖν, ἐλπίζει μου ἡ ψυχὴ τῇ ἐπιθυμίᾳ μου μὴ παραλελοιπέναι[1] τι τῶν ἀνηκόντων εἰς σωτηρίαν. 2. ἐὰν γὰρ περὶ τῶν ἐνεστώτων ἢ μελλόντων γράφω ὑμῖν, οὐ μὴ νοήσητε διὰ τὸ ἐν παραβολαῖς κεῖσθαι. ταῦτα μὲν οὕτως.[2]

XVIII

1. Μεταβῶμεν δὲ καὶ ἐπὶ ἑτέραν γνῶσιν καὶ διδαχήν. Ὁδοὶ δύο εἰσὶν διδαχῆς καὶ ἐξουσίας, ἥ τε τοῦ φωτὸς καὶ ἡ τοῦ σκότους. διαφορὰ δὲ πολλὴ τῶν δύο ὁδῶν. ἐφ’ ἧς μὲν γάρ εἰσιν τεταγμένοι φωταγωγοὶ ἄγγελοι τοῦ θεοῦ, ἐφ’ ἧς δὲ ἄγγελοι τοῦ σατανᾶ. 2. καὶ ὁ μέν ἐστιν κύριος ἀπὸ αἰώνων καὶ εἰς τοὺς αἰῶνας, ὁ δὲ ἄρχων καιροῦ τοῦ νῦν τῆς ἀνομίας.

XIX

1. Ἡ οὖν ὁδὸς τοῦ φωτός ἐστιν αὕτη· ἐάν τις θέλων ὁδὸν ὁδεύειν ἐπὶ τὸν ὡρισμένον τόπον, σπεύσῃ τοῖς ἔργοις αὐτοῦ. ἔστιν οὖν ἡ δοθεῖσα ἡμῖν γνῶσις τοῦ περιπατεῖν ἐν αὐτῇ τοιαύτη. 2. ἀγαπήσεις τὸν ποιήσαντά σε, φοβηθήσῃ τόν σε πλά-

---

[1] τῇ ἐπιθυμίᾳ μου μὴ παραλελοιπέναι τι τῶν ἀνηκόντων εἰς σωτηρίαν ℵͨG, μὴ παραλελοιπέναι τι ℵ*C.

[2] With the addition of the doxology the Latin version comes here to an end.

XVII

1. So far as possibility and simplicity allow an explanation to be given to you my soul hopes that none of the things which are necessary for salvation have been omitted, according to my desire. 2. For if I write to you concerning things present or things to come, you will not understand because they are hid in parables. This then suffices.

XVIII

1. Now[1] let us pass on to another lesson and The two teaching. There are two Ways of teaching and Ways power, one of Light and one of Darkness. And there is a great difference between the two Ways. For over the one are set light-bringing angels of God, but over the other angels of Satan. 2. And the one is Lord from eternity and to eternity, and the other is the ruler of the present time of iniquity.

XIX

1. THE Way of Light is this: if any man desire The Way to journey to the appointed place, let him be zealous of Light in his works. Therefore the knowledge given to us of this kind that we may walk in it is as follows:—
2. Thou shalt love thy maker, thou shalt fear

---

[1] Here begins the section taken from the " Two Ways," cf. p. 309.

σαντα, δοξάσεις τόν σε λυτρωσάμενον ἐκ θανάτου·
ἔσῃ ἁπλοῦς τῇ καρδίᾳ καὶ πλούσιος τῷ πνεύματι·
οὐ κολληθήσῃ μετὰ τῶν πορευομένων ἐν ὁδῷ
θανάτου, μισήσεις πᾶν, ὃ οὐκ ἔστιν ἀρεστὸν τῷ
θεῷ, μισήσεις πᾶσαν ὑπόκρισιν· οὐ μὴ ἐγκαταλίπῃς ἐντολὰς κυρίου. 3. οὐχ ὑψώσεις σεαυτόν,
ἔσῃ δὲ ταπεινόφρων κατὰ πάντα· οὐκ ἀρεῖς ἐπὶ
σεαυτὸν δόξαν. οὐ λήμψῃ βουλὴν πονηρὰν κατὰ
τοῦ πλησίον σου, οὐ δώσεις τῇ ψυχῇ σου θράσος.
4. οὐ πορνεύσεις, οὐ μοιχεύσεις, οὐ παιδοφθορήσεις. οὐ μή σου ὁ λόγος τοῦ θεοῦ ἐξέλθῃ ἐν ἀκα-
θαρσίᾳ τινῶν. οὐ λήμψῃ πρόσωπον ἐλέγξαι τινὰ
ἐπὶ παραπτώματι. ἔσῃ πραΰς, ἔσῃ ἡσύχιος, ἔσῃ
τρέμων τοὺς λόγους οὓς ἤκουσας. οὐ μνησικακήσεις
τῷ ἀδελφῷ σου. 5. οὐ μὴ διψυχήσῃς, πότερον ἔσται
Deut. 5, 11   ἢ οὔ. οὐ μὴ λάβῃς ἐπὶ ματαίῳ τὸ ὄνομα κυρίου.
ἀγαπήσεις τὸν πλησίον σου ὑπὲρ τὴν ψυχήν σου.
οὐ φονεύσεις τέκνον ἐν φθορᾷ, οὐδὲ πάλιν
γεννηθὲν ἀποκτενεῖς. οὐ μὴ ἄρῃς τὴν χεῖρά σου
ἀπὸ τοῦ υἱοῦ σου ἢ ἀπὸ τῆς θυγατρός σου, ἀλλὰ
ἀπὸ νεότητος διδάξεις φόβον θεοῦ. 6. οὐ μὴ
γένῃ ἐπιθυμῶν τὰ τοῦ πλησίον σου, οὐ μὴ γένῃ
πλεονέκτης. οὐδὲ κολληθήσῃ ἐκ ψυχῆς σου μετὰ
ὑψηλῶν, ἀλλὰ μετὰ ταπεινῶν καὶ δικαίων ἀναστραφήσῃ. τὰ συμβαίνοντά σοι ἐνεργήματα ὡς
ἀγαθὰ προσδέξῃ, εἰδώς, ὅτι ἄνευ θεοῦ οὐδὲν
γίνεται. 7. οὐκ ἔσῃ διγνώμων οὐδὲ γλωσσώδης,[1]

---

[1] γλωσσώδης ℵ, δίγλωσσος CG ; G also adds παγὶς γὰρ
θανάτου ἐστιν ἡ διγλωσσία (from *Apost. Const.*) "for to be
double-tongued is the snare of death."

thy Creator, thou shalt glorify Him who redeemed
thee from death, thou shalt be simple in heart, and
rich in spirit ; thou shalt not join thyself to those
who walk in the way of death, thou shalt hate all
that is not pleasing to God, thou shalt hate all
hypocrisy ; thou shalt not desert the commandments
of the Lord.   3. Thou shalt not exalt thyself, but
shall be humble-minded in all things ; thou shalt not
take glory to thyself.   Thou shalt form no evil plan
against thy neighbour, thou shalt not let thy soul be
froward.   4. Thou shalt not commit fornication,
thou shalt not commit adultery, thou shalt not commit sodomy.   Thou shalt not let the word of God
depart from thee among the impurity of any men.
Thou shalt not respect persons in the reproving of
transgression.   Thou shalt be meek, thou shalt be
quiet, thou shalt fear the words which thou hast
heard.   Thou shalt not bear malice against thy
brother.   5. Thou shalt not be in two minds whether
it shall be or not.   "Thou shalt not take the name of
the Lord in vain."   Thou shalt love thy neighbour
more than thy own life.   Thou shalt not procure
abortion, thou shalt not commit infanticide.   Thou
shalt not withhold thy hand from thy son or from
thy daughter, but shalt teach them the fear of God
from their youth up.   6. Thou shalt not covet thy
neighbour's goods, thou shalt not be avaricious.
Thou shalt not be joined in soul with the haughty
but shalt converse with humble and righteous men.
Thou shalt receive the trials that befall thee as good,
knowing that nothing happens without God.   7. Thou
shalt not be double-minded or talkative.   Thou

ὑποταγήσῃ κυρίοις ὡς τύπῳ θεοῦ ἐν αἰσχύνῃ καὶ
φόβῳ· οὐ μὴ ἐπιτάξῃς δούλῳ σου ἢ παιδίσκῃ ἐν
πικρίᾳ, τοῖς ἐπὶ τὸν αὐτὸν θεὸν ἐλπίζουσιν, μή
ποτε οὐ μὴ φοβηθήσονται τὸν ἐπ᾽ ἀμφοτέροις
θεόν· ὅτι οὐκ ἦλθεν κατὰ πρόσωπον καλέσαι, ἀλλ᾽
ἐφ᾽ οὓς τὸ πνεῦμα ἡτοίμασεν. 8. κοινωνήσεις ἐν
πᾶσιν τῷ πλησίον σου καὶ οὐκ ἐρεῖς ἴδια εἶναι·
εἰ γὰρ ἐν τῷ ἀφθάρτῳ κοινωνοί ἐστε, πόσῳ μᾶλλον
ἐν τοῖς φθαρτοῖς ; οὐκ ἔσῃ πρόγλωσσος· παγὶς
γὰρ τὸ στόμα θανάτου. ὅσον δύνασαι, ὑπὲρ τῆς
ψυχῆς σου ἁγνεύσεις. 9. μὴ γίνου πρὸς μὲν τὸ
λαβεῖν ἐκτείνων τὰς χεῖρας, πρὸς δὲ τὸ δοῦναι
Deut. 32, 10;
Ps. 17, 8,
Prov. 7, 2 συσπῶν. ἀγαπήσεις ὡς κόρην τοῦ ὀφθαλμοῦ σου
πάντα τὸν λαλοῦντά σοι τὸν λόγον κυρίου.
10. μνησθήσῃ ἡμέραν κρίσεως νυκτὸς καὶ ἡμέρας,
καὶ ἐκζητήσεις καθ᾽ ἑκάστην ἡμέραν τὰ πρόσωπα
τῶν ἁγίων, ἢ διὰ λόγου κοπιῶν καὶ πορευόμενος
εἰς τὸ παρακαλέσαι καὶ μελετῶν εἰς τὸ σῶσαι
ψυχὴν τῷ λόγῳ, ἢ διὰ τῶν χειρῶν σου ἐργάσῃ
εἰς λύτρωσιν ἁμαρτιῶν σου. 11. οὐ διστάσεις
Deut. 12, 32 δοῦναι οὐδὲ διδοὺς γογγύσεις· γνώσῃ δέ, τίς ὁ τοῦ
μισθοῦ καλὸς ἀνταποδότης. φυλάξεις ἃ παρέ-
λαβες, μήτε προστιθεὶς μήτε ἀφαιρῶν. εἰς τέλος
Deut. 1, 16; μισήσεις τὸ πονηρόν. κρινεῖς δικαίως. 12. οὐ
Prov. 31, 9 ποιήσεις σχίσμα, εἰρηνεύσεις δὲ μαχομένους
συναγαγών. ἐξομολογήσῃ ἐπὶ ἁμαρτίαις σου.
οὐ προσήξεις ἐπὶ προσευχὴν ἐν συνειδήσει πονηρᾷ.
αὕτη ἐστὶν ἡ ὁδὸς τοῦ φωτός.

shalt obey thy masters as a type of God in modesty and fear; thou shalt not command in bitterness thy slave or handmaid who hope on the same God, lest they cease to fear the God who is over you both; for he came not to call men with respect of persons, but those whom the Spirit prepared. 8. Thou shalt share all things with thy neighbour and shall not say that they are thy own property; for if you are sharers in that which is incorruptible, how much more in that which is corruptible? Thou shalt not be forward to speak, for the mouth is a snare of death. So far as thou canst, thou shalt keep thy soul pure. 9. Be not one who stretches out the hands to take, and shuts them when it comes to giving. Thou shalt love "as the apple of thine eye" all who speak to thee the word of the Lord. 10. Thou shalt remember the day of judgment day and night, and thou shalt seek each day the society of the saints, either labouring by speech, and going out to exhort, and striving to save souls by the word, or working with thine hands for the ransom of thy sins. 11. Thou shalt not hesitate to give, and when thou givest thou shalt not grumble, but thou shalt know who is the good paymaster of the reward. "Thou shalt keep the precepts" which thou hast received, "adding nothing and taking nothing away." Thou shalt utterly hate evil. "Thou shalt give righteous judgment." 12. Thou shalt not cause quarrels, but shalt bring together and reconcile those that strive. Thou shalt confess thy sins. Thou shalt not betake thyself to prayer with an evil conscience. This is the Way of Light.

XX

1. Ἡ δὲ τοῦ μέλανος ὁδός ἐστιν σκολιὰ καὶ κατάρας μεστή. ὁδὸς γάρ ἐστιν θανάτου αἰωνίου μετὰ τιμωρίας, ἐν ᾗ ἐστιν τὰ ἀπολλύντα τὴν ψυχὴν αὐτῶν· εἰδωλολατρεία, θρασύτης, ὕψος δυνάμεως, ὑπόκρισις, διπλοκαρδία, μοιχεία, φόνος, ἁρπαγή, ὑπερηφανία, παράβασις, δόλος, κακία, αὐθάδεια, φαρμακεία, μαγεία, πλεονεξία, ἀφοβία θεοῦ. 2. διῶκται τῶν ἀγαθῶν, μισοῦντες ἀλήθειαν, ἀγαπῶντες ψεῦδος, οὐ γινώσκοντες μισθὸν δικαιο-

Rom. 12, 9

σύνης, οὐ κολλώμενοι ἀγαθῷ, οὐ κρίσει δικαίᾳ, χήρᾳ καὶ ὀρφανῷ οὐ προσέχοντες, ἀγρυπνοῦντες οὐκ εἰς φόβον θεοῦ, ἀλλ' ἐπὶ τὸ πονηρόν, ὧν μακρὰν καὶ

Ps. 4. 2
Is. 1, 23

πόρρω πραΰτης καὶ ὑπομονή, ἀγαπῶντες μάταια, διώκοντες ἀνταπόδομα, οὐκ ἐλεῶντες πτωχόν, οὐ πονοῦντες ἐπὶ καταπονουμένῳ, εὐχερεῖς ἐν καταλαλιᾷ, οὐ γινώσκοντες τὸν ποιήσαντα αὐτούς, φονεῖς τέκνων, φθορεῖς πλάσματος θεοῦ, ἀποστρεφόμενοι τὸν ἐνδεόμενον, καταπονοῦντες τὸν θλιβόμενον, πλουσίων παράκλητοι, πενήτων ἄνομοι κριταί, πανθαμάρτητοι.

XXI

1. Καλὸν οὖν ἐστὶν μαθόντα τὰ δικαιώματα τοῦ κυρίου, ὅσα γέγραπται, ἐν τούτοις περιπατεῖν. ὁ γὰρ ταῦτα ποιῶν ἐν τῇ βασιλείᾳ τοῦ θεοῦ δοξασθήσεται· ὁ ἐκεῖνα ἐκλεγόμενος μετὰ τῶν ἔργων αὐτοῦ συναπολεῖται. διὰ τοῦτο ἀνάστασις,

XX

1. BUT the Way of the Black One is crooked and full of cursing, for it is the way of death eternal with punishment, and in it are the things that destroy their soul : idolatry, frowardness, arrogance of power, hypocrisy, double-heartedness, adultery, murder, robbery, pride, transgression, fraud, malice, self-sufficiency, enchantments, magic, covetousness, the lack of the fear of God ; 2. persecutors of the good, haters of the truth, lovers of lies, knowing not the reward of righteousness, who "cleave not to the good," nor to righteous judgment, who attend not to the cause of the widow and orphan, spending wakeful nights not in the fear of God, but in the pursuit of vice, from whom meekness and patience are far and distant, "loving vanity, seeking rewards," without pity for the poor, working not for him who is oppressed with toil, prone to evil speaking, without knowledge of their Maker, murderers of children, corrupters of God's creation, turning away the needy, oppressing the afflicted, advocates of the rich, unjust judges of the poor, altogether sinful.

XXI

1. IT is good therefore that he who has learned the ordinances of the Lord as many as have been written should walk in them. For he who does these things shall be glorified in the kingdom of God, and he who chooses the others shall perish with his works. For this reason there is a resurrec-

διὰ τοῦτο ἀνταπόδομα. 2. ἐρωτῶ τοὺς ὑπερέ-
χοντας, εἴ τινά μου γνώμης ἀγαθῆς λαμβάνετε
συμβουλίαν· ἔχετε μεθ᾽ ἑαυτῶν εἰς οὓς ἐργάσησθε
τὸ καλόν· μὴ ἐλλείπητε. 3. ἐγγὺς ἡ ἡμέρα ἐν ᾗ
Is. 40, 10 συναπολεῖται πάντα τῷ πονηρῷ· ἐγγὺς ὁ κύριος
καὶ ὁ μισθὸς αὐτοῦ. 4. ἔτι καὶ ἔτι ἐρωτῶ ὑμᾶς·
ἑαυτῶν γίνεσθε νομοθέται ἀγαθοί, ἑαυτῶν μένετε
σύμβουλοι πιστοί, ἄρατε ἐξ ὑμῶν πᾶσαν ὑπόκρισιν. 5. ὁ δὲ θεός, ὁ τοῦ παντὸς κόσμου
κυριεύων, δῴη ὑμῖν σοφίαν, σύνεσιν, ἐπιστήμην,
γνῶσιν τῶν δικαιωμάτων αὐτοῦ, ὑπομονήν.
6. γίνεσθε δὲ θεοδίδακτοι, ἐκζητοῦντες τί ζητεῖ
κύριος ἀφ᾽ ὑμῶν, καὶ ποιεῖτε ἵνα εὑρεθῆτε ἐν
ἡμέρᾳ κρίσεως. 7. εἰ δὲ τίς ἐστιν ἀγαθοῦ μνεία,
μνημονεύετέ μου μελετῶντες ταῦτα, ἵνα καὶ ἡ
ἐπιθυμία καὶ ἡ ἀγρυπνία εἴς τι ἀγαθὸν χωρήσῃ.
ἐρωτῶ ὑμᾶς, χάριν αἰτούμενος. 8. ἕως ἔτι τὸ
καλὸν σκεῦός ἐστιν μεθ᾽ ὑμῶν, μὴ ἐλλείπητε
μηδενὶ ἑαυτῶν,[1] ἀλλὰ συνεχῶς ἐκζητεῖτε ταῦτα καὶ
ἀναπληροῦτε πᾶσαν ἐντολήν· ἔστιν γὰρ ἄξια.
9. διὸ μᾶλλον ἐσπούδασα γράψαι ἀφ᾽ ὧν ἠδυνήθην, εἰς τὸ εὐφρᾶναι ὑμᾶς. σώζεσθε, ἀγάπης
τέκνα καὶ εἰρήνης. ὁ κύριος τῆς δόξης καὶ πάσης
χάριτος μετὰ τοῦ πνεύματος ὑμῶν.

Ἐπιστολὴ Βαρνάβα.

[1] αὐτῶν GL, ἑαυτῶν NC.

tion, for this reason there is a recompense. 2. I beseech those who are in high positions, if you will receive any counsel of my goodwill, have among yourselves those to whom you may do good; fail not. 3. The day is at hand when all things shall perish with the Evil one; "The Lord and his reward is at hand." 4. I beseech you again and again be good lawgivers to each other, remain faithful counsellors of each other, remove from yourselves all hypocrisy. 5. Now may God, who is the Lord over all the world, give you wisdom, understanding, prudence, knowledge of his ordinances, patience. 6. And be taught of God, seeking out what the Lord requires from you, and see that ye be found faithful in the day of Judgment. 7. If there is any memory of good, meditate on these things and remember me, that my desire and my watchfulness may find some good end. I beseech you asking it of your favour. 8. While the fair vessel[1] is with you fail not in any of them, but seek these things diligently, and fulfil every commandment; for these things are worthy. 9. Wherefore I was the more zealous to write to you of my ability, to give you gladness. May you gain salvation, children of love and peace. The Lord of glory and of all grace be with your spirit.

The Epistle of Barnabas.

[1] *i.e.* while you are in the body.

*Printed in Great Britain by
Fletcher & Son Ltd,
Norwich*

THE LOEB CLASSICAL LIBRARY

VOLUMES ALREADY PUBLISHED

Latin Authors

AMMIANUS MARCELLINUS. Translated by J. C. Rolfe. 3 Vols.

APULEIUS: THE GOLDEN ASS (METAMORPHOSES). W. Adlington (1566). Revised by S. Gaselee.

ST. AUGUSTINE: CITY OF GOD. 7 Vols. Vol. I. G. E. McCracken. Vols. II and VII. W. M. Green. Vol. III. D. Wiesen. Vol. IV. P. Levine. Vol. V. E. M. Sanford and W. M. Green. Vol. VI. W. C. Greene.

ST. AUGUSTINE, CONFESSIONS OF. W. Watts (1631). 2 Vols.

ST. AUGUSTINE, SELECT LETTERS. J. H. Baxter.

AUSONIUS. H. G. Evelyn White. 2 Vols.

BEDE. J. E. King. 2 Vols.

BOETHIUS: TRACTS and DE CONSOLATIONE PHILOSOPHIAE. Rev. H. F. Stewart and E. K. Rand. Revised by S. J. Tester.

CAESAR: ALEXANDRIAN, AFRICAN and SPANISH WARS. A. G. Way.

CAESAR: CIVIL WARS. A. G. Peskett.

CAESAR: GALLIC WAR. H. J. Edwards.

CATO: DE RE RUSTICA. VARRO: DE RE RUSTICA. H. B. Ash and W. D. Hooper.

CATULLUS. F. W. Cornish. TIBULLUS. J. B. Postgate. PERVIGILIUM VENERIS. J. W. Mackail.

CELSUS: DE MEDICINA. W. G. Spencer. 3 Vols.

CICERO: BRUTUS and ORATOR. G. L. Hendrickson and H. M. Hubbell.

[CICERO]: AD HERENNIUM. H. Caplan.

CICERO: DE ORATORE, etc. 2 Vols. Vol. I. DE ORATORE, Books I and II. E. W. Sutton and H. Rackham. Vol. II. DE ORATORE, Book III. DE FATO; PARADOXA STOICORUM; DE PARTITIONE ORATORIA. H. Rackham.

CICERO: DE FINIBUS. H. Rackham.

CICERO: DE INVENTIONE, etc. H. M. Hubbell.

CICERO: DE NATURA DEORUM and ACADEMICA. H. Rackham.

CICERO: DE OFFICIIS. Walter Miller.

CICERO: DE REPUBLICA and DE LEGIBUS. Clinton W. Keyes.

CICERO: DE SENECTUTE, DE AMICITIA, DE DIVINATIONE. W. A. Falconer.

CICERO: IN CATILINAM, PRO FLACCO, PRO MURENA, PRO SULLA. New version by C. Macdonald.

CICERO: LETTERS TO ATTICUS. E. O. Winstedt. 3 Vols.

CICERO: LETTERS TO HIS FRIENDS. W. Glynn Williams, M. Cary, M. Henderson. 4 Vols.

CICERO: PHILIPPICS. W. C. A. Ker.

CICERO: PRO ARCHIA, POST REDITUM, DE DOMO, DE HARUSPICUM RESPONSIS, PRO PLANCIO. N. H. Watts.

CICERO: PRO CAECINA, PRO LEGE MANILIA, PRO CLUENTIO, PRO RABIRIO. H. Grose Hodge.

CICERO: PRO CAELIO, DE PROVINCIIS CONSULARIBUS, PRO BALBO. R. Gardner.

CICERO: PRO MILONE, IN PISONEM, PRO SCAURO, PRO FONTEIO, PRO RABIRIO POSTUMO, PRO MARCELLO, PRO LIGARIO, PRO REGE DEIOTARO. N. H. Watts.

CICERO: PRO QUINCTIO, PRO ROSCIO AMERINO, PRO ROSCIO COMOEDO, CONTRA RULLUM. J. H. Freese.

CICERO: PRO SESTIO, IN VATINIUM. R. Gardner.

CICERO: TUSCULAN DISPUTATIONS. J. E. King.

CICERO: VERRINE ORATIONS. L. H. G. Greenwood. 2 Vols.

CLAUDIAN. M. Platnauer. 2 Vols.

COLUMELLA: DE RE RUSTICA. DE ARBORIBUS. H. B. Ash, E. S. Forster and E. Heffner. 3 Vols.

CURTIUS, Q.: HISTORY OF ALEXANDER. J. C. Rolfe. 2 Vols.

FLORUS. E. S. Forster.

FRONTINUS: STRATAGEMS and AQUEDUCTS. C. E. Bennett and M. B. McElwain.

FRONTO: CORRESPONDENCE. C. R. Haines. 2 Vols.

GELLIUS. J. C. Rolfe. 3 Vols.

HORACE: ODES and EPODES. C. E. Bennett.

HORACE: SATIRES, EPISTLES, ARS POETICA. H. R. Fairclough.

JEROME: SELECTED LETTERS. F. A. Wright.

JUVENAL and PERSIUS. G. G. Ramsay.

LIVY. B. O. Foster, F. G. Moore, Evan T. Sage, and A. C. Schlesinger and R. M. Geer (General Index). 14 Vols.

LUCAN. J. D. Duff.

LUCRETIUS. W. H. D. Rouse. Revised by M. F. Smith.

MANILIUS. G. P. Goold.

MARTIAL. W. C. A. Ker. 2 Vols. Revised by E. H. Warmington.

MINOR LATIN POETS: from PUBLILIUS SYRUS to RUTILIUS NAMATIANUS, including GRATTIUS, CALPURNIUS SICULUS, NEMESIANUS, AVIANUS and others, with " Aetna " and the " Phoenix." J. Wight Duff and Arnold M. Duff. 2 Vols.

2

MINUCIUS FELIX. Cf. TERTULLIAN.

NEPOS CORNELIUS. J. C. Rolfe.

OVID: THE ART OF LOVE and OTHER POEMS. J. H. Mosley. Revised by G. P. Goold.

OVID: FASTI. Sir James G. Frazer

OVID: HEROIDES and AMORES. Grant Showerman. Revised by G. P. Goold

OVID: METAMORPHOSES. F. J. Miller. 2 Vols. Revised by G. P. Goold.

OVID: TRISTIA and EX PONTO. A. L. Wheeler.

PERSIUS. Cf. JUVENAL.

PERVIGILIUM VENERIS. Cf. CATULLUS.

PETRONIUS. M. Heseltine. SENECA: APOCOLOCYNTOSIS. W. H. D. Rouse. Revised by E. H. Warmington.

PHAEDRUS and BABRIUS (Greek). B. E. Perry.

PLAUTUS. Paul Nixon. 5 Vols.

PLINY: LETTERS, PANEGYRICUS. Betty Radice. 2 Vols.

PLINY: NATURAL HISTORY. 10 Vols. Vols. I–V and IX. H. Rackham. VI.–VIII. W. H. S. Jones. X. D. E. Eichholz.

PROPERTIUS. H. E. Butler.

PRUDENTIUS. H. J. Thomson. 2 Vols.

QUINTILIAN. H. E. Butler. 4 Vols.

REMAINS OF OLD LATIN. E. H. Warmington. 4 Vols. Vol. I. (ENNIUS AND CAECILIUS) Vol. II. (LIVIUS, NAEVIUS PACUVIUS, ACCIUS) Vol. III. (LUCILIUS and LAWS OF XII TABLES) Vol. IV. (ARCHAIC INSCRIPTIONS)

RES GESTAE DIVI AUGUSTI. Cf. VELLEIUS PATERCULUS.

SALLUST. J. C. Rolfe.

SCRIPTORES HISTORIAE AUGUSTAE. D. Magie. 3 Vols.

SENECA, THE ELDER: CONTROVERSIAE, SUASORIAE. M. Winterbottom. 2 Vols.

SENECA: APOCOLOCYNTOSIS. Cf. PETRONIUS.

SENECA: EPISTULAE MORALES. R. M. Gummere. 3 Vols.

SENECA: MORAL ESSAYS. J. W. Basore. 3 Vols.

SENECA: TRAGEDIES. F. J. Miller. 2 Vols.

SENECA: NATURALES QUAESTIONES. T. H. Corcoran. 2 Vols.

SIDONIUS: POEMS and LETTERS. W. B. Anderson. 2 Vols.

SILIUS ITALICUS. J. D. Duff. 2 Vols.

STATIUS. J. H. Mozley. 2 Vols.

SUETONIUS. J. C. Rolfe. 2 Vols.

TACITUS: DIALOGUS. Sir Wm. Peterson. AGRICOLA and GERMANIA. Maurice Hutton. Revised by M. Winterbottom, R. M. Ogilvie, E. H. Warmington.

TACITUS: HISTORIES and ANNALS. C. H. Moore and J. Jackson. 4 Vols.

3

TERENCE. John Sargeaunt. 2 Vols.

TERTULLIAN: APOLOGIA and DE SPECTACULIS. T. R. Glover. MINUCIUS FELIX. G. H. Rendall.

TIBULLUS. Cf. CATULLUS.

VALERIUS FLACCUS. J. H. Mozley.

VARRO: DE LINGUA LATINA. R. G. Kent. 2 Vols.

VELLEIUS PATERCULUS and RES GESTAE DIVI AUGUSTI. F. W. Shipley.

VIRGIL. H. R. Fairclough. 2 Vols.

VITRUVIUS: DE ARCHITECTURA. F. Granger. 2 Vols.

Greek Authors

ACHILLES TATIUS. S. Gaselee.

AELIAN: ON THE NATURE OF ANIMALS. A. F. Scholfield. 3 Vols.

AENEAS TACTICUS. ASCLEPIODOTUS and ONASANDER. The Illinois Greek Club.

AESCHINES. C. D. Adams.

AESCHYLUS. H. Weir Smyth. 2 Vols.

ALCIPHRON, AELIAN, PHILOSTRATUS: LETTERS. A. R. Benner and F. H. Fobes.

ANDOCIDES, ANTIPHON. Cf. MINOR ATTIC ORATORS.

APOLLODORUS. Sir James G. Frazer. 2 Vols.

APOLLONIUS RHODIUS. R. C. Seaton.

APOSTOLIC FATHERS. Kirsopp Lake. 2 Vols.

APPIAN: ROMAN HISTORY. Horace White. 4 Vols.

ARATUS. Cf. CALLIMACHUS.

ARISTIDES: ORATIONS. C. A. Behr. Vol. I.

ARISTOPHANES. Benjamin Bickley Rogers. 3 Vols. Verse trans.

ARISTOTLE: ART OF RHETORIC. J. H. Freese.

ARISTOTLE: ATHENIAN CONSTITUTION, EUDEMIAN ETHICS, VICES AND VIRTUES. H. Rackham.

ARISTOTLE: GENERATION OF ANIMALS. A. L. Peck.

ARISTOTLE: HISTORIA ANIMALIUM. A. L. Peck. Vols. I.–II.

ARISTOTLE: METAPHYSICS. H. Tredennick. 2 Vols.

ARISTOTLE: METEOROLOGICA. H. D. P. Lee.

ARISTOTLE: MINOR WORKS. W. S. Hett. On Colours, On Things Heard, On Physiognomies, On Plants, On Marvellous Things Heard, Mechanical Problems, On Indivisible Lines, On Situations and Names of Winds, On Melissus, Xenophanes, and Gorgias.

ARISTOTLE: NICOMACHEAN ETHICS. H. Rackham.

4

ARISTOTLE: OECONOMICA and MAGNA MORALIA. G. C. Armstrong (with METAPHYSICS, Vol. II).

ARISTOTLE: ON THE HEAVENS. W. K. C. Guthrie.

ARISTOTLE: ON THE SOUL, PARVA NATURALIA, ON BREATH. W. S. Hett.

ARISTOTLE: CATEGORIES, ON INTERPRETATION, PRIOR ANALYTICS. H. P. Cooke and H. Tredennick.

ARISTOTLE: POSTERIOR ANALYTICS, TOPICS. H. Tredennick and E. S. Forster.

ARISTOTLE: ON SOPHISTICAL REFUTATIONS.
On Coming to be and Passing Away, On the Cosmos. E. S. Forster and D. J. Furley.

ARISTOTLE: PARTS OF ANIMALS. A. L. Peck; MOTION AND PROGRESSION OF ANIMALS. E. S. Forster.

ARISTOTLE: PHYSICS. Rev. P. Wicksteed and F. M. Cornford. 2 Vols.

ARISTOTLE: POETICS and LONGINUS. W. Hamilton Fyfe; DEMETRIUS ON STYLE. W. Rhys Roberts.

ARISTOTLE: POLITICS. H. Rackham.

ARISTOTLE: PROBLEMS. W. S. Hett. 2 Vols.

ARISTOTLE: RHETORICA AD ALEXANDRUM (with PROBLEMS. Vol. II). H. Rackham.

ARRIAN: HISTORY OF ALEXANDER and INDICA. Rev. E. Iliffe Robson. 2 Vols. New version P. Brunt.

ATHENAEUS: DEIPNOSOPHISTAE. C. B. Gulick. 7 Vols.

BABRIUS AND PHAEDRUS (Latin). B. E. Perry.

ST. BASIL: LETTERS. R. J. Deferrari. 4 Vols.

CALLIMACHUS: FRAGMENTS. C. A. Trypanis. MUSAEUS: HERO AND LEANDER. T. Gelzer and C. Whitman.

CALLIMACHUS, Hymns and Epigrams, and LYCOPHRON. A. W. Mair; ARATUS. G. R. Mair.

CLEMENT OF ALEXANDRIA. Rev. G. W. Butterworth.

COLLUTHUS. Cf. OPPIAN.

DAPHNIS AND CHLOE. Thornley's Translation revised by J. M. Edmonds: and PARTHENIUS. S. Gaselee.

DEMOSTHENES I.: OLYNTHIACS, PHILIPPICS and MINOR ORATIONS I.–XVII. AND XX. J. H. Vince.

DEMOSTHENES II.: DE CORONA and DE FALSA LEGATIONE. C. A. Vince and J. H. Vince.

DEMOSTHENES III.: MEIDIAS, ANDROTION, ARISTOCRATES, TIMOCRATES and ARISTOGEITON I. and II. J. H. Vince.

DEMOSTHENES IV.–VI: PRIVATE ORATIONS and IN NEAERAM. A. T. Murray.

DEMOSTHENES VII: FUNERAL SPEECH, EROTIC ESSAY, EXORDIA and LETTERS. N. W. and N. J. DeWitt.

DIO CASSIUS: ROMAN HISTORY. E. Cary. 9 Vols.

5

DIO CHRYSOSTOM. J. W. Cohoon and H. Lamar Crosby. 5 Vols.

DIODORUS SICULUS. 12 Vols. Vols. I.–VI. C. H. Oldfather. Vol. VII. C. L. Sherman. Vol. VIII. C. B. Welles. Vols. IX. and X. R. M. Geer. Vol. XI. F. Walton. Vol. XII. F. Walton. General Index. R. M. Geer.

DIOGENES LAERTIUS. R. D. Hicks. 2 Vols. New Introduction by H. S. Long.

DIONYSIUS OF HALICARNASSUS: ROMAN ANTIQUITIES. Spelman's translation revised by E. Cary. 7 Vols.

DIONYSIUS OF HALICARNASSUS: CRITICAL ESSAYS. S. Usher. 2 Vols. Vol. I.

EPICTETUS. W. A. Oldfather. 2 Vols.

EURIPIDES. A. S. Way. 4 Vols. Verse trans.

EUSEBIUS: ECCLESIASTICAL HISTORY. Kirsopp Lake and J. E. L. Oulton. 2 Vols.

GALEN: ON THE NATURAL FACULTIES. A. J. Brock.

GREEK ANTHOLOGY. W. R. Paton. 5 Vols.

GREEK BUCOLIC POETS (THEOCRITUS, BION, MOSCHUS). J. M. Edmonds.

GREEK ELEGY AND IAMBUS with the ANACREONTEA. J. M. Edmonds. 2 Vols.

GREEK LYRIC. D. A. Campbell. 4 Vols. Vol. I.

GREEK MATHEMATICAL WORKS. Ivor Thomas. 2 Vols.

HERODES. Cf. THEOPHRASTUS: CHARACTERS.

HERODIAN. C. R. Whittaker. 2 Vols.

HERODOTUS. A. D. Godley. 4 Vols.

HESIOD AND THE HOMERIC HYMNS. H. G. Evelyn White.

HIPPOCRATES and the FRAGMENTS OF HERACLEITUS. W. H. S. Jones and E. T. Withington. 4 Vols.

HOMER: ILIAD. A. T. Murray. 2 Vols.

HOMER: ODYSSEY. A. T. Murray. 2 Vols.

ISAEUS. E. W. Forster.

ISOCRATES. George Norlin and LaRue Van Hook. 3 Vols.

[ST. JOHN DAMASCENE]: BARLAAM AND IOASAPH. Rev. G. R. Woodward, Harold Mattingly and D. M. Lang.

JOSEPHUS. 10 Vols. Vols. I.–IV. H. Thackeray. Vol. V. H. Thackeray and R. Marcus. Vols. VI.–VII. R. Marcus. Vol. VIII. R. Marcus and Allen Wikgren. Vols. IX.–X. L. H. Feldman.

JULIAN. Wilmer Cave Wright. 3 Vols.

LIBANIUS. A. F. Norman. 3 Vols. Vols. I.–II.

LUCIAN. 8 Vols. Vols. I.–V. A. M. Harmon. Vol. VI. K. Kilburn. Vols. VII.–VIII. M. D. Macleod.

LYCOPHRON. Cf. CALLIMACHUS.

Lyra Graeca, J. M. Edmonds. 2 Vols.

Lysias. W. R. M. Lamb.

Manetho. W. G. Waddell.

Marcus Aurelius. C. R. Haines.

Menander. W. G. Arnott. 3 Vols. Vol. I.

Minor Attic Orators (Antiphon, Andocides, Lycurgus, Demades, Dinarchus, Hyperides). K. J. Maidment and J. O. Burtt. 2 Vols.

Musaeus: Hero and Leander. Cf. Callimachus.

Nonnos: Dionysiaca. W. H. D. Rouse. 3 Vols.

Oppian, Colluthus, Tryphiodorus. A. W. Mair.

Papyri. Non-Literary Selections. A. S. Hunt and C. C. Edgar. 2 Vols. Literary Selections (Poetry). D. L. Page.

Parthenius. Cf. Daphnis and Chloe.

Pausanias: Description of Greece. W. H. S. Jones. 4 Vols. and Companion Vol. arranged by R. E. Wycherley.

Philo. 10 Vols. Vols. I.–V. F. H. Colson and Rev. G. H. Whitaker. Vols. VI.–IX. F. H. Colson. Vol. X. F. H. Colson and the Rev. J. W. Earp.

Philo: two supplementary Vols. (*Translation only.*) Ralph Marcus.

Philostratus: The Life of Apollonius of Tyana. F. C. Conybeare. 2 Vols.

Philostratus: Imagines; Callistratus: Descriptions. A. Fairbanks.

Philostratus and Eunapius: Lives of the Sophists. Wilmer Cave Wright.

Pindar. Sir J. E. Sandys.

Plato: Charmides, Alcibiades, Hipparchus, The Lovers, Theages, Minos and Epinomis. W. R. M. Lamb.

Plato: Cratylus, Parmenides, Greater Hippias, Lesser Hippias. H. N. Fowler.

Plato: Euthyphro, Apology, Crito, Phaedo, Phaedrus, H. N. Fowler.

Plato: Laches, Protagoras, Meno, Euthydemus. W. R. M. Lamb.

Plato: Laws. Rev. R. G. Bury. 2 Vols.

Plato: Lysis, Symposium, Gorgias. W. R. M. Lamb.

Plato: Republic. Paul Shorey. 2 Vols.

Plato: Statesman, Philebus. H. N. Fowler; Ion. W. R. M. Lamb.

Plato: Theaetetus and Sophist. H. N. Fowler.

Plato: Timaeus, Critias, Clitopho, Menexenus, Epistulae. Rev. R. G. Bury.

Plotinus: A. H. Armstrong. 7 Vols. Vols. I.–V.

PLUTARCH: MORALIA. 16 Vols. Vols I.–V. F. C. Babbitt. Vol. VI. W. C. Helmbold. Vols. VII. and XIV. P. H. De Lacy and B. Einarson. Vol. VIII. P. A. Clement and H. B. Hoffleit. Vol. IX. E. L. Minar, Jr., F. H. Sandbach, W. C. Helmbold. Vol. X. H. N. Fowler. Vol. XI. L. Pearson and F. H. Sandbach. Vol. XII. H. Cherniss and W. C. Helmbold. Vol. XIII 1–2. H. Cherniss. Vol. XV. F. H. Sandbach.

PLUTARCH: THE PARALLEL LIVES. B. Perrin. 11 Vols.

POLYBIUS. W. R. Paton. 6 Vols.

PROCOPIUS. H. B. Dewing. 7 Vols.

PTOLEMY: TETRABIBLOS. F. E. Robbins.

QUINTUS SMYRNAEUS. A. S. Way. Verse trans.

SEXTUS EMPIRICUS. Rev. R. G. Bury. 4 Vols.

SOPHOCLES. F. Storr. 2 Vols. Verse trans.

STRABO: GEOGRAPHY. Horace L. Jones. 8 Vols.

THEOCRITUS. Cf. GREEK BUCOLIC POETS.

THEOPHRASTUS: CHARACTERS. J. M. Edmonds. HERODES, etc. A. D. Knox.

THEOPHRASTUS: ENQUIRY INTO PLANTS. Sir Arthur Hort, Bart. 2 Vols.

THEOPHRASTUS: DE CAUSIS PLANTARUM. G. K. K. Link and B. Einarson. 3 Vols. Vol. I.

THUCYDIDES. C. F. Smith. 4 Vols.

TRYPHIODORUS. Cf. OPPIAN.

XENOPHON: CYROPAEDIA. Walter Miller. 2 Vols.

XENOPHON: HELLENCIA. C. L. Brownson. 2 Vols.

XENOPHON: ANABASIS. C. L. Brownson.

XENOPHON: MEMORABILIA AND OECONOMICUS. E. C. Marchant. SYMPOSIUM AND APOLOGY. O. J. Todd.

XENOPHON: SCRIPTA MINORA. E. C. Marchant. CONSTITUTION OF THE ATHENIANS. G. W. Bowersock.